Streamers and Bucktails
The Big Fish Flies

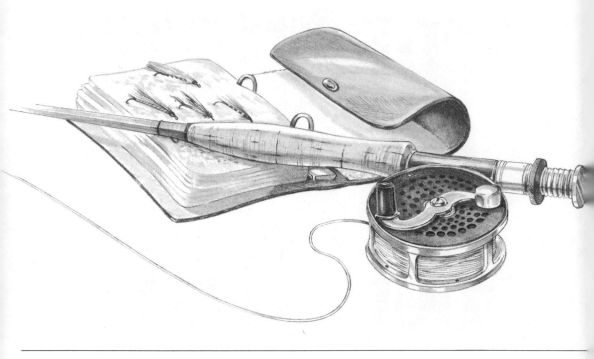

Illustrated with pencil drawings by Bill Elliott
and pen-and-ink drawings by Milton C. Weiler

Joseph D. Bates, Jr.

STREAMERS AND BUCKTAILS

The Big Fish Flies

Alfred A. Knopf

NEW YORK 1979

To
my wife
Helen Ellis Bates
again:
with devotion

THIS IS A BORZOI BOOK
PUBLISHED BY ALFRED A. KNOPF, INC.

Copyright © 1950, 1966 and 1979 by Joseph D. Bates,
Jr. Illustrations Copyright © 1979 by Bill Elliott and
Joseph D. Bates, Jr. All rights reserved under Interna-
tional and Pan-American Copyright Conventions.
Published in the United States by Alfred A. Knopf,
Inc., New York, and simultaneously in Canada by Ran-
dom House of Canada Limited, Toronto. Distributed
by Random House, Inc., New York.

Grateful acknowledgment is made to Ray Sparrow,
Photography, Springfield, Massachusetts, for use of
color plates.

Library of Congress Cataloging in Publication Data

Bates, Joseph D., Jr.   [Date]
  Streamers and bucktails, the big fish flies.

  Includes index.
  1. Flies, Artificial. 2. Fly tying. 3. Fly
fishing. I. Title.
SH451.B29   1979   799.1'2   79–2163
ISBN 0–394–41588–4

Manufactured in the United States of America
First Edition

Contents

Part One:
Freshwater Streamer Fly Fishing   2

1. Why More and Bigger Fish Take Streamers   5

A wilderness trip for brook trout—Why big trout get that way—Simulating bait fish with fur and feathers—Why fish take streamers—Bits about bass—How to fish streamers—A tactic for brown trout—Will artificials outfish bait?—Fishing an undercut bank—Tips about marabous—Locator flies—Imitators versus attractors—How to select streamers—Advantages of flies being "true to pattern"—Essentials of a good fly—Eastern and western types—The "big fish flies"

2. How Fly Fishing's Most Versatile Method Began   19

Importance of presentation—The streamer fly's ancient beginning—Uses by American Indians—The start of sport fishing in America—Theodore Gordon's contributions—Fort Wayne Bucktail—Trude Bucktail—Maine's earliest streamers—New York State types—More about Maine—Rooster's Regret and its progeny—When does a hair fly become a bucktail?—Definitions of streamers and bucktails—Development of a bucktail—Streamer and bucktail construction—Development of a streamer—Suggestions to beginners—How to learn streamer fly dressing

3. Tips on Fishing Streamers in Fast Water   34

The color perception of fish—Light and water conditions—How stream flow guides fly selection—Tips on tackle—Importance of reading the water—Barren water and holding water—Notes on how water temperatures affect fishing—The upstream cast—The quarter upstream cast—Working the fly—Fishing the tail of a pool—The cross-stream cast—Values of the floating line—Variations in cross-stream casting—The quarter downstream cast—The downstream cast—Fishing feeding positions—Fishing riffles—Why change the fly?—A few general rules

Illustrations

Color Plates

Tables

Introduction

Of all the artificial flies anglers collect, dress, trade, treasure, and use—wets, dries, nymphs, and streamers—*only one type* hooks more and bigger fish consistently all season through in both fresh and salt water. This is the type intended to represent bait fish—streamers and bucktails, often called "the big fish flies," because they are the meat and potatoes in the larders of trophy and near-trophy tackle busters everywhere, worldwide, in lakes, rivers, ponds, oceans, estuaries, and bays—wherever such big fish are found.

These are what this book details—how to choose and use streamers and bucktails under all conditions, and how to distinguish correct ones from those which might politely be termed "variations." Here are precise instructions for dressing about five hundred of the most reliable patterns, with twelve full-page plates showing nearly two hundred of them in accurate color, most all dressed by the originators themselves.

As an angler who fishes for fun and usually releases whatever he hooks, I admit and recommend the virtues of the dry fly or nymph when they seem appropriate. Nothing is more fun than to drop a tiny floater precisely, watch it bob merrily in the current, and see a fish rise to take it. Such opportunities unfortunately occur only part of the time because weather and nature must be suitable for hatches. Dry flies and nymphs aren't noted for hooking the biggest fish, although they occasionally do. The lunkers and trophies we seek rarely expend much energy chasing hors d'oeuvres. They usually prey on more robust fare—the bait fish and similar substantial mouthfuls represented by bucktails and streamers. That's a reason why the big ones get that way! Also, we don't find terrestrials and ephemerals in salt water. The big ones there also favor bait fish almost exclusively, and therefore they slam streamers to the exclusion of most everything else.

Thus, the type of artificial used by fly-rodders most often, most everywhere, is the feather-dressed streamer or the hair-dressed bucktail, usually lumped as "streamers" for convenience. This is the type to choose, if you're choosing only one!

This book is the culmination of half a century of fascination with this subject, and the winnowed augmentation of two popular predecessor volumes—*Streamer Fly Fishing in Fresh and Salt Water,* published in 1950, and *Streamer Fly Tying & Fishing,* published in 1966. Both of these books have been widely praised and have been accepted as the authoritative sources on streamer fly patterns and fishing methods. While such praise pleases an author, the credit here should go to the experts with whom I have been privileged to fish over the years—the early pioneers who took me under their wings, gave me examples of their original patterns, and told me their fishing secrets. This book gives the dressings of their originations in such detail that any reasonably proficient fly tyer can copy them accurately.

During the past decade, patterns, preferences, and methods have changed so much that an entirely new book is needed. While the old masters of the art are gone, their major accomplishments are retained here as the bedrock of the art. Added to their teachings are those of the newer experts, such as Stu Apte, Dan Blanton, George Grant, Larry Green, Hal Janssen, Lefty Kreh, and Dave Whitlock, plus others whose streamer flies, fly types, and angling methods offer new conceptions to make fishing more successful and more fun.

Most of the patterns in this book are given in Part Four, in alphabetical order, but there are a good many other patterns given in Parts One, Two, and Three, in chapters where they are relevant. The quickest way to find a given pattern is to use the index at the back of the book.

Readers who don't find fly patterns they seek should realize that any book which tried to include everything would become cluttered with trivia. Doubtless the patterns they look for are variations of standard ones found herein, or are intentionally excluded in favor of others quite similar and considered more valuable. Every attempt has been made to provide all the basics whose descriptions can be published "true to pattern" as their originators intended them to be. Being true to pattern also means, however, that they must have the elements of quality, character, and style, so these points are stressed in the detailed dressing instructions.

With that, let's delve into the book. I hope that the lore of streamer flies and fishing will provide as much fun and success for you as it has for me.

Joseph D. Bates, Jr.
Longmeadow, Massachusetts

Streamers and Bucktails
The Big Fish Flies

Part One
Freshwater Streamer Fly Fishing

1

Why More and Bigger Fish Take Streamers

As THE LITTLE AIRCRAFT circled into the wind over the wilderness lake, the young angler looked down upon Maine's spruce-carpeted emerald hills and glistening cobalt lakes with delighted fascination. Beeches, maples, and other hardwoods, sprinkled among the expanses of green, shimmered with the golds, pinks, and russets tinted by early frosts. Nestled deeply in the verdant forest was the familiar pool below the old log dam; a tiny white V of current showing where lusty trout so often flashed to the fly. Nearby, in a grassy clearing, a small gray rectangle marked the patched log cabin on the point—both clearing and cabin relics of logging operations early in the century.

When the young angler glanced down the wing of the turning plane a small figure emerged from the cabin, looking up and waving. It was the old angler, and this was another of their cherished reunions.

The smoothly droning aircraft then skimmed low over the forested shore, descending in the direction of the cabin across the lake. The engine's whine decreased as the plane leveled off and its pontoons touched the lake's wavelets with a mild bump and a shower of spray. Then came a higher pitch as the pilot increased speed, bumping wave crests toward the cabin's gravel beach. Near it, the engine coughed silent as the pontoons lightly scraped the gravel. The old angler, a cheery grin on his weatherbeaten face, secured the craft with ropes through the ringbolts of the pontoons. The door swung open and the young angler climbed out, quickly walking a pontoon to hand to the other man a sleeping bag, rod case, and other

1–1 The familiar pool below the old log dam.

luggage. The greeting between the two showed the warmth of mutual admiration and respect. Each of these fishing vacations broadened the younger man's angling knowledge and skill.

"Now that we've caught up on the high spots of the news from home," the old angler later said, "why don't you run the canoe down to the dam and catch a pair of trout for dinner? I'll stay here and finish frying this batch of doughnuts. I guess you won't mind a little late-afternoon fishing, and you never seem to get your fill of wild pink-fleshed brookies, fresh from the water and fried to a nice golden brown."

After their meal the two men pulled ancient rockers to the railing of the porch and lighted their pipes while dark shadows crept in from the far shore and the sun's pink afterglow grew fainter beyond the darkening hills toward the west. All was wrapped in silence save for the occasional whickering of a pair of loons far out on the placid blackening silver surface of the lake.

"Nice pair of trout you brought back," the old angler remarked. "Each was a bit over a pound, so I guess you selected them. You must have released some others."

"There's a thing about that I don't quite understand," the young man replied. "I'd rather fish dry flies or nymphs. You always prefer streamers.

You always catch bigger fish, on average, than I do, except when I do it your way and change to streamers. I used a dry fly for half an hour, mostly downcurrent close to the log cribbing. The old dam is falling apart—won't last more than a few years more. Anyway, I took several small trout on the dry fly and released them. Then I shifted to a streamer—a silver-bodied white marabou with peacock topping—and fluffed it down the same run. Bang! I was fast to a much bigger trout. I tried it again. Bang! I hooked another. That was the pair I brought back. What I can't understand is this. Why didn't those bigger trout take the dry fly? I'm sure they must have seen it."

The older man chuckled and shifted his feet on the porch's cedar railing. "Maybe there are two kinds of all varieties of trout—the smart ones and the dumb ones," he replied. "The smaller ones wear themselves out by chasing tidbits like dry flies. The big ones get that way by waiting for food to come to them. They usually spurn the tidbits in favor of meat and potatoes. By that, I mean substantial food like shiners and sculpins and maybe salamanders or crayfish or eelets.

"A noted ecologist gave me an explanation I'll accept," the old angler went on. "Big trout get that way because they are smart enough to know how to capture a maximum amount of food with a minimum amount of effort. Direct comparisons can be made between what trout eat and the energy they use to catch it, because both can be expressed in calories.

"So we arrive at a very simple formula. A trout's growth equals its intake of food divided by the energy expended to catch it. If the trout, or any other kind of fish, can capture a lot of food with the use of only a little energy, that trout will grow faster. If energy used is greater than intake, the fish loses condition. It doesn't grow and, at best, becomes thin. With an abundance of easily available food and the sense to concentrate on the meat and potatoes, trout no more than three or four years old could attain a weight of over ten pounds. These big ones are found in lakes and rivers in many places in the world. On the other hand, you and I have fished beaver ponds and such places where the trout are all little ones. There may be too many, or they have to use too much energy to catch their food. They never grow much.

"And so big trout," the old angler continued, "have inherited the ability to use a minimum of energy to acquire a maximum of food. They specialize, tending from time to time to concentrate on one type of food to the exclusion of all others. A smelting trout, for example, usually ignores everything else and can only be taken by using smelt as bait or by using a streamer fly that represents a smelt. Many big trout concentrate on sculpins, which are much more abundant than one might think. They do this because sculpins are easy to catch and provide substantial meals.

"Thus, in discussing artificials, I think we have to conclude that streamers and bucktails usually are by far the best flies for taking big fish. They

7

represent the main course—the meat and potatoes—in the diets of the lunkers. Of course, we sometimes catch big fish on dry flies and nymphs, and when a hatch is on, I'm all for that. Generally speaking, however, we'll hook more of the big ones more often on streamers and bucktails. Bear in mind a proven statistic: bait fish outnumber all other bottom-dwelling residents by ten to one in ninety percent of all American streams."

While the old angler refilled his pipe the young one said, "You gave me some excellent advice a few years ago when I asked how to select bucktails or streamers for specific situations. You told me to lie on a dock and to watch the bait fish swimming down below, then to imitate them in size, colors, flash, and action by selecting and fishing a streamer fly as nearly like them as possible. That's good advice for anyone, and I've followed it often when fishing in different places.

"I didn't realize there are so many kinds of bait fish. By watching them I know the blacktail shiner is very prevalent and that it can be represented by a silver-bodied fly with a wing of green over white, as can the rock shiner. The redhorse shiner's characteristic is its red-orange fins, so I'd select a streamer such as a Golden Darter or maybe a Mickey Finn for it. On the other hand, we have bait fish with dark lateral lines, such as weed shiners and blacknose dace, so we need a fly with a dark median stripe for them. The fly called Black Nosed Dace is of course a good one, or a silver-bodied one with a sparse wing of white under black under brown. Since smelt are the prevalent bait fish in many lakes, I use the Gray Ghost or Supervisor quite often. Then, too, there are bait fish with vertical bars, like the barred killifish, and streamers with grizzly hackles are good to represent them. I learned by watching that each kind of bait fish has pronounced characteristics of colors, size and shape, and that some show more flash than others. If we work under the supposition that our game fish are hungry, the closer we can imitate their favorite bait fish, the better off we will be."

"You also know," the old angler said, "that big fish don't strike at streamers only because they are hungry, although that is the best assumption to start with. They also strike because of anger, or curiosity, or playfulness. We can group these three reasons together and use an entirely different set of tactics, because a fish will strike the same fly regardless of the reason it does so."

"Bass are suckers for streamers," the young angler joined in, "and I have great fun using unusual methods for them. We have a bass pond near home, with plenty of lily-pad coves, and banks with laurel growing out over the water. These bass love crazy streamers, but I don't know which of your four reasons makes them take them. I use large regular-shank hooks and tie several long saddle hackles over the rear of the shank—sometimes on a silver or chenille body, or even on a bare hook. Colors don't matter much, but the hackles should be floppy. It's the action that counts. Just splash the fly down close to shore or near some cover. Let it splay on the surface a few seconds; then pull it under and strip it in—sometimes fast, sometimes slow. If there's an old bucketmouth nearby, it will have it. Once I had two bass on at once!"

"Not on one fly!"

"Sure! A little bass no longer than the fly struck and hooked itself. As I turned to talk to my partner the rod tip jerked down and line began to rip off the reel. It was about as strong a run as even a salmon could make. Impossible for such a little fish to do such a thing, I thought. Then the line went slack and I reeled in the badly damaged little bass. An old lunker had taken it but finally let it go. I never saw the big fish—wish I had. It must have been a whopper!"

The old man chuckled. "That never happened to me with bass, but years ago it did with trout," he said. "A fingerling hit the fly and a big one took the little one so deep that I landed both. I released the four-pounder, but the little fellow was beyond repair. All kinds of bass will take streamers—sometimes on top, sometimes deeper. Little bass bugs are fun, too, and more or less effective at one time or another. Did you ever fish streamers over bass beds during spawning time? The bass hit them from anger, because they want to get them out of the way."

"Isn't that poor sportsmanship?" the younger man asked. "Taking bass off their beds?"

"Not usually. When Mama Bass has done her stuff, then Papa Bass takes over and the female finds something else to do. In many lakes there are so many that some should be harvested. I release them anyway, unless I want a big one for dinner."

"So, in that case, we add the protective instinct to the four reasons," the young angler remarked. "I don't suppose we can separate hunger from curiosity, and it doesn't matter. But I've seen trout strike from playfulness. While sitting beside a pool, I saw another angler release an undersized trout. He didn't do it properly, and the little one flopped around near surface, trying to get upright. A bigger trout came up and hit it but didn't take it. As it drifted down the pool two others did the same thing—not hungry, not angry, probably not curious, so it must have been from playfulness. Can you use the same fly for all four reasons?"

"Sure you can," the old man said. "But for that, some flies are better than others. Let's take a marabou streamer; for example, the Ballou Special, which is so popular in Maine, or one of Polly Rosborough's Silver Garland Marabous, which are very famous out west. This type of fly can be fished to imitate a minnow exactly. The Ballou Special, for instance, has a silver tinsel body to represent the silvery underbelly of a smelt. When it is wet, the white marabou wing provides lifelike action to the fly, at the same time giving it the substance and color of a smelt's body. The peacock topping imitates the smelt's dark-greenish back, the jungle-cock cheeks look like head and gills, and the bit of red bucktail and golden pheasant crest seem to add to the illusion. All the fisherman needs to do is to make it *act* like a smelt. If it darts away like a terrified bait fish when a big game fish is

9

nearby, the hungry game fish will have it in no time. It must be fished so fast that all the game fish sees is a flash of color, shape, and action.

"Now take this same fly when the fish are not hungry," the older man went on. "To be specific, let's take an actual instance of brown trout fishing in a New York State stream. The anglers I was with knew that a big brown trout lay near some cover by the bank. They had tried naturals of all sorts, but the trout didn't react to a thing. I thought I'd see if I could make him angry enough to strike, so I went in about sixty feet above him and cast the marabou streamer across-stream with sixty feet of line. A small rainbow took it on the swing and I had to cast again. I guided the fly to a few feet above where I thought the big trout lay and left it there. Then I lighted a cigarette. The fly worked in the current near the bank, but the trout wouldn't take it. I kept slowly raising and lowering my rod tip and could imagine the fly's marabou wing fluffing and closing in the water. I'd let it drift down a few feet and then bring it up again, keeping the rod tip and the fly busy. Just before I finished the cigarette the big brownie struck. He weighed five pounds and two ounces. Now, surely that trout wasn't hungry, and the fluffy marabou streamer was not being fished to imitate a bait fish. The trout stood the thing jerking near his nose as long as he could. Then he got mad and struck at it. It took five minutes, nearly. With brown trout it often takes that long, but by the time five minutes have gone by he will either strike or go away. Usually you can make a rainbow trout angry much quicker. It just goes to illustrate that there are two types of reasons fish will take a streamer, and there are two basic ways to fish them, plus a lot of variations. Unless we have evidence to the contrary, it seems preferable to start with reason number one—the hunger motive—and match the pattern and action to the local bait fish. If that fails, try reason number two—anger, curiosity, or playfulness. Then, almost any fly will do; but some are better than others. It's the way you fish 'em that counts."

The night grew colder, and the two friends went indoors. While the old angler lighted lamps, the young one threw some logs on the fire and assembled several coils of monofilament on the table for tying leaders. The old man pulled up a chair, put a soft cushion into it, and sat down to watch the work.

"I think your comments about the four reasons why fish take streamers and bucktails explain more than you have said," the young angler remarked as he tightened a Perfection Loop in a heavy strand of the leader material. "If we are using small wet or dry flies or nymphs, or even live bait, it strikes me that we can appeal only to a fish's sense of hunger. How can he get angry or curious about any of these things? How could he get playful?'

10

The old angler chuckled softly. "That's another reason why I like streamers," he said. "It's pretty hard to appeal to a fish with a dry fly or wet fly or nymph if he isn't hungry. It's pretty hard to make him angry or curious or playful with a worm or a grasshopper or a half-dead shiner. But slap a streamer fly or bucktail in his territory and make it dart around like a strange little fish on the prowl, and the old tackle buster is likely to tear over and chew it to pieces! He will not want to eat it, but he will strike at it and then try to spit it out."

"I think that's the territorial instinct," the young man said. "We notice that many animals, birds, and even fish stake out their territories and try to drive invaders away. Fish such as trout and bass do it, too. The strongest ones take the best places, and if one is caught or moves away, another will move into the choice spot and will protect its right to be there. If a smaller fish moves in too close, he's had it! If a streamer fly is fished in too close the angry fish strikes it. So we chalk up another reason for fishing with streamers. It's one of the reasons why they are called 'the big fish flies.' "

The old angler dropped another log on the fire, turned over his cushion, and picked up one of the leaders the young angler had made. He inspected the strengths and lengths of the sections and the manner in which the knots were tied. He carefully coiled the leader, secured the end, and approvingly placed the finished product near the lamp with the others.

"When we know how to select streamers of the right size and shape, with suitable colors and flash for the conditions under which we are fishing, and when we know how to fish streamers properly under those conditions, we can take big fish with them anywhere at any time of year," he commented. "But one of the best times here in the north is in early spring when there is a minimum of insect life on the streams. If one knows how, he might have some success with nymphs, but in very cold water the fish are too lethargic to strike at the small stuff. They will react more surely to something that seems to represent a square meal. You have to know where the fish are lying, or make an educated guess at it, and fish almost on the bottom to work the flies close to their noses. When water is uncomfortably cold for fish they won't go far to take anything—even bait."

"That reminds me of an argument I had with a young doctor who said that anyone using bait, such as worms or shiners, could outfish a streamer-fly fisherman anytime," the young angler replied. "So I took him up on it on a stream of his selection. He drifted bait downcurrent while I tried to dredge bottom with slightly weighted streamers. He hooked a few trout, but I scored better, and with bigger ones. Why? Well, for one reason, he was changing bait pretty often, while I kept my fly in the water. For another, I could make longer casts and cover more of the hot spots. He would assume that a fish or two should be lying behind a midstream rock, or under a fallen log, or under an undercut bank on the far side, but most of the time he couldn't reach that far or couldn't present his bait properly. Then I would try the same place, dropping the streamer far enough upstream so it would sink deeply enough by the time it reached the hot spot. When I activated it there I often got a strike."

"The arguments about bait versus streamers probably never will end,"

11

the old angler said. "My points would be that fly fishing is more fun and that fly fishermen can release unwanted fish. When they are caught with bait they usually take it too deep and can't be released unharmed. Whether or not one method gets more action than the other seems inconsequential. The days are long gone when we could afford to waste trout. Sportsmen fish for fun, not for meat. Fly fishing seems to most of us to provide more fun. We usually get plenty of action and a big one or two to bring home if we need them."

He stood up and glanced out at the black sky sprinkled with bright stars and a few high clouds in the clear chilly night. "Should be a good day tomorrow. Let's get some sleep and get up early. There's a place I want to show you."

After a breakfast of bacon and eggs, with strong coffee and a plate of the doughnuts the old man had made, the two anglers stowed rods and a pack basket in the canoe and paddled to the dam. Leaving the craft there, they took the trail downstream, pausing now and again to look at the rocky outlet and the fast water. Half a mile's walk brought them to where the stream widened placidly at its inlet into Third Lake. No habitations were on the lake then. The trout were wild and unmolested. There were the remains of a spruce-bordered clearing where a lumber camp had once stood, and the rotting hulk of an old bateau; part of its planking had been used for firewood in a crude fireplace made from rocks brought from the beach. The old man came here often.

"You'll notice that the stream has gouged out the far bank," he said. "I'm sure there are some good trout under it. Wade out until you get an easy cast. The bottom on this side is a bit muddy, but firm. Put your back cast high to miss the alders." Then he settled comfortably with his back against the old bateau to see what his young friend would do.

The young angler fished diligently for half an hour and released a few small trout. Then he returned. "I'm sure you can do better," he said sheepishly.

"You could have done better," the older man chided. "You were reaching the bank, but you were letting the current whip the fly, and it was whipping before it got deep enough. You should mend your line more often to maintain proper fly speed. Few trout will bother with a whipping fly. I know there are big fish there. Let me show you."

The old angler selected a small but fluffy bright-red marabou streamer, secured it to his leader, and waded out. His cast, angled a bit upstream, almost touched the far bank. Immediately he flipped his rod tip against the current to put an upstream loop in his line. The fly drifted placidly and sank out of sight. Each time the current bowed the line slightly, he mended it again. Suddenly he gave an audible "Ah!" and raised his rod tip. He was fast to a brilliant male brook trout of nearly two pounds. He kept the fish and waded ashore.

12

"I've got my lunch," he smiled. "Now you go and get yours. I don't want to spoil the water for you."

While the young man was gone the older one collected dead wood and built a fire. He put two handfuls of coffee into a blackened pot he had filled with water and rested it on the edge of the flames. He took two packets of vegetables, sealed in foil, from his basket and put them near the heat. When the coffee came to a boil he added a little cold water to settle the grounds and removed it from the heat when it came to a boil again. He kept glancing at the younger man out in the stream and was pleased to see him hook and release several trout.

The young man returned with a trout for lunch. They cleaned and seasoned them, sealed them in foil, and set them on the hot ashes, turning each of the four packets occasionally. They poured coffee and enjoyed lunch. While eating it the young man said, "I haven't used marabou streamers very often because they don't seem to represent much of anything, and I noticed that you just drifted yours, without working it to any extent."

"There are things about marabou streamers that some people don't understand," the old angler replied. "When you tie them or buy them, be sure the wing isn't so long that it can wrap around the hook. The light fibers can catch and matt in the barb. Be sure the fly isn't overdressed. Soak it and check its shape when wet. Unless the fly is hanging downstream we don't need to work it much, or any at all. The fibers are so fluffy that the current will work them. The fly on a dead drift in any current will pulsate by itself, but when it's towed, it's no better than anything else. Thus, I wouldn't troll with them unless I worked the rod tip all the time. Marabous have an action all their own, if you let them work. Then they look alive. True, they don't exactly represent anything, but they do have lots of action. Many anglers swear by them, and tie them in all sorts of bright and dark color combinations. They are highly effective attractor patterns."

"I always thought that exact imitation was the goal we're working toward," the young man said. "And then you take this bright-red thing and catch big trout with it!"

"Trout often go for a touch of red. That run under the bank was very shady, so I wanted a fly that would appear dark and give a better silhouette. Probably a black one would have done as well."

"Now I'm rather confused," the young man admitted. "Tell me more about attractor patterns. I think you sometimes call them locator flies. There are imitators and attractors. Are all either one thing or the other?"

"Some quite obviously are either one or the other, but some have characteristics of both types. The well-known Mickey Finn is a good example of an attractor, although many fishermen think it resembles a little sunfish. Attractor patterns are just that. In color, at least, they don't imitate anything, because they usually are too bright. Because of the brightness, fish often will come up and look at them when they might not notice the

13

more somber imitators. If a fish shows interest but doesn't take, the idea is to change to an imitator and go after him again. An attractor might wake him up and an imitator might hook him. Attractor patterns are good during high or discolored water conditions because they can be seen better then. There's no exact division between the two types. Some have characteristics of both, such as the Black Ghost and the Edson Tigers, for instance. It's not what we see that counts; it's the way the fish see it. When water is low and clear, a fairly small imitator pattern, selected as we have discussed, should be ideal. When water is high or dark, a larger and brighter fly may be called for—one with a pronounced silhouette. Excellent examples of the two types were dressed by Carrie Stevens, of Upper Dam, Maine. Her Gray Ghost is an imitator, and perhaps the most famous streamer ever originated. Her Colonel Bates is an attractor, bright-yellow, white, and silver, with touches of gray, brown, and red. Many anglers tell me that these make an unusually effective pair in waters where the predominant bait fish are smelt. If one doesn't do the business, the other one should. I have found it to be true."

The two men soaked the embers of their luncheon fire with water from the lake. They stowed their refuse in the pack basket, leaving no trace of their visit to the little clearing. They spent a pleasant afternoon experimenting with barbless streamers of various patterns and sizes, hooking many trout but killing none. When the sun's pink disc nicked the western evergreen hills, they returned along the muddy trail by the stream to the upper lake and paddled home.

The old angler enjoyed dressing flies when he had nothing more important to do. His kit of hooks, furs, feathers, tinsels, threads, and other items littered a crude but sturdy table in the corner of the cabin. He was such a noted expert at the art that fishermen everywhere contrived to acquire examples of his workmanship and often kept them as treasures under the impression that they were too valuable to fish with. When he sat down to copy Lew Oatman's Golden Darter, the young man produced his own fly book bulging with streamers and asked the expert for comments.

The old man fingered them carefully, poking one and then another. Occasionally he selected one and held it up to the lamp, then replaced it in the fly book.

"Streamers are made to catch fishermen as well as fish," he observed.

"I tied many a long time ago," the young man said. "Some I bought and some were given to me. What do you think of them?"

"You can discard about half of them," the older angler said. "You can select a couple dozen of the others and with them you can hook any kind of fish that swims in fresh water in New England. Of course, in other regions you'd need different types, although a few should do well most anywhere. You have the same trouble as most fishermen. You've got collectoritis. Fun, though, isn't it?"

The young man contemplated his treasured collection. He knew that

14

many were unnecessary and never used, but he loved them, and they took up negligible room and weight. "Better too many than too few," he thought; and then aloud he said to the older man: "You say that a couple dozen streamers or bucktails will do as well up here as a great many. Which would you select?"

The old man smiled broadly. "A couple dozen should do, but there aren't many anglers who would be content with so few. A list of patterns and sizes will be of little help unless we first know how to tell a good streamer from a poor one. You and I can dress our own flies, but many anglers can't, or they lack the time to bother with it. They must buy them. Unless they can tell the good ones from the poor ones, they are in trouble before they put their money on the counter. What are the indications which distinguish a good fly from a poor one?"

"Shape," the young man ventured, "and color combination—and quality."

"To an extent correct, but not entirely," said the old angler. "Quality is important, and we shall define it better as we go along." He selected a battered streamer from his fly box and tossed it on the table.

"That streamer has quality," he said. "You wouldn't believe how many trout and salmon have been caught with it. Fish can't pull it apart. Dealers should let buyers tug at flies a bit to be sure components are firmly wound and cemented in place. Usually, though, flies come in envelopes, so one has to trust the integrity of the dealer. On the other hand, you can estimate quality by inspecting details. Is the head nicely finished? If the fly has a tinsel body, do any gaps in winding let thread show through? Do tail and wing curve properly? Is the fly true to pattern?"

"Some people argue about this true-to-pattern business," the young man interjected.

"When a person wants a fly of a certain pattern, he should get it just the way its originator made it, not modified for economy or because of the whim of the dealer. 'True to pattern' means that the pattern has been well tested, and that it works. A modified version may not. I always advise beginners to insist on flies being true to pattern. If they are learning fly dressing they should copy patterns exactly. Later on, and with reason, they can modify them any way they wish, but they should have reasons for what they do. That's their business, and it's part of the fun of making flies. A fly which isn't true to pattern lacks quality because it isn't what it's supposed to be. Nothing of quality is built with the wrong parts or with missing parts.

"The essentials of a good fly," the old angler continued, "are form, flash, and action. Of course, color is important, but that is decided by pattern. Form is more important than color. Flash is more important than color, and action is more important than all of them. Fish usually take streamers because they represent bait fish, yet many streamers which anglers make or buy lack the form of any known fish. Sometimes, in marabou patterns, for example, this is intentional, but not usually. We find streamers

15

dressed with stiff neck hackles which, even when wet, make the fly too wide at the head. An excess of hackle throat or collar, or an excess of underbody, often contributes to this. We find streamers with wings out of proportion, or so heavily dressed that they won't sink properly or may not swim upright. Most flies are badly overdressed, anyway. They lack the trim, streamlined appearance of the forage fish they are made to imitate. Two of the most effective flies I know of are the Rev. Smith's Sidewinder and Pin Fish. You can't dress 'em any thinner than that, and it's amazing the way they appeal to fish. Form is a matter of proportion, and proportion is dictated by the fish we desire to imitate and the type of water we desire to fish."

"The type of water we desire to fish seems important," the young man remarked. "Good form in western bucktails seems to call for a high wing and heavier dressings, as in steelhead patterns. However, here in the east, we seem to prefer sparser dressings with wings that hug the bodies, such as in the Edson Tigers, for example."

"Right you are," the old angler said, "and there are reasons we can sink our teeth in. Western bucktails usually are fished in fast, turbulent rivers which require a fly to be dressed more heavily in order to be seen more clearly. The swift current pulls down the high wing and forces the fly to take a streamlined appearance without masking the flash of the body. Western flies mostly are fast-water ones; ours in the east mostly are the opposite. Hackling makes a difference, too. A well-hackled fly sinks slowly or may be hard to sink. One with only a tiny beard, or none at all, sinks much quicker. Both eastern and western types have proper form for the types of water for which they are made.

"Now, let's rehearse the element of flash," the older man went on. "Flash also is dictated by water conditions and the conditions of light and weather. When you watch the minnows in a quiet pool you may not notice them until they turn to pick up a speck of food. Then you see a flash from their silvery bodies. Flash is what makes you notice them, and it is what attracts game fish to them, too. Flash similarly helps to attract game fish to streamers, but you then need form and action to make them strike. Flash is a relative matter. We need lots of it when streams are high or discolored in order to make fish see the fly at all. That is why many streamers and bucktails are dressed with oval silver ribbing over the flat tinsel or are dressed with bodies of Mylar piping or have Mylar strips mixed in their wings. Fluorescent butts or bits of fluorescence in the wings accomplish a similar purpose. We need less flash under clear water conditions or in small streams or on bright days. It is possible to select flies which have too much flash under such conditions. Too much flash could scare fish rather than attract them."

16

The old angler filled his ever-present pipe, lighted it, and gazed critically at the Golden Darter he had nearly finished. He whipped the thread to secure the head and carefully applied varnish to it. While doing this he commented reflectively, "What we have said pretty nearly covers the element of action. The fly must have action suitable to the water where it is being fished. In fast water the current may provide much of the action. In slack water, action is provided by the fly and by the angler who fishes it. If it is a bucktail, the hair wing must act 'alive' rather than cling to the body in a sodden mass. It must 'breathe' as the angler works it in the water. The quality and quantity of hair and the way it is applied to the fly helps, or detracts from, the lifelike action which the angler can give it. If it is a streamer, the feather wing must accomplish the same purpose. That is why most fly dressers prefer saddle hackles for wings rather than neck hackles. Saddle hackles are more streamlined and flexible. They react in a more lifelike manner to the action of the water and of the angler. They are more translucent. Some slack-water streamers are dressed with a splayed wing, for example, so that the V thus formed in the wing will open and close as the fly is fished, giving added action. Fine strands of marabou do the same thing. The hackle throat or the underbody may add even more. All of these things we have been discussing influence the choice of the fly we select for the type of water we intend to fish. Form, flash, and action are all-important. Color selection and color combination are important too, but they are least important of all! You see, when you delve into this, you instinctively learn the ground rules of why more and bigger fish so consistently take streamers, and how to choose and use streamers in taking them.

"Now," the old gentleman added, "this Golden Darter is for you. Try it tomorrow and catch a big one with it!"

"This fly never will see the water," the young man said appreciatively. "I'm going to label it and set it in a little plastic case as a memento of the wonderful days I've spent with you."

The old man stood up, stretched a bit, and gazed out upon the lake. Then, turning, he remarked, "Of course there's a lot more to be said, and we'll get to it eventually. We have talked a bit about trout, landlocked salmon, and bass, but we realize that all game fish in fresh and salt water take streamers because, all during the year, the bait fish they imitate are their most substantial food. Atlantic salmon take streamers, although maybe as a change-of-pace fly, because Atlantics are said not to feed in fresh water. Pacific salmon take them, and almost every game fish in the ocean does—usually more avidly than anything else under conditions where fly fishing makes sense. One of the greatest angling sports in the world is to hook striped bass on flies, although some may insist that tarpon or bonefish or snook or something else is preferable. We used to think that we couldn't hook sailfish on flies, but it has been done countless times.

"So," he added, "have fun with your dry flies or nymphs when you want to. There are times when I prefer them myself. But just bear in mind this important fact. If you want to catch big fish consistently all during the season and almost regardless of conditions, you should try to learn all you

17

can about fishing with streamers and bucktails, because they represent meat and potatoes in the diets of game fish. They are 'the big fish flies.' "

Some who read this book surely will ask who the young angler and the old angler are. To satisfy their curiosity it should be stated that the young angler could have been myself, because I have enjoyed many a discussion such as this in a place such as is described. If he were meant to be myself, the word "young" would have an element of wishful thinking in it unless the conversation took place many years ago, as a part of it most certainly did. It could be that the "young angler" is he who reads this page. Youth is a relative state anyway, and the Red Gods give an ample share of it to those who enjoy fishing.

The old angler is the important one, and he is a composite of many famous fishermen I have been privileged to know. The remarks he has made in this chapter are true remarks, uttered by one and endorsed by others. What they have agreed upon would be true even if I had not enjoyed enough years with the streamer fly and the fly rod to prove these things to my own satisfaction. Whether or not I am old enough to have the wisdom of the old angler, I surely am old enough to enjoy a bit of reminiscence. It is pleasant to ponder upon the fireside talks I have had with some of the truly great in American angling—Herbie Welch, Pete Schwab, Bill Edson, Joe Stickney, Ray Bergman, and Joe Brooks are only a few. It is because I know that these, and others less well known, have endorsed the old angler's remarks that I feel it of value to write them. The opinion of one man is only as good as his experience, but the opinions of many can become so stabilized as to be contributions of considerable value to angling knowledge.

Importance of presentation—The streamer fly's ancient beginning—Uses by American Indians—The start of sport fishing in America—Theodore Gordon's contributions—Fort Wayne Bucktail—Trude Bucktail—Maine's earliest streamers—New York State types—More about Maine—Rooster's Regret and its progeny—When does a hair fly become a bucktail?—Definitions of streamers and bucktails—Development of a bucktail—Streamer and bucktail construction—Development of a streamer—Suggestions to beginners—How to learn streamer fly dressing

2 How Fly Fishing's Most Versatile Method Began

DURING THEIR CONVERSATION the old angler advised the younger one to select bucktails or streamers which imitate the prevalent bait fish as accurately as possible in size, in form or shape, in flash, and in color. Then he advised the younger man to imitate their action with his rod and line, saying that the action given to a streamer or bucktail is more important than its other characteristics. Color is important, and we should copy the colors of prevalent bait fish as closely as possible, as he said—realizing, however, that clearness of water, or the lack of it, has an effect on color which should be considered. Even far-out colors, as in some attractor patterns, have their place in inducing disinterested fish to strike when exact imitations are being ignored.

If the old angler had been talking less about flies and more about fishing, then he might have said that presentation is the most important element in success, because flies must be cast properly to locations where big fish are expected to be before the elements of fly selection and imparted action become relevant. When fish are hungry they are easy to please. What separates expert anglers from inept ones is the thoughtful combination of the various elements that attract strikes when fish are sophisticated or disinterested. These are matters which should become clearer as we go along.

Insofar as catching fish is concerned, the history of streamers and bucktails obviously is of minor importance. It does, however, illustrate the point that properly dressed flies of these types have evolved through many years of trial and error, culminating in numerous basic and successful patterns which modern fly dressers may adapt to their own purposes as they desire. A quick résumé of the past, as given here, should interest most readers.

We have it on good authority from an Italian author named Aelian, who lived between the years A.D.170 and 230, that way back then the Macedonians used artificial flies to catch fish with speckled skins. Evidently the popular pattern was one which was supposed to imitate a terrestrial looking something like a wasp or bee, and which was called a *hippouros.* Thus, the fly was called the False Hippouros. According to Aelian's book, "They fasten red [crimson red] wool round the hook, and fix on to the wool feathers which grow under a cock's wattles, and which in color are like wax," or, in another translation, "are brought up to the proper color with wax." This account goes on to say that their rods were six feet long, with lines of the same length.

Some modern students think that the two feathers, which were supposed to act as "wings," made the fly a streamer, regardless of whatever it was supposed to be, because the feathers were "secured" to the hook and evidently were not wound on as a collar or were not palmered. Such a fly in those days had to be simple and crude.

From that ancient start nothing of importance happened, that we know of, for nearly fifteen hundred years, when Dame Juliana Berners' famous *Treatise* was published in 1496. This included a dozen then-popular patterns of artificial flies, but they were wet flies, and not properly streamers.

It is certain that the American Indians used crude flies which could be called streamers during the first half of the nineteenth century. Explorers report having seen bone and hair lures, somewhat similar to the modern bucktail, in use among the Alaskan Eskimos (see Alaska Mary Ann Bucktail in Part Four), but how old they are is unknown.

Sport fishing in America is a development of the nineteenth century. Before that fish were caught only for food, and refinements in tackle were almost unknown. In 1833 Dr. Jerome V. C. Smith, in the second part of *The Fishes of Massachusetts,* described standard patterns of flies (chiefly English) and advised the angler to learn to tie his own. Apparently the sport of fly fishing was well established in parts of the United States by that time. In 1849 Frank Forester (Henry W. Herbert) described taking shad in fresh water on "a gaudy fly." Although these are but two of many instances of early fly fishing, the sport did not become more than regionally popular until after 1850, and the development of the streamer fly and the bucktail followed that of other types of flies. So we must skip to the latter part of the nineteenth century to learn anything valuable about streamers and bucktails from an angling point of view.

Those conversant with the history of flies will not be surprised to learn that the great Theodore Gordon, father of the American dry fly, was one of the first to dress and to experiment with the bucktail and streamer fly

20

as we know it today. For this valuable bit of research we are indebted to John McDonald, who edited the papers of Theodore Gordon and published them in *The Complete Fly Fisherman* (New York: Charles Scribner's Sons, 1947), a book of the greatest interest and value to every serious fly fisherman. Mr. McDonald has allowed me to quote these pertinent lines from Gordon's notes:

January 24, 1903: " . . . Some years ago we tried [for pike] some flies on an entirely different principle, our notion being to turn out something that would have great life and movement and resemble a small bright fish in colouring. If you could see one of these large flies played, salmon-fly fashion, by a series of short jerks of the rod top, and notice how the long fibres expand and contract, how the jungle fowl feathers (in a line with the hook) open and shut, you would see at once that it must be very attractive to any large game fish. White and silver predominate, but are toned down by long badger hackles and jungle fowl feathers. . . . We have taken, with a companion, sixty pike in an afternoon with these flies. Usually the big fish prefer the fly well sunk, but it is more sport when the fish can be seen when they rise. . . . They will kill all kinds of game fish, salmon included."

The fly Gordon mentioned in 1903 as having been evolved and tried "some years ago" was one of his various versions of the Bumblepuppy, which is discussed in detail in Part Four of this book. There it will be noted that Roy Steenrod, a lifelong friend and fishing companion of Gordon's, wrote to the author, "I know that Gordon was tying these flies *as early as 1880.*"

In a note written by Gordon on April 25, 1903 (as quoted in McDonald's book), he said, "The 'Bumblepuppy' is great medicine—there is no doubt of that, after years of trial. Attach a well-made specimen to the end of your cast and play it in clear water. You will see at once that it is very much alive and shows up wonderfully. If jungle-fowl feathers are put on, they should open and shut with each movement of the fly. Years ago I sent samples of this fly, dressed salmon fly fashion, to the Editor [of the *Fishing Gazette*], but it is difficult to induce anglers to try new patterns if they are peculiar or display combinations not usually approved of."

Gordon's correspondence with the editor of the *Fishing Gazette* may have borne fruit, or it may be that the next allusion to streamer flies and bucktails was developed independently. In either case, six years or so after the emergence of the Bumblepuppy, John P. Hance, of Fort Wayne, Indiana, brought forth a long hair-wing fly for bass called the Fort Wayne Bucktail. I am indebted to Harold H. Smedley, author of *Fly Patterns and Their Origins* (Muskegon, Mich.: Westshore Publications), for research on the subject. In a perusal of old bound copies of *Forest and Stream* magazine, he found a letter written by Hance to its editor describing the Fort Wayne Bucktail. Mr. Smedley comments in his book as follows: "The orange body was bound with gold. The tail was red, yellow, and a strip of wood duck feather. A large lock of deer hair extended as a wing beyond the end of the tail and was the

21

most prominent part of the fly. This hair was not put on like a hackle but like a wing. It is dated 1886." Mr. Smedley told me that this description is just as Hance wrote it.

Those of us who love to fish for striped bass with the fly rod and saltwater streamer flies may be interested to know that Gordon seems to have been one of the first to try this also, because on July 19, 1915, he wrote to a friend: "The striped bass of the American coast is one of the finest game and food fishes in the world. On the same tackle he makes longer runs and fights as well as the Atlantic salmon. Large striped bass were at one time fished for at the Falls of the Potomac with large flies. I have killed them with Bumblepuppy flies. I sent you patterns years ago."

Also in 1913, in a letter to Roy Steenrod, Gordon wrote, "I have taken bass, bream, rock fish, perch, sun fish; pickerel, etc. on Bumblepuppies, not to mention big trout in the Esopus. Good when they are feeding on minnows."

In these early days, despite the work of pioneers such as Gordon and Hance, it appears that this new type of fly was so little known that others considered they had originated it independently. For example, William B. Sturgis, in his book *Fly Tying* (New York: Charles Scribner's Sons, 1940), quoted a memorandum commenting on the fact that a bucktail was tied in 1901 from the hair of a red spaniel and some worsted taken from a rug. This account is given correctly in George Grant's book *Montana Trout Flies* (privately printed, see page 194), in which he says:

"The Trude Bucktail was originated by Carter H. Harrison, once Mayor of Chicago, while visiting the A. S. Trude ranch near Big Springs, Idaho, in 1901.

"The fly was first tied in jest on a muskie hook, a wing of hair from a red spaniel, and red worsted from a cabin rug. It looked so good, however, that it was later tied with a fox squirrel wing, red yarn body ribbed with flat silver, and a red rooster hackle, no tail.

"Bill Beaty, one of Montana's first professionals, added a tail of red goose wing section, and covered the wool base with red floss silk. The hackle was bushy as it was intended to cover the area where the wing was tied on, and it was always inclined toward the rear.

"Cliff Wyatt, a renowned western fly tyer, dressed a wet fly version of the Trude by retaining the fox squirrel wing, changing the body to orange chenille ribbed with oval gold tinsel, and making the hackle and tail from guinea hen feather fibers."

Dan Bailey later tied the Trude as a dry fly. The original bucktail version appears in Color Plate III.

In 1902, during a week or two of guiding an English angler who was fishing for trout and landlocked salmon on Maine's famed Kennebago Stream, Herbert L. Welch, nationally known as a guide, artist, taxidermist, and fly caster, tied several flies to imitate smelt. He showed me one in his studio on Mooselookmeguntic Lake. Herbie related that there were no long-shanked hooks in those days and, rather than make the flies with ordinary short hooks, he cut down and reforged bluefish hooks for the job. This was inspired by the fact that the Englishman had brought along several very lovely Silver Doctor salmon flies which were size 6/0, much too large for Kennebago fishing. They were useless as they were and seemed much too beautiful to discard. With the reforged bluefish hooks (originally made four or five inches long, so that the sharp teeth of the bluefish could not cut the leader) and the long multicolored feathers of the abnormally large salmon flies, Herbie made several streamers which took big fish. There is no doubt that he arrived at the idea independently, and there is no question that these flies were the most elaborate and beautiful streamers produced up to that time.

Other records show that William E. Scripture, Jr., a lawyer of Rome, New York, dressed bucktails in 1907. Soon after this the killing power of the new long flies began to become regionally known as anglers traveled from place to place leaving samples for other fly dressers to copy and adapt to their own requirements.

2–1 The Scripture bucktail.

One of the grand old gentlemen of American angling was Harvey A. Donaldson, the famed firearms expert from Fultonville, New York. In letters written to me in 1958 he enclosed three ancient bucktails,* with the following comments:

"Strange as it may seem, my first fly fishing was done with a brown and white bucktail fly, so I was using bucktails before 1900. Our Mohawk River [in the Mohawk valley of New York State] was famous for smallmouth bass and we caught plenty with bucktails. One of the flies I am sending you I believe was tied around 1875, maybe earlier. Note the fat body and the hook. These were Pennell hooks from England. At that time, no long-

---

*The bucktail which Mr. Donaldson states is dated 1875 has a short red wool tail with a fat buglike body wound (evidently) with silver wire. The wing is a bunch of natural dark brown bucktail about twice as long as the hook.

The two bucktails of 1893 vintage are dressed as follows. No. 1 has a short red wool tail with a body of black thread windings over and almost concealing the wool, ribbed with silver wire or narrow silver tinsel. The wing is natural brown bucktail over white bucktail, about twice as long as the hook. No. 2 has a tail of olive green wool with a body of the same wound with white thread as a ribbing. The wing is natural brown bucktail over white bucktail about twice as long as the hook. Both flies are crudely dressed. Mr. Donaldson relates that he often tied flies while standing in a stream. Comparison of the Donaldson bucktails with the Scripture bucktails indicates that they are quite similar.

shanked hooks were available. Around 1905 I used bucktails on the Mohawk River above Rome, New York, for *big* brown trout. It was at this time that I met and fished with Bill Scripture. I knew his brother but never met his father, who was a judge and an old-time bird hunter.

"The only reason we used feathers instead of bucktail was for fishing in fast water. We found that long white feathers tied back to back and thus curved outward (as in the Ordway pattern) gave a lot more action, and the big brook trout really went for them. This started about 1898 when my fishing companion, a lawyer from Fultonville, New York, named Leonard F. Fish, decided we needed something with more action than the bucktails in the swift water below Wakeley Flow Dam on the Cedar River. The cook had been cleaning some chickens, so we tried tying some feathers on top of the bucktails. This didn't work, so I eventually tied four feathers (two on each side, back to back) on a bare hook. That really worked! We used these flies *only* in fast water.

"The reason the old flies I'm sending you have lasted so long is that I was taught to use fine tobacco dust sprinkled over the flies to preserve them from moths. This does not evaporate like moth balls, and it keeps flies for years. The other two bucktails enclosed were tied before 1893."

There are many who have had the impression that the streamer fly and bucktail originated in the state of Maine. While this does not seem to be so, it is certain that the fly tyers, anglers, and guides of Maine did much to promote the great popularity which these flies enjoy today. Their start in Maine seems to have taken place on Grand Lake Stream prior to 1910, because in the April 1910 issue of *National Sportsman* magazine an army officer, Brigadier Philip Reade, writes: ". . . There was a time when the chanticleers of Grand Lake Stream used to rule the yards with uplifted white tails; but their pride was crushed when a guide named Alonzo Stickney Bacon demonstrated that hen's long feathers made attractive lures for ouananiche (landlocked salmon). This is how it came about.

"Alonzo was in his canoe, fishing with artificial flies. He could not get a rise. He was seated on a cushion filled with hen's feathers. There was a hole in the cushion and a long white feather protruded. Alonzo plucked the feather from the cushion; tied it to a hook, and used it as a lure. The ouananiche took it with avidity. Other fishermen copied the lure. Soon in all the barnyards of the plantations all of the hens were rifled of their caudal appendages, and the stream was flecked with anglers using a long straggly fly, misnamed by Boston flymakers the Morning Glory. All things great are wound up with some things little, but I am convinced that this recital is true. The fly makers of the great cities adorn the hook with white bristles in addition to the white hen feathers. The Grand Lake Stream people cut off these whiskers when sports let them. The lure is supposed, when jiggled in rapid water, to look to fish like a smelt."

It may be true that Alonzo Bacon tied the first streamer used in Maine, although I daresay that there are those who will dispute it. Whether this was his original idea or a suggestion from a sportsman who learned of the new "long flies" somewhere else probably will never be known. In any event, the genesis of the streamer fly, insofar as Maine is concerned, seems to be at Grand Lake Stream—now, as then, a favorite angling water for big trout and landlocked salmon, the famous *Salmo salar sebago* of Maine.

Just as Theodore Gordon's Bumblepuppy was tied in many patterns, so were the original streamer flies of Grand Lake Stream. They usually were identified by the rather apt name Rooster's Regret, which meant almost any fly which was tied from the long feathers picked up around the henhouses of the farms along the stream. Mr. A. W. Ballou, originator of the Ballou Special (the Maine version of the marabou streamer), sent me a rather ancient fly which he said was the first streamer he ever saw and ever used; it was tied by an Indian guide on Grand Lake Stream. It is made from two or three curved mallard body feathers crudely laced to a hook with string. I do not doubt that it caught fish, but I must say that it appears that the trout and salmon of those days were a lot less sophisticated than they are now!

Evidently the colors of these early streamers mattered very little, although white seemed to predominate. The colors were the simple barnyard colors, and the shape and action of the fly were what interested the fish. In those days simplicity seemed to serve the purpose, and in many instances this still is true today. There are guides on the Miramichi who insist that the best salmon fly is made by tying black bear hair to a bare hook. The guides say that they catch more fish on these simple flies than they do on the fancy patterns which the sports give them. The basic requirement in their minds is long hackles or hair to give form and action. They do admit, however, that when few fish are in the river, a bit of added flash from tinsel or silk seems to enhance the result.

From here on, the family trees of streamers and bucktails become rather complicated. In the cases of those flies which are of special interest, I have added to the detailed specifications for their dressings whatever historical notes seem to be of value. The fly dressers of Maine were quick to exploit the new flies, and the fly dressers of other states, either independently or in imitation, followed suit. In the years that have gone by, the prolific result has brought the joy of acquisition to countless fishermen, at the same time confounding their minds and depleting their pocketbooks. How much these many patterns have aided their fishing is a question rather hard to decide. Without doubt there are far too many. Some are extremely valuable, designed with science and knowledge. Others are mere brainstorms of pretty colors, conceived by fishermen or fly dressers who wish to become fathers of what they hope may someday become famous patterns. This book gives authentic and detailed dressings for several hundred streamers and bucktails which are of sufficient value or of enough national or regional prominence to make their inclusion seem advisable. In selecting this rather large number, many others of seemingly lesser importance were left out. Even so, from this group about two or three dozen could be selected which would provide good fishing to any angler, for any species of fish, anywhere in the United States.

As an example of this, let us start with the lowly Rooster's Regret, when one of its versions was so crudely fashioned by a guide on Grand Lake Stream from several white hackles stolen from a Leghorn and a bare hook with a bit of thread. This fly was made beautiful and legitimate by a Maine angler who added silver tinsel to the hook and embellished the wing with red shoulders. The fly, still called the Rooster's Regret, took more fish than its cruder forebear because the tinsel and the more carefully selected feathers enhanced its form, flash, and action.

Professional fly dressers always are on the lookout for worthwhile patterns. This one was made even more salable by Gardner Percy, who, until his death in 1949, was the proprietor of the Percy Tackle Company of Portland, Maine, and the most prolific of that state's fly tyers. Mr. Percy added a white throat and silver ribbing, calling the now fully developed creation the Colonel White. This was because the fly reminded him of the famous Colonel Fuller, except that it had a white wing instead of a yellow one.

Shortly after this accomplishment a gentleman from New Hampshire came to the Percy Tackle Company and said that he wanted some Colonel White Streamers, but he wanted them dressed with splayed wings in order to give the fly greater action in slow water. Mr. Percy did as requested and, liking the adaptation, put it in his list of patterns. He called it the Ordway in honor of the gentleman from New Hampshire.

Following this occurrence, G. D. B. Bonbright, president of the Seaboard Airline Railway, was going tarpon fishing in Florida. As a pioneer in fly fishing for tarpon, Mr. Bonbright recognized the value of the color combination for this type of fishing. He commissioned Steward Slosson, then a famous fly dresser for Abercrombie & Fitch Company in New York, to dress the fly on tarpon hooks. It is probable that during the conference a few added refinements were decided upon, because the fly emerged beautiful to behold. A tail was added of red and white duck wing sections, and a short golden pheasant crest feather was included for good measure. Above the wing appeared a topping of a long golden pheasant crest feather. Horns of blue macaw tail fibers and cheeks of jungle cock completed its embellishment.

The fancy fly became known as the Bonbright. It caught many tarpon, was included in the Abercrombie & Fitch catalogs, and was copied for the use of all who desired to fish with such a combination of brilliant and rare plumage. That it caught more tarpon than the Colonel White or the Ordway would have is very much open to doubt. That it pleased a wealthy gentleman more is a foregone conclusion.

Eventually the fame of the Bonbright reached Boston, by way of Florida and New York. In Boston a tackle dealer by the name of L. Dana Chapman thought it very pretty, as in truth it was. Perhaps not knowing its name, he sent an order to Percy to make up a few dozen, tied on freshwater hooks for the trout and salmon of Maine. I am sure that Percy must have recognized his former baby, even in its new silks and satins, but in any event he named it the Dana and it is known by that name in Maine today.

The sequel to the story is short, and I trust that there will be no occasion to add to it in later years. I purchased a Dana from Percy and dressed a few duplicates. One spring in the 1930s I went into the Allagash country of Maine to fish for trout. My guide was Ross McKenney, so famed as a woodsman that he later taught the subject at Dartmouth College. I gave Ross a sample of my home-tied Dana and he gave it to Bert Quimby, who at that time was second only to Gardner Percy in Maine's professional production of streamer flies. Next year the identical fly emerged in Quimby's catalog, but now it was called the Ross McKenney. The Bonbright, Dana, and Ross McKenney are identical in dressing. All have stemmed from the Colonel White and the Ordway, whose common parent was the Rooster's Regret, conceived on Grand Lake Stream!

Thus new flies are born, some to reach lasting fame and others to be deservedly ignored. Perhaps the vast number of good, bad, and indifferent patterns is a reason why no one before now has attempted to evaluate and classify them in a book such as this!

In understanding the dressings and uses of streamer flies and bucktails, just as in learning a language or a business, it is most convenient to start with elementals. With an understanding of these, it is simpler to understand which variations in dressings are necessary and helpful and which are not. Even the simplest dressings vary in their suitability for taking certain species of fish under certain definite weather, water, and seasonal conditions. That is a subject in itself, and it will be dealt with in this book. It seems logical to understand the dressings first and then to learn how to use them most profitably.

The pedigree of the Bonbright and its less glamorous relations was given largely to indicate these two points: that patterns in streamers and bucktails have become unnecessarily voluminous and complicated, and that it is not necessary to use complicated patterns in order to catch fish. Many elaborate patterns are very successful, perhaps even more so than simpler ones. Anglers enjoy their beauty, and they have confidence in them. Enjoyment and confidence are primary factors, making expensive and detailed patterns worth their higher price, regardless of whether or not something simpler could do as well.

The point where a hair fly becomes a bucktail and a feather-winged fly becomes a streamer is an arbitrary one. Peter J. Schwab, the famous angler and writer, defined it this way: "A hair fly becomes a bucktail when the wings are roughly twice the length of a *standard*-length hook and thus give pronounced swimming action to the lure." This is generally true, and his definition applies to feather-winged streamers as well as to hair-winged bucktails.

27

A hair-wing fly may be termed a bucktail, even though the wing is scarcely longer than the hook, provided that the hook is sufficiently long so that the fly, in action in the water, gives the effect of a swimming bait fish rather than of an insect or something else. This is true of feather-winged streamers as well. As an example we may take the two Edson Tigers, which are acknowledged by everyone to be bucktails and to imitate bait fish. When these are correctly dressed, the hook is abnormally long, such as 4X or 5X. The hair wing is scarcely longer than the hook. This is to prevent the hair from being able to catch under the bend of the hook while the fly is being fished. (An alternative, widely used in saltwater patterns, is to apply the wing even as far back on the hook's shank as its bend to prevent the possibility of similarly fouling the wing.)

It would seem more logical to consider as bucktails any hair fly, regardless of size, which is of a shape that gives it the appearance of a bait fish in the water. Streamers should enjoy a similar definition except that their "wings" are predominantly composed of feathers.

Of course there are both hair-winged flies and feather-winged flies which are so shaped that they can be fished by one method to imitate a bait fish and by another to imitate an insect. There is no doubt that the familiarly termed "wet flies" of many types are taken by fish to be tiny bait fish when the water current or the angler makes them appear so. Such cases may be decided by determining what they are made to represent. There are few which can escape falling into one classification or the other.

The terms "streamer flies" and "bucktails" are loosely used by many fly dressers and writers. It seems suitable to define the streamer fly as a fly possessing a predominantly *feathered* wing and having shape and action which are intended to represent a bait fish. As such, a streamer may have a bit of hair of any length dressed over or under the hook. If the feathered part of the wing predominates, it should be termed a streamer. By the same token, a bucktail would be a fly possessing a predominantly *haired* wing, whose shape and intended action are to represent a bait fish. It may have a feathered topping or shoulders (and frequently does), at the same time remaining a bucktail. A hair-wing fly of this type is called a bucktail regardless of the kind of hair used. Both streamer flies and bucktails are known as "flies" even though the term may not be strictly correct. The words have become common in usage and are convenient. Since the necessary repetition of the words "streamers" and "bucktails" may become tiresome in this book I occasionally have grouped both types under the name of "streamers" for the sake of simplicity, and I do not mean to destroy their individuality by so doing.

The simplest of all such flies is the single-color bucktail. Normally it is dressed on a hook 2X, 3X, or 4X long, but it can be dressed on a short hook if the wing is made long enough to provide minnowlike action. Usually the body of the hook is concealed by silver tinsel, because the majority of bait fish have a silver underbody. It may, however, be dressed with tinsel of another color, silk, chenille, wool, or other materials. The wing is a small bunch of hair of any sort or color provided that it gives suitable appearance and action. If the hooks used are 2X or 3X long, the wing should be about one and a half times as long as the hook. Shorter or longer hooks will require that the wing be longer or perhaps shorter than this.

The single-color bucktail need have no tail, throat, shoulder, topping, or other embellishment. If it is correctly dressed with a suitable amount and color of hair, it will catch fish—a surprising number of them. The colors to be chosen and the reasons for selecting them will be discussed as we go along.

Although such a bucktail surely will catch fish, I am convinced that the addition of a few more refinements will make it more successful, because these refinements aid in giving it the appearance of a minnow. However, I would prefer a simple fly such as this, if it is suitably dressed, to a more elaborate one, which is so badly tied that it is relatively lacking in the inherent form, flash, and action that are so necessary to tempt strikes.

A difficulty found when bucktails or streamers are dressed with wings which are very long or with hooks which are too short is that, while fishing the fly, the wing may foul itself by catching under the bend of the hook. Since this ruins fly action, we must watch for it. A way to prevent it in dressing bucktails on short hooks is to tie the wing on over the end of the shank of the hook where the tail would be; perhaps over the bit of color composing the tail. To avoid short strikes this part of the wing usually shouldn't be very long. Then, using the same amount of hair, tie in the wing behind the eye, as usual, making it overlap only slightly the part of the wing included in the tail. This provides a double-wing bucktail as in the Blonde series. To prevent the same difficulty with streamers, add a bit of fairly stiff hair under the feathered wing for it to rest on.

In passing on to more complex or elaborate bucktails, the fly dresser can go in either of two directions, or in both of them at the same time. He can build up the wing in two, three, or more colors, or he can embellish the fly with tail, throat, shoulders, and other decorations. My preference in the matter is merely individual judgment, but it has been sufficiently successful so that I shall discuss the steps in the order of their importance to me, leaving it to others to change them if they wish.

Fish in relatively unfrequented waters, certain pond fish, and many saltwater fish usually will strike the simplest bucktail or streamer just as readily as one which is more ornate. When fish learn to be suspicious of anglers and their flies, greater attention must be given to the dressing and selection of the flies and the ways in which they are used. Whether or not the single-color bucktail will obtain results, it always has seemed to me that the double-color bucktail is better because it more nearly gives the impression of the dark back, light midsection, and glistening underbody common to most bait fish. The double-color bucktail is made by applying the same total amount of hair as in the single-color fly, but the hair is composed of

The blacknose dace

The Black Nosed Dace Bucktail when dry

The same fly when wet

2–2 Comparison of actual bait fish and its imitation when dry and when wet.

two distinct colors, one added on top of the other. Normally the darker color is on top. Thus, while the single-color bucktail may be dressed with white or brown or yellow or some other effective color, on a silver-tinseled hook, for example, the double-color bucktail may have brown over white, black over white, yellow over white, red over white, red over yellow, black over brown, or many other similar combinations. The single-color often is good. The double-color usually is better.

The next step is to add shoulders or cheeks or both. (The names of the parts of a fly are included with a drawing at the beginning of Part Four.) The shoulders imitate the head and gills of the bait fish, and the cheeks represent the eyes. Cheeks normally are the tips of feathers from a jungle cock neck, since these best seem to convey the illusion. Jungle cock is expensive and sometimes difficult to obtain, so many fly tyers leave it off or substitute an imitation or some other bit of feather for it. Shoulders normally are the tips of body feathers, dyed or natural, from ducks or other birds. They should conceal the fore part of the wing to between a quarter and a third of its length. Either shoulders or cheeks add greatly to the appearance and effectiveness of the fly, but the inclusion of them both is more of a luxury than a necessity.

Next in importance is the throat and/or the tail. The throat, with or without the shoulders, adds to the appearance of the fly and enhances the illusion of gills. It normally is rather short, not heavily dressed, and its stiff fibers are made to splay out so that they will "work" in the water, providing added action to the fly. The throat also is referred to as a "collar" or a "beard." A collar consists of part of a hackle wound on where the wing is applied, usually with only two or three turns, or more if the pattern calls for them. A few windings of thread can be applied over the base of the collar to slant the fibers backward as much as desired and to make the collar more secure. Before doing this the top half of the collar can be pulled down and then secured so that the throat is dressed in a lower semicircle. This helps to partially mask the shoulders, or substitute for them, and can provide an

30

attractive effect. At the same time the splayed throat pulsates in the water to enhance the fly's effectiveness.

A smaller number of windings (usually one or two) of two hackles of different colors can be applied, either mixed or one in front of the other, for an even better effect. Very few patterns call for this. Collars almost always are of hackle, but they can be of spun-on hair, as in Muddlers.

A beard usually is a small bunch of hackle fibers pulled from the feather and tied in under the base of the wing. A beard also can be a small bunch of hair, such as bucktail. It often is as long as the wing and then acts as an underbody, partially masking the fly's body, which then is normally of tinsel. This underbody or underwing provides the lower color of the fly and suggests the belly of a bait fish, so it should be of a light color such as white or yellow. When a dressing calls for a throat, it can be applied either as a collar or as a beard. When it calls for a collar or a beard, it is a specific instruction to do as noted. In addition to providing the illusion of gills, or perhaps pectoral fins, the throat enhances the action of the fly and gives a more finished appearance.

The tail may be of very short hair, but usually it is a small bunch of hackle fibers or a section (or combination of sections) of a feather. It adds color and attractiveness, and some anglers feel that it seems to provide the illusion of the tail of the fish. This last, if taken from the fish's point of view, always has appeared to me to be doubtful. I am sure that it adds color and attractiveness, but otherwise its inclusion seems superfluous.

A topping adds to the appearance and effectiveness of many streamer flies and bucktails. Frequently it is a few strands of peacock herl, as long as the wing, but it may be of other materials. I doubt that many of these "other materials" do very much to catch fish.

It usually is important to add tinsel ribbing when the body of the fly is made from chenille, silk, or similar substances, because the tinsel provides the flash which makes the fly noticeable to the fish. If the body is of tinsel, the added ribbing enhances the flash by providing additional reflecting surfaces. This usually is an advantage, but on bright days in clear water it may not be so. If the dressing of the fly includes no tinsel in body or ribbing, a bit may be added as a tag.

The patterns of many elaborate streamers and bucktails call for butts, horns, and the feathers of rare birds for toppings and for other embellishments. To my mind, these are decorations only. They make the flies beautiful and thus please the fishermen, but I am sure they make no difference whatsoever to the fish. Butts are supposed to represent the egg sacs of flies which imitate insects. Horns correspond to their "feelers," if they have any. Quite obviously these have no place in flies made to represent bait fish, but they occasionally are added for decoration.

31

A third color, or even a fourth, may be added to the bucktail wing at any stage of the game. This has resulted in such simple and extremely effective flies as the Mickey Finn and the Black Nosed Dace. An additional color often assists in the imitation of certain minnows, particularly those having a dark lateral line or stripe. On some flies the inclusion of topping (usually peacock herl) takes the place of another color of hair in the wing.

The steps in embellishing the streamer fly are almost identical with those in embellishing the bucktail. Many streamer patterns call for adding a very small bunch of bucktail (or other hair) under or on top of the hook shank, or both, to help develop the desired color scheme. If the hair is applied on top of the hook, as we have noted, it helps prevent the wing from fouling under it. Streamer wings usually are dressed with four neck or saddle hackles of identical size, although the outer two may be somewhat shorter than those in the middle and/or of a different color, as in the Supervisor, for example. A topping of a few strands of peacock herl represents the dark backs of bait fish and adds to attractiveness. A topping of golden pheasant crest adds a bit of flash to the fly and helps to "frame" the wing, but this is confined to fancy flies where the desire is more to please fishermen than fish. If used, the golden pheasant crest feather should be selected to reach the end of the fly's tail, and it should be exactly over the back of the fly to frame both sides of it.

This book contains the names of many illustrious anglers and fly dressers who have contributed authentic dressings and/or methods to its pages. The majority of the flies herein listed are patterns which resulted from many years of study and streamside experience. Wherever possible, I have gone to the source to obtain the authentic pattern of each fly, and have tried to explain each pattern so it can be copied exactly without the necessity of seeing a correct example. I have been gathering this explicit information for over thirty years. The year 1950 saw the publication of *Streamer Fly Fishing.* As years go by, new fly patterns, new fishing methods, and new techniques evolve. Thus, in 1966, the book was reborn and brought up to date as *Streamer Fly Tying & Fishing.* Now, a little more than ten years later, a wealth of new experiences and new information are included in the current volume.

If I may make three suggestions to younger anglers who are interested in dressing their own flies, I would say that it is most important to start by trying to copy established patterns. As an amateur fly dresser myself, I used to make the error of trying to "invent" new patterns. Before I learned the wisdom of accepting the experience of others, I had made many pretty but illegitimate flies, most of which I never found very successful. It is fun to improvise if we have good reason to do so, but it seems more advantageous to copy authentic patterns that are of proven value.

As a young angler I began a collection of flies tied by the originators of the patterns. These, now numbering many hundreds, have been the greatest aid in tying my own flies properly. Even if this book accomplishes what I hope it will, my second suggestion is that anglers and fly dressers should obtain, as occasion permits, authentic dressings from the finest fly tyers, keeping this collection properly labeled and intact for future reference. If the fly dressers and their patterns are well known, as many of them surely will be, the collection will become more valuable with age, affording inestimable assistance and pleasure to its possessor.

Lastly, the best way to become an expert fly dresser is to join a group of others with the same interest, and to participate actively in it. Club members teach each other new techniques, trade fly dressing materials, know where the best fishing spots are—and they have fun! The outdoor writer of the local newspaper should know about nearby groups and should help prospective members to join and get acquainted. There is a very valuable international group which publishes an instructive magazine on fly dressing called the *Roundtable* and which is composed of many regional groups. It is called the United Fly Tyers, or UFT. The cost of joining is small and the advantages are great. Write them at P. O. Box 723, Boston, Massachusetts 02102.

Tips on Fishing Streamers in Fast Water

Dᴜʀɪɴɢ ᴛʜᴇ ᴄᴏɴᴠᴇʀsᴀᴛɪᴏɴ between the old angler and the younger one, two statements were made which are correct but perhaps confusing. The old angler advised his protégé to watch the prevalent bait fish and to select flies which match them as closely as possible in coloration, as well as in form, flash, and action. Then he said that color is the least important of the four requisites. How important is it to select a fly which represents the color characteristics of bait fish? The answer is that it is more important under certain conditions than under others. So, what are the conditions?

Authors of some of the older angling books have advanced the theory of "bright fly for bright day, dull fly for dull day." Others have said they would be content (as far as color goes) with only three patterns: a bright one, a dull one, and one in between. These authors were correct, as far as they went, but they didn't go far enough.

When the angler fishes his fly between the fish (or where they should be) and the sun, the fish's perception of the fly may be blinded or dazzled a bit so that all it may see is a bit of flash or action, if it notices anything at all. If one holds a fly against a bright light, this will be obvious. What we need then is a dark fly, because it presents a better silhouette which the fish can see in the glare more easily.

On the other hand, when the angler fishes his fly where the fish is between it and the sun, the fish's perception of the fly is not blinded, because it sees the fly reflected by the sun. So what we need then is a lighter

34

fly, or one with more tinsel. In this case, in clear water, the fish can see the fly clearly, so we should select one which imitates prevalent bait fish as closely as possible. Such flies usually contain some light colors and probably a tinseled body.

Of course, water conditions play a part in fly selection. When water is low and clear a smaller fly may do better, and conversely when it is high and discolored. In the latter case fish can notice a bigger fly better, and perhaps a brighter one.

Light conditions also play a part. As light increases, try a lighter fly with more tinsel in it. As light decreases, try a darker fly with less tinsel. On overcast days a fly in the medium range of color intensity, such as with some gray, brown, or orange, might do best. When light fails, on a very dark day or at night, a black fly usually is ideal because its silhouette is more noticeable.

Two comments may support the latter contention. During World War II, demolition divers (frogmen) looking up at the hulls of ships reported that white hulls were the most difficult to see, and black hulls the easiest. Hunters watching bird dogs near dark know that light-colored ones are hard to see, but that dark or black ones can be noticed more clearly.

This provides a few guidelines in selecting imitator patterns versus attractor types. Most of our fishing is done when streams are clear and their flow low or moderate. Try imitator patterns along the guidelines which have been suggested. If these don't do well, put on an attractor, which may wake fish up. If they look at the fly but don't take it, go back to an imitator again, which they may then take. If these tactics fail, the fault may not be with the fly; it may be with our presentation, the action being given to it, or the depth at which we are fishing.

When streams are not clear, or when they are high, larger and brighter, or much darker, patterns should work best because fish see them easier under adverse conditions. The clue then is to experiment.

Stream flow also is a factor in fly selection. Fast mountain streams require flies with high wings because they give better action in swift currents. Low-winged patterns are better in slow streams and in lakes.

If we want flies to sink quickly, and don't want to weight them, sparsely dressed ones with less neck hackle should be better. Most streamers sink faster than most bucktails. Deer hair, being hollow, is more buoyant than the hairs of most other animals.

When we ponder these various rules and opinions well enough to understand them, we may be able to look at scores of streamers or bucktails in a fly book and notice one, saying to ourselves, "That's the one for now." We can fish it with confidence, which is a big help. In any event, knowledge helps in selecting a few from many. If we could carry all this far enough to fathom fishes' minds, we might have the sure answer, but that would spoil the fun of fishing!

Since this book is for people with more than a modicum of angling

35

experience, let's reduce tips on tackle to a minimum. Except for use in brushy streams, I prefer rods that are sensibly long rather than unreasonably short. The new graphites, such as those of standard top quality made by Cortland or Scientific Anglers, are ideal if one can afford them; in fact, I would recommend raiding the piggy bank if necessary to acquire one. For one of several reasons, their lightness in proportion to length makes constant casting less tiresome and much more pleasant.

The fly lines offered by these two firms also are of exceptional value. In thin water, a floater should fish the fly deep enough. In deeper water, use a floater with a sinking tip. Since streamers and bucktails normally are relatively large, these lines in weight-forward types are best. When extra-long casts (rarely necessary on streams) are needed, we might consider shooting heads in the above types. The Sunset Line and Twine Company pioneered in these, and offers excellent ones, along with its "memory-free" solid filament shooting line for backing.

Leaders usually need be no longer than the rod, or not much longer. My favorite here is Cortland's Twin Tip, which comes with a butt section and two tip sections. When one tip is used up, just tie on the other and/or use monofilament extensions of proper strength for the size of fly and fishing conditions.

With this tackle or something similar and with fly selection narrowed down, let's review streamer fishing tactics for flowing water. Most areas of any stream are devoid of sport fish because they congregate in the relatively few places which provide concealment, suitable water temperatures, adequate oxygen, and easy access to food supplies. Too many anglers innocently waste time fishing barren water instead of concentrating on spots greater knowledge would indicate to be productive.

Many years ago, when an older angler took me under his wing, he taught me a lesson I'll never forget, one which is well worthy of being passed along to others. He took me to a wilderness pool on a famous trout stream and watched me rig up and wade in while he sat on a log and placidly puffed on his pipe. After several casts I looked to see where the old gentleman was, and noticed he still was there but had an admonitory frown on his face. I waded ashore and came to him.

"Aren't you going to fish?" I asked.

"Not here," he said. "You've spoiled the pool. You were wading where the fish were, and you should have noticed them scooting for safety. Now, you sit down here by me for a while and we'll let this pool get back to normal. In the meantime you won't mind if I tell you a few things.

"When you approach water you plan to fish, you'll do better to stay concealed while you look the situation over. Take all the time necessary to examine the water to decide where the trout should be and to plan your casting strategy. Look for the places you'd select to be resting in if you were a trout, or a salmon, or any other game fish. If you stay quiet for a while, you may see fish or the signs they make when they are feeding. You waded out to get in back of a boulder to fish the tail of the pool, and you didn't notice that two nice trout were lying back of the rock. I saw them go for cover, and you should have assumed that fish would be there.

"This is a real good pool, so let's do what you should have done in the first place—sit here for a while and look over the situation. The stream at the head of the pool breaks over those rocks into deeper water. The main current flows in, but some of it swirls into that little eddy. This forms an edge of current, and fish should be lying in or near the edge because the water is deep enough to conceal them and because food drifting down-stream passes close to the edge. It's a feed lane.

"Over there," the old man continued, pointing to the place, "the current in high water has undercut the bank enough for good concealment. Bushes shade the spot, and terrestrials such as grasshoppers drop from them into the water to provide food. Drift your streamer as close to the bank as you can, and you'll have to mend your cast often so the fly won't whip.

"Now, cross-stream, over there, you'll see an old stump the undercut bank dumped into the pool many years ago. A fly worked closely and carefully there should get a take. Farther down a little brook trickles in, so small that it looks like a spring hole. The grass is lusher there, so you should notice it. Later on, when the water is warmer, several trout should be lying in that cooler spot, but maybe not now. An Edson Dark Tiger got me a three-pounder there last August. Between here and there you'll see boils in the current indicating big rocks down deep. Fish your fly deep all around each of them. Don't bother with the tail of the pool now, because I see no feeding activity there. Since there's no concealment, I wouldn't expect fish to feed in the tail until dark, but the gravel bottom indicates it might be a good spot then.

"The pool is settling down now, but let's give it a few minutes more. If you'll look for the longish dark spot I see back of the rock where you were fishing, you'll see that one of the trout has returned. The other should move in presently. Leave them for later. Work the upper edge first, then the undercut bank. Keep low. Fish slow. I'll stay here for a while and watch."

Although this lesson occurred a few decades ago it is one I always remembered. Several minutes devoted to reading the water can save many fruitless casts and can make more of them productive. The story is true, as well as I can remember it now. The time was late June and the place was Maine's Kennebago Stream. The old gentleman was Herbie Welch, originator of the Black Ghost, a famous artist and taxidermist of trout, and one of the greatest anglers who ever lived. Whenever I think of what the old angler said in this book I often think of Herbie but, as I have explained, the old angler is a composite of several of similar fame.

37

Reading the water,* whether it be brook, stream, river, pond, lake, estuary, bay, or ocean, is the principal key to fishing success; more so than casting ability, choice of fly, or anything else. It is essential to develop the ability to sense where fish should be so that the fly can be presented to such places with maximum chances of success. Most of us, being more or less specialists in one kind of fish or another, in one type of water or another, should not find this very difficult. It may be helpful to review some of the typical places where fish hold in streams, because good holding water is the same most everywhere.

Too many fishermen work their lures in water they should assume to be barren, unless there is evidence to the contrary. Consider a stream as a tunnel through which water flows. Since fish seek the best available combination of protection and quiet water where they don't have to exert themselves, they usually are not in the faster water in the center of the tunnel. Except when feeding on the surface, they are at the sides and bottom of the tunnel, where they do find this combination. So why do so many fishermen work their lures in midstream or at middepth when the fish should be elsewhere? Where is elsewhere? Elsewhere is holding water where there is protection; either the protection of depth or of obstacles which provide concealment. Let's define holding water.

While standing knee-deep in a stream, bend over and put your hand beside one of your boots. The current is swift there because it is unimpeded. Now put your hand either just in front of or just behind the boot. The current is slow there because the boot breaks the flow, providing a quieter pocket in front of as well as behind the boot. A big rock or a ledge or stump or anything else that breaks the flow, such as a log jam or a bridge abutment, makes a larger pocket of quiet water. Fish can rest in these quiet pockets with minimum exertion; so little, in fact, that they can be seen lying there barely moving fins or tails. This is holding water. Another type is where the current forms an edge, as between the fast flow and a backwater or an eddy. The best holding water is where there is protection of depth, such as rocks on the bottom of the stream, or of anything fish can hide under, such as ledges, undercut banks, or tree roots. Fish leave holding water only to feed or when alarmed, so nearness of a food supply, such as a feeding lane, makes good holding water even better. Since there are many impediments such as these on the bottoms and sides of many parts of streams, currents are slower in these places, and feeding can be done with minimum exertion. Small fish usually occupy minor holding spots, while bigger ones take the major ones. If a big fish is taken from a major holding position, another big one soon will occupy it, driving smaller fish away. Anglers remember good holding positions where they have taken big fish because they later take others from the same places.

Another factor in finding fish concerns water temperatures, which we

*See my book *How to Find Fish and Make Them Strike* (New York: Harper & Row, 1974).

will learn more about in the next chapter. This can be important in deciding where fish should be in streams and how to fish streamers for them as conditions change during the season. Like people, fish are very sensitive to water temperatures, and they go to places where they are most comfortable, if they can.

Let's consider the eastern brook trout for example. It is most comfortable in water of about 57° F. but tolerates water in the 47° to 68° range. In early spring the trout's metabolism is so slow that they practically cease to feed. They lie on the bottom of pools or other deep areas in the warmest water they can find, which is at the lowest part of their toleration range, and they take food or lures languidly, if at all. Streamers must be fished slowly and close to bottom. As water warms toward its optimum temperature of about 57°, trout become highly active and are found in such places as have been discussed. As water exceeds its optimum temperature, trout go where they can find it cooler. This usually is at brook mouths where colder water flows down, but it may be in visible spring holes near shore or in invisible ones deep in the stream. Anglers search for spring holes because they can be hot spots in summer.

Brown trout and rainbow trout have similar tolerant ranges, but they prefer water about 5° warmer. Brown trout seem to prefer water slower than rainbows like but faster than brook trout like. It helps to understand water temperatures preferred by various species in order to fish streamers in the right places and at suitable depths. Many anglers consider water temperatures so important that they carry thermometers and use them frequently.

Given reasonable knowledge of what types and sizes of streamers to select for various conditions and where to fish them in streams, we should find basic casting suggestions of value in order to put the fly in the right place and to fish it at the proper speed and at the desired depth. Students of angling know there are many casting methods and combinations, but we can simplify them here by limiting them to five which should accomplish the purpose.

The upstream cast is used to sink the fly deeply, as in bottom dredging in streams where water temperature is below the optimum, thus causing fish to lie deep in runs or pools. A floating line with sinking tip should suffice except where a sinking or fast-sinking one is needed for abnormal depth. Select a fly that sinks easily; probably a streamer without a collar, or a bucktail with a wing of minimum buoyancy, such as squirrel rather than deer hair. If weighting is allowed, a little would help. One of the weedless types mentioned in Chapter 9 or a jig fly as described in Chapter 10 may be needed to prevent hangups.

To fish the streamer fly upstream the wading angler directs it over midstream boulders or other holding water and allows it to sink while recovering line fast enough to keep the fly moving slightly faster than the current, so that it will appear natural and so that he can feel a strike when

39

it occurs. It is necessary to work the fly with a lifelike motion, because it will not simulate a minnow when it is being washed downstream headfirst. In a fast-moving stream this combination is so difficult to accomplish satisfactorily that I usually give it up, unless deeply sinking the fly to bottom-feeding fish is the prime objective. In a slow-moving stream the operation is much easier and more likely to be successful.

This type of cast works better when it is curved either to the right or to the left, depending on where the best holding water is. Remember that the fly goes where the rod tip sends it. Before the forward cast drops the fly to the water, move the rod tip one way or the other and notice that the fly curves in the same direction that the rod tip is moved. A bit of practice is necessary to learn how much tip movement to give it. Thus, if a cast is made just to the right of a midstream boulder and the fly is curved to the left, the fly will drop into the holding water above the boulder and will drift close beside it and into the edge of the holding water below it. Such a cast, when delivered far enough upstream from the holding water, should sink the fly deeply into it, where good fish should be lying. This cast has been called a curve cast and is useful in keeping the leader out of direct line with the fly, so the leader is less apparent to the fish. It is handy in upstream casting,

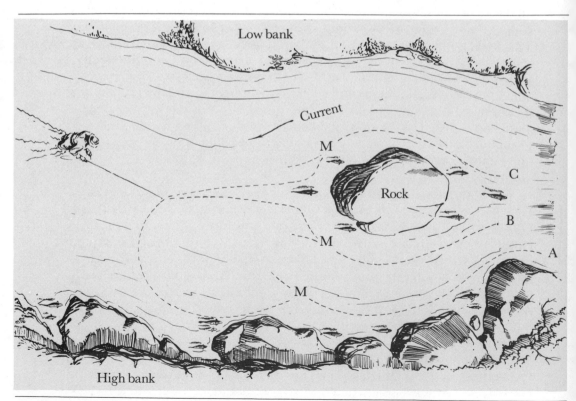

3–1 The upstream cast.

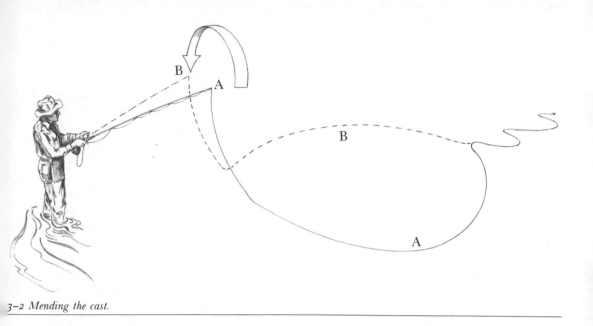

3–2 *Mending the cast.*

and for many other purposes, such as working the fly in a feeding lane.

A typical situation in upstream casting is illustrated in Figure 3–1. The angler sees on his right some large rocks and a deep run near them where some of the stream current is directed to the right bank. He may correctly assume that fish are lying deep in the protection of the rocks near the fast water of the current. He therefore makes a reasonably long cast to a point such as *A* where the current moves into a deep run near the bank, and he allows the fly to be borne into the run toward the bank by the current. As the fly drifts downstream, he simulates the action of a minnow by raising and lowering his rod tip to give the fly a series of short and erratic jerks. Each time he lowers his rod tip he recovers sufficient line to keep himself in control of the fly. The raising of the rod tip is done in a series of sharp and short twitches rather than in a sweeping motion.

In fishing across a current to slower water beyond, as in the cast to the far right to position *M,* the faster current will put a downstream bow in the line, which will pull the fly downstream much faster than it should be fished. Unless this is corrected, the excess speed of the fly usually repels fish rather than attracting them. To correct this, the angler "mends" his line. That is, he keeps the line on or very near the surface and, by a flip of the rod tip in the opposite direction from that which the bowed line is taking, he reverses, or partially reverses, the bow in the line, as shown in Figure 3–2, thus regaining control of the line from the current and allowing the fly to be fished in a normal manner. Mending the line under such circumstances is of extreme importance.

Abnormally large rocks in a stream are favorite sanctuaries for fish. They lie in the protection of the slack current around the rock, usually just above it or on its downstream side in the position shown in Figure 3–1.

41

Thus, a cast to a position above the rock to point *B* will direct the fly deep into the water near where the fish are presumed to be. As the fly begins to pass by the rock, it may be possible, if a sufficient length of the line is on top of the water, to mend the line to the left to keep the fly as near to the downstream side of the rock as possible. This should throw that part of the floating line which is nearest the rod into the current to the left of the rock. This current should pull the line to the left and direct the fly through the quiet fish-holding area on the downstream side of the rock.

When one side of the rock has been covered, the other side should be fished in a similar manner, as is indicated by the cast to position *C*. Mending the line is an alternative to making a new cast. Sometimes this is advisable in cases where low overhanging branches make it impossible to place the fly near the bank by ordinary means. Many very large fish are found in the protection of rocks near shore, so these places should not be ignored in favor of midstream locations.

It often happens that a fish will follow a lure and not take it unless the method of fishing the lure is varied. Therefore, just before the cast is completed, anglers often find it of value to change the action of the fly by giving it a series of longer and slower, or shorter and sharper, motions before it gets near enough to be picked up from the water. I have seen many cases where this change of action brought a quick strike from a good fish, his indecision probably being settled by a feeling that his prey was about to escape.

In all degrees of current swiftness, and particularly under very fast water conditions, *the quarter upstream cast* has several advantages. It usually makes it possible to fish from the bank in places where it is not desirable to wade. It allows the fly to sink deep in the water. It gives the angler better control of his line and his fly. Being fished more nearly broadside to the current, the fly drifts in a more natural manner, tempting more strikes with a minimum of manipulation of the fly. Its main purpose is to allow the fly to sink. Therefore, on completion of the cast the fly should usually not be fished immediately but should be allowed to drift and sink on a fairly slack line until just before it reaches a place where a fish may be expected.

There is a spot on Vermont's White River where a big brown trout habitually lives below the large rock shown in Figure 3–3. Other smaller trout usually rest in the protection of the fallen tree slightly downstream. An angler with whom I was fishing noticed the big trout one evening but could not catch it, so the next morning it fell to my lot to try it with a bucktail. After casting for it from downstream I walked up to position *A* and made a quarter upstream cast to point *C*, allowing the fly to drift deep and pass by the big rock. The water was cold and slightly muddy from spring rains. The fly took the path of the upper broken line in the sketch, but the current took it away before it could pass near enough to the downstream face of the rock. Since I had cast directly into the position previously, I

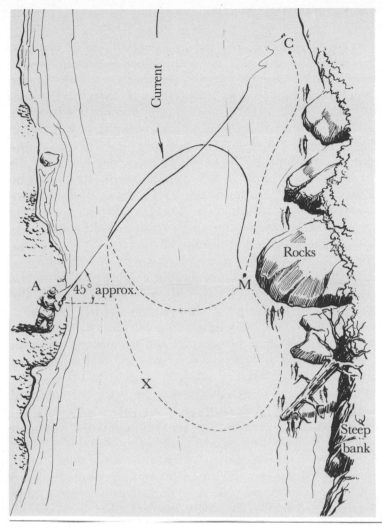

3–3 *The quarter upstream cast.*

assumed that I had put the fish down, so I went farther upstream and returned an hour later to try for it again.

On the next cast I mended the line at point *M* so that the fly was carried nearer to the pocket than in the previous cast. The fly passed out of the pocket and drifted by the fallen tree in the curve shown by the lower dotted line. When the fly had reached point *X*, I noticed that a big trout was following it. It came along directly behind the fly, seemingly interested, but rather obviously suspicious. When I saw it in pursuit of the little brown-and-white bucktail, I gave it a series of short, quick jerks rather than using the slower method I had adopted previously. The trout immediately became more interested, increasing its motion to stay directly behind the fly. At this point I had about given up the idea that the trout would take it, since it was now so close that my presence must have been noticed. Just before

43

I had to take the fly from the water, I gave it several even shorter and sharper twitches, and the trout took it less than fifteen feet from the rod tip. It weighed nearly four pounds, but did not put up a fight of any consequence. Evidently the water was so cold that it was extremely logy and disinclined to feed. It was only the extreme variation in fishing the fly which seemed to make the trout take it, and my opinion was that it was not as smart as most big brown trout are supposed to be.

Undoubtedly it was the big trout I had been fishing for, in spite of the fact that another angler took another fish from the same position next morning, in addition to several smaller brook trout from around the fallen tree. Usually a good holding position does not go vacant for long. The fallen tree always is an excellent spot for smaller fish, but the fly must be worked within a few inches of the log to make them take it.

When a streamer fly or bucktail swings in the current on a tight line, it drifts broadside or quartering to the current, which will keep it in motion with little or no help from the angler. We can note a similarity between this maneuver and the frequent habit which minnows have of drifting downstream for a short distance quartering against the current. In the case of a streamer fly or bucktail drifting in this manner, the fish may not strike the fly even though it may be observing it, but it is probable that it will strike when additional action is imparted.

When a fly is drifting in the proper current, too much action given to it by the angler may drag it from the current into a less favorable location. In such a situation it usually seems wise to try a complete drift, without giving the fly added motion. In this case its nearness to suitable rocks or the river bank may be more desirable than increased action in a less desirable path. I believe in fishing out the cast first and allowing the fly to complete its swing and hover for a minute or so in the current downstream. At this point it pays to work the fly rather energetically. It frequently happens that a fish will follow the fly on the swing, and will take it only when the swing has been completed and there is a change in the fly's motion as the line trails downstream. If there is no strike at this point, it is well to vary the action of the fly as much as possible while retrieving the line. The indecision of many fish can be overcome in this manner, as in the case of the brown trout mentioned above.

The upstream cast and the quarter upstream cast have so many means of employment that no book could ever list all the typical situations which arise from time to time. So I shall confine myself to relating a single example. There have been repeated instances of it happening. Usually it recommends the use of the dry fly, but this book is about streamers and bucktails and they will serve just as well.

In stream fishing the angler may come upon a situation where trout are feeding in the tail of a pool. They may be picking up nymphs or hatching flies, and it is possible that they will be feeding rather selectively. A small

44

bucktail or streamer often works well even in a case such as this. It happened, for example, one year when I was fishing a small wilderness stream in Maine. The deep upper part of the pool provided little action, but there seemed to be activity in the shallow water where the tail of the pool fanned out. I walked through the brush and waded into the riffles below, so as not to disturb the water. From this position several minutes' inspection showed four or five large trout feeding on the bottom, their tails and dorsal fins occasionally showing. After locating the fish, I made a quarter upstream cast to a spot just above the nearest one. The fly worked in front of it without its seeing the leader, and it took it instantly. I coaxed it over the lip of the pool and netted it there so as not to disturb the others. Then I cast for the next nearest fish and ultimately took three before those remaining had moved away.

I enjoy most of all *the cross-stream cast,* as shown in Figure 3–4, because it is adaptable to shallow water or to deep water when fish are feeding near the surface. With this cast I like to use a floating line so that I can mend it at will. One can see the fly and watch the strike of the fish, all of which adds greatly to the fun of angling.

The cross-stream cast may be used from the side of a deep pool, as is indicated in the sketch. It may be used across a stream or river just as well. In this case, and ordinarily, the angler will elect to fish the nearby water first, casting to points *B, C, D,* and *E* before he makes a final cast to point *F.* He may try a few casts with a slack line and allow the fly to explore the depths of the pool. He also may allow the fly to swing on a tight line until all of the fishable water is covered, or until the fly has been borne downstream to point *H,* where it should be worked for a few moments before being retrieved. In doing this he will find it advantageous to so handle his line that the fly will work close to the rock at position *G,* because a rock such as this is an excellent place to find large trout.

I think the floating line should be used in surface fishing with streamers more commonly than it is. With it one can pick up the fly almost at will, if occasion demands it, without disturbing the water. If the leading portion of the line sinks, this is of minor consequence. When one can watch the line on the water, the position of the fly is clearly indicated. In a slack-line cast, the motion of the line often will indicate a strike before it is felt by the angler. The floating line allows the shallow spots to be fished without the line becoming caught up on the obstructions which may be a few inches underwater in the stream. This allows us to fish over shallow rocks where it would not be possible otherwise.

With the floating line I like to use a leader about nine feet long. A short leader restricts operations and frequently discourages a fish which might strike. A longer leader is often inconvenient and usually unnecessary. The nine-foot leader allows a streamer or bucktail to be fished to a depth of a foot or so, which is usually sufficient when fish are feeding on or near the

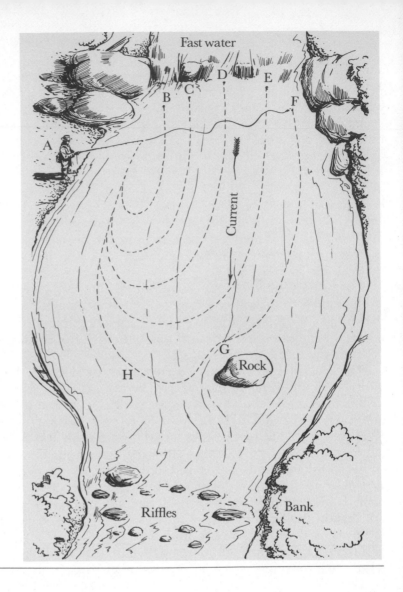

Fast water

D
E
B
C
F
A
Current
G
Rock
H
Riffles
Bank

3–4 *The cross-stream cast.*

surface. At this depth the floating line will not hamper the action of the sunken fly, particularly since a few feet of the leading portion of the line will most likely be underwater.

There are two variations in cross-stream casting which I have found very successful when suitable situations present themselves. The first has to do with working an undercut bank on the far side. Big fish like undercut banks and usually lie as far under them as they can get, but they are watchful for substantial food and ready to dart out for it. Let's offer them a marabou pattern, weighted if the water is deep, and let's fish it drifting broadside to the current. We don't need to give action to marabou streamers, because currents will fluff them enough to simulate ample activity. I usually prefer

46

a medium-sized black one because it provides an excellent silhouette, but any color should get results. If crayfish inhabit the stream an orange one might do, or even red, yellow, or pink.

Cast the streamer across, or a bit up and across, trying to put it as close to, or as far under, the bank as possible. Let it drift under the surface, mending the line as often as necessary to keep it drifting broadside without any tendency to whip. Continue the free drift as long as possible; then repeat the same tactic a little farther downstream. Marabou streamers are most effective for dead-drifting undercut banks, but other patterns, such as imitators, often do well. So many big fish are taken this way that it is a favorite wherever it seems practical.

The other variation is a little more difficult to do properly, but equally effective when done so. It is the best way to work an eddy or the edge of a backwater on the far side of the stream. The object is to keep the streamer or bucktail in the eddy or edge as long as possible. The problem is that we have faster water between here and there which will whip the fly out unless we do something to prevent it. The answer is to make quick repeated mends to the line. This mending must be fast and constant in order to keep the fly in position. If the mending is applied with proper force it will not move the fly to any extent, but the action of the mending and of the currents will keep the fly darting in about the same location long enough to interest the lunkers that should be lying there. Of course a fish may strike the fly instantly, but many delay such action, possibly under the presumption that if it is a streamer rather than a bait fish, it wouldn't remain in the same position for so long.

The *quarter downstream cast* is useful when it is desirable to cover a definite position more or less downstream or to cover holding water in an obstructed area such as where a tree has fallen into the current. If one wishes to fish a rock or run, for example, it may be unnecessary to cover other parts of the water. Avoid casting directly to the spot to be fished if it is possible to place the fly several feet away and to use current and rod to work it into the desired position. The principal value of the quarter downstream cast is to land the fly in a current which will swing or drift it into the hot spot. This cast is valuable in covering riffles, a pool, or any obstructed area from upstream. Examples of it are illustrated in the casts to positions *B* and *D* in the sketch in Figure 3–5.

The remaining of these five casts is the *downstream cast,* which also has rather distinct advantages. The depth and turbulence of the water decide the choice between a floating line, a floater with a sinking tip, and a sinking line to fish the fly at the desired level. When buying a reel it is helpful to purchase one or two extra reel spools so that this choice of lines can be available. As shown in Figure 3–5, one of the uses of this cast is to work the fly between obstructions (in this case, rocks) in order to fish positions which could not be reached as well with cross-stream casts. Quite obviously

47

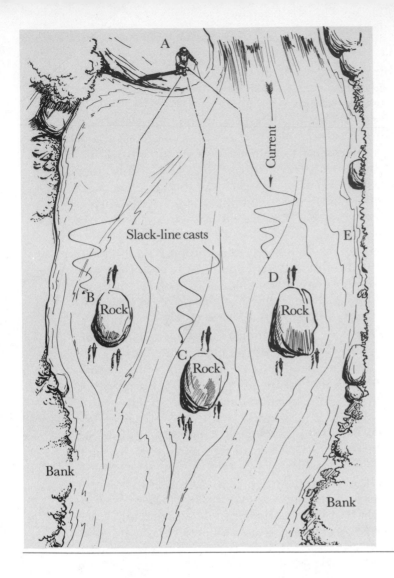

Current

Slack-line casts

A

B
Rock

C
Rock

D
Rock

E

Bank

Bank

3–5 *The downstream and quarter downstream casts.*

the downstream cast is the opposite of the upstream cast and may be used in covering similar positions. Of course the upstream cast tends to sink the fly much deeper.

In Figure 3–5 the angler is on a jutting ledge, attempting to cover the holding positions in the sketch. He makes a cast as near the left bank as possible and allows the fly to swing and to work the water at point *B*. He may let out line and try to reach the fish on the downstream side of the rock, and undoubtedly he has first covered the position on the upstream side. When this is done to his satisfaction, he will cast to point *C* and allow the current to fish the fly between the two rocks, extending and shortening his cast or the length of his line to explore the upstream area first and then work the lower positions. When he casts to point *D*, the current will immediately move his fly to the right of the middle rock, and by letting out

48

a bit of line he can reach the fish on the right of its lower side. After this, he should lay a cast to spot *E* and allow the current to swing the fly to the left to fish the nearby rock on that side.

In a previous discussion of the marabou streamer, we mentioned the fact that a fish may rise to a streamer and be seen to be interested in it even though it will not take it. Midstream rocks provide ideal spots for such a thing to happen when fish are not hungry, or if the appearance of the lure does not appeal to them. I should like to make the point again that when an extra-good feeding position is noticed, it should not be fished superficially and too quickly passed by. If there is good reason to think that a worthwhile fish is there, try to induce it to strike by repeatedly working the streamer in front of it. When I find such a place I usually make it a point to light my pipe and not to stop fishing the place until the pipe goes out. When we think of the time it takes to explore a stream, five minutes does not seem too long to invest in fishing a good feeding position. In any event, the practice has paid dividends in big fish that other anglers did not catch because they preferred to hurry to newer places around the bend.

If this does not work, it is well to drop the lure back a few feet and then make it undulate forward by an upward sweep of the rod tip. This causes the fly to sink down into the current and then to work upward like a minnow trying to reach the surface in a current that is too swift for it. To cover the water thoroughly, this may be done in alternation with moving the rod from side to side while gradually recovering line by the hand-twist method preparatory to regaining it for a new cast.

When one can fish a split riffle, there is a great deal of advantage in wading the riffle and casting to the bank rather than attempting to fish from the bank. In riffle fishing the large game fish normally are near the midstream rocks or along the deep runs and protected positions of the shore. In fishing from the bank the angler often is at a distinct disadvantage, because he is on top of the good spots before he sees them; the situation is just the opposite when he is able to wade the riffles.

The motion of a sick or injured minnow can easily be duplicated with the streamer fly. When an actual one is observed, it will be seen to drift and waver, occasionally to summon its strength and try to dart for cover, only to lose its balance and repeat the procedure. The point cannot be stressed too strongly that the easiest way to learn the various methods of making a streamer or bucktail act like a live or injured bait fish is to devote a considerable amount of time, perhaps in the often unproductive noonday period, to watching the various bait fish and fishing a bucktail nearby, trying to achieve an action that is a reasonably accurate simulation of the minnows' varying action in the water.

49

It may also be well to repeat here the point that once a suitable fly has been selected, it is more advantageous to change the method of fishing it than to change the fly itself too often. I have fished with anglers who use a fly for a few minutes and then impatiently break it off and try a new one.

The result is that they spend too much time fussing with their tackle and too little time working their fly in the water.

I have noticed, as others have, that big trout (and other fish, too) have a habit of traveling in pairs all year through. When an abnormally big fish is taken, it is well to keep on covering the same water. Very frequently another can be caught. In watching the actions of a hooked fish, I have often seen the rather frantic behavior of another which followed the hooked fish in. Perhaps it is too disturbed to be caught, but very often it is there.

When one angler is fishing an ordinary wet fly or dry fly and another chooses to use streamers or bucktails, it is better for the former to fish ahead, followed by the latter. A streamer fisherman frequently can spoil the water for a wet-fly or dry-fly man, but the opposite rarely is the case. Many of us have followed anglers using small flies and have taken large fish right behind them. A trout often will strike at a small fly only once, but it may come for a streamer again and again. Perhaps it thinks that it has lost it the first time and when it comes into its field of vision again it assumes that it is injured and makes a renewed attempt to take it.

Let's conclude this chapter by reviewing a few general rules which may serve as the essence of streamer and bucktail fishing in fast water. Study the bait fish and try to copy them in form, flash, size, and particularly in their action. Sparsely dressed flies usually are more effective than overdressed ones. When in doubt as to size, use the smaller one. Fish the fly into position instead of casting to it. When water is cold, fish the fly slowly and close to bottom. Before fishing, take time to read the water and to plan how to fish it. Spot the probable holding positions and concentrate on them rather than fishing aimlessly at middepth. If a bucktail or streamer is fished in the right places at the right times, it is almost certain to produce more than its share of bigger fish.

4

Tips on Fishing Streamers in Slack Water

WE HAVE OBSERVED that fish are like people in that they seek comfortable temperatures and an easily available food supply. If we link this up with knowledge of the predictable seasonal changes in the water temperatures of ponds and lakes and a basic understanding of where food supplies should be found in them, we can learn to fish where fish should be, rather than wasting time working our streamers and bucktails where they shouldn't be. This knowledge is more important than the tactics we use and the kinds of flies we select.

The predictable seasonal changes in the water temperatures of ponds and lakes first were noticed by the famous naturalist and author Henry David Thoreau in about 1850, when, noting the warm surface waters and the coldness of the depths of Massachusetts' Walden Pond (where he lived his hermit-like existence for several years), he observed, "How much this varied temperature must have to do with the distribution of fish in it! The few trout must oftenest go down in summer."

Thoreau was the father of the science of limnology, or the study of lakes and other inland waters. In the more than one hundred years since his observation we have learned how to coordinate our knowledge of lakes and ponds with the temperature and food requirements of sport fishes, to the great benefit of angling success. Let's see how this works.

The first important point is that fish are cold-blooded. This means that they assume the temperature of the water in which they live. They have no

51

option. In warm water they are warm; in cold water they are cold. If the temperature is uncomfortable they move away in search of a more suitable area. Trout, for example, are reasonably comfortable in water between 47° F. and 68° F. If water is colder or warmer they grow sluggish. At about 75° F. their metabolism is so slow they cease to feed. This dependence on temperature is absolute. In water above 80° F. a ravenously hungry trout will starve with food all around it. In the comfortable or tolerant range of between 47° F. and 68° F. each species of trout has an affinity for an ideal temperature—about 63° F. for brown trout, 62° F. for rainbow trout, and 57° F. for brook trout. Find these approximate temperatures in ponds or lakes and trout should be there near a handy food supply. When surface waters are too warm, fish will rest deeper where they are more nearly ideal, but they may temporarily come into warmer surface waters to feed, often in the evening and during the night when surface waters are cooler. Opposite is a table giving the tolerant and ideal temperatures for prominent species of freshwater fish.

The second important point is that we can learn to find these temperatures in ponds and lakes. This has a lot to do with the behavior of inland waters during the season, and the main part of the point is that water is maximumly dense (heaviest) at 39.2° F. Water either warmer or colder than this rises toward the surface, which is the reason waters in northern climes don't freeze solid in winter.

In winter, while ice covers most northern inland waters, they remain at 39.2° F. in the depths. The increasing warmth of spring makes the ice soft and spongy, and winds break it up. The breakup, or "ice-out," may happen quickly and attract fishermen, who might be better advised to wait until surface waters warm to the maximum density of 39.2° F. At this temperature all water in the pond or lake is of the same density, so winds can mix it; thus one hears it said that the lake has "turned over." This is the start of good spring fishing, because fish come to the surface to look for food there. Where on the surface are they most often found?

Since this temperature is well below the tolerant ranges of most species, they look for warmer water. They find it in the shallows, very close to shore, where the sun has warmed it a bit more. At this time trout and landlocked salmon can be in such shallow water that their dorsal fins protrude while they are lying on the bottom. The trick then is to move the boat slowly along the shoreline so an average cast can put the fly within inches of shore. Try a small imitator pattern first, and fish it slowly, because fish are less active than they will be when the water is warmer.

When two people are casting flies from the same boat they can cause trouble unless the casting is coordinated. One man always waits to make his cast until the other one is fishing his cast in. A way to do this is shown in Figure 4–1. The angler in the stern has cast to a fallen tree, which should be a good lie for fish. As he fishes his cast in to point X, the angler in the bow casts to point A, between two large rocks. As he completes fishing his

52

TEMPERATURE-ACTIVITY TABLE FOR FRESHWATER FISH

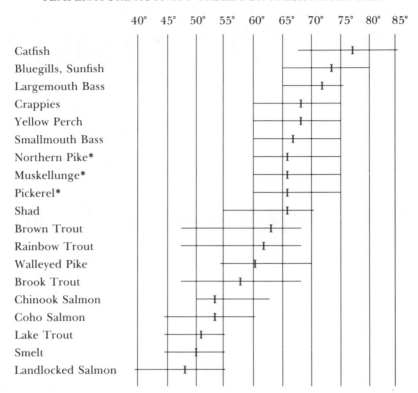

	40°	45°	50°	55°	60°	65°	70°	75°	80°	85°
Catfish								I		
Bluegills, Sunfish							I			
Largemouth Bass							I			
Crappies						I				
Yellow Perch						I				
Smallmouth Bass						I				
Northern Pike*						I				
Muskellunge*						I				
Pickerel*						I				
Shad						I				
Brown Trout					I					
Rainbow Trout					I					
Walleyed Pike				I						
Brook Trout				I						
Chinook Salmon			I							
Coho Salmon			I							
Lake Trout		I								
Smelt		I								
Landlocked Salmon		I								

Note: "I" indicates ideal temperature. While this may vary somewhat in various regions, this chart should be followed unless regional data suggest variation. The horizontal line indicates tolerant temperature range. Fish usually will not take lures well outside of this range.
*Members of the pike family, which includes northern pike, muskellunge, and the various pickerels, are much less fussy about water temperatures than other species. While the range shown for them is the optimum one, they usually will take lures when the water is slightly warmer or very much colder.

cast, the rearward angler may try the same place—because a difference in the fly or in its manner of presentation could tempt a strike where the first angler has failed.

When the aft angler has completed his cast to point *A,* the boat's progress will permit the forward angler to cast to point *B.* By thus alternating casts, only one line is in the air at a time to prevent possible tangles. Also, all the good spots can be easily and alternately covered. In the case of a strike the boat would be allowed to drift while all nearby positions would be fished more thoroughly.

What shoreline areas are best to fish when the pond or lake is too big to try them all? Try the downwind side, because airborne food which drops into the water drifts there also. Select parts of the shoreline that are rela-

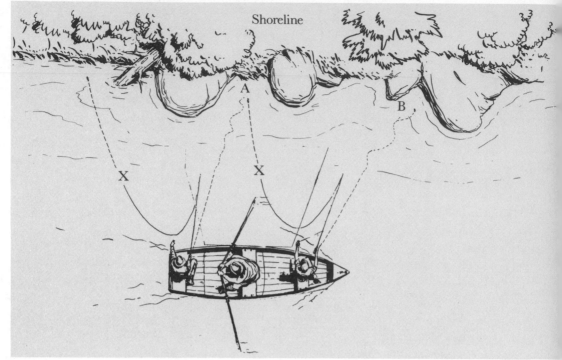
Shoreline

A

B

X   X

4-1 Covering shoreline from a moving boat.

tively shallow and offer the protection of rocks, logs, bushes, or grasses. In addition to offering protection in warmer water such places provide food, such as bait fish. Similar conditions are found close to islands, points of land, and ledges.

Week by week the increasing warmth of spring adds to the depth of the warmer water preferred by game fish, so they become more active in expanding areas which may cover the entire water's surface. Following winter's hibernation they are ravenous for food and follow schools of bait fish, such as smelt. Since smelt run up entering streams to spawn, good fishing areas, particularly at this time, are stream mouths and perhaps the streams themselves. Near-surface trolling in these areas should be good, as well as casting from shore. This is best in areas where the surface is mildly choppy from wind action, often called a salmon ripple.

In casting from shore the *fan-casting method* explores the water thoroughly, as shown in Figure 4–2. The angler methodically covers the nearby area first so he won't disturb that farther out. For example, starting at his left, he makes a series of short casts to his right until all the area about twenty feet from his rod tip has been covered. He fishes one cast near the surface, retrieving with short jerks of the rod tip, and then tries another deeper, retrieving more slowly. Retrieving speed usually is slower when the water is below optimum and faster when water temperature is more nearly ideal. He covers this nearby area to his satisfaction, as indicated by casts

54

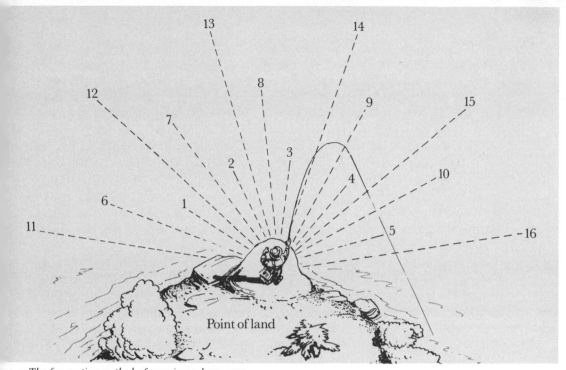

13   14
8
12   9   15
7
3
2   4
6   1   10
11   5   16

Point of land

4–2 The fan-casting method of covering a large area.

1 to 5 in the sketch; then he repeats the same procedure several feet farther out, as shown by casts 6 to 10, and then still farther out, as indicated by casts 11 to 16. If he gets a strike he concentrates on that area and depth. If he doesn't he moves somewhere else.

Toward the end of bait-fish spawning the little fish leave the streams and proceed in large schools along the shore, of course followed by game fish. Alert anglers often see the bait on calm days because it spasmodically flurries the surface when game fish drive it up. If one boat finds a school, there soon is a concentration of several, so good fishing can be found in this way also. The bait often remains in stream channels, which may extend far out into the lake. A topographical map of the area is helpful to locate such channels.

The spawning habits of game fish also help to locate them. While this information is too extensive to cover here, it can be found in *McClane's Standard Fishing Encyclopedia* (New York: Holt, Rinehart and Winston). As an example, rainbow trout spawn in the spring and may be found concentrated near or in stream mouths (and in the streams themselves), when the water is between about 50° F. and 60° F. (These temperatures vary somewhat in various geographical areas.) While lake trout are fall spawners, we have seen that they enjoy very cold water, and they often feed in shallow coves in early spring.

As the season progresses, surface waters continue to become warmer

55

and thus become lighter, so they remain on the surface while the colder water stratifies beneath. The stratification of cold-water lakes (and sometimes ponds) has had such extensive coverage in other publications that we will only touch upon it here. What happens is very important in finding fish. The warm water forms a surface layer of between a few feet and many feet deep, depending primarily on the lake's size. The cold water, being heavier, lies at the bottom. Between the warm surface layer and the cold depths is a relatively thin mixed layer called the thermocline. In summer, game fish occupy the thermocline level or the level just below it, wherever they can find their optimum temperatures. Since they want to be near a food supply they concentrate in areas where the thermocline touches land at such depths along the shore and around islands, etc. In summer this is the path of good trolling. How do we find it?

If we want to avoid guesswork we find it with a topographical map and a depth thermometer, such as the "Depth-O-Plug" available in tackle shops. Mark a cord with knots at three-foot intervals or so and lower the thermometer to gradually increasing depths, noticing the temperature at each depth. Readings will indicate warm water down to a certain depth, where the temperature then drops quickly. This is the thermocline level. Let's suppose that this fairly quick experiment (which need not be repeated very often) shows that the rapid drop in temperature is at a depth of between twenty and thirty feet. Use a crayon to color between these depth contours on the topographical map. It shows the depth and path of good fishing. We'll learn how to troll at this depth later on.

In fly casting we need a high-density (fast-sinking) line and probably a weighted fly. Since we will need to make long casts to fish this depth as far as possible, an extra-fast-sinking shooting head attached to solid-filament memory-free shooting line (such as Sunset's Amnesia) should be ideal. Use the countdown method to find the proper depth before fishing in the fly. A line's rate of sinking (in feet per second) should be provided by the manufacturer.

For those of us who are not particularly interested in fishing flies deep, alternatives are available for finding fish in summer. One of these is stream mouths where cold water pours in, usually providing compatible temperatures as well as a food supply. The channels of some streams continue out into the lake, so casts should be made far out, and perhaps deep, after trying the visible part of the mouth. Too many anglers anchor their boats in the invisible part of the mouth over where the fish are (or were) and cast to the visible part when the fish may be in deeper water. Other stream mouths may spread out in the form of a delta. In this case there probably is a sharp dropoff, and the best fishing usually is over this.

Another alternative is spring holes, if they can be found. Some, welling up from lake bottom, are discovered by accident, and many have become famous. Others can be seen along shorelines, where a trickle of water and lush vegetation reveal them. Their cold water can harbor large concentrations of trout in summer, often in very shallow water. Discoverers of springs in deep water usually keep them top secret. One on a remote lake in Canada gave me my biggest brook trout.

We had been fishing that lake with good success but hadn't landed one of the brookies of over six pounds that were supposed to be there. While cruising along the shore one afternoon I noticed a lush little cove clogged with drifted timber. "Let's try that spot," I said to the French Canadian guide.

He shook his head. "No fish there. I find you good place," he said. The "good place" harbored many trout, but they all were small ones.

After an early dinner I took a canoe to the little cove. The soft evening breeze wafted toward it, so I let the canoe drift in until it lightly touched the floating timber. I put on a smeltlike little Sidewinder and cast it out close to the outer logs, allowing it to sink a little before twitching it in. A strong swirl and a jarring strike indicated a big fish.

The cove was a maze of logs and stumps, both floating on the surface and littering the bottom in about ten feet of transparent water. The trout had to be worked away from all that lest the leader become snarled in the tangle. I applied all the tension that seemed safe to pull it to deep water. It dove repeatedly, but never deep enough, combining short runs and swirls on the surface until it eventually lay exhausted within reach. I was able to slide thumb and forefinger over its gill covers and lift it into the canoe. It was a male, humpbacked with fat, and brilliant with spawning colors. My pocket scale said it weighed six and a quarter pounds. I laid the trophy on a towel on the floor of the boat and spent minutes admiring its beauty.

"Where there's one there may be two," I suddenly thought, and, after resting the place until my pipe went out, I sent the tiny streamer on its mission again. Casts out toward the lake proved fruitless, but another one close to the logs brought another hard strike. After a battle similar to the first, the trout was brought to boat. It also was a male, the same size as the other. I watched it feebly fanning in the water while I worked the fly loose with pliers so it could swim away. Perhaps another angler on another day enjoyed the same thrill of catching that trophy. Anyway, I took the first fish to Haines Landing on the way home so Herbie Welch could mount it for me. It still decorates my den, and Herbie said it was the last he ever mounted.

A third alternative is evening fly fishing in the shallows. Since food is more abundant there than in the thermocline area, hungry fish will tolerate the too-warm surface water for a short time, when it becomes cooler in the evening and at night, in order to find an easy meal. Rocky places are likely larders. As darkness approaches, a streamer or bucktail which is predominantly black should do best, and it can be larger than clear-water patterns used during daytime.

Why do fish fool with fakes? Why do they strike at streamers so often even though real food is abundant? For an answer we could read what the great naturalist Charles Darwin had to say in his proven precept of the survival of the fittest. Animals which become deformed or otherwise unfit are not allowed to live. Fish strike at bait fish which act unusual and/or look unusual even while they leave schools of minnows alone. No streamer or bucktail ever can be made to act or to look absolutely natural. This divergence from naturalness may be a reason why big fish take streamers so readily, even those which we might consider far-out ones, such as attractor and marabou patterns.

Trolling with streamers and bucktails is a way of life for some and a relaxing change of pace for others. Use an inexpensive, long and stiff rod for this, rather than one of your best ones. We know that in spring fish can be taken near surface, and that in summer the best fishing usually is deeper

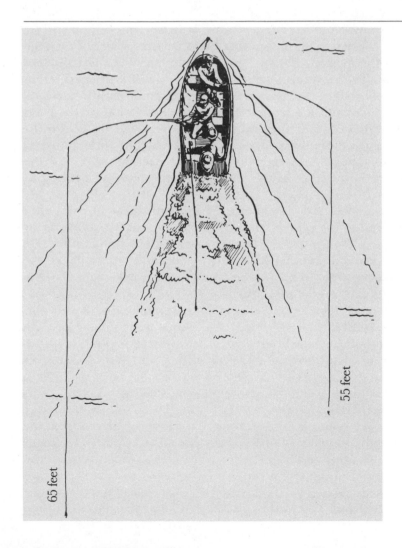

4–3 *Trolling two
or three lines.*

down. Regardless of this, a good trolling method is shown in Figure 4–3.

In this drawing three rods are being used. The person running the boat finds it most convenient to troll his fly at the end of the wake off the stern. If only two fishermen were involved he could troll that way or as one of the two others are doing. Fish often are attracted to the wake of a boat, and they may come to the middle fly as it rides in the wake. If they don't like the looks of it, one of the two outboard ones may appeal to them when they follow along. When fish are taking near the surface, there may be no need to put lead on the leaders or to use fast-sinking lines, but going deeper with at least one of the lines is a good experiment. After a strike or two you'll know what works best. Note that the three lines are being trolled at varying distances. This keeps flies separated and makes them visible to more fish. Most anglers seem to agree that the best speed is about four or five miles per hour, or as fast as a man can walk. A rule is to troll longer lines when the surface is calm than when it is rippled.

Since proper trolling speed is hard to estimate, because of winds and currents, an inexpensive speed indicator such as a "Trolex" is helpful. This is merely a weight attached to a cord with the other end of the cord tied to a pointer on a dial; this unit is affixed over the side of the boat. When the boat is stationary, the weight, cord, and pointer are vertical and the pointer indicates zero speed. When it is moving, the weight and cord trail behind, becoming more nearly horizontal as the boat picks up speed; this speed being registered by the pointer on the dial. Such units are easy to make, but buying one eliminates the tediousness of calibration.

On getting a strike, notice the speed at which the fish was hooked, and stay with it. In near-surface trolling it is better to go in a snakelike pattern than in a straight line, even while trying to keep a certain distance offshore. Thus, speed will vary, letting the lures ride higher or lower and allowing the boat to cover more ground.

Since streamer and bucktail fly selection varies so much according to where we are fishing, the species we are fishing for, and the unpredictable changes or whims in patterns regionally popular, no one can suggest sure solutions. As far as northeastern angling in lakes is concerned, we do note that certain established patterns popular a few decades ago are equally so today. These fall into three classes for near-surface trolling, and each class could be tried to see which clicks at the moment. One is the very small and sparse imitator patterns such as the Sidewinder, Pinfish, and any of Lew Oatman's favorites, shown in Color Plate XI. Another is the intermediate sizes in both imitators and attractors such as the Gray Ghost, Black Ghost, and Herb Johnson Special. The third is the bigger tandem trollers (discussed in Chapter 11); the Nine-Three, Supervisor, and Red Ghost are worthy of mention and probably will be so for years to come. If this small group doesn't get results, the fault is not fly selection. Although born in the northeast, these patterns should be effective anywhere in fresh water, except that the larger ones are not appropriate for the smaller pond fish.

59

While styles in flies vary somewhat from year to year, most of them are influenced by basic patterns such as these. Some readers may not be familiar with the newcomer called the Red Ghost, fathered by Ray Salminen, a dedicated angler and fly dresser of Acton, Massachusetts. When I wrote *Streamer Fly Tying & Fishing* I bragged a bit that its eight color plates (made from my flies under my supervision) were absolutely true to color. One knowledgeable angler picked me up on this, saying that the wing of Carrie Stevens' Gray Ghost should be gray instead of slightly pink. I inspected the actual fly and the color plate (Plate II) had reproduced it exactly. Over the years the wing had faded a bit and had turned pinkish.

The anecdote might not be worth relating except that several anglers copied the fly in the plate and made the wing even more pink. This proved so successful that the Pink Ghost was born. This didn't stop there, though. Ray Salminen figured that if pink was an improvement (I doubt that it was), why wouldn't red be even better? The Red Ghost now is an established pattern in New England, and it may be successful, particularly under dark conditions, because it presents a better silhouette. If so, I suggest that black would be even better, but don't call it the Black Ghost because there already is one!

We know that when trolling streamers in summer we may need to get down to the thermocline area to find fish, and we have learned where this is. Fast-sinking or extra-fast-sinking lines are necessary, such as Scientific Anglers' Wet Cel Hi-D, or a high-density shooting taper attached to twenty- or twenty-five-pound-test memory-free solid-filament shooting line such as Sunset's Amnesia. Some anglers think that lead-cored lines are needed to search the depths in big lakes. If this is so, or when it is, try a leader of monofilament such as just mentioned which is at least *one hundred feet long,* and add about ten feet of much lighter monofilament between it and the fly so this can be broken loose in case of a severe hangup. By this means one can reel in the heavy line and have the pleasure of playing the fish on the lighter monofilament.

While we know how to find thermocline depth, how do we know how much line to let out to get the fly down there? Variable factors such as line weight make it necessary for each angler to solve this independently. If you don't get a hangup once in a while, you're probably not fishing deep enough, or near enough to bottom on the path of good trolling. When you do get hung up, get directly over the spot and measure its depth by measuring the vertical line. With this information you can compensate, and, when you know how much line to let out to reach proper depth, you can mark the line there to decrease hangups.

There is a general rule which isn't much good, but better than nothing. When a boat is going at normal trolling speed a weighted line will sink about one foot for each five feet of its length. Thus, to get down to thirty-five feet, which is about average thermocline depth in medium-sized lakes, we'll have to measure out one hundred and seventy-five feet, or about fifty-eight yards, of line. If lead-cored line is used, this would be nearly six colors. To check depth we can troll toward shallower water until the lure catches and then measure this depth with a marked plumb line or an electronic instrument.

The increasing cold of fall gradually cools surface water until it reaches maximum density of 39.2° F. again. At this time the reverse of the spring turnover happens, because again all the water in the lake is of the same temperature, or density, and thus can be mixed by wind action. At this time the fish which have been in the depths again come to the surface and provide good fly fishing there under conditions similar to those found in the spring.

This marks the approach of spawning time for many species of game fish, including brook trout, brown trout, lake trout, landlocked and coho (silver) salmon, and (in some rivers) steelhead. Lake trout (togue, or mackinaw, or gray trout) breed over gravel or rocky bottoms, where they can be trolled for and, in some cases, fly-fished for if the lakes are shallow. They strike at streamers with minimum discrimination, but medium sizes seem best. The others for the most part congregate at river and stream mouths, where they will take streamer flies and bucktails as avidly as they did in the spring.

Ponds vary between cold-water ones in the north, cool-water ones, including farm ponds and many other man-made impoundments, in middle latitudes, and warm-water ones in the south. Each has different characteristics, which, in border areas, often overlap.

Cold-water ponds usually are rocky or gravelly and often have forested shorelines. Treat them as little lakes, using small imitators or attractors if they contain trout and bigger, more spectacular patterns if they hold bass. One species usually eliminates the other. I know of several such ponds in a small group. All exclusively contain trout except one, which holds an abundance of bass, but no trout. The bass, both largemouth and smallmouth, like large flies of the Blonde or marabou types splatted down as close to the brushy shoreline as possible.

Some cold-water ponds may be relatively shallow, often containing many underwater springs and an abundance of weeds, which rarely grow very near to the surface. One such is a favorite, with a lawnlike bottom of lacy green weeds about two feet thick. The secret seems to be to use a slowly sinking line and to use the countdown method to settle the streamer just above the weeds, then to strip it in very fast. My favorite fly there is the Miller's River Special, but several of Lew Oatman's patterns are very effective. In warm-weather fishing we notice that some small areas provide many strikes, while all the others offer none at all. This probably is due to underwater springs. We went swimming there one warm afternoon and found the water rather tepid except in a few areas where it was chillingly cold.

I make a distinction between cold-water ponds and cool-water ones

61

because, unlike the former, the latter have temperatures in the high 60s and areas containing dense patches of emerging weeds such as cattails, grasses, lily pads, and so forth. Being usually too warm for trout, they are ideal for smallmouth and largemouth bass, pickerel, and various kinds of panfish.

An easy way to fish such grassy waters is to cast along a weed line, making shorter casts and gradually extending them as far as convenient, thus not spoiling the water farther on. If one wants pickerel, almost any common streamer will do, but these fish seem to prefer lighter colors such as white and yellow.

Another way is to fish the holes in the weeds, because bass like to lie along their edges. Large weedless patterns as described in Chapter 9 are handy here because the flies can be cast onto lily pads and pulled off—a bassy tactic sure to provoke strikes.

The extremely abundant, easy-to-catch, and delicious members of the panfish "family" include bluegills (bream), crappies, rock bass, yellow perch, and the common sunfish. One of the best ways to get a youngster interested in becoming an angler is to turn him loose on these spunky little fighters with a very light rod fitted with a floating line with sinking tip and a leader tapered very fine. Look for panfish near docks, in quiet coves, near weed patches, and in other spots offering protection. Use the smallest streamers or bucktails in imitator patterns, as well as attractors such as the Mickey Finn. Fish these slow and deep.

Since warm-water ponds are in southern regions they usually do not freeze over in winter and they maintain fairly constant temperatures of between 60° F. and 75° F. all year round. These ponds (and lakes) often are shallow, with great clumps of grasses. Others are deep and sprinkled with stumps, cypress knees, and brush piles. A favorite southern species is the crappie, or calico bass, which prefers the substantial protection of submerged logs, brush piles, wharfs, and rock bars. If one favors streamers and bucktails (which may not always be the most suitable type of lure), small minnow imitations work best, usually in spring when large schools congregate before spawning. During the year the best fishing is at dusk.

Fishing Maine's famous Upper Dam Pool—Record trout and salmon—Birth of the Gray
Ghost—Carrie Stevens' originations—Herbie Welch and his streamers—Joe Stickney's patterns—Bill Edson's Tigers—Kennebago Stream—Reasons for fishing decline—Carrie Stevens Day—How Mrs. Stevens dressed her Gray Ghost—The most popular Stevens patterns
—"Shang" Wheeler—Lew Oatman's imitator flies—Sam Slaymaker's trout simula-
tions—Other important eastern streamers

5

The Saga of the Gray Ghost, and Other Prominent Eastern Streamers

F OR ABOUT FIFTY YEARS around the turn of the last century Maine's Rangeley Lakes area was the locale of the finest eastern brook trout fishing in the
United States, if not in the world. Center stage for this piscatorial bonanza
was the renowned Upper Dam Pool, where a newly built stone-cribbed log
dam deepened and enlarged the pure water of Lake Mooselookmeguntic
and flumed it into the big pool before it swirled on its course into Richard-
son Lake below.

Fly fishing for trout was good all summer, even in hottest weather,
because the water rushing through the dam's spillways became cooled and
aerated, thus tempting the big trout to run up into the pool and to stay
there, feasting on smaller fry washed over the dam.

In those early days fish under three pounds weren't considered keepers.
Five pounds was about average; seven-pounders were common, and one
gentleman landed a whopper weighing in at nine pounds and eleven
ounces. The date was September 23, 1897.

Here, too, the famous Gray Ghost was born, along with many other
streamer and bucktail patterns still very popular today. The Rangeley area
was the developing ground of the streamer fly, descending from such
revered names as Carrie Stevens, Herbie Welch, Joe Stickney, and Bill
Edson—all old friends and fishing companions, but all much older than I.
This writer was sort of a mascot for the bunch.

At the beginning of the Rangeley era, in 1860 or so, this part of Maine
was a wilderness traveled only by Indians and a sprinkling of trappers and

63

timber cruisers, plus a few adventurous sportsmen from cities to the south. These anglers spread the word about the fabulous fishing in the Rangeley region. Logging crews moved into this wilderness in the 1860s and built sturdy log dams to flume logs from one lake to another. Arriving at a new lake, the logs would be boomed together into immense rafts which were slowly towed by steamboats to the next dam on their way to the mills. The pools below all these dams were havens for trout, but Upper Dam is the most historic one.

Toward the end of the century the comfortable way to reach Upper Dam was by the newly built railroad from the south, which then terminated at the thriving lumbering town of Bemis, situated under the rise of ground at the southern end of Mooselookmeguntic Lake. If you were very rich you could arrive in your private railway car. Less so, you could enjoy Pullman service from cities such as Washington and New York. During the fishing season it wasn't uncommon to see several private cars parked on the siding at Bemis. The black servants on the cars relaxed in primeval luxury while the tycoons enjoyed their fishing. They and the transient lumberjacks formed a sort of mutual admiration society, because usually the one type never before had seen the other.

While the guides were moving gear from the cars to the small steamboats for the trip to Upper Dam, the tycoons could amuse themselves by casting a Parmachenee Belle, a Dark-Tipped Montreal, or a Silver Doctor from the dock, which was close by the outlet of Bemis Stream. Big trout lay in the outlet. History says they averaged about six pounds.

While the sports sipped cold drinks and watched the wilderness shore-line drift by, the five-mile trip by steamer from Bemis was livened by backwoods stories and guides' reports about the fishing. Upper Dam was a comfortable place. Tucked amid the spruce and birch on the northern side of the great pool nestled a row of several log cabins leased by wealthy anglers. Nearby was a white, wide-porched hotel where other fishermen stayed. Not much more was there except that a walk across the dam brought one to the warden's camp and to the summer home of Carrie Stevens, who dressed her famous flies there while her husband, Wallace, helped with the guiding.

The fly fishermen at Upper Dam observed strict protocol in boating and angling methods. You had to act properly and fish properly, or you just weren't "in." All fish were taken on flies and, usually, with the most expensive tackle. Even the mere mention of bait might get you drummed out of camp.

During the log drives (which usually happened earlier in the season, before the tycoons arrived) about all one could do was to sit on the porch and discuss the "big one that got away." He was a trout often referred to as Pincushion Pete, and was reputed to weigh twelve pounds or so, depending on who was telling the story. Traditionally, he would slam the fly, race under the dam, and break the leader around the piling. Some said he had

5-1 *Upper Dam Pool in the 1940s.*

5-2 *Upper Dam's wide-porched hotel and some of the cabins.*

5–3 *A bit of the action at Upper Dam Pool. (Photo: Maine Development Commission)*

five flies in his face, while others insisted on up to fifteen.

The newcomers, of course, didn't believe this. So the proud host would "prove" it by taking his guest to a damp little building under the downstream side of the dam. After carefully descending to the lower level, he quietly would pull up a trap door in the floor to expose the dark, swirling waters under the dam's apron below.

"Look down," he would say, smirking.

On hands and knees the neophyte would cautiously peer down into the blackness lighted only by reflections from outside. There, in the backwater under the dam, he would see dozens of giant trout placidly cruising and resting.

"Good God! Look at them!" he would exclaim in righteous awe. "Let's get our rods and go fishin'."

The guides, contentedly puffing pipes in the shade of the cabins while waiting for their sports to appear, would pick up expensive rods made by Thomas, Payne, or Leonard; would shoulder large nets and lead their anglers across the grassy clearing down to the floating dock. When the fishermen were comfortably seated in swivel chairs with cushions, the guides would unhitch the Rangeley boats from dock rings and allow them to drift in the clockwise current of the pool. Caught by swift water rushing down the dam's flumes, each boat would make a quick circuit until the guide, with instant precision, dropped anchor to place his boat as near as possible to where the pool's clockwise current split from that going down the thoroughfare. Then he would thoughtfully inspect his sport's tackle, hand it to him, and light his pipe again.

Although most of these men were excellent casters, not much experience was necessary. They laid out their flies to the best of their abilities and, except for working the rod tip a bit, could let the current do the rest.

In those days action wasn't long in coming. There would be a solid hit and a fish would be on. If its run toward the sanctuary of the dam took it too near other boats, the guide would pull anchor and let his craft drift into an area less thickly populated. There the angler would leisurely play his fish, tell the guide when to net it, and hold it up for the admiration of friends. Unless it was considered a trophy or was needed for the table, it usually was released. If it broke loose (as many did) it promptly was dubbed the one and only Pincushion Pete and instantly reached the estimated weight of about eleven pounds.

Although the biggest fish usually were taken by boats, smaller ones abounded near the rockwork of the dam. Others could be taken by rather sporty wading among the rocks in the fast water over the lip of the pool. Even as late as the 1920s, when I first fished there, trout of varying sizes could be hooked on cast after cast in the current's edges behind the rocks.

Before the turn of the century old records show that only eastern brook trout were taken. After that, landlocked salmon made their appearance, and the size of the trout year by year became smaller. In the 1920s it wasn't unusual to hook salmon of six pounds or so, and occasional ones were bigger. Most of us then tried for salmon because it was so much fun to watch them jump. One smaller fish of four pounds or so went into the air fourteen times by actual count. It deserved its freedom and got it.

In this wilderness setting, fragrant with spruce and woodsmoke, the famous Gray Ghost Streamer was born on July 1, 1924—the date when fashions in flies partially shifted from wets and drys to streamers and bucktails. As we know, its originator was Carrie G. Stevens, whose husband, Wallace, was a popular guide at Upper Dam. Carrie was a milliner by trade, and thus a lady definitely in the know in the field of feathers. No one ever taught her how to tie a fly, and until she endowed my book *Streamer Fly Tying & Fishing* with her secrets, she never would show anyone how she did it.

Her sudden inspiration for the Gray Ghost was to dress a fly to imitate a smelt, because smelt are the predominant food fish in the Rangeley Lakes region. Her first attempt was a crude version of her later beautiful development of the pattern. But during the first hour of its testing she landed several fish, including a six-pound, thirteen-ounce brook trout that took first prize and other honors in the *Field & Stream* magazine's competition of that year.

The talk around the potbellied stoves that night was about one subject only, and you know what it was! The tycoons in the cabins and the others in the hotel ordered Gray Ghosts as fast as Carrie could dress them and took them home to proudly pass around. The new fly was launched—

67

probably the most famous streamer pattern ever originated.

Almost none of the Gray Ghosts sold nowadays are dressed as Carrie did it, and therefore many of us feel they aren't as effective. Her method is given later in this chapter.

Carrie Stevens originated at least twenty popular streamer fly patterns, plus at least as many others in color combinations designed to favor friends. She dressed most of them as art forms, rather than in an attempt to imitate various species of bait fish. She did them all by the same method, and they were effective more because of shape or form than because of colors or components. One, said by others to be second only to the Gray Ghost in value, is the Colonel Bates, originated by her during World War II. Since this is an attractor pattern the two are said to be a good pair.

At Haines' Landing, on the eastern shore of Mooselookmeguntic, there stood a wide-porched log-cabin-type store owned and run by Herbert L. Welch—an artist who had studied in Paris, the world's greatest taxidermist of trout, a famous guide, and one of the finest anglers who ever lived. Herbie's store sold fishing tackle and related items, also including exotic and regional furs, carvings, etc. Back of it, along a short boardwalk, was his neat studio. The store was a mecca for anglers during the first part of this century, because Herbie was famous, garrulous, and very informative on many subjects, especially angling. A wicker basket filled with Carrie Stevens' flies was always on a counter, each fly neatly carded and named in her own handwriting. Many of us wish we had had the foresight to buy them all, because Carrie's originals are coveted museum pieces today!

I was granted the privilege of fishing with Herbie Welch many times, and I soaked up his genial wisdom. He originated several streamer patterns. Among the most prominent are the Black Ghost, Jane Craig, and Welch Rarebit.

The streamer fly may not have originated in the Rangeley area, but it received its greatest development there. We have noted that, in his writings, Theodore Gordon mentions a streamer he called the Bumblepuppy (there were several versions by the same name), which he used "before 1903." In 1902, however, Herbie Welch was guiding an English angler who wanted to use his 6/0 Silver Doctor Atlantic salmon flies for Rangeley's fish. There were no long-shanked fly hooks in those days, and these ultra-large flies were of course too big, but they gave Herbie an idea. He reforged some bluefish hooks (originally made four or five inches long, so the sharp teeth of bluefish couldn't cut the leader) and cut them down to proper length. He removed the wings of some of the Silver Doctors and used the long feathers on the remade bluefish hooks, thus arriving at acceptable streamers for Rangeley fishing, as we reported when discussing the history of streamer flies in Chapter 2.

Another great name in the Rangeley area is that of Joseph S. Stickney. Joe was an architect who became a warden supervisor so he could enjoy more fishing and the pleasures of the woods. His famous originations are the Supervisor (1925), the Lady Doctor (1926), and the Warden's Worry (1930). The Supervisor is a smelt imitator of such great value that it competes with the Gray Ghost in effectiveness. Originally it was tied without a peacock herl topping. When this was added the fly was called the Imperial Supervisor. This topping added so much to the fly's ability that it now is merely called the Supervisor and the topless earlier version is all but forgotten.

Joe's other two originations are great trout takers, but there is a question whether their wings are long enough to qualify them as streamers. The Lady Doctor (Joe's wife was an M.D.) is nearly as complicated as a classic Atlantic salmon pattern, and it would be considered rather bright nowadays. If my memory serves me he dressed it to resemble a bee. The Warden's Worry is duller and very simply dressed. In New England it is a perennial favorite.

69

Among the many others who developed famous flies in the Rangeley area, the name of William R. Edson also stands out because his two Edson Tigers still are prominently listed in northeastern fly catalogs. I like the Edson Dark Tiger much better than the Edson Light Tiger, but that may be a matter of opinion.

Reading clockwise from top left:
5-5 Herbert L. (Herbie) Welch,
5-6 William R. (Bill) Edson,
5-7 Joseph S. (Joe) Stickney.

Here again, what you're able to buy probably isn't exactly what Bill Edson originated, and it may not be as effective. Bill preferred (for these flies) extra-long (5X long) Sproat hooks in sizes from 4 to 10, of which 6 and 8 are recommended. The wing should be sparse, with hairs of nearly equal length. It should hug the top of the body and should be short enough not to catch in the bend of the hook if it should turn under it while being fished. These two patterns (particularly the Dark Tiger) are excellent subjects for beginners in fly tying because they are easy to dress and effective to fish with, regardless of the species you're after.

The Rangeley area was an angler's heaven for about a hundred years after white men first realized what they had there. The fishing was fabulous everywhere until a rapid decline became apparent about 1950. Before then, in the fall during spawning time, one could part the alders, quietly peek into a brook, and find it so full of trout that the bottom was hidden. I remember a September day when Herbie Welch, Bill Edson, and I fished Kennebago Stream, which empties into Rangeley Lake. We were wading, and so many trout and salmon were running up that some passed between our legs! (We had a hard time hooking many because they had other business in mind.) Most lakes had log dams at their outlets. One could lay a fly downcurrent in the pool below and see several big trout or salmon flashing for it. On one week's trip to Rangeley before World War II I hooked (by tally) one hundred large trout and salmon on the same fly (a Ballou Special). Then I gave it to a friend, who took nineteen fish with it on the last day of our trip! Nearly all were released.

Except for rare instances, such as pure luck or being on private water, those fruitful days are about gone. We can go to the Rangeley region now and perhaps enjoy what we now call "good fishing," but that's because we don't realize how good it used to be.

The number of fishermen has multiplied, and they now can drive on networks of new roads to formerly remote places. Outboard motors whisk anglers from place to place quickly, and aircraft can land them on formerly wild lakes. Portable refrigerators tempt them to kill more fish, and freezers keep them for months when they get home. Fishing tackle has been improved and more effective methods have been developed. There is a "get it while you can" element among us which has little or no respect for fish and game laws. Groups of anglers such as Trout Unlimited and the Federation of Fly Fishermen, plus smaller groups everywhere, try to protect and improve our fishing. Fortunately, in some cases, we are successful.

The governor of Maine officially proclaimed that Saturday, August 15, 1970, would be designated Carrie Gertrude Stevens Day. Hundreds of anglers and friends collected on the shore of Rangeley Lake to pay her tribute, and I was asked to give the eulogy. Following that a metal plaque in her memory was embedded beside her spring across the carry from where she lived at Upper Dam. I set up a rod and fished the pool for an hour. The sturdy old dam was still there, showing signs of age. The cabins of the tycoons were gone, and so was the quaint white hotel. The damp little building with the trap door, through which we looked for Pincushion Pete, was gone, too. Mine was the only boat on the pool, and the fishing was very poor.

My heart bled for future anglers because they would never see Upper Dam as it used to be and would never enjoy the fabulous fishing that once was there. Future anglers, however, will doubtless fish, and fish successfully, with these famous flies originated during those halcyon days at Upper Dam.

Upper Dam Pool lives in the hearts of anglers who never have been there because it was there that Carrie Stevens originated her famous flies and her individual method of dressing them. She specialized in trolling flies tied on long (5X and 6X) hooks, as well as tandem-hooked trolling streamers, but her flies in smaller sizes were (and still are) appropriate for casting. Here are her secrets, using the Gray Ghost as an example.

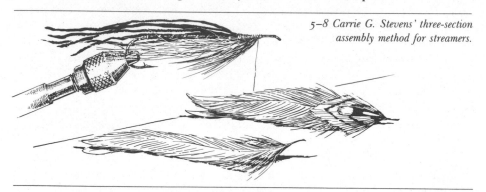

5–8 *Carrie G. Stevens' three-section assembly method for streamers.*

She dressed each fly by combining three separately assembled sections, making up dozens of each section at one time. The body and each side of the wing were made separately. To assemble either of the two sides of the wing, she would first prepare the shoulder of a Ripon's silver pheasant (narrow-banded) body feather and would firmly cement it to the jungle cock cheek by coating the entire underside of the jungle cock with cement. Then she would prepare and lay on the two olive gray saddle hackles, cementing all four together where they would be tied in. Many assembled and firmly cemented right and left sides would be made at one time by this means. Because of the cementing, the jungle cock rarely pulled out of place or became detached in use.

The dressing of the body was also unique. The tying thread was made tacky by wax, an extra piece of which was always stored in a convenient place where it would be kept warm by body contact. She wound the underbody on the hook with white thread, because other colors would affect the color of the silk overbody when wet. The overbody of the Gray Ghost was yellow-orange silk, rather than red-orange, and she stopped dressing the overbody four-fifths of the way to the head of the fly, leaving one-fifth dressed only by the white tying thread. She applied the narrow flat silver-tinsel ribbing sparsely to allow three-fourths of the silk overbody to show.

Now the throat was tied in. A small bunch of white bucktail extending beyond the barb of the hook was tied in under the rearward part of the white underbody. This surrounded the white underbody and was applied here so it would point backward, rather than backward and downward. Immediately ahead of this a small bunch of white hackle (all of approximately the same length) was tied in. Then, over this, one heavy golden pheasant crest feather was tied in as a topping, so that it would be as long as the wing and would arch upward over the back of the body to meet the end of the wing. The white thread at this point was tied off and black thread was substituted for it. Using the black thread, a small golden pheasant crest feather was tied over the white hackle throat so that it extended backward half the length of the hook shank, curving upward. This completed the body.

Identical but opposite right- and left-wing assemblies one and a half times as long as the hook were then selected from the two piles she already had made, and these two sides were laid on one at a time so the shoulders covered the forward underbody windings and so that the upper sides met and combined at the top but allowed the throat to show. These assemblies were tied in usually more on the sides of the body than on top to achieve this effect. (The ribs of the feather assemblies were not scored.)

Carrie always dressed her flies with a two-color head, which she used as a trademark or signature. To do this, she covered all of the quill with black thread and, in winding backward, tied in a piece of orange thread. She finished the head with black thread, then whip-finished three or four turns of the orange thread in the middle of the head to make a three-section head of black, orange, and black. A light coat of lacquer then was applied to the head, but not enough to conceal the orange collar. Finally, she adjusted the dressings as necessary, especially pulling up the golden pheasant topping just enough for it to show.

We have heard of fly dressers who copy the Stevens patterns to the extent of also imitating her two-color-head trademark. While copying the patterns is commendable, copying her trademark is not. It makes the copied fly a counterfeit and only causes misrepresentation and confusion.

Among Mrs. Stevens' more popular patterns are the Allie's Favorite, Blue Devil, Colonel Bates, Don's Delight, General MacArthur, Golden Witch, Gray Ghost, Greyhound, Green Beauty, Morning Glory, Shang's Favorite, Shang's Special, White Devil, Wizard, and Yellow and Black. The correct dressings are given in Part Four.

As a final historical note to the saga of the famous Gray Ghost we add that the "Shang" named in two of the above flies was the Hon. Charles E. (Shang) Wheeler, former state senator of Stratford, Connecticut, and one of the greatest duck-decoy carvers who ever lived. Before Carrie Stevens ever dressed her first fly, Shang, knowing that she had been a milliner, gave

73

her a few boxes of long-shanked streamer fly hooks and suggested that she might use her spare time to tie flies. Shang and I fished together many times at Upper Dam Pool. His suggestion and the gift of the hooks was how the whole thing started. Some of Carrie's dressings are illustrated in Color Plate II.

Two other streamers from Maine which have stood the test of time are the marabou-winged Ballou Special, originated by A. W. Ballou, and the horizontal-winged Nine-Three, by Dr. J. Hubert Sanborn. Notes on them are included in Part Four.

One of the greatest of innovators of eastern streamer patterns was Lew Oatman, of Shushan, New York, who pioneered in developing feathered imitations of the forage fish common to that area. Although his work has become rather obscured by time his seventeen patterns are still excellent for trout and bass, are attractive and simple to dress, and are well worth copying and using by tyro or expert. They are shown in Color Plate XI.

Both Lew Oatman's flies and his angling methods were based on his conception of sound reasoning. A few of his notes in letters he wrote to me just before his death in 1958 should be of interest:

"The basic purpose of a bucktail or a streamer fly is to resemble a small forage fish. With plenty of opportunity to study the actual feeding habits of game fish, I concluded that this type of fly would be most effective, day in and day out, all season through, and under practically all conditions. Since I was familiar with the species of small fish the big ones seemed to like, and that were more or less common, I looked for patterns to imitate them. Aside from patterns designed in Maine to imitate the smelt, my search was unproductive.

"It is possible to design a fly of almost any combination of materials and colors that may take fish, but imaginative patterns lack the ingredient of sound reason. Mother Nature offers us patterns in the forage fish she created that are not only graceful and beautiful in color and design but are also easily recognized as real tasty bits by our game fish.

"Among the forage fish are found some species with the subdued coloring that is effective for wary trout in the clearest waters, and others that serve better as attractors when that type may be needed. So a fly tyer should be satisfied if he can imitate nature's patterns to a reasonable degree without attempting to surpass her creative ability.

"Working along this line, the resulting patterns have turned out to be very effective. Once the technique of handling this type of fly is learned, and confidence gained in its use, an angler can take his share of fish all season long with selections from this group. There are several species of forage fish more or less similar in coloring, including the longnose dace, and some of the suckers, chubs, and shiners. These generally have light bellies and lower sides, with darker backs. They are imitated fairly well by either the Ghost Shiner pattern or the old brown-and-white or black-and-white bucktail, depending on the shade of back wanted. Thus, there isn't much point

74

in attempting to imitate each of these species individually. Being a practical fisherman, I have tried to boil down the number of patterns as much as possible.

"In fishing streamers and bucktails, the type of water also should be considered. When it is of medium depth with deep pockets, or when it is turbulent, fairly large flies can be used. Violent action should be given to them, even slapping them down to attract attention.

"When waters are quieter or shallower, a sparser, more subdued, more natural fly is likely to be more effective, and the action given to it should be gentler. In deep, quiet pools and in lakes or ponds it often is necessary to let the fly sink very deep and to retrieve it slowly, by inches.

"Some of my patterns, such as the Silver Darter, Golden Darter, Gray Smelt, and Ghost Shiner, when tied in small sizes, often will take rising trout when they won't take a dry fly. Of course many anglers won't use streamers or bucktails in low, clear water, but I find them effective. It is important to cover the water thoroughly, because under such conditions trout scatter and lie in unexpected places. In summer fishing over sophisticated trout a very slight rod or line action imparts considerable motion to the fly. But keep it working in the water, rather than in the air!"

Following in the footsteps of the revered Lew Oatman, a knowledgeable angler from Lancaster, Pennsylvania, named Sam Slaymaker II, adopted a different but equally sensible approach to the development of exact imitations. Knowing that trout in streams where they spawn have no compunction against devouring their own young, Sam developed three bucktails to imitate their young: the Little Brown Trout, Little Rainbow Trout, and Little Brook Trout. He says: "My first step was to have two small hatchery fish—a brook and a brown—cast into clear plastic prisms. By manipulating these, the fish's colors could be viewed separately. This made it easier to find materials which would come closest to duplicating each color. The brown's hues appeared less varied than those of the brook, so I started by tying a bucktail to look like a young brown trout. From back to belly the colors had to be dark brown, blending into a lighter brown and finally into a creamlike white. Since the fish's speckles appeared yellow and orange-red, these colors had to be lightly mixed with the brown.

"My coloration was achieved by using dark squirrel tail on top, receding into a lighter shade of it mixed sparingly with strands of yellow and reddish orange dyed bucktail. The body was white spun wool wrapped with thin copper-wire ribbing which served to promote the quality of iridescence common to fish under water. The cheeks were jungle cock, and the tail came from a breast feather of a ring-necked pheasant."

The Little Brown Trout became so successful for taking big brown trout that Sam developed the other two trout patterns. All three did so well that they have been featured in several national magazines as well as in his book *Tie a Fly, Catch a Trout* (New York: Harper & Row, 1976). The dressings are given in Part Four.

Other eastern streamers of historic importance include Theodore Gordon's Bumblepuppy, Arthur B. Flick's Black Nosed Dace, Harold N. Gibbs' Gibbs Striper, and John Alden Knight's Mickey Finn. The dressings and notes on these also are included in Part Four.

Novices often become frustrated by the plethora of streamer and bucktail patterns offered by dealers and recommended in magazine articles and books. Many of the newer patterns are excellent, and the best of them are included herein. Let's not, however, forget the old standbys. They have stood the tests of time and should be basic ingredients in modern fly selection.

6

Streamer Fishing the Rocky Mountain High Country

W<small>E PARKED THE CAR</small> off the macadam above the beaver meadow. While setting up fly rods we paused to view the awesomely magnificent bright June panorama before us. Reaching high into the blue heaven, the towering jagged peaks of Wyoming's Grand Tetons brilliantly reflected their creamy mantle of snow into the azure lake below. The lake was bordered by lush meadows sprinkled with clumps of bushes where a few moose were feeding. The green was interwoven with myriad narrow waterways made deep and placid by a complex of brush dams expertly engineered by the beavers. My host said that this tributary of the Snake River was a haven for several varieties of big trout.

The green of the meadow bordering the path to the stream was brightly sprinkled with the red of Indian paintbrush, the blue of dwarf delphinium, and the bright yellow of balsam root, all of which vied with other varieties to provide rainbows of bright colors. Crowning this, skimming the majestic peaks, scatters of puffy white cumulus clouds drifted lazily through the blue.

We three separated, each to have to himself more water than he could fish properly in a week. I wandered along the slowly flowing depths of the stream, noting its undercut banks and looking for signs of rising fish. Ahead, the depths widened out into a gravel riffle which looked so promising.that I circled some willows in an attempt to approach unseen. Peering carefully through the branches, I snapped to rapt attention. Cruising aim-

77

lessly over the gravel in shallow water were several trout, all obviously over two pounds!

The line was a white floater attached to a long and fine leader terminating with a small Muddler Minnow. A careful cast dropped the fly ahead of and beyond a trout, allowing it to sink slightly as I worked it in front of the leading fish, which paid no attention. Two more casts with the same fly also were ignored. Several offerings of a Stonefly Nymph brought no response.

Quietly backing away, I rested the spot while tying on a finer tippet and a No. 14 Ginger Quill. The tiny dry fly drifted properly over a few of the fish, but none reacted in the slightest. Nothing worked.

"Any luck?" a low voice behind me inquired. My host had approached, a fat rainbow in his jacket. He said he had released three others.

"You think they didn't see you, but they probably knew you were there," he said. "These cruising trout are very hard to hook. In a spot like this we sometimes score by using a weighted Muddler or a Sculpin pattern. Let it sink to the bottom and leave it there until a cruising fish approaches. Then gently twitch it a bit and let it sink again. This calls for patience, but it gets results. Come with me and I'll show you an easier place."

Deeper water proved more fruitful. Weighted streamers drifted under undercut banks often brought savage strikes, particularly when allowed to sink and then retrieved with fast jerks. These methods hooked several trout, including five of over two pounds—two rainbows, two brown trout, and a handsome brookie, all of which were released.

On another day we fished the famous Firehole River in Yellowstone Park. Here again I was left to my own devices for a few hours, but enjoyed the scenery more than the fishing. This is near Old Faithful Geyser, which erupts its column of steam and hot water on periodic schedule to the great delight of tourists clustered safely around its edge. The whole area is sprinkled with smaller geysers, fumaroles, and other steam vents emanating from the earth's rocky surface.

My way to the river led over a crusty area of bubbling hot-water pools and small fissures from which steam wafted. Being an easterner unused to such places, I was apprehensive. There was an elk trail, which I followed under the theory that if an elk hadn't broken through, neither would I.

Many Rocky Mountain rivers are unsuitable for streamers, and the Firehole is one of them, because of its grassy bottom in so many places. Streamers in some areas often take very creditable fish, but grassy streams mainly produce better with the dry fly. No one method is a sure cure for everything.

78 Some of the grassiest streams are the spring creeks. These amazing little rivers suddenly erupt from the earth fully fledged, crystal-clear, and rich in nutrients encouraged by their birth deep in limestone caverns. We fished one near Sun Valley, Idaho.

This smoothly flowing river has a sturdy gravel bottom easily wadable over knee-deep except for the grasses, whose immense patches of green

-1 The Firehole River, with steam vents in the distance. (Photo: Bud Lilly)

5-2 Fishing the edge of a current on the Big Hole River. (Photo: Bud Lilly)

fronds rise to the surface and lie on it. One has to plan his path through the open spaces or the least of the grasses to find a good position from which to cast the dry fly to rising trout. This is intriguing fishing, but it isn't for streamers because of the grasses, so we won't dwell on it.

I haven't fished the highest of the high country, but am told that tiny dry flies, nymphs, and shrimp imitations far outclass streamers because of the lack of bait fish at these altitudes. This isn't true farther down.

The famous trout streams are in the moderately high country—the Gibbon and Firehole, which flow into the wide Madison near West Yellowstone; the Yellowstone, Big Hole, Henry's Fork, Snake, and many others. In many of these streams western anglers fish what they call "pocket water," or what others refer to as "edges of current," or "comfort zones," as discussed in Chapter 3. They learn to "read the water" to locate submerged rocks as well as visible ones, because they know that trout frequent the moderate flow above and behind such obstructions just as they do in eastern streams. They know that properly weighting the fly and controlling the speed of the drift or swing is essential in big streams, and they use proper lines to fish the flies at the desired levels.

This kind of water is the home of bait fish such as various minnows and sculpins (the latter discussed in Chapter 14), so it is ideal for streamers and bucktails. Bud Lilly, popular guide and tackle-shop owner in the West Yellowstone area, says that sculpin and minnow imitations account for some of the largest trout taken each year.

With this bonanza of good fishing in the Rocky Mountain area, and particularly in the states of Idaho, Montana, Wyoming, and Colorado, it is natural that several fly dressers there became nationally or internationally famous for their skill and inventiveness. One is Dan Bailey, a transplanted easterner whose fly and tackle shop is a mecca for all fishermen who pass near Livingston, Montana. Among many other accomplishments Dan is renowned for his improvements in Muddlers, as noted in Chapter 14. Another is Alfred C. Troth, of Dillon, Montana, who also deals in flies and who originated the Troth Bullhead described in the same chapter and shown in Color Plate VI.

During several decades of fascination with fishing flies and fly fishing I have noted numerous tyers without great ability who proudly announce that they have "created" a pattern or two. It seems more modest to say they "originated" it, if they did, and to leave creation to the Deity. If anyone deserves the accolade of "creator" in fly dressing it is a supreme artist in his field named George F. Grant, of Butte, Montana, who was kind enough to honor this book with his handiwork as shown in Color Plates III and VI.

George Grant developed and perfected well over a dozen patterns of the various large black or dark brown stonefly nymphs, hellgramites, etc. referred to locally as "mossbacks" which are based on the hand-woven "Mite" hair flies originated and patented by Franz B. Pott, of Missoula, Montana. Grant originated the process of making woven-hair-hackle dry

PLATE I Flies Designed Primarily As Baitfish Imitations

1. Emerald Minnow
2. Spot-tailed Minnow
3. Silver Minnow
*Originated and dressed by
Keith C. Fulsher*

4. Little Brook Trout
5. Little Brown Trout
6. Little Rainbow Trout
*Originated by Samuel R.
Slaymaker II.
Dressed by the Weber Tackle
Company*

7. Jesse Wood
*Originated by Jesse Wood.
Dressed by Ray Bergman*

8. Black Nosed Dace
*Originated and dressed by
Arthur B. Flick*

9. Grizzly Prince
*Originated and dressed by
Austin S. Hogan*

10. Marabou Perch
*Originated and dressed by
Arthur W. Fusco*

11. Hornberg
*Originated by Frank Hornberg.
Dressed by the Weber Tackle
Company*

12. Polar Chub
*Originated and dressed by
E. H. Rosborough*

13. Muddler Minnow
*Originated and dressed by
Don Gapen*

14. Leech
*Originated and dressed by
Frier Gulline*

15. Silver Minnow
*Originated by Al Giradot.
Dressed by Maury Delman*

16. Miracle Marabou
Blueback Shiner

17. Miracle Marabou
Longnose Dace
*Originated by Robert Zwirz
and Kani Evans.
Dressed by Gladys Zwirz*

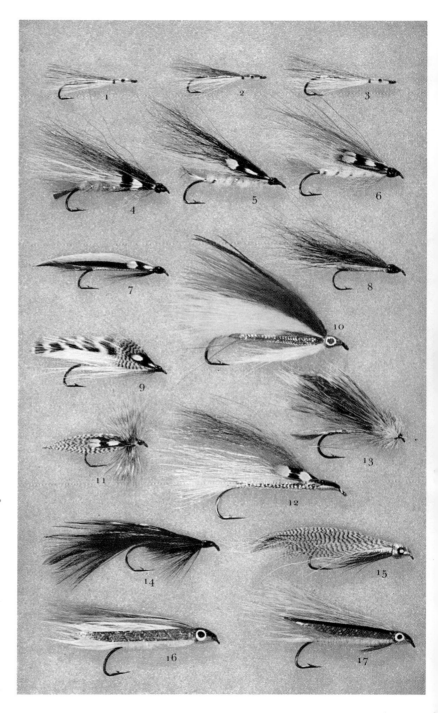

PLATE II Original Patterns by Mrs. Carrie G. Stevens

1. Wizard
2. Golden Witch
3. Blue Devil
4. Don's Delight
5. Shang's Favorite
6. Colonel Bates
7. Gray Ghost
8. General MacArthur
9. Green Beauty
10. Morning Glory
11. Allie's Favorite
12. Shang's Special
13. Greyhound

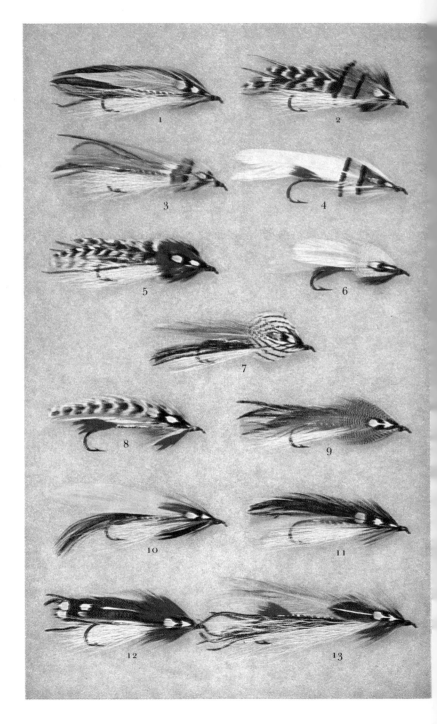

The patterns on this plate were originated and dressed by Mrs. Carrie G. Stevens

PLATE III Streamers of the Rocky Mountain High Country

1. Trude
2. Fox Squirrel (Red)
3. Picket Pin
4. Bloody Butcher
5. Dr. Mummy
6. Canadian Killer
7. Murder Orange
8. Dark Spruce
9. Big Hole Demon
10. Platte River Special
11. Gray Squirrel (Yellow)
12. Integration
13. Wyatt's Squirrel
14. Badger Royal
15. Western Doctor

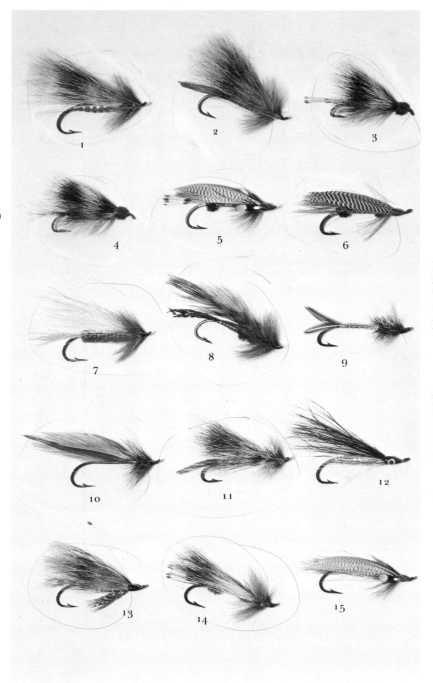

Dressed by George F. Grant, Butte, Montana

PLATE IV Prominent Western Freshwater Patterns

1. Alaska Mary Ann
*Originated and dressed by
Frank Dufresne*

2. Ashdown Green
*Originated by Ashdown H. Green.
Dressed by Fin, Fur, &
Feather, Ltd.*

3. Thor
*Originated and dressed by
C. Jim Pray*

4. Bellamy
*Originated by George B. Bellamy.
Dressed by Peter J. Schwab*

5. Royal Coachman
*An English pattern,
dressed by the author*

6. Black Demon
*Originated and dressed
by C. Jim Pray*

7. Chappie
*Originated and dressed
by C. L. Franklin*

8. Carter's Dixie
*Originated and dressed
by C. Jim Pray*

9. Umpqua Special
*A northwestern pattern dressed
by Don C. Harger*

10. Owl Eyed Optic
*One of a series originated
and dressed by C. Jim Pray*

11. Improved Governor
*Of English origin,
dressed by C. Jim Pray*

12. Railbird
*Originated by John S. Benn.
Dressed by C. Jim Pray*

13. Spruce
*Originated by A. & C. Godfrey.
Dressed by Dan Bailey*

14. Orange Steelheader
*Originated and dressed
by Fred A. Reed*

15. Red Phantom
*Originated and dressed
by E. H. Rosborough*

16. Atom Bomb
*Originated by George
and Helen Voss.
Dressed by E. H. Rosborough*

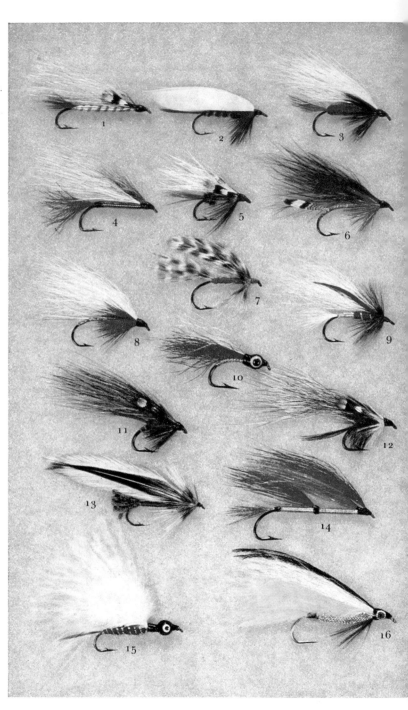

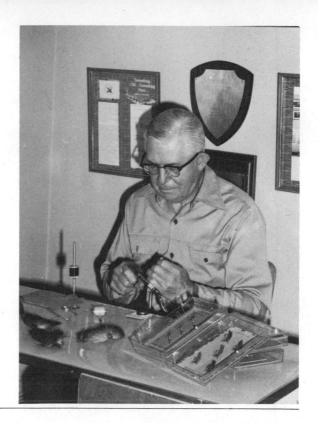

6–3 Famous conservationist and
fly dresser George F. Grant.

flies and is responsible for many other accomplishments, such as using
woven-hair hackles on streamers and bucktails rather than the usual feather
collars.

His reproductions of sculpins (see Color Plate VI) are also remarkable.
In addition to all this George is a noted conservationist and the author of
two very valuable books on these subjects (the titles and Grant's address
are given in a footnote on page 194).

Rocky Mountain streamers and bucktails were developed principally for
big rivers, such as the Madison, using methods similar to those for steelhead and Atlantic salmon. The trout are big, and so are the flies, which
often are weighted and distinguished by heavily dressed flaring wings. In
one of his books *(Montana Trout Flies)* Grant says, "Fly historians tell us that
the first squirrel tail flies were tied in Idaho about 1901, and it is reasonable
to believe that they were in use in western Montana within the next few
years. The Fox Squirrel (Red Body) and the Gray Squirrel (Yellow Body),
tied in the traditional Trude style with the hackle put on after the wing,
were as popular and effective in the first fifty years of this century as the
Muddler Minnow is today.

"The success of these flies led Jack Boehme, the great Missoula, Montana, fly tyer, to utilize the tail hair of the native ground squirrel (gopher),
and thus the famous Picket Pin patterns were born about 1915. They are
just about as popular today as they were in the early years, but the ground

81

squirrel has not fared as well and these flies are now usually winged with tail hair of the eastern gray squirrel."

It is evident that streamer flies of the Rocky Mountain states differ considerably from general patterns, so we present here the tying instructions for fifteen of the most important as this book is being written. All were dressed for this purpose by Mr. Grant and are shown in Color Plate III. We should add that George Grant does not produce flies for sale. When obtainable as gifts they are cherished as rare collectors' items. Since the Trude is the ancestor of the series, we will start with it. Its history is told in Chapter 2.

TRUDE
HOOK SIZE: 2 or 4, 3X long
HEAD: Red
BODY: Red yarn, quite full and tapered
RIBBING: Wide silver tinsel
WING: A fairly large bunch of red squirrel tail hair tied long to show the dark band
THROAT: Several turns of a red rooster's hackle tied full and inclined to the rear after the wing has been applied

Carter H. Harrison, the originator of this pattern in 1901, says, "I have tied other Trude flies using green, yellow, and blue yarn and have also made flies with wings of hair from *gray squirrels.*" This indicates that gray squirrel tail was used early in the 1900s.

FOX SQUIRREL (Red Body)
HOOK SIZE: 2 or 4, 3X long
HEAD: Red
TAIL: A section of a goose wing quill dyed scarlet extending slightly beyond the bend of the hook
BODY: Red floss, quite full and tapered
RIBBING: Oval or flat gold tinsel
WING: A fairly large bunch of fox squirrel tail, well flared out
HACKLE: Several turns of a light brown hackle tied full and inclined to rear after the wing has been applied

This pattern obviously is a variation of the Trude and is the forerunner of the well-known Red Abbey Atlantic salmon fly. Many fly tyers prefer oval to flat tinsel because it can be seated more securely on the tapered body.

82

GRAY SQUIRREL (Yellow Body)
HOOK SIZE: 2 or 4, 3X long
HEAD: Red
TAIL: A section of a goose wing quill dyed scarlet extending slightly beyond the bend of the hook
BODY: Yellow floss, quite full and tapered

RIBBING: Oval or flat silver tinsel

WING: A fairly large bunch of gray squirrel tail, well flared out

HACKLE: Several turns of a gray grizzly hackle (badger often is used) tied full and inclined to rear after the wing has been applied

PICKET PIN

HOOK SIZE: 4 or 6, 3X long (Mustad #9672)

THREAD: Black Nymo, size A

TAIL: Golden pheasant tippets (three to five), quite long

BODY: Medium flat gold tinsel

HACKLE: About six turns of a medium brown saddle hackle palmered from tail over whole of body

RIBBING: Yellow waxed tying thread or fine gold wire

WING: A fairly large bunch of gray squirrel tail, well flared out

COLLAR: White tip hair of gray squirrel over wing only

HEAD: Several turns of peacock (or ostrich) herl, full

This is a famous pattern by Jack Boehme, of Missoula, Montana. The original was tied with gopher tail hair. This little ground squirrel was referred to as a "picket pin" because it looked like a tether stake when sitting upright. The body of the fly has been tied in several variations, but none is as effective as this original. It suggests a variety of western trout food and is an all-season favorite.

The tail hair of a Columbian ground squirrel (gopher) shows markings of white, black, white, while that of the gray squirrel is white, black, gray. When using gray squirrel a collar of white squirrel tip hair can be tied over the gray portion, resulting in a wing that is white, black, white, like the original.

BLOODY BUTCHER

HOOK SIZE: 4 or 6, 3X long (Mustad #9672)

THREAD: Black Nymo, size A

TAIL: A very small bunch of mixed scarlet and yellow hackle fibers, quite long

BODY: Wound with peacock herl

HACKLE: About six turns of a scarlet and a yellow saddle hackle palmered together over whole of body

RIBBING: Fine gold wire

WING: A fairly large bunch of gray squirrel tail, well flared out

COLLAR: White tip hair of gray squirrel over wing only (see Picket Pin for detail)

HEAD: Several turns of peacock (or ostrich) herl, full

83

The scarlet and yellow body hackle should be "doubled" or "blended" together prior to tying in by the tips at the tail end of the fly, and then wound on as a single hackle, wet-fly style, over the peacock-herl body.

This is an important variation of the Picket Pin and is fully as effective. The name evidently refers to the scarlet in the body hackle.

DR. MUMMY
HOOK SIZE: 4 to 8, 2X long (Mustad #9671)
THREAD: Black Nymo for body; red for head, size A
TIP: A few turns of narrow flat gold tinsel
TAIL: Golden pheasant tippets (three to five), quite long
BUTT: Peacock herl, fairly full
BODY: Black floss, thinly dressed, not tapered
RIBBING: Medium oval gold tinsel
THROAT: Two or three turns of a hot orange hackle applied as a collar
UNDERWING: A few fibers from a cock pheasant's center tail feather, extending slightly beyond bend of hook
OVERWING: A gray mallard flank feather tied on flat, or roofed (see below)
CHEEKS: Jungle cock

Select a mallard side feather longer and wider than seems necessary. Tie flat on the bare quill with two turns of thread and then pull the feather forward slowly until the proper length of wing is achieved. This will give the compact, low-profile wing proper for this very attractive pattern.

The fly was originated about 1930 by William L. Beaty, one of Montana's earliest commercial fly dressers and inventor of the Beaty Patented Locking Reel Seat for fly rods. It was a particular favorite on big rivers during cloudy water conditions when bright classics such as the Silver Doctor, Royal Coachman, and Jock Scott also were popular. It was named for a Dr. Mummy, from Denver, who asked Bill Beaty to tie the pattern for him.

CANADIAN KILLER
HOOK SIZE: 4 to 8, 2X long (Mustad #9671)
THREAD: Red Nymo, size A
TIP: A few turns of narrow flat gold tinsel
TAIL: A very small bunch (eight to ten) of brown hackle fibers extending well beyond bend of hook
BUTT: Peacock herl, fairly full
BODY: Scarlet floss, thinly dressed, not tapered
RIBBING: Medium oval gold tinsel
FRONT BUTT: Peacock herl, fairly full
THROAT: Two or three turns of a medium brown hackle applied as a collar
UNDERWING: A small bunch of bucktail or polar bear hairs dyed scarlet, extending slightly beyond bend of hook
OVERWING: A teal side feather tied on flat (see the Dr. Mummy pattern for method)

While the originator of this fly is unknown, there is a reasonable similarity between it and the Canadian teal-wing patterns described by the late Roy Patrick in his *Pacific Northwest Fly Patterns,* and one of them could have served for the basis for this one.

When Georgetown Lake, west of Anaconda, Montana, was one of the best trout lakes anywhere, the method of fishing this fly was a combination of fly casting and trolling. The fly was cast from a slowly moving boat that pulled it just under the surface until it was retrieved and another cast was made.

MURDER ORANGE
HOOK SIZE: 4 to 6, 3X long (Mustad #9672)
THREAD: Black Nymo, size A
TIP: Fine flat gold tinsel (optional)
TAIL: A small bunch of deep orange polar bear hair extending well beyond bend of hook
BODY: Thickly wound with deep orange chenille
WING: A bunch of white bucktail (in the original) or white polar bear, extending to end of tail and widely flared (see below)
HACKLE: Several turns of a dark brown hackle (in the original) or of a deep orange hackle, applied as a collar and slanted backward

To make the fly more visible it is best to apply the wing in reverse style, which will cause it to stand up higher. This is done by tying in the wing *first* with the hair tips pointing forward over the eye of the hook. When the rest of the fly is completed the wing then is reversed to normal position and tied down so it flares widely. This method, often used on bucktails, also provides a much smaller and neater head as well as a very secure wing. The hackle is wound on *after* this is done.

The origin of this fly is obscure but it may have been originated by Dave Stratford, a tackle dealer and guide who lived in Dillon, Montana, to compete with Jack Boehme's Bloody Butcher. While this is a true bucktail, several of the flies described here were made to simulate a large insect called the salmon fly which hatches in great profusion from western rivers in the spring. We don't know whether fish considered it an insect or a bait-fish imitation but it was a very popular and effective pattern which still is used to a minor extent.

DARK SPRUCE (MONTANA)
HOOK SIZE: 6 to 12, various lengths
HEAD: Black
TAIL: About four strands of peacock sword feather, quite long
BODY: Rear half red floss, built up toward middle to merge with front half; front half peacock herl
RIBBING: Fine gold oval tinsel over rear half only

85

WING: Four gray grizzly hackles dyed medium brown, set at about 30°
over body

HACKLE: A gray grizzly hackle dyed medium brown, applied ahead of
wing and slanted backward

This perennially popular pattern is dressed in various areas in so many
variations, both wet and dry, with regular or splayed wings, that it might
be considered a type. This is the Montana dressing. For others see the
Spruce Streamer and its variations in Part Four. The original was tied in
1918 or 1919 by Bert and Clarence Milo Godfrey (probably more or less
in collaboration) of Seaside, Oregon, for sea-run cutthroat trout. The Godfrey brothers tied the wet patterns quite full on regular-weight Sproat
hooks. Their various originations were noted for simplicity and the absence
of hard-to-find materials. The fame of the fly quickly spread beyond the
eastern Rockies and into Alaska and Canada. It now is popular everywhere,
fished wet, like a nymph, at varying depths, as well as in a dry version in
sizes 10 to 24.

In his *Montana Trout Flies* George Grant comments, "The body of the
original fly was made of peacock herl with a red tip like the old Governor
pattern, and the wings were badger hackles, often splayed or forked. The
fly was first used in its original form by Montana fishermen, who later
changed the body to include a rear half of silver tinsel while retaining the
peacock herl in front. They also gradually replaced the badger wing hackles
with grizzly. The Montana Spruce was born when the Plymouth Rock hackles used for wings were dyed a medium brown to provide a better imitation
of the mottled sculpin but whether or not trout take it for such is open to
question. It has been quite generally replaced by the Spuddler when a
specific sculpin imitation is desired."

BIG HOLE DEMON

HOOK SIZE: 2 to 10, 2X or 3X long

HEAD: Black

TAIL: Two jungle cock body feathers, splayed (or a few fox squirrel
tail fibers)

BODY: Rear half, silver tinsel; front half, black chenille

HACKLE: A badger hackle heavily palmered over the chenille

Some dressers apply silver tinsel as far forward as two-thirds of the
body, and add a ribbing of oval silver tinsel. One version also is all jet black
(with silver rear half). Another calls for a tail of fox squirrel and a grizzly
hackle (with silver rear half).

The original was the black pattern, tied by Pete Narancich, of Sheridan,
Montana, about 1965, more or less on a whim. Arthur M. Taylor, of Phoe-
nix, Arizona, who provided Pete Narancich's originals for this book, says,
"This was a real killer between 1965 and 1970 but since then has not been
as effective although it still does take fish. Pete felt the grizzly was somewhat

6–4 *Fishing a lake in the scenic high country. (Photo: Montana Fish & Game Department)*

the best, while I think the all-black is. One day during those years when I was on the Big Hole River with Joe Brooks, I gave him some of these flies. He tried them and readily admitted it was 'one heck of a new pattern.' Joe gave some to Dan Bailey to try on the Yellowstone and both felt that the Big Hole Demon was a very special fly for southwestern Montana."

PLATTE RIVER SPECIAL
HOOK SIZE: 1/0, 2X long
HEAD: Black
BODY: None (see below)
WING: Four broad bright yellow spade hackles, with a broad medium
    brown spade hackle on each side
HACKLE: A brown and a bright yellow hackle mixed, collared in front
    of wing and tied back slightly

This is the standard version, although there are many variations. Presumably it was originated about 1951 by Bud Miller, of Casper, Wyoming. Note that the brown shade used in the wings and hackle is medium brown —*not* Coachman brown. The fly is not weighted. It is intended to simulate the western sculpin, a prevalent bait fish in the Platte River area.

On the Miracle Mile section of Wyoming's North Platte the fly is dressed as above but on size 2 or 4 Limerick hooks. During the spring months red hackle often is substituted for the yellow and seems to be more effective for rainbow trout.

Michael Gula, of Hank Roberts Sport Shop in Boulder, Colorado, says that the most popular dressing in his area is the standard version with a body of gold Mylar piping or tinsel on 4X long Mustad #79580 hooks.

Sometimes the wings are applied concave sides out to flare and provide more action. The addition of a brown floss body is another variation.

A final variation to be mentioned here is called the Big Horn Special. It is the standard version except that the hackle is clipped in the Muddler fashion. This pattern for the Platte River sometimes substitutes black hackle for brown and/or red for the yellow.

TRUEBLOOD'S INTEGRATION
HOOK SIZE: 2 to 8, 2X long
HEAD: Black (painted white eye, black pupil optional)
BUTT: Tie down excess of Mylar body with red thread (black is conventional)
BODY: Silver Mylar tubing slipped over built-up tapered floss or wool underbody
WING: Black over white bucktail, flared, a bit longer than the hook
THROAT: A small bunch of white bucktail, the longest hairs extending to point of hook

This pattern was developed by Ted Trueblood, of Nampa, Idaho, famous sportsman and writer for *Field & Stream* magazine. Its name is obvious, and it is one of the few flies in the Rocky Mountain area using Mylar tubing to form the body.

WYATT'S SQUIRREL (Red)
HOOK SIZE: 2 to 8, 2X long
HEAD: Black
TAIL: A small bunch of guinea fowl feather fibers of medium length
BODY: Wound with medium yellow-orange chenille, built up and tapered
RIBBING: Fine gold oval tinsel
THROAT: A moderate bunch of guinea fowl feather fibers extending about two-thirds of body length
WING: A bunch of fox squirrel tail hairs extending to end of tail and well flared (gray squirrel often is used)

This popular western pattern was originated by Clifford Wyatt, of Santa Monica, California, and formerly of Ogden, Utah—famous fly caster, fly dresser, and rod builder, now deceased. The reason for the dressing is obscure, but many western anglers consider it of great importance. When tied with a gray squirrel wing it is known as Wyatt's Squirrel (Gray).

BADGER ROYAL
HOOK SIZE: 2 to 8, 2X long
HEAD: Red
TAIL: A small bunch of golden pheasant tippet fibers
BUTT: Wound with peacock herl, fairly thick
BODY: Thinly wound with scarlet floss

FORWARD BUTT: Wound with peacock herl
WING: A bunch of badger hairs extending to end of tail
HACKLE: Several turns of a red rooster's hackle, slanted slightly
   backward

This prominent Big Hole River pattern is merely the Royal Coachman Bucktail with a badger-hair wing.

WESTERN SILVER DOCTOR
HOOK SIZE: 2 to 8, 2X long
HEAD: Red
TAIL: A small bunch of yellow polar bear hair or similar of medium
   length
BUTT: Red chenille or wool
BODY: Flat silver tinsel
RIBBING: Fine oval silver tinsel or thread
THROAT: A few turns of a hackle dyed dark blue and slanted backward
UNDERWING: A very small bunch of mixed red, yellow, and blue
   bucktail or polar bear extending nearly to end of tail
OVERWING: A mallard flank feather tied on flat, as long as the
   underwing
CHEEKS: Jungle cock, rather short

Here again, select a feather for the overwing which is a bit larger than called for. After tying the quill down with two turns of thread, pull the quill forward to the desired length, thus compacting it a bit so it will act as a roof for the underwing.

This is merely one of several Atlantic salmon patterns that were adapted to western fishing conditions but not to the extent that their ancestry was completely disguised. Such patterns were used almost exclusively on the Madison River during the 1920–40 period when frequent water releases from Hebgen Dam often caused the river to become muddied, making brightly colored flies necessary so they could be more readily seen by trout. These flies are useful today under similar conditions.

Western streamers usually are tied with hair wings, and squirrel tail hair is used to a greater extent than bucktail. Hackle-winged streamers are rare and bear little resemblance to their more streamlined eastern counterparts. Wings are set high for better movement in fast water, this position usually being achieved through reverse tying or the use of bulky body materials. Wingless patterns such as the Big Hole Demon may not be true streamers, but are intended to represent small forage fish. The dividing line between streamers and other types cannot always be clearly defined. For example, the same fly might be taken at one time for a forage fish and at another time for a stonefly nymph, since these are very prevalent and very large. The way the fly is being fished must influence the matter.

89

7

Freshwater Tactics for the Pacific Coast

ANGLERS FALL IN LOVE with favorite rivers and are never blamed for affairs with others on the side. Rivers are beautiful and tempting, each in individual ways. Nestled in rocky gravel, dressed in shades of green, and decorated with fronds and flowers, they sparkle happily in sunshine, sulk in misty grayness, mutter angrily or burble peacefully, always talking, always active, always beckoning with suggestive invitations sometimes unfulfilled. Anglers who fall in love with rivers cherish their individualities and strive to understand them intimately. Luckily for wives, rivers aren't very cuddly and don't know how to cook.

Joe Brooks and I fell temporarily in love with California's Klamath even though he was wedded to Montana's Madison while I had a thing going with a bounteous stream in southwestern Iceland. He was faithful to the Madison until he died. I make annual visits to the Laxá i Kjos but I must admit that her streamy sister, Langá, is a rather titillating temptation.

Joe and I first viewed the curvy Klamath from a bluff near Happy Camp while we were spending a month together getting to know a few of the steelhead and salmon rivers in Oregon and northern California under the guidance of two Portland experts named Don Harger and Chandler Brown. In this area the beautiful Klamath tumbles sinuously down a rocky gorge forested with sycamores, evergreens, and oaks to linger from time to time in a succession of deep pools and graveled riffles delightful but challenging to fishers of the fly.

Our camp on the Klamath was on a rise of ground overlooking the shining river as it snaked with disarming smoothness through the rocky pine-and-fir-covered hills. We were there in late September and early October when there was enough frost in the crisp night air to turn the aspen leaves the color of burnished gold, shining brightly against the deep greens of the hillsides. Thirty miles upstream from our base of operations the dam of the California-Oregon Power Company acts as a barrier to the upriver migrations of the steelhead and salmon as well as to the downstream travels of the large resident rainbow trout and the few brown trout which occupy the river from there to its source in the reedy expanses of large and boggy Klamath Lake. Thus, as a steelhead river, the Klamath begins at Copco Dam. From Copco to Seiad Valley, seventy-five miles downstream, a good road borders the river and makes excellent fishing easily available. This was the part of the river where we fished for steelhead.

The first runs of fish come into the river in late August and arrive in the Happy Camp area about the second week in September. These steelhead are small; called "half-pounders" locally, they are what Atlantic salmon anglers would refer to as "grilse." They rarely exceed five pounds, but are noted for their stamina and spectacular jumping ability. The big ones and the salmon work upstream later.

The peacefulness of this section of the Klamath is disarming. In a matter of twenty minutes it can turn from a low-water stream into a raging torrent, swift and deadly for all but the rambunctious steelhead resting behind the boulders which breast its rocky riffles. As the turbines at Copco produce power the dam releases water, causing the river to rise once a day from a few inches to about twenty in as few minutes. Many an unsuspecting angler, gingerly wading a deep riffle in the middle of the stream, has been swept from his feet by the flood, and there are those who have not lived to tell of it, despite warning signs erected by sportsmen's clubs.

Anglers therefore note markers on the shoreline and leave the river when they disappear. Another warning is globs of foam drifting down. The flood waters travel at about three and a half miles an hour, so upon meeting them at one point, fishermen can drive downstream for five or ten miles and have an hour or two more of low water before the rise again overtakes them.

Steelhead fishing is much better when the water isn't high. The fish migrate upstream during high water and are difficult to locate and to interest in a fly when they are traveling. High water makes many of the riffles unwadable. It becomes discolored and makes it less likely that the steelhead will notice a lure. Even during low water, long casts of about eighty feet often are needed to enable anglers wading the riffles to reach some of the favorite resting places of the fish near the deeper bank.

Resting places for steelhead are nearly identical to those for trout, as discussed in Chapter 3—edges of current, pocket water, and the lower part of the tails of pools where the gravel curves upward. This is because the top water is faster, while the bottom water is slowed by obstructions. Some

91

7-1 *The Klamath from a bluff near Happy Camp. (Photo by author)*

anglers maintain that steelhead do not rest *in back* of boulders because there is less upstream vision for them and less surface agitation, so they can be seen more easily by enemies. Resting spots in front of boulders are thought to protect the rear. In spite of this opinion I have had success in both locations.

Riffles known usually to contain fish are termed "holding riffles" because they have the depth and speed of current desirable to the fish, together with the necessary rocks and back eddies which break the force of the current and thus induce the steelhead to rest in them. Their location may be a factor also, in that when they lie above a long run of fast water the fish may be more tired and thus more apt to tarry there.

Holding riffles are known as either "early" or "late" ones, the names pertaining both to the season and to the time of day. Some riffles which are good early in the season are barren of fish later on, and vice versa. Water level and the speed of the current have a lot to do with this. Proper current speed seems to be about as fast as a man can walk, which can be estimated by the drift of objects floating on the surface. Thus, when the river is low in the early fall, the steelhead may prefer the narrow riffles, which are deep, while in the late fall or winter when the river is running full, these places may be too fast and too deep, and the favored riffles, or "late riffles," may be the wide ones where the current was too slow and the depth too shallow earlier in the season.

Many anglers will not fish certain "hot" riffles except at definite times of day, maintaining, for instance, that Slippery Riffle is no good in the morning, while Pinetree Riffle is fishable only before noon. One explanation for this is the position of the sun on the water. When the fly is between the sun and the fish, they feel that the glare on the surface is such that it cannot be seen clearly. Advocates of this theory prefer to fish riffles at the time of day when the sun is behind the fish (which will be facing upstream) rather than in front of them. A somewhat similar belief is that too much glare on the water is not conducive to good fishing, so that riffles are fished at a time of day when they are in the shadow of the bordering hills.

Anglers usually wade the riffles quarter downstream casting, first trying shorter casts and then gradually extending them to cover all the good holding areas. When the fly completes its swing and starts to hang downstream, they work it there in case a fish may have followed and might be enticed to take. When more than one angler is fishing a riffle, they follow one another at safe intervals, being set by the leading person, who is duty-bound to maintain reasonable progress. When a fish is hooked, other anglers get out of the way, and the lucky one returns to the rear of the line.

Following the influx of small steelhead come bigger ones and schools of silver (coho) salmon. In some rivers (including the Klamath) also come the giants of them all, the lordly king (Chinook) salmon, which can reach a weight of about fifty pounds and can be taken on tiny flies as small as 8s and 10s, if one is sufficiently skillful! These three superb species of game fish enter the rivers on rising water at various times, depending on the rivers and the weather, reaching into midwinter.

In an attempt to avoid generality the Klamath has been briefly described merely as an example (albeit a very good one) of the host of northwestern coastal rivers harboring these challengers to the angler and his fly tackle. While every river is different, angling methods are pretty much the same. The Klamath also was selected because it is more or less on the dividing line between the popularity of winged patterns, which are used to the north, and wingless ones, used to the south—except that winged ones may be used in the south too during high or discolored water for greater visibility.

We found that in rivers such as the Klamath and the Deschutes, the steelhead even quite far upriver were reasonably bright fish. However, the majority of steelheading is done very close to the mouth of a river, because the fish often become stale and get what is referred to as "lockjaw" the farther up the river they go. The best steelheading is in tidal waters, lagoon areas, and within about ten miles from the mouth of a river. After spawning,

93

7–2 *Steelheading on the lower Deschutes. (Photo by author)*

most steelhead return to the ocean, unless interfered with, perhaps to return again as bright and bigger fish, some reaching weights of over twenty pounds. All the salmon, on the other hand, deteriorate and die after spawning.

The holds preferred by steelhead and salmon vary significantly in rivers. Unlike steelhead, both coho and Chinook salmon rest in deep pools, which are often fished from small anchored boats (prams) using fly tackle accommodating line sizes between 10 and 12. These lines when necessary are fast-sinking ones, including lead-core shooting heads. Sometimes the flies also need to be weighted.

Silver (coho) salmon are one of the most challenging of all game fish. They average about ten pounds and rarely exceed fifteen, but provide aggressive battles with many spectacular jumps. Anglers in the estuaries usually troll for them and find schools by noticing bird action. Flies are colorful bucktails such as the Candlefish, Coronation, and Herring, or one of the very popular Mylared white streamers like Lefty's Deceiver. Fly-rodders fish in the rivers, especially when trollers in the estuaries interfere with the action there. The action for them happens when the bar separating the river from the estuary is opened by the increasing flow of water due to rains.

When the salmon are in a taking mood they will hit most any reasonable pattern of fly, although each angler has his favorites, some of the best of which are described later in this chapter. Pacific salmon patterns usually are simple, with long tails and no wings, but normally with bright collars. Size is more important than color, but the "bright fly, bright day—dark fly, dark day" theory seems to hold, with perhaps a more neutral pattern or two in between. The heavy-wire hook sizes average between 4 and 6 but may be smaller.

Similar (or the same) flies and sizes are used for king (Chinook, or tyee) salmon, which sometimes reach weights of about fifty pounds. Most of the fly fishing for them is in the deeper pools upstream from the tidal estuary. Presence of fish often is indicated by boils or broaching on the surface. A good area is the top of a pool where its water starts to slide into the riffle, from three to six feet deep. Except possibly for our eastern Atlantic salmon, which rarely reach such weights, Chinooks provide the most exciting and challenging freshwater fly fishing on the North American continent.

Some readers may question the inclusion of steelhead and wingless Pacific salmon flies in a book about streamers and bucktails. While I admit that they may be in the gray area, many anglers feel the book would be incomplete without them. For example, Hal W. Janssen, a prominent fly dresser and steelheader and sales manager of the Sunset Line and Twine Company, of Petaluma, California, which manufactures some of the best lines for this sport, says, "Even though these patterns do not have the traditional wing of bucktail or hackle feathers, we would have to classify them in the streamer category due to their methods of use and imitative theory."

Styles in flies for these anadromous fish change rapidly. When my *Streamer Fly Tying & Fishing* was published in 1966, it included the authentic dressings of twenty-two then-prominent patterns. They also are included in Part Four of this book, partly for their historic value—they were originated by such noted experts of yesteryear as Peter J. Schwab, C. Jim Pray, Fred Reed, and George McLeod—and partly because some of them, such as the Skykomish Sunrise and the Thor, are still among the very best. For convenience of reference the other twenty patterns, in alphabetical order, are the Bellamy, Black Demon, Black Gordon, Bobby Dunn, Carter Fly, Carter's Dixie, Chappie, Improved Governor, Orange Steelheader, Owl Eyed Optic, Paint Brush, Princess, Queen Bess, Railbird, Silver Demon, Silver and Orange, Stevenson's Special, Umpqua Special, Van Luven, and Wood Pussy.

The style then was for winged flies. As has been noted, it still is, to an extent, from the Klamath River northward. Southward to the steelhead's southern limit near Santa Cruz the style is predominantly for wingless flies, although wings often are desirable for greater visibility under high-water conditions.

When my comprehensive book *Fishing* was published in 1974, it included a color plate of twenty-two steelhead patterns, most of which are as popular now as they were then. West Coast experts have nominated thirteen steelhead and/or salmon patterns for this book (including the ever-popular Skykomish Sunrise and Thor), some of which were illustrated in the previous work. I doubt that more are needed and am sure that fewer would do. The authentic dressings of these patterns follow:

BLACK COMET

HOOK SIZE: 4 to 8, black salmon
THREAD: Black
TAIL: A small bunch of straight black hair a bit longer than the hook, and cocked up slightly
BODY: Silver tinsel Mylar, with a turn taken under the tail to hold it up
HACKLE: A few turns of a black hackle a bit wider than the gap of the hook and slanted backward slightly
HEAD: A pair of small silver bead-chain eyes applied just back of eye of hook by winding thread in the figure-eight manner

The silver tinsel Mylar used for the body also is called "Poly Flash" or "Poly Glitter." This is the first of several Comet patterns and was originated by Virgil Sullivan, of Guerneville, California.

The Golden Comet has the same silhouette, with a tail of orange fluorescent bucktail, a gold body, orange or orange and red hackle, bead-chain eyes, and a red head.

BOSS

HOOK SIZE: 4 to 8, black salmon
THREAD: Black
TAIL: A small bunch of straight black hair a bit longer than the hook and cocked up slightly
BODY: Black floss, fairly full
RIBBING: Fine oval silver tinsel, with two turns taken under the tail to hold it up
HACKLE: A few turns of an orange-red hackle a bit wider than the gap of the hook and slanted backward slightly
HEAD: A pair of small silver bead-chain eyes applied just back of eye of hook by winding thread in the figure-eight manner

This first of several Boss variations was originated by Grant King, of Guerneville, California. In his tackle shop on the bank of the Russian River, Grant experimented with shad patterns and found that Pacific shad would take flies readily, as they had been doing on the East Coast long before this. His experimentations indicated that steelhead and salmon also prefer patterns of this type, a discovery which partly revolutionized styles in such flies, as this chapter indicates.

This pattern can be modified by applying small hackle-tip wings in

7–3 Hal Janssen shows a forty-four-pound Chinook salmon.

either black or orange for use under high-water conditions.

BLACK BOSS

This fly is the same as the Boss except that the hackle is black. Thus, the fly is entirely black and silver. It is one of Grant King's originations.

FLAMING BOSS

HOOK SIZE: 4 to 8, black salmon
THREAD: Black
TAIL: A small bunch of straight black hair a bit longer than the hook and cocked up slightly
BODY: Fluorescent red yarn or floss
RIBBING: Fine oval silver tinsel, with two turns taken under the tail to hold it up
HACKLE: A few turns of an orange-red hackle a bit wider than the gap of the hook and slanted backward slightly
HEAD: A pair of small silver bead-chain eyes applied just back of the eye of the hook by winding thread in the figure-eight manner

97

This is another of Grant King's patterns. It can be modified by adding small hackle-tip wings in either black or orange-red to make the fly more visible in high water.

BRINDLE BUG

HOOK SIZE: 4 to 8, black salmon

HEAD: Black

TAIL: Two medium brown hackle tips, splayed, about the length of the gap of the hook

BODY: Two sections of medium chenille, one black and one yellow, wound on alternating to provide a full beelike banded effect

HACKLE: About four turns of a medium brown hackle, fairly long

This fly and the Silver Hilton are, as this is being written, the leading favorites on the Klamath and Trinity rivers and are very effective elsewhere. Some anglers substitute brown for black in the body, while others dress the fly with a fluffy red tail of medium length, such as fluorescent red marabou.

EGG FLY

HOOK SIZE: 4 to 8, black salmon

THREAD: Black

TAIL: A small bunch of straight black hair a bit longer than the hook, and cocked up slightly

BODY: Silver tinsel Mylar (Poly Flash, or Poly Glitter), with a turn taken under the tail to hold it up

FORWARD BUTT: Several turns of red chenille to make a butt of salmon-egg shape and size immediately back of the hackle

HACKLE: A few turns of a black hackle a bit wider than the gap of the hook and slanted backward slightly

HEAD: A pair of small silver bead-chain eyes, as on the Black Comet

This pattern is the Black Comet with the simulation of a salmon egg behind the hackle.

FALL FAVORITE

HOOK SIZE: 4 to 8, black salmon

HEAD: Red

BODY: Oval silver tinsel

THROAT: A few turns of a bright red hackle extending nearly to the bend of the hook

WING: A moderate bunch of bright red bucktail (or similar hair) extending a little beyond the bend of the hook

98

This is one of the top steelhead patterns and is even better for salmon in the Eel River and north of it into the Smith River in the upper part of

California. The Smith River is famous for giant Chinook salmon. The fly also is dressed in low-water style.

GOLDEN GOOSE

HOOK SIZE: 6 to 8, regular
HEAD: Red
TAIL: A small bunch of straight black hair a bit longer than the hook
BODY: Gold oval silver tinsel with one turn under the tail to hold it up slightly
HACKLE: A few turns of an orange-red hackle a bit wider than the gap of the hook and slanted backward slightly

This steelhead and salmon fly was originated by Bill Schaadt, famous salmon angler of Monte Rio, California. Except for the black tail and lack of bead-chain eyes it is very similar to the Golden Comet.

PINK THOR

HOOK SIZE: 6 to 8, regular
HEAD: Red
TAIL: A fairly short and small bunch of the fluffy base fibers of a red hackle, or red marabou tips
BODY: Orange wool or floss, not built up
RIBBING: Fine oval gold tinsel
HACKLE: Three or four turns of a narrow natural grizzly hackle

This silver salmon pattern was originated by famous angler and writer Larry Green, of San Bruno, California, and is one of his favorite patterns.

SALMON HACKLE YELLOW

HOOK SIZE: 6 to 8, regular
HEAD: Red
TAIL: A fairly short and small bunch of the fluffy base fibers of a red hackle, or red marabou tips
BODY: Medium yellow chenille
HACKLE: Three or four turns of a red hackle, moderately long

This is another salmon pattern originated by Larry Green.

SILVER HILTON

HOOK SIZE: 6 to 8, regular, or chrome-plated (Mustad #3908C)
HEAD: Black
TAIL: A small and fairly long bunch of grizzly hackle or teal breast fibers
BODY: Fine black chenille
RIBBING: Oval #14 silver tinsel

99

WING: Two grizzly hackle tips extending slightly beyond the bend of
the hook

HACKLE: Two or three turns of a grizzly hackle of moderate width

This fly and the Brindle Bug are top patterns on the Klamath and Trinity
rivers, as well as elsewhere along the northern Pacific coast.

It has been noted that flies for the Klamath River and northward largely
remain as classic patterns and that most of them are winged, while popular
flies southward of the Klamath usually are wingless except for high-water
use. The change from classic to modern there came from experimentation
with (wingless) shad flies, which resemble East Coast patterns except for
their colors. It was found that these, in the brighter colors, were superior
for steelhead and salmon.

Why the brighter colors, which seem to represent nothing natural in
their tones of yellow, orange, and red, as well as black?

The black, of course, provides an excellent silhouette, and seems best
for dark days. Someone said, "Why imitate shrimps with orange or red
when their actual color, when alive, is a brownish green?"

The answer may be found in *McClane's Standard Fishing Encyclopedia*,
wherein it is stated that the color of various shrimp species varies widely.
Brown shrimp are usually a reddish brown color, with tinges of blue or
purple. Pink shrimp seem to vary according to geographic locality, some
being light brown, others pink or lemon yellow. White shrimp are generally
a grayish white, and are variously tinged about the tail and legs with green,
red, and blue. The sea bob is usually red or pinkish red. Royal red shrimp
are usually deep red all over, but sometimes are only a gray-pink. It is well
known that the pink or red flesh of fish is due to the fact that they have been
feeding on crustaceans such as these. Does this explain the affinity of
steelhead and salmon for flies in these colors? It may!

A few readers will remember the often-printed opinion that salmon (and
steelhead) don't feed after entering fresh water. More recent research has
revised this slightly. While Atlantic salmon don't feed then out of hunger,
they do take bits of food from instinct, even though they may try to spit
them out instead of swallowing. This is very fortunate for fly fishermen, and
Pacific anadromous species may do the same to a greater extent.

Another reason for fish taking flies is pugnacity: the instinct to kill the
little intruder that is seemingly alive in order to get it out of the way.
Because of the savage strikes we so often get with small flies from big fish,
this theory appeals to me. It doesn't matter, except that it may help to
account for color popularity in Pacific salmon and steelhead flies. Of course
this is a debate which could be extended, but we don't have to do it here.

The Rocky Mountain area differs from the Pacific coastal area mainly
because the rivers in the latter harbor fish that are anadromous, so they
have been the feature of this chapter. Fishing methods and flies for other

7–4 A twenty-two-pound striped bass taken on a Whistler Streamer. (Photo: Don Blanton)

species are quite similar on both sides of the Continental Divide, so we may not need to add much to what was said in the preceding chapter. There are three bait-fish imitations, however, which are important because they represent species peculiar to rivers of the western slopes, so their patterns are given here.

TAHOE REDSIDED MINNOW
HOOK SIZE: 4 to 8, 2X long
THREAD: White
BODY: Medium oval silver tinsel
THROAT: Applied as an underwing, a very small bunch of white
    bucktail mixed with a very small bunch of blood-red bucktail one
    and a half times as long as the hook
WING: A very small bunch of the same blood-red bucktail, over which
    is a small bunch of black bucktail or other hair, and over this a
    very small bunch of brownish hair, all about as long as the
    underwing
HEAD: Painted black on top, with red lateral line and white bottom; an
    eye of yellow with large black center is added

This imitation of the bait fish of the same name was dressed for this book by Hal W. Janssen, mentioned earlier in this chapter. Hal favors the practice of extending the colors of streamers and bucktails into the head with applications of paint, as noted in this fly and the one which follows. This recommended head decoration adds greatly to the attractiveness and abil-

101

ity of the fly. He says, "This is very popular in the Truckee River drainage and the streams running into and out of Lake Tahoe, as well as Pyramid Lake, in Nevada, for the giant cutthroat trout that are there."

SACRAMENTO RIVER HARDHEAD
HOOK SIZE: 4 to 8, 2X long
THREAD: White
BODY: Medium oval silver tinsel
THROAT: Applied as an underwing, a very small bunch of white bucktail mixed with a very small bunch of blood-red bucktail one and a half times as long as the hook
WING: A very small bunch of yellow bucktail, over which is a larger bunch of dark brown bucktail
HEAD: Painted black or dark brown on top, with a red lateral line and white bottom; an eye of white with a large black pupil is added

This Janssen pattern represents a prominent western-slope bait fish known as the "Sacramento pike" or "hardhead," which is the young of the squawfish, one of the largest of the minnow family. Hal Janssen says, "This bucktail also imitates a form of bait fish which we refer to as a 'Hitch,' which is very common in all our streams and lakes in the Sierras." Eastern anglers who travel to this area to fish for big cutthroat trout and other species will find that Sam Slaymaker's Little Brown Trout is a good substitute.

JANSSEN MARABOU EEL
This pattern is a stacked-tie method of dressing often used in saltwater patterns but here used for fresh water with natural grayish brown marabou found near the legs of large game birds such as pheasants and turkeys.

Using a No. 2 long-shanked hook and thread of a color similar to the wing, tie in a small bunch of marabou about one and a half inches long (for this size) as a tail. As soon as this is tied down and varnished, tie in another similar bunch on top of the hook immediately forward of the tail and so close to it that no gap is noticeable. Continue tying in bunches of marabou in this manner until the head is reached—about eight bunches in all. Finish the head to complete the fly.

Hal Janssen, who provided the pattern, says, "This fly, fished in this larger size or a bit smaller size, has been successful in the Trinity River, where it has produced some very outsized brown and rainbow trout. It is best fished early in the morning or late in the evening and has been an excellent producer on some of our larger lakes.

102

"You will note that there is no weight in the Marabou Eel. I prefer to keep it this way and enjoy fishing it on a medium-sinking or extra-fast-sinking line, preferably one made by Sunset. I have used this type of fly in olive and black and, in some instances, have altered the colors to make simple but very effective imitator patterns."

I might add that when one knows the lie of a big brown trout, the fly can be floated and twitched over it on a floating line to simulate a swimming mouse. Of course it will soon sink, but it should provide a strike before then! I have hooked very large brown trout using similar methods.

Part Two

How to Dress Freshwater Streamers and Bucktails

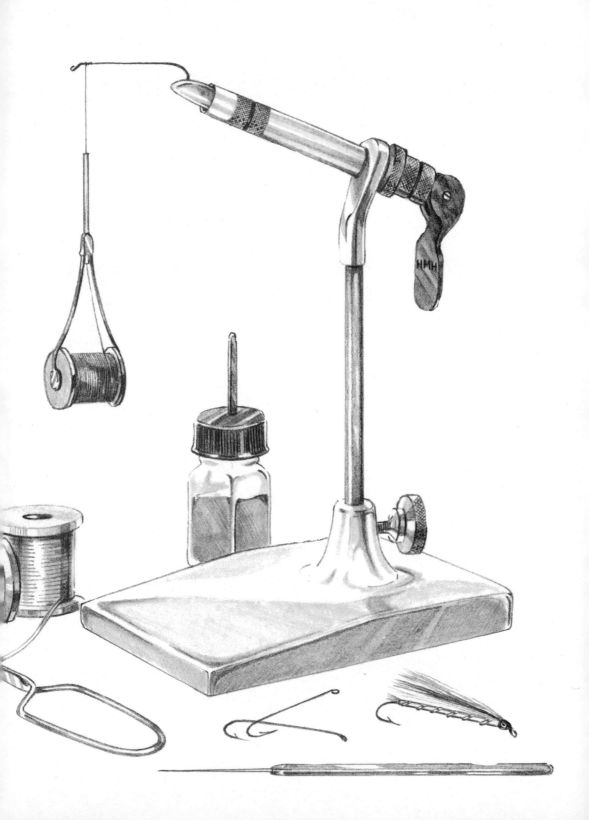

8

Variations in Dressing Techniques

In a corner of the little cottage on a rocky point where the stream merged into the lake, the old surgeon, while waiting for dinner, was carefully tying a few flies he hoped would hook big trout at first light next morning. The battered table was littered with colorful or shining bits and pieces of dressing materials taken from the kit he always carried on fishing expeditions.

A red-and-white silver-bodied bucktail was in the vise, ready for the application of cheeks, which the old gentleman was preparing so differently that the younger angler pulled up a chair to watch. Two gray mallard breast feathers had been stripped to tips no larger than a little fingernail. What intrigued the younger man was that the surgeon was coating a tip with rubber cement by pulling it between thumb and forefinger between which a drop or two of the cement had been applied. The old man was the epitome of contentment and concentration as he blew on the feather to be sure it was coated so properly that all fibers were securely joined.

"Brook trout seem to go for a bit of red," he observed, seemingly to no one in particular.

"Why is it that doctors of medicine are so 'with it' on fly dressing and fishing?" the younger man interjected. "No matter where I go in angling circles, I seem to meet many doctors—so many that they must have a special reason for liking this sort of thing."

"Doctors spend long hours under great pressure because their patients' well-being rests on every decision and every incision they make," the surgeon replied. "Fishing, or getting ready for it, takes their minds off whatever is past, and offers a refreshing change of pace. Herbert Hoover, one of our only three presidents who enjoyed fishing, said that it washed one's soul in pure air, and I guess I couldn't put it any better than that.

107

*8–1 Arthur C. Mills, Jr.'s
Life-Action Bucktail.*

"Now, let's not discuss doctors; let's talk about this. Do you remember reading in old fishing books about Arthur C. Mills, Jr., and his Life-Action Bucktail?* He had the idea of tying on cheeks in reverse, so they splayed outward, to give the fly more action and to simulate pectoral fins. I note, however, that water currents pull the fibers together, so much of the action is lost. This rubber cement seals the fibers in their original shape while letting the cheeks pulsate. Varnish could make them too brittle, but rubber cement is waterproof and lets them remain flexible. This simulation of pectoral fins is popular in making flies that represent sculpins, so let's put these little cheeks, or fins, on and see how they work. The idea can be used to improve most any bucktail or streamer."

The doctor laid one of the reinforced feathers splayed outward against the fly's body and parallel to it, made a turn of thread, and applied the other on the opposite side. After making two more turns of the thread, he pulled the quills forward until the fibers gathered enough to make the cheeks cup-shaped. He added a bit of lacquer and finished the head.

"Looks good," he commented. "I'll tie three more so we'll each have a couple. They should hook a few big ones tomorrow."

In experimenting with the idea later, I noticed that the application of rubber cement to some breast feathers leaves the ends a bit sawtoothed. They can be left that way or, when the cement is partially dry, the jagged ends can be pinched together to make them even more cup-shaped.

This chapter draws together various bits and pieces of information to give readers ideas for experimentation. It may be like going to a cocktail party where trays of goodies are being passed. You can accept the ones that appeal to you and leave the rest alone.

I must assume that readers of this book have at least a basic knowledge of fly dressing, because that subject requires a volume all its own. Fortunately there already are many, so I'll merely try to set down what other authors haven't mentioned and recommend some of the best current books in the list below. Since each offers different suggestions, it is helpful to

*Arthur C. Mills, Jr., of the historic New York City tackle shop of William Mills and Son, originated this pattern in 1932 or 1933, the first one to feature outwardly splayed cheeks in simulation of gills or pectoral fins. The fly had an embossed silver tinsel body, a red bucktail underwing (throat), and a wing of red over white bucktail, all of equal length. The outwardly splayed cheeks each were a gray or white over a red breast feather a third as long as the body, the red feathers being nearly concealed by the white or gray ones. The head was black.

acquire a library of several. Innovative angling books by capable authors have a way of appreciating in value, so you can enjoy your library and also have the satisfaction of knowing that, in time, it should be worth much more than you paid for it.

Bay, Kenneth E. *Salt Water Flies.* Philadelphia and New York: Lippincott, 1972.

Boyle, Robert H., and Whitlock, Dave. *The Fly-Tyer's Almanac.* New York: Crown, 1975.

Gerlach, Rex. *Creative Fly Tying & Fly Fishing.* New York: Winchester Press, 1974.

Grant, George F. *The Art of Weaving Hair Hackles.* Butte, Montana: Privately printed, 1971.

Jorgensen, Poul. *Dressing Flies for Fresh and Salt Water.* New York: Freshet Press, 1973.

Jorgensen, Poul. *Modern Fly Dressings for the Practical Angler.* New York: Winchester Press, 1976.

Leiser, Eric. *The Complete Book of Fly Tying.* New York: Knopf, 1977.

Shaw, Helen. *Fly Tying.* New York: Ronald Press, 1963.

Veniard, John. *Fly Dresser's Guide.* London: A. & C. Black, 1952.

Veniard, John. *A Further Guide to Fly Dressing.* London: A. & C. Black, 1965.

Experts have valid preferences among *streamer hooks,* but those less skilled may find these comments helpful.* When originators of patterns given herein specify hook sizes and types, this book gives them. Ordinarily, streamers and bucktails should be dressed on either Limerick or Sproat hooks with turned-down eyes (preferably turned-down *looped* eyes) in regular strength, 3X long. Ringed eyes (which turn neither up nor down) should be used only for flies which will be attached to snaps, rings, or spinners (an exception being some of the reverse-tied bucktails such as those in the Thunder Creek series). In freshwater angling there is little choice between the Limerick and Sproat bends. The Sproat is bent into a rounder curve than the Limerick. My preference is for the Limerick, partly because the straight stem and the narrow bend help to prevent the hook from sawing about and pulling loose, but largely because it seems to be superior for penetration and strength.

Unless otherwise noted it is recommended that all bucktails and streamers be dressed on 3X long hooks, usually using the bronze finish for fresh water and either noncorrosive nickel, cadmium, gold plate, or stainless steel for salt water. These brightly plated hooks sometimes add to attrac-

109

---

*For additional information, see *A History of the Fish Hook,* by H. J. Hurum (London: A. & C. Black). Published for O. Mustad & Son, this 148-page book ignores other hook manufacturers, but it provides a detailed history and explanation of hook making from earliest times to the present, and is excellently illustrated with drawings and photographs.

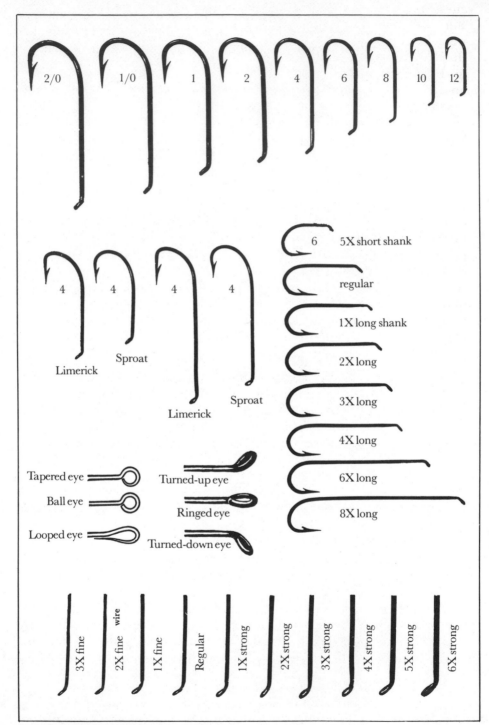

110

8–2 Mustad-Limerick Hooks (actual size).

tiveness and glitter in fresh water. I have an affinity for black-enameled Atlantic salmon hooks for many patterns, perhaps only because they seem more attractive.

In some cases extra-long patterns are specified, such as 4X long or 5X long. But the extra length gives fish more leverage with which to work themselves loose.

As shown in Figure 8–2, the lengths of hooks are based on the "regular" or normal length, which is in proportion to the size of the hook. A hook "2X long," for example, is one which is as long as a regular hook two sizes larger. A hook "4X long" is as long as a regular one four sizes larger. A hook "2X short" is as long as a regular one two sizes smaller, and so forth.

A similar situation holds true for strengths. Each larger size of hook is made on a proportionately larger diameter of wire. A hook which is "2X strong," or "2X stout," is made on the strength of wire normally used for a hook two sizes larger. A hook "1X light," or "1X fine," is made on the strength of wire normal for a hook one size smaller.

Both Limerick and Sproat hooks have straight bends; that is, they lie flat with the point bending neither to the right nor to the left. A straight-bend hook is preferable for bucktails and streamers because it rides on a level keel in the water and has less tendency to twist or to spin than offset-bend hooks do. Some anglers prefer offset types, thinking they offer better hooking ability. If they are used they should be *double offset* for the above reason.

Hooks lighter than regular are used on flies where buoyancy is desired and exceptional strength is unnecessary. Hooks stronger than regular are used for their qualities of quicker sinking or for abnormally strong fish, such as steelhead, which might straighten a lighter hook, particularly in the fast waters where they frequently are found.

A primary reason for losing hooked fish is that anglers are careless about keeping points sharp. Before hooks are packed for sale, machines dump them in bins for heat treating, thus perhaps dulling the fine points. Canny anglers always carry sharpening stones or files and touch up points to needle sharpness before each use.

Modern technology provides a wide range of *hair materials* for bucktails which adds many new and valuable choices to the natural ones. The natural ones, of course, include bucktail, polar bear, Arctic fox, badger, numerous varieties of squirrels, and so on. One of the keys to selection is buoyancy. For example, some parts of the hair from a deer are hollow and very buoyant, while other parts and the hair from other animals are much less so. If we want flies to sink quickly, several factors contribute to it, such as less buoyant hair, heavier hooks, and sparser dressings of wings and throats, as well as weighted bodies.

Artificial hair in varying lengths and a wide selection of attractive colors can be obtained as scraps from furriers and coat makers. A benefit of belonging to a fly-tying group is that members find sources of supply for

111

natural and artificial hair and often bring in enough of one thing or another to last the whole group for years to come. Since most artificial hair is very fine it is excellent for mixing colors, but it usually should be combined with natural hair to add stiffness.

Among the wealth of new patterns (particularly for salt water) given in this book there are references to several nylon or nylon-like man-made materials such as colorful nylon and crimped nylon filaments, Dynel, and fluorescent items of several sorts. These challenges to fly-dressing ingenuity are readily available in shops and from catalog houses catering to fly tyers. Old-fashioned metallic tinsels, which tarnish unless lacquered, are being replaced by Mylar, both plain and embossed, which won't tarnish.

Mylar tinsels in silver, gold, and many colors are available in various widths for fly bodies, and strips can be cut from sheets if need be. Fine Mylar tinsel is excellent for adding flash to wings. Loop several turns (as you would wind a leader) around two or more fingers (according to size of coils desired) and tie it in at the head of the fly; then cut the coils at their opposite side and trim the strands for proper length. This is easier than applying lengths separately.

Another suggestion: Double a small sheet of plain or embossed Mylar and cut it with scissors to an elongated wing shape a little longer than the hook. You now have two opposite wing sections which can be tied in at the head to conceal the hook body, which then doesn't need to be dressed. The hair wing is tied in beside and over this. The wings should taper upward a bit beyond the bend of the hook so as not to interfere with the barb. Another method is to dress the wing (and throat, if desired) and then to apply the Mylar wings. In this case the Mylar flares out a little; in the former method its two sides are compacted. The Mylar can be tinted with any of the many colors available in waterproof felt-tipped markers. A black lateral line often is effective.

Mylar tubular cord or piping, formerly introduced for ladies' hats, etc., is available wherever fly-tying materials are sold. It comes in several sizes and colors, including gold and silver. This is an innovation offering many varieties of very lifelike bodies, as the following examples show. Let's first make a Mylar-bodied bucktail in any desired color combination, as seen in Figure 8–3. The seven easy steps are:

(1) Wind thread down the hook's shank and tie in the tail. (2) Build up the body and (3) taper it slightly with either chenille, wool, or polyethylene foam. Lead can be added, as explained in Chapter 10, before the body is built up. Cut a section of piping to proper length (as long as the hook's shank from eye to tail) and remove the cotton core by holding one end between the thumb and forefinger of one hand and compressing or peeling the outer shell down toward the stationary end with the other hand, thus exposing an end of the core, which is pulled out and discarded. (4) Apply a few drops of lacquer to the front end of the filler material. (This will seal

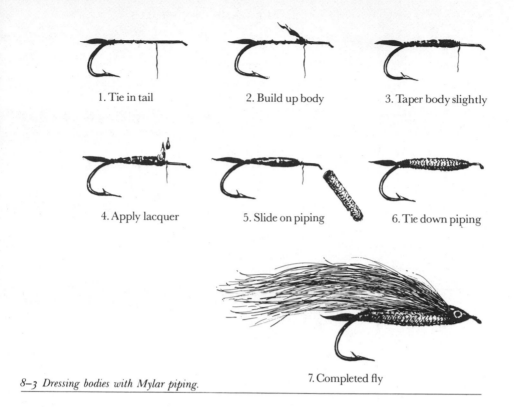

1. Tie in tail   2. Build up body   3. Taper body slightly

4. Apply lacquer   5. Slide on piping   6. Tie down piping

7. Completed fly

8–3 Dressing bodies with Mylar piping.

the piping in place and facilitate sliding the piping over the body.) (5) Slide the piping over the hook's eye and over the built-up body until it reaches the tail. (6) Tie down the piping at both ends with winding thread to make neatly tapered ends, completing both with a whip finish. The rear end will resemble a butt, so the thread, covering the rear of the piping as well as the winding at the tail, can be of any color, such as black or red. This winding covers the frayed ends of the piping, which may have needed to be trimmed a bit. Give the body and windings two coats of lacquer, either tinted or clear.

(7) Now the throat can be applied, as usual, and the wing can be added to finish the fly in any combination the tyer desires. The Mylar body can be tinted with a waterproof felt-tip marker before lacquering, if desired. This offers a wide range of pattern possibilities in a bucktail type which looks very like a bait fish and therefore is extremely effective.

To further illustrate the versatility of bodies of Mylar tubing let's look at three patterns by the prominent angler and fly dresser Louis F. Lopez, of the Long Beach (California) Casting Club.

113

LOPEZ SCULPIN
HOOK SIZE: 2 to 10, 6X long, ringed-eye
THREAD: White Nymo, size A
LEAD: .021-inch-diameter lead wire

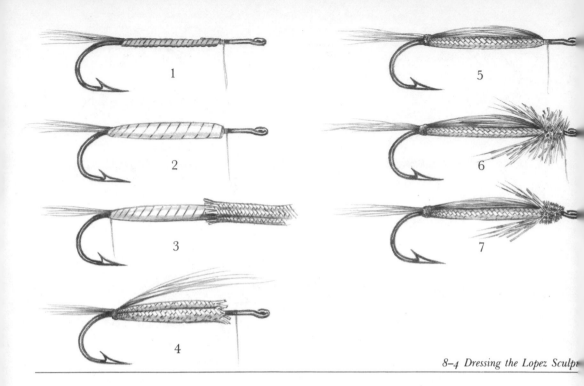

TAIL: A small bunch of brown bucktail extending slightly beyond
   bend of hook
BODY: Silver Mylar tubing colored with a yellow waterproof felt-tip
   marker; coat this with clear head cement
BACK: Brown bucktail
COLLAR AND HEAD: Natural deer body hair spun on and trimmed
   sculpin-style (see Chapter 14)

The above dressing illustrated by the sketches in Figure 8–4 is explained
as follows: (1) Tie on the tail and wrap as much lead around the shank as
desired. (2) Build up underbody with polyfoam, leaving a quarter-inch head
space. (3) Saturate underbody with head cement and slip Mylar tubing over
the underbody, tying it in at the tail while trimming the frayed ends. (4) Tie
on the bucktail back, leaving tips to add to the tail, and whip-finishing it at
the rear. Tie down the Mylar tubing at front and trim ends. (5) Bring
bucktail forward tightly; tie off, and trim ends. (6) Spin on deer hair for
collar and head. (7) Trim the head to flattened shape, sculpin-style. Trim
tail, if desired.

   The above is Louis Lopez' brown sculpin. Since some sculpins are more
of a green color, he gives this variation:

TAIL: Dark part of a bucktail dyed green
BODY: Colored with a green marker
BACK: Dark part of a bucktail dyed green
COLLAR AND HEAD: Deer body hair dyed olive

114

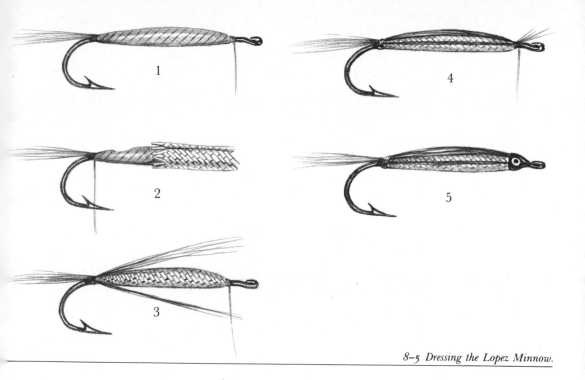

This sculpin dressing, as well as Lopez' minnow and anchovy dressings, was published in the United Fly Tyers magazine, the *Roundtable,* issue of September–October 1975, in which the author says, "This fly can be tied in various colors by changing the color of the bucktail and the deer body hair used. A little red can be dubbed over the Mylar tie-down at the head space before the hair is spun on. This gives a gill effect."

LOPEZ MINNOW
HOOK SIZE: 4 to 12, 6X long, ringed-eye
THREAD: White Nymo, size A on larger sizes, prewaxed 8/o on smaller ones
LEAD: .021-inch lead wire (optional)
TAIL: A small bunch of brown bucktail
BODY: Silver Mylar tubing over built-up polyethylene foam base
BACK: About ten to fifteen brown bucktail hairs
LATERAL LINE: About ten to fifteen bucktail hairs in color to suit minnow being imitated
HEAD: Thread color, with yellow-and-black eye

The above dressing illustrated by the sketches in Figure 8–5 is explained as follows: (1) Tie on the tail and build up the underbody. (2) Saturate the underbody with head cement; slip on the Mylar tubing, tie down at tail, and trim ends. (3) Tie on bucktail on both sides for lateral line and bucktail on top for back. (4) Bring lateral material along sides and tie down. Bring back material over top and tie down. Avoid covering lateral line. (5) Build a

115

minnow-shaped tapered head and paint eye, and trim tail to desired size.

This dressing is a type which can be altered to imitate various bait fish. Try brown over black for dace, green over pink for rainbow trout, brown over orange for brown trout, green over black for other bait fish, etc.

LOPEZ ANCHOVY

HOOK SIZE: 4/0-4, 6X long, ringed-eye
THREAD: White Nymo, size A
LEAD: Desired size lead wire (optional)
TAIL: White bucktail covered by all materials on back
BODY: Large silver Mylar tubing over the built-up underbody
BACK: Peacock herl over blue bucktail over green bucktail
HEAD: Thread color with yellow eye and black pupil

Steps in tying this pattern illustrated by the sketches in Figure 8–6 are explained as follows: (1) Tie on a small bunch of white bucktail at the tail. Build up the underbody. (2) Saturate the underbody with head cement; slip the Mylar body over it; tie down at tail, and trim ends. (3) Tie in ten to twelve green bucktail hairs on each side with tips extending to end of tail. Do the same with a similar amount of blue bucktail on top, and then four to six peacock herls on top of that. Whip-finish these at rear; tie down Mylar at head, and trim ends. (4) Bring the green bucktail snugly along both sides and tie down at head. Do the same with the blue bucktail and then the

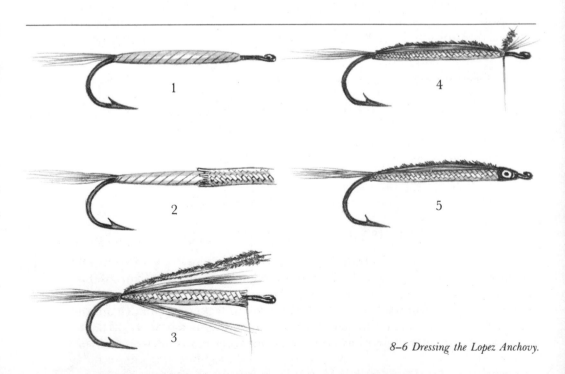

8–6 Dressing the Lopez Anchovy.

peacock herl on top. (5) Build a minnowlike head and paint the eye, and trim the tail as desired.

This of course is a saltwater fly, so noncorrosive hooks should be used. It is productive because anchovies are food for a wide variety of saltwater game fish. The colors can be varied to resemble other baits.

Since one of these flies is a sculpin or muddler pattern it should be of interest to mention here that an alternative to the trimmed head of deer body hair is *rabbit fur,* spun on and built up to desired size. This can be trimmed as usual for muddlers and sculpins. An advantage is that it is much less buoyant than deer hair, and it may be easier for some readers to apply.

The value of *fluorescent materials* in fly dressing often is understated. When used with restraint—less on bright days, more in discolored water or when fishing deep—they act as excellent attractors and often bring strikes when other flies might be ignored. Color seems to make little or no difference, but green, red, and yellow are very effective. Try fluorescent floss for butts and/or use a doubled thread or two mixed into wings. Avoid the misconception that if a little is good, a lot is better. The reverse is true. Too much can be worse than none at all.

In applying *marabou for wings,* Tom Watson, of Sayre, Pennsylvania, reminds us that wetting the fibers before application makes them easier to work with. Since the suggestion is excellent, let's look at it using his favorite all-purpose streamer as an example: the Marabou Dace, which imitates the blacknose dace, the most common minnow found on many eastern trout streams. Tie on a body of fine oval silver tinsel or silver Mylar tubing. With a glass of water handy, dip a small bunch of white marabou fibers in the water and remove excess water between thumb and forefinger. Tie this in as a wing and top it similarly with the same amount and length of black marabou, and then with brown. This straightens the fibers and shows how the fly will look when wet. Watson says, "Don't make the marabou extend past the hook too far, or the fish may strike short." A red yarn tail is optional.

This brings up a suggestion for painting heads to carry body and wing colors into the heads. On the above fly, for example, the underpart of the head could be painted white or silver, with a black medial line, and with the top of the head brown. Painted eyes often are effective. Such decorations add to the attractiveness of the fly and can't detract from its efficiency.

Since fly dressers enjoy experimenting, why not do so with *roofed patterns?* This book contains only four, as such: the Dr. Mummy, the Canadian Killer, and the Western Silver Doctor in Chapter 6 and the Cowee Special in Part Four. This type is so attractive and so effective that it should be used more widely.

A roofed pattern is one with a large flank feather applied flat over a sparse hair wing so that the sides curve downward, tentlike, to roof the wing. There is a simple way to do it. Dress any bucktail as usual, but make

117

the hair wing quite scant, no more than half the usual amount. Take a larger flank feather (such as gray mallard) than you think you'll need and tie it in on top of the wing with two turns of thread. Grasp the tip extending beyond the turns and pull the feather forward through the turns, thus curling the forward fibers around the body slightly, causing them to curve downward on each side equally. Pull the feather enough to give it the desired length and finish the fly. Feathers selected should be identical on both sides to provide a balanced roof. Such a fly pulsates differently than usual streamers do, and so may be effective as a change of pace. Examples are shown in Color Plate I and in Color Plate III.

Another interesting variation, much used in New Zealand and Australia, but not popular here yet, is what might be called the *sliced skin wing* as described for the New Zealand Rabbit Fly in Chapter 13. This is a wing sliced from the skin of any appropriate fur of reasonable length, such as rabbit. With the skin fur side down, use a straightedge and razor blade to cut very narrow strips with the grain of the fur. Cut from a strip a piece twice as long as the shank, or even a bit longer, and trim it to a V on each end. With the grain of the fur (the way the hairs slant) extending toward the rear, tie the forward V in securely at the head. The ribbing has been tied in at the tail, but not wound on. Wind this on through the separated hairs to the head, thus binding down the fur. Use a pointed instrument to free any hairs caught under the ribbing. The part of the hair extending beyond the bend of the hook is not tied down and acts as a tail.

This type of fur wing offers a different pulsating action than others. It is popular in countries under the Southern Cross, and may become so in northern latitudes.

Reverse-tied bucktails, popularized in recent years by the Thunder Creek series and by George Grant's dressings of squirrel tail patterns (see Chapter 6), have more going for them than so far has been published. We'll have to thank Carrie Stevens for this idea, as well as for her famous Gray Ghost, because she evidently was the first to do it long before World War II.*

Beginning near the rear of the hook, she wound the body evenly and compactly with red thread, which then was lacquered. At a point slightly behind where the wing usually is tied in she fastened two saddle hackles upright in the usual manner. Just forward of this she tied in one or more bunches of bucktail with the tips pointing *forward.* The bucktail was pulled uniformly around the hook and the ends were trimmed off as near as possible to where they were tied in. The winding was carried forward to just behind the eye and then was brought back at least three-sixteenths of an inch, where two half hitches were made. The base was then lacquered.

---

*Since Carrie Stevens lacked access to the classics it seems certain that she arrived at this idea independently. However, William Blacker, in his *Art of Fly Making* (London, 1855), describes tying in wings with the feathers' roots to the rear, and many Irish fly dressers of that era did similarly. I find no old record of the reverse tying of hair because the use of feathers predominated then.

At this point the bucktail was gathered back tightly and evenly, so that it concealed all of the winding done previously. The thread was brought through the bucktail at a convenient place and the bucktail was lashed down by a few turns of thread secured by a two- or three-turn whip finish. These turns of thread thus gave the effect of a band. The thread and the bucktail forward of it were saturated with varnish. The bucktail should be nearly as long as the feathers and should be thick enough to nearly conceal the shank of the hook, without overdressing the fly.

Mrs. Stevens believed very correctly that this reverse-tied bucktail made a stronger fly. She tied many of them in whatever colors seemed to suit her customers. She gave me several when I visited her at Upper Dam at the outset of World War II. One had a white underbelly and a wing of brown over orange, not unlike the Black Nosed Dace.

Carrie Stevens didn't realize that her innovation could do much more than provide a stronger wing. George Grant proved that, by tying down the reversed bucktail a little differently, the bucktail (he favors squirrel) could be made to fluff out in a cone shape for the added pulsation advisable in fast streams. Another innovative angler named Edward L. Haas showed that the wing could be made even stronger and that it could be cocked back at any angle the tyer desires. His methods will be described later in this chapter.

Early in the 1960s a banker from Eastchester, New York, named Keith C. Fulsher, improved on Carrie Stevens' idea by developing and testing his Thunder Creek series of exact bait-fish imitations, some of which are shown in Color Plate I. These indicate a continuing trend in streamer and bucktail design away from the earlier large, often overdressed, gaudy flies toward smaller, more streamlined patterns—a trend noticeable elsewhere in the development of the tiny and sparsely dressed streamers and bucktails so successful in heavily fished waters where game fish are usually relatively small.

Keith's series of four primary patterns and three secondary ones are so unusual that they deserve special attention. The difference between them and the more conventional patterns is caused by the way the bucktail dressing is attached to the hook, which in turn leads to the shaping of the head and body. Color and proportion are important, providing a minnow imitation both rugged and lifelike, with a head in proper proportion to the body and with an eye placed in correct position on the head. The few turns of red thread at the neck provide the little flash of red so often seen in a

119

live minnow as its gill covers open and close. Placing the bucktail completely around the hook adds an important third dimension and, at the same time, largely conceals the hook.

Tying the bucktails in the Thunder Creek series is relatively simple. Since a favorite is the <u>Silver Shiner</u>, let's use it as an example. Hook sizes 8 and 10, 6X long, are preferred, using ringed-eye hooks to act as an extension of the head. With red tying thread, dress the hook shank with flat silver tinsel. A small bunch of brown bucktail is tied to the top of the hook so that the tip ends extend *forward* of the hook eye. (In tying on the hair, slightly more room than normal is left for the head area, and the length of the hair should be such that when the tip ends are folded back toward the hook bend, they will extend slightly beyond the bend.) When applying the hair, allow it to rotate to cover the top 180 degrees of the hook shank, and trim the butt ends at the base of the head area. In binding the bucktail down, wrap the tying thread over the hair right up to the eye of the hook; then return the thread to the base of the head and cement the wrappings.

To dress the underside, turn the hook over in the vise and, using a small bunch of white bucktail, perform the same operation as with the brown hair, allowing the white to cover the bottom 180 degrees of the hook shank. Use bucktail sparingly because sparseness is most important.

The next step is to return the hook to its upright position and completely reverse all of the bucktail by folding it back tightly along the hook shank, so that in this reversed position it is firmly against the underwrappings of tying thread in the head area. In doing this, keep the two colors of hair separate, and be sure that they completely surround the hook.

Now bring the tying thread through the hair at the base of the head and wind several turns, ending with a whip finish. This completes the fly except that several coats of clear lacquer should be applied to the head, followed by the painting of a yellow eye with black dot on each side of the center of the head.

When a lateral stripe is needed (as in the Black Nosed Dace), tie on a few black bucktail hairs conventionally on each side after the hook shank has been dressed. The Black Nosed Dace can be improved further by applying a narrow line of black lacquer along both sides of the head from the hook eye to the base of the head, following the dividing line of the brown and white hair. This is done prior to applying the eye, which is then centered on this line. (These black head markings blend in with the black hair previously put on and create an imitation with the exact markings found on the actual minnow.)

120

With the above method, one's imagination is the only limitation in developing new patterns. In fishing, the fly should be kept constantly in darting motion to provide minnowlike appearance and action in the water. The flies are most effective when thoroughly soaked, because the bucktail tends to streamline better and assume the minnow shape it is made to represent.

Below are dressing instructions for Keith Fulsher's Thunder Creek series. (Three patterns are illustrated in Color Plate I.)

THUNDER CREEK SERIES

Name	Hook Shank Covering	Lateral Stripe	Back[1]	Stomach[1]	Eye
Primary Patterns					
Black Nosed Dace	Silver tinsel	Black bucktail	Brown bucktail	White bucktail	Yellow lacquer with black lacquer pupil
Golden Shiner	Yellow tinsel	Yellow bucktail	Brown bucktail	White bucktail	Yellow lacquer with black lacquer pupil
[2]Red Fin Shiner	Deep pink fluorescent floss	None	Brown bucktail	White bucktail	Yellow lacquer with black lacquer pupil
[2]Silver Shiner	Silver tinsel	None	Brown bucktail	White bucktail	Yellow lacquer with black lacquer pupil
Secondary Patterns					
Emerald Minnow	Green tinsel	None	Brown bucktail	White bucktail	Yellow lacquer with black lacquer pupil
Satin-Fin Minnow	Blue fluorescent floss	None	Brown part of blue bucktail	Pale yellow bucktail	Yellow lacquer with black lacquer pupil
Spot-Tailed Minnow	Gold tinsel	None	Brown part of green bucktail	White bucktail	Yellow lacquer with black lacquer pupil
Sentimental Pattern					
Mickey Finn	Silver tinsel	Red bucktail	Yellow bucktail	Yellow bucktail	Yellow lacquer with black lacquer pupil

[1]This material also forms the head.
[2]The Silver Shiner imitation duplicates the female and immature fish of the silver or common shiner species, while the Red Fin Shiner imitation duplicates the mature male fish of the common shiner species.

Fly dressers who are self-taught may have a harder time learning, but they often discover new methods of exceptional value. One of these was Carrie Stevens. Another is the above-mentioned Edward L. Haas, a successful businessman who retired to Forks of Salmon, California, to enjoy the quiet life and the excellent fishing nearby. Ed Haas ties flies (mainly steelhead patterns) as a retirement business. After studying his innovative methods many readers will want to try them, while others will seek his flies because they are as indestructible as such things can be. Despite this, they feature the smallest of heads and are as effective as they are beautiful.

Selection of hooks is important. They must be single ones of medium hardness with looped (returned) eyes. Atlantic salmon patterns are most suitable. This is a reverse-tied method in which the butts of hair and/or feathers are wedged between the hook shank *and* return loop in reverse manner and tied down that way while the body is being dressed. Then the wing is returned to normal position. The number of turns of thread against it decide its angle over the shank. Fewer turns keep the wing high; more tie it down lower. A wing tied in this manner will never twist or turn or change its set, so this part of the fly is indestructible except for normal wear and tear. The method should become clear by following the sketches in Figure 8–8 and Ed Haas' explanation:

"Pry the return loop open from the rear with the blade of a small knife —about one thirty-second of an inch is sufficient. Attach the thread on the shank of the hook just beyond where the return loop ends and then take two or three loose loops to the right but still on the shank alone so that the foremost loop will be where you want to tie down the hair wing. Hang the thread on the far side of the hook. (Use the finest thread you can handle.)

"Even up the hairs for the wing and place them on the top of the hook with the tips facing forward with the left-hand thumb and forefinger holding them in position. Take two turns of thread over the loop eye and shank and hairs. These turns do not have to be tight as they will be tightened later.

"Hold hairs on top of hook in position with left forefinger and with the thumb of right hand pull the butts forward and down so that the wing is now nearly vertical and the hair is between the shank and the return loop. Try to leave space between the front of the hair and the eye of the hook so that if a Turle knot is used the tippet will rest on the bare hook and not on the threads when the fly is in use.

"Take two tight turns of thread in front of the wing and at the same time keep the butts below the hook by pressing the return loop and the shank together with the thumb and forefinger of the left hand.

"Push the hair together toward the front against the two turns of thread and take the thread to the rear of the wing and bind down the hair in tight close turns, all the while keeping the hair tucked in between the shank and the return loop until the return loop has been covered, and then take a couple of turns on the shank to anchor the hair. Trim the hairs at an angle to form a base for the body.

"Tie in the hackle by the butt just behind the wing and take the thread to the rear where the tail will be tied in and the body completed. Wind on the hackle and take the thread to the front of the wing. Bind down the wing by turns of thread to the left until the proper angle of the wing is obtained. Finish off with a whip knot and varnish the head. I always use at least three coats of varnish so that all threads are completely covered.

"Depending on the malleability of various hooks and the slipperiness of different hairs there will be small modifications, but this is the basic method.

"Although I use English hooks, a Mustad #36890 is an excellent one on which to practice as it is extremely malleable.

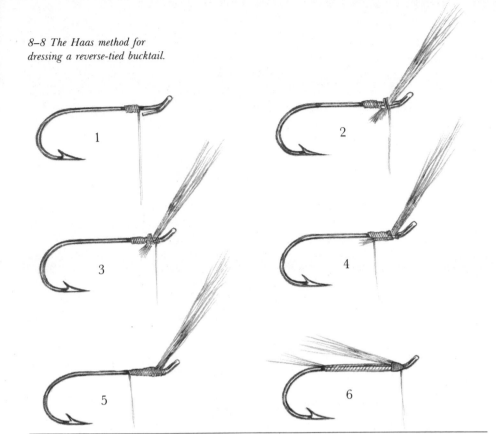

8–8 The Haas method for dressing a reverse-tied bucktail.

"Bucktail is not a good hair to use for this type of wing except on the larger sizes as the butts are usually too large to insert into position. Excellent hairs are squirrel, Arctic fox, stone marten, and skunk, while calf is a good all-around hair for general use. Each of these hairs is handled in a slightly different manner due to the slipperiness of the hair.

"The difference in attaching various hairs is mainly a different number of turns of thread and whether the thread is wound on with one to four turns and whether the turns are taken to the left or the right of the previous winding of thread. None of this is important if one merely wants to make a durable fly but the proper turns will reduce the size of the head."

Other comments taken from our correspondence should be of value:

"The body material of embossed silver tinsel is attached near the eye (with the wing in reversed position) and then taken down to the tail and then brought back toward the head as far as possible and tied off. Then the body, if desired, can be tinted or colored with a waterproof felt-tipped pen, such as deep orange, and given three coats of Cellire. (This celluloid varnish dries slowly, so each coat must be allowed to dry overnight.) After drying, the thread is attached behind the hairs and then brought to the front of the hair wing and the wing is tied down."

123

This is for a tailless fly. To add a tail: "The tail is tied in just beyond where the return loop ended and the tail is bound down with thread taken to the rear in close tight turns to the left to where we want the body to end at the rear, and a turn is taken beneath the tail to raise it and spread it a little. Then the thread is brought back to the front to where the tinsel is tied in and the body double-wrapped.

"Each fly head is given three coats of Cellire and three coats are also put on the tinseled bodies, so a tinseled fly takes an elapsed time of six days to complete, while other types of bodies require only three days due to the slow drying qualities of Cellire."

Ed Haas is a perfectionist. This perfection becomes obvious in the attractiveness and durability of his work. He has a favorite steelhead pattern called Protein because the name was on a food box used to store his flies. His comments following the formula indicate the reason for its inclusion here.

PROTEIN

HOOK SIZE: 4 to 12, 2X to 4X long, returned-eye, Atlantic salmon type
HEAD: Red
TAIL: Scarlet hackle fibers
BODY: Silver tinsel double-wrapped and then colored deep orange
    with a felt-tip pen and then given three coats of Cellire, a celluloid
    varnish. A hot orange chenille is used for a duller body or a
    fluorescent chenille or wool for heavy or murky water.
THROAT: Scarlet hackle, two or three turns (optional)
WING: Black or dark brown. Wing extends to just beyond the bend of
    the hook. Natural black squirrel, a very fine hair, is used for still
    water. Black-dyed ground squirrel, bear, or stone marten is used
    for faster water so that the maximum action of the wing is evident
    regardless of the type of water.

"This fly with the practical variations was originated by Ed Haas for the Salmon River, which is usually a moderate-sized crystal-clear stream which feeds into the Klamath. This fly has unquestionably been the most productive for the past seven years, and I have been fortunate enough to spend over two thousand hours a year for the past fifteen years trying an infinite number of different patterns. Before I started experimenting I was of the opinion that the color of a fly was of relatively small importance, but I now know that an orange body with a dark wing is by far the most effective combination on the Salmon, and the fly is also used on the Klamath and numerous other rivers. In the smaller sizes it is also extremely effective on rainbow trout. The fly is most productive when fished with small jerks of an inch or so with the rod held at an angle of ninety degrees from the fly, and this is accomplished by tapping the line with a forefinger where the line leaves the reel. This method eliminates all tendencies to grab the line or fail to release immediately at the time of a strike and also allows the rod

124

tip to take the initial shock instead of the reel."

When *Streamer Fly Tying & Fishing* was written in 1966, I predicted that the famous series of Blonde bucktails "in smaller sizes should do well for *many freshwater species.*" Since this point seems to have been missed it is being stressed here instead of in the chapter on southeastern saltwater patterns. The Blonde type is a "breather" fly whose high wing pulsates in action. In suitable sizes, it will take most any kind of freshwater or saltwater fish anywhere.

I use it for all species of trout on regular-length hooks as small as size 10, with the wing and tail about twice as long as the hook. In addition to the established colors I like a peacock wing and white tail, an all-orange, and an all-red, the latter two sometimes being fluorescent. The fly in medium-large sizes is excellent for all species of bass, and there seems to be no reason why it shouldn't be an excellent salmon and steelhead pattern. Don't confine dressings to bucktail. Also try squirrel, fox, and other moderately long hairs. I haven't yet adapted it to feathers, but intend to, sometimes splaying either the tail, the wing, or both.

Al Troth, of Dillon, Montana, who originated the Troth Bullhead discussed in Chapter 14, favors large sizes (such as 3/0) for big trout in big rivers. He ties his Blondes very thin and long, with a high profile, and has records such as having taken and released thirty trout from four to nearly nine pounds in one day!

This pattern was originated in the late 1940s by Homer Rhode, Jr., for

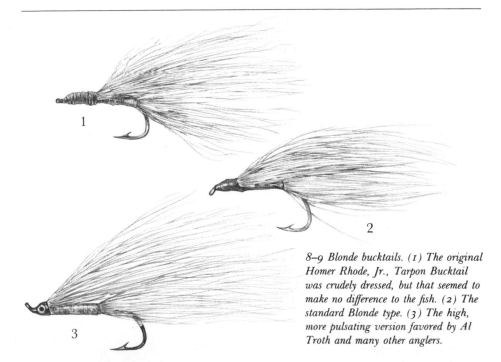

8–9 Blonde bucktails. (1) The original Homer Rhode, Jr., Tarpon Bucktail was crudely dressed, but that seemed to make no difference to the fish. (2) The standard Blonde type. (3) The high, more pulsating version favored by Al Troth and many other anglers.

125

tarpon, and was then called the Homer Rhode, Jr., Tarpon Bucktail. Homer and Joe Brooks and I used it in the 1950s and 1960s in Florida for several saltwater species. Joe became so entranced with its success that he renamed the type and wrote about it extensively under names such as the Strawberry Blonde, Platinum Blonde, and others which will be described. They sometimes were referred to as the Brooks Blondes, but Joe disclaimed that because, while he popularized the series, he didn't originate it.

Tying Blonde patterns is easy. Use any regular-length hook and apply a bunch of bucktail as a tail. This tail is about three times as long as the hook, and forms the build-up of the body, thus adding to its security. The body is relatively short, usually of silver, either embossed or plain, or of Mylar tubing. The wing is another bunch of bucktail (or other long hair) of similar size and length, so the wing is as long as the tail, or nearly so. Take a few turns of thread around the wing to hold it up at least thirty degrees from the body. Heads usually are black, with a painted eye and pupil.

Following are the established colors for either fresh or salt water:

	Tail	Wing
Strawberry Blonde	Orange	Red
Platinum Blonde	White	White
Honey Blonde	Yellow	Yellow
Black Blonde	Black	Black
Pink Blonde #1	Pink	Pink
Pink Blonde #2	White	Pink
Argentine Blonde	White	Medium blue

The upside-down streamer—Keel-hook streamers—Monofilament loop guards—Two ways
to make wire guards—A rubber-band expedient—What colors do fish see best?—
Water clarity and light penetration—Keys to fly selection

9

Ways to Make Streamers Weedless

FLY-RODDERS HABITUALLY become specialists in one form of freshwater or
saltwater fishing or another, the choice often due to propinquity. Fishing
for the basses, especially the smallmouth and largemouth varieties, is the
dominant sport of many. Some consider the fly rod an inadequate instrument, while others insist it offers more challenge and more fun. Undoubtedly it does, where conditions make its use sensible. Among the latter
anglers, a portion favor popping bugs while others opt for streamers because they regard them as "the big fish flies," good takers everywhere, all
season long.

Unlike trout, which can be frustratingly selective, bass, when in the
mood, strike viciously at anything moving. Although some streamers do
better than others, because of individual characteristics, there are few specific bass patterns as such, for this reason. Any large fly could be called a
bass fly because it can hook bass on occasion, even though it is intended
for tarpon, salmon, trout, or whatever, and regardless of what it is supposed
to represent. Bass consider anything moving and catchable to be edible,
even small birds and animals.

Despite all this, there are secrets of successful selection of streamers and
bucktails for bass (as well as other weedy habitués, such as pickerel). Some
are of construction to make the flies able to swim among pads, grasses, and
snags at varying depths and with enticing action. The basis of proper
construction, then, is to make the flies as nearly weedless as possible. There
are several ways to do this, of which some are more acceptable than others.

127

Figure 9–1 shows an *upside-down streamer,* which also can be dressed as
a bucktail. Merely put the hook in the vise upside down and tie the fly that
way, the purpose being to protect the barb with hair and/or feathers
enough to prevent it from snagging. After dressing tail and body we could
start the wing with a bunch of hollow bucktail applied to surround the barb

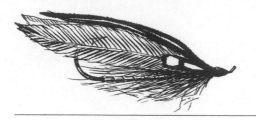

*9–1 The weedless streamer,
or upside-down fly.*

of the hook. Since hollow bucktail is buoyant, this induces the fly to ride barb upward. A little lead on the shank counteracts buoyancy. A wide and stiff neck hackle or two could be applied as a collar to help push the fly away from obstructions. A tail is not needed except perhaps for added color. (Bass like a touch of red.) Wing hackles can be tied in before or after applying the hair. Splayed wings work well.

In dressing such a fly, consider the depth at which it usually will be used. One to be worked near the surface requires little or no lead, while one intended to sink deeper and faster needs more.

When the *keel hook* was invented it was promoted as the "weedless wonder." Keel-hook streamers and bucktails, with their boat-shaped hook design, which makes the barb ride on top, were demonstrated by casting them into trees and brush and pulling them out easily with almost never a hangup. After an initial flurry of popularity the pattern went into limbo because fishermen distrusted its hooking ability due to the point and barb being parallel with the eye of the hook. Keel hooks now are used widely, but many anglers think they can be improved by bending the point and barb outward to an angle of about thirty degrees from the line of the eye of the hook, as Figure 9–2 shows.

With this improvement, keel-hook flies are nearly as effective as standard bends, and they are virtually weedless when dressed properly, as noted for upside-down types. With them it is better not to set the hook quickly on a strike. Instead, gradually tighten the line and, when the fish

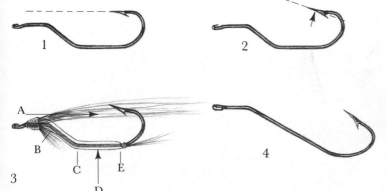

9–2 Tips on dressing keel hooks. (1) Hook as provided. (2) Barb bent up about thirty degrees for better hooking. (3) Dressed hook. Center of buoyancy is at A, center of gravity at D. Body runs from B to E; weight can be added between C and E, if desired. (4) A central draught hook.

is felt, *then* sink the barb with a moderate twitch.

Since streamers dressed for bass often contain more materials than those for other fishes, such as trout, it may be helpful to stress that the lighter ingredients, such as bucktail, should be predominantly on top. Otherwise, the fly could swim upside down.

Another way to make streamer hooks weedless, or nearly so, is to tie them with a *monofilament loop*. Before dressing the fly, tie in four or five inches of hard monofilament, securing the front end with thread wound back to the start of the hook's bend, where the tail will be applied. Let this extend backward until the tail, body, and wing are dressed, but before putting on the throat or collar. At this point curve the monofilament around the hook's bend and point and tie it in under and just behind the eye, using two or three turns of thread. Now, check and adjust to be sure the monofilament guard curves slightly outward from the hook's point, and directly below it. Then lash the monofilament down securely back of the eye; snip off the excess, lacquer the windings, and apply throat or collar to partially hide the loop.

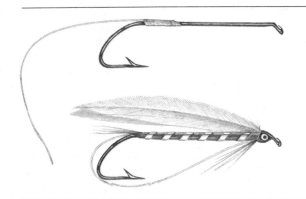

9–3 Monofilament-loop weed guard.

Since various brands and sizes of monofilament vary in stiffness, and because it becomes limper when soaked, we must decide for ourselves what type and diameter to use. If we select a hard type (used for leader butts) such as offered by the Mason Tackle Company (Otisville, Michigan 48463), an average-size streamer hook, such as a No. 4, could have its point protected adequately by monofilament of about thirty-pound test, or .027 diameter.

With the proper choice of monofilament, this weed guard works as well as any and permits better hooking than some of the others being described here. It is shown in Figure 9–3. It can be snipped off easily for open-water fishing.

Finally, let's discuss *two ways to use wire to make streamers weedless.* These can be done easily by amateur fly dressers with fine-tip round-nosed pliers and some very fine stainless-steel wire that will provide proper spring and

129

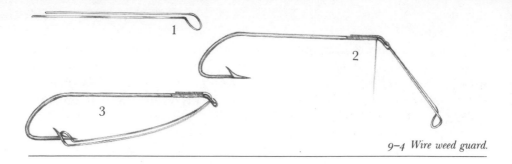

9-4 Wire weed guard.

rigidity. The wire is available from tackle shops, particularly those catering to saltwater sportsmen.

Cut off about six inches of wire and, with both ends nearly together, use the pliers to compress the bend into a tight U as shown in Figure 9–4. Bend about a sixteenth of an inch of the apex of the U upward slightly. Thread both wire ends through the eye of the hook and set the upcurved U end over the point of the hook just forward of the barb to obtain the exact length of the guard. Bend the ends of the wire along the top of the hook's shank and hold them tightly in place; then release the doubled wire from the hook's point and push it forward, out of the way, as shown in the middle sketch.

Lash down the two wire ends over the hook's shank, trimming them if desired. This lashing with tying thread should be at least half an inch long for a large hook about size 2. Lacquer the windings. Check the weed guard for proper length. The tip should rest over the point of the hook but should not be able to be pushed back over the barb, as shown in the bottom sketch. The upturned end helps to skid the wire over weeds, holding them away from the point.

Now push the weed guard forward again so the fly can be dressed without its interference. This done, set the guard over the hook's point to complete this easy operation.

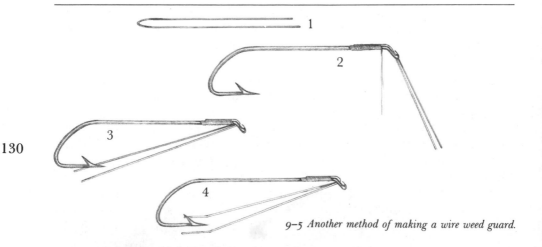

9-5 Another method of making a wire weed guard.

An alternate way to make a wire weed guard is shown in Figure 9-5. The same length of wire is doubled as before but its apex is not bent. Push the apex through the hook's eye from below, bending down about half an inch of the doubled wire tightly against the hook's shank and lashing it down securely. Cement the windings, as before. Dress the streamer (or bucktail). Now bend both wires backward toward the barb so that a wire is on each side of it, a quarter of an inch or so away from it and slightly below it. Test the spring of the wires by pushing them upward slightly to be sure they will guard the hook's point from weeds. If the wires' spring is light they may need to be pushed down a bit more. Trim both wires to the bend of the hook. Optionally, as shown in the bottom sketch, the wires can be set (bent) farther away from the shank and their ends bent parallel to it beside the point of the hook. Trim the wires to a distance between barb and bend, and test their spring, as above.

If fine stainless-steel wire with the proper amount of spring is used, the fashioning of these weed guards is very simple. Admittedly, they are a bit of a nuisance in casting, but are very necessary when fishing amid pads, grasses, and other obstructions. The payoff is to cast the fly to a pad or weed clump back of a clear spot and to pull the fly off into it, letting it rest there a moment before activating it. With luck there will be a boiling splash as a big bass rushes to grab the lure. This surely is better than the alternative of casting a non-weedless fly the same way and having to go in to free it, thus spoiling the water, when the fly catches on something, as it usually does.

What do we do in similar situations when our weedless streamers have been left at home? A rubber band will help to protect the barb from foulups, but two things are necessary. The hook's eye must be large enough to permit the rubber band to be threaded through it. Streamers tied for bass fishing often are on hooks with suitably large eyes, or they can be dressed on such hooks. Second, you must find small, thin bands of the right size, and these bands should have tension suitable to several lengths of hooks.

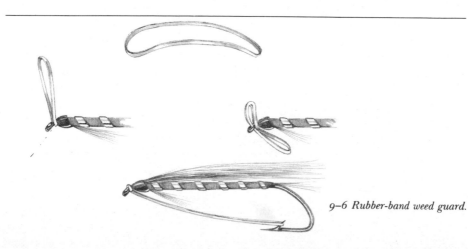

131

9–6 Rubber-band weed guard.

As shown in Figure 9–6, collar a band over the hook's shank just behind the eye and, holding it there, push the other side of the band through the eye from the top, then pull it tight from below. Stretch the band toward the hook's bend and catch it over the barb. As noted, we need a rubber band sized to do this and have proper tension.

If there is difficulty in pushing the band through the hook's eye it can perhaps be pulled through by using a length of thread or fine monofilament. Loop this through the band and thread the ends through the eye. Then pull on the finer material to draw the band through the hook's eye.

Since bass usually strike from hunger at anything small enough to ingest, including animals and birds hapless enough to be available, as well as bait fish, frogs, and various other water dwellers, it is obvious that appropriate flies are quite different from, for example, those suitable for trout. Imitator patterns in streamers take fish, but attractors normally do better, particularly if they are breather types, with splayed wings, or even floppy soft-hackled monstrosities usually reserved to tempt tarpon. Big bass strike at action, so the more of it the better, no matter what it is supposed to represent, if anything.

Color in streamers or bucktails can be important under certain conditions, as we will see, but color rarely is as critical as anglers seem to think. Size is more important, and action is even more so. When bass aren't in a striking mood, try varying the size, shape, or silhouette of the lure, rather than worrying about color. Try varying the lure's action, too, because this can be most important.

Although I downplay the importance of colors, there are facts all anglers should know about them in relation to what fish see, because evidently fish see, or don't see, colors in two ways, depending on the intensity of light. While the information I'll mention resulted from experiments with certain species, such as perch, there is no reason to think it doesn't apply to others, such as trout, salmon, and bass, because eye structure seems to be the same in all.

This subject intrigued me many years ago when I read about it in *Salmon and Sea Trout,* written by Sir Herbert Maxwell in 1898, wherein he quoted from a book called *Study of Fishes,* published much earlier. In 1973 Mark Sosin, a famous angler and author, covered the matter more definitively from the anglers' standpoint.* From these writings and others some interesting facts can be obtained to help decide what colors of flies to use, when, and why.

The retina in the eye of a fish has two types of receptor cells, which are used alternately depending on the intensity of light. One type are cone cells, which are used in bright daytime. These are color receptors. The other type are rod cells, used at night or when light is dull. Rod cells are about thirty times as sensitive as cone cells, but detect *only black and white.*

132

*Mark Sosin and John Clark, *Through the Fish's Eye* (New York: Outdoor Life—Harper & Row, 1973).

This seems to confirm what anglers long have suspected, because we usually favor bright flies on bright days and flies with sharp silhouettes, such as black or white, on dull days or at night.

Water clarity or light penetration also affects the fish's perception of color. In murky water, light penetration is filtered out in about ten feet, while in clear water the light penetration is about three times as much. From Mark Sosin's book we learn that in clear water, ten feet deep, flies of a red color penetrate to a maximum of only 6.5 percent; orange, 50 percent; yellow, 73 percent; and green, 88 percent. White is a component in many flies because it is detectable in poor light and at major depths. Bass seem to have an affinity for red, but this near-surface color is of little value in deep or murky water unless white is combined with it. Black provides the best silhouette, and is best under conditions of poor visibility.

Thus, for bass, as well as for other species, opinions in some of the older angling classics seem to agree with more modern scientific findings. Famous angling authors of books about popular species such as trout, salmon, and bass seem to agree that color is of minor importance except as it is affected by light intensity and water clarity. Several, including most angling authors who have expressed opinions in print, say that three color types of flies should do for all fishing conditions: a bright fly, a dark fly, and one in between, such as gray.

This is a controversy that has been going on for generations, and the little that is written here, or the lot in Mark Sosin's book, won't settle it, partly because all of us enjoy colorful flies and enjoy trying various patterns. In summary, however, we see that color, or color contrast, as far as bass are concerned, has some importance, but not as much as we might suspect. Fly size and, more particularly, fly action is the principal key to selection, and weedless hooks help to fish flies successfully where most of the action is!

10

Streamer-Jigs, and Other Weighty Suggestions

THE ANGLER RELAXED on a flat rock by the little river, his wadered feet cooling in a gravel-strewn backwater, while he waited for his partner to appear for lunch. On a rise of ground across the stream in what once had been a clearing bounded against the woods by an ancient stone wall was the remains of a habitation, now merely a stone-lined cellar hole filled with bushes and vines.

In this solitude, far from the noises of civilization, a family of homesteaders once had lived, eking out a bare existence from the boulder-strewn western Massachusetts soil. The angler enjoyed thinking of what life must have been like then, a century or more ago, when this remote area bustled with large farms and small factories powered by the stream beside which he rested. The gurgling river and the forested hillsides evidently had changed very little, but the industrial revolution had driven away the inhabitants generations ago.

What was the fishing in this placid pool like then? Surely much better than now. "I'll bet the kids who lived over there used to catch twelve-inch brookies with worm-baited hooks and willow switches any time they wanted to," the angler thought enviously, remembering the few small trout he had released that morning without hooking even one that could be considered a keeper.

The angler's gaze shifted to the nearby backwater, where he idly watched a small school of black-striped minnows dipping down while feeding on the mossy rocks of the bottom.

"They feed like bouncing jigs," he thought, "dipping down to eat, darting a little distance, and then dipping down again."

This made the angler's reflections turn to jigs. He had used them in salt water often enough. How could they be made to work in fresh water, castable with a fly rod? After all, when one has to bump bottom to hook trout, the flies usually must be weighted. Why weight the body in the middle, causing it only to sink? Why not weight it at the head, like a jig, so it will sink and dip down headfirst, just as the minnows do? Why settle for simple jig dressings which attract more than imitate, when they can be dressed as established streamer or bucktail patterns, which do more of both?

When the angler's companion appeared from upstream this chain of thought was broken, but not forgotten. On wakeful nights it appeared again and again. Being a writer on matters piscatorial, the angler corresponds with various people of kindred pursuits, sometimes to mutual advantage. And so it happened that one day he received in the mail a collection of jigs expertly made by a gentleman in Ontario named Loring A. Dodge.

Now, friend Loring is a construction engineer by profession, and thus skilled in the arts of tinkering, especially as they apply to anything having to do with catching fish. He is noted as the regional expert on various angling techniques, and the relatively heavy jigs he sent to the angler were gems in their class. The angler, whose avocation is writing in between fishing seasons, is inadequate at tinkering with metals, even if time permitted. So why not get someone to do the job who knows how?

And thus it happened that the angler (who, you may have guessed, is this author) and Loring Dodge collaborated toward the perfection of streamer-jigs. Collaboration may not be the proper word, because Loring did all the work, while I generously provided the criticism.

In letters I wrote to Loring over a year and a half ago these comments are noted: "I never have seen small jigs dressed as named patterns of streamer flies or bucktails; they should work better than plain hair jigs. . . . Should be light enough to be cast with a fly rod. . . . Better than leading the body of the fly, as the weighted head wants to dive, and the fly can be fished in a more lifelike manner, as a small bait fish grubs on the bottom. I presume that a sixty-fourth of an ounce is as small as we should go, and that a sixteenth of an ounce is as heavy as one should cast."

Loring Dodge graciously accepted the challenge, and what follows, as far as streamer-jigs are concerned, is entirely his. So far, he has labored for more than a year on the project, and volumes of correspondence have passed between us. While research is continuing, I stream-tested streamer-jigs last summer with sufficient success to know that this little innovation has very definite advantages. We are convinced that properly weighted and properly dressed streamer-jigs can be worked along or near stream bottoms when necessary to hook some of the big fish that habitually lie there so often. Since the hook rides bend and barb upward, hangups are much

135

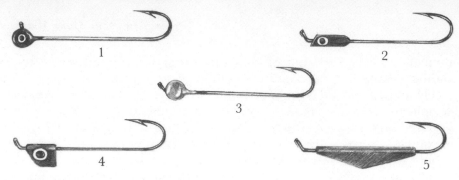

10–1 Typical streamer-jig types. (1) Doll head, (2) Bullet head, (3) Shot head, (4) Rudder head, and (5) Keel head. Still another head type has been tested with success: Two small pieces of metal (round, oval, lozenge-shaped, or arrow-shaped) are cemented together horizontally over and under the shank and far enough back so wing and throat can be applied. The throat can be two or more breast feathers tied on flat (horizontally) under the head to cover its underside. Horizontal heads settle more slowly and thus are useful in shallow water or over weeds.

less frequent. Muddlers, for example, should be worked as close to bottom as possible, where the actual species lives. This is an ideal way to do it, but it is by no means confined to them. It works also when fish are deep in lakes. With a slight and slow jerking retrieve the streamer-jig dives on a slack line and moves forward and upward on a tightening one—just the action so often desired. Furthermore, the dressings in established streamer and bucktail patterns enhance the lifelike appearance of this type of fly.

Amateurs may adapt the information in this chapter to their personal uses. Professionals should contact Loring Dodge, because he has accumulated information too involved for inclusion here, and also has applied for certain protections on his methods of manufacture following his many months of research.*

Figure 10–1 shows five typical streamer-jigs before dressing. The Rudder and Keel heads are made from sheet lead, and will be described first. The Shot head is simplest—merely a split shot split enough to be crimped around the hook after being cemented in place. The Bullet and Doll heads are lead castings, possibly superior to the others, but requiring molding, which some anglers won't want to bother with.

Hooks on all models are from 6X to 8X long, usually in sizes 4, 6, and 8. The 6X Irish Limerick is a good pattern, or the 8X Mustad #94720, which has a Model Perfect bend, with steel soft enough to allow bending the shank to fit a mold to make Doll heads. Mackerel hooks in 8X length also are appropriate.

Sheet lead, available from plumbing-supply outlets or hobby shops, is ideal in sixty-fourth-inch thickness, which weighs one pound per square foot. It can be cut easily into one-inch strips and smaller. One square inch weighs a ninth of an ounce, half of this weighs an eighteenth of an ounce, and half of this weighs a thirty-sixth of an ounce. Sheet lead can be pounded

136

*Loring A. Dodge, P.O. Box 666, Elliot Lake, Ontario P5A 2P9, Canada.

thinner and comes in a variety of hardnesses. A thirty-sixth of an ounce is a good size to start with on a hook such as a No. 4 because this weight casts nicely and sinks readily in all but the strongest currents. After making a sample or two, readers will have their own ideas about this, partly influenced by their tackle. A thirty-sixth of an ounce is, however, about the maximum advisable for fly-rod use, and weighting of about half of that should be better in mild currents.

Lead will oxidize, causing a thin, dull gray film on the surface. This can be burnished off easily with fine steel wool until the surface is clean and shiny, thus making glue, paint, and lacquer adhere properly. Avoid breathing lead dust and getting it into scratches in the skin. After burnishing, wash lead and hands in water and laundry soap.

To make a Rudder head let's take a size 4 or 6 hook 6X or 8X long and put it in the vise bend upward. Wrap tying thread in close coils where the lead will be applied, to help it hold better. Cut a strip of lead about three-eighths of an inch by three-quarters of an inch and partially fold it over into a rough square. Apply cement to thread and to inside fold of lead.

Any two-component epoxy cement is satisfactory, but Plastic Steel epoxy repair cement is preferred because it fills any loose spots in the bend.

Fit the doubled, cemented lead over the shank of the hook, leaving a little room behind the eye for dressing a collar or beard. Complete the fold with finger pressure, keeping both sides of the lead as even as possible. Use parallel-jaw pliers (preferably) to apply *light* pressure to squeeze both sides of the lead together. Wipe off excess cement now, because this will be difficult after it hardens. If it does harden it can be removed with acetone. Too much pressure with the pliers may squeeze the lead out of shape. Optionally, the lead can be kept in the grip of the pliers until the cement hardens by winding a large rubber band tightly around the handles or by using a spring-loaded clothespin. Put a bit of paper between jaws and lead so the clamps won't adhere to the lure if cement is squeezed out. It is efficient to make several Rudder heads at a time, putting them through the various steps together.

When the cement has hardened, the lead can be trimmed to desired shape with small scissors. The Rudder head shown in Figure 10-1 works nicely but it could be trimmed less deeply—cut in a semicircle, in a V, or whatever the maker desires. Experiments show the shape shown to be a good one. After trimming, the head can be smoothed of sharp edges or burrs with fine sandpaper or a small file.

With the cement hardened, the next step is to give the head a final cleaning in preparation for the primer and sealer. Just give it a quick rub with fine steel wool (such as is used in polishing furniture or gun stocks) to remove any flecks of glue or other residue. The Rudder head now can be dressed and used as it is, if we don't want to paint it.

The instructions for the next steps, applicable to jigs of any kind, may seem a bit involved, but they result in a tough color finish that won't fleck.

137

or rub off as easily as casual finishes do. They are worth the effort, and dozens of the heads can be run through the steps in an evening.

The first step in finishing is to dip the heads in a combination primer and sealer which can be obtained in white or clear (for other colors). White is satisfactory because other colors can be applied over it if desired. In these experiments a primer-sealer called X-I-M was used, made by X-I-M Products, Inc., 1169 Bassett Road, Westlake, Ohio 44145, and usually available at paint stores. This dries quickly, makes paint adhere well, and prevents flaking and blistering. One dipping will do, but two are recommended.

The next step in painting the heads is to apply color and varnish. For color, Flecto Varathane was used, a plastic enamel available in various colors. The final varnish coat was Flecto Varathane Varnish. These are made in the United States by the Flecto Company, Inc., of Oakland, California, and in Canada by Flecto Coatings, Ltd., of Richmond, British Columbia. Loring Dodge says, "Once you get the hang of all this, you can do hundreds in an evening!" He also recommends two light coats, rather than a single thick one.

Now, those inclined to be artistic can apply eyes and any other features desired, such as a fine red slash on the rear of the head to simulate gills. To make an iris for an eye, use a simple round dowel about an eighth of an inch in diameter. Dip it in a bit of paint which has intentionally been dropped on a piece of waxed paper, or a similar surface, and touch it to the center of the head. The iris usually is yellow. After this dries, apply the pupil, in black, in the same manner but with a dowel about a sixteenth of an inch in diameter. The slim, tapered wood handles of inexpensive paintbrushes make ideal dip sticks, and are available in all sizes.

When eyes are dry a final dip in Flecto Varathane Varnish improves the appearance and protects the enamel from bumps and bruises. We usually favor black for all heads because it is a neutral "color" and won't distract the fish from the rest of the fly. When doing white flies, that color should be used. Steelheaders or bass fishermen may prefer red or yellow.

Now to dress the Rudder head. Follow any established pattern, tying in the materials back of the head, except for the collar or beard, which can be applied ahead of it. The collar helps to conceal the head, while providing a bit of added action. The dressing of the body, of course, should help to conceal the bend and barb of the hook.

We don't need to use lead entirely and, rather than painting the heads, may prefer them in gold or silver color.

To do the Rudder or Keel head in gold color, obtain some extremely thin brass sheeting and cut and bend it to size, as discussed above. Ideal thicknesses are ten thousandths (.010) for brass and five thousandths (.005) for copper. Since brass is rather difficult to cut, this should be done accurately before insertion. It should be burnished before using, but need not be lacquered unless desired, because we may want it dull, and it always can be burnished to brightness with fine steel wool. Apply it to the hook the

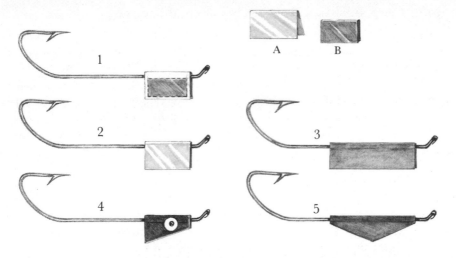

10–2 *Rudder and Keel heads of sheet-metal with optional lead inserts. A lead insert* (B) *can be cemented between sides of bent sheet brass, copper, or aluminum* (A) *as shown in sketch 1. Trim heads as shown in sketches 2 and 3 to obtain shapes shown in sketches 4 and 5.*

same way as for lead. Optionally, a lead insert can be cemented between the bends of the brass, as shown in Figure 10–2. This need not be fitted exactly because it can be trimmed and smoothed after the cement has set.

To do these heads in a silver color merely use part of an aluminum beer can, applied exactly the same as the brass.

To make a Keel head merely follow the directions for the Rudder head, trimming the keel as indicated in the illustrations, or as desired. Although the keel is set forward on the shank, this type of head won't dive as readily as the Rudder. It does keep the fly upright and can swim it on or very close to bottom, where the keel can help to bounce it over obstructions, thus helping to make it weedless. In silver or gold finish the keel imitates the belly of a bait fish and may offer an improvement over two very popular Pacific saltwater patterns: the Silver Beer Belly and the Golden Beer Belly. In motion, the Keel head (or body) very closely resembles a darting bait fish. It is an excellent basis for dressing Muddlers.

Keel-fly hooks offer weighting alternatives that make fast-sinking patterns even more weedless than the above. Wright and McGill's Eagle Claw keel hooks are sold everywhere in bronze finish (#1213) in sizes 12 to 2, and in stainless steel (#1213SS) in sizes 6 to 3/0. As Figure 10–3 shows, weights can be applied with sheet lead, trimmed as desired, or with split shot, to the bow of the hook or to the keel. Forward weighting of course makes the fly dip headfirst, while keel weighting causes it to settle. It has been recommended that the point and barb should be bent upward at an angle of about thirty degrees for better hooking. The weighting may or may not interfere with the body dressing, or may replace it, depending on how it is applied. This is a minor matter because the principal dressing is the wing, put on at the neck of the hook.

139

Some of us enjoy the challenge and relaxation of tinkering, while others, like this writer, can't seem to find the time or inclination. The latter will settle for Shot heads, which can be applied to hooks quite simply. Merely open a split shot a bit more, if necessary, and crimp it on near the eye, using a drop of two-component epoxy cement for a firm bond. Weight distribution should be mainly below the upturned hook. If the shot is put on about a quarter of an inch behind the eye this space can be used for a collar to partly mask the shot. The shot can be slightly flattened, and can be painted any desired color (as previously described) and decorated with a painted eye and pupil. In this case no collar is necessary, and all the dressing can be put on behind the shot. This provides an effect similar to Jim Pray's historic Optic Bucktails, formerly very famous for steelhead, and described later in this chapter. Since Shot heads cause the fly to ride with bend and barb upward, this variation may be superior in some cases because it provides more freedom from snagging.

Finally, in these several variations of making streamer-jigs, we come to two models cast from lead: the Doll head and the Bullet head.

The *Bullet-head streamer-jig* looks exactly like its name except that the front is slanted backward at an angle of about forty-five degrees to improve appearance and efficiency. These heads are small in diameter—not over an eighth of an inch for hook sizes 2 to 6, and weighing not over a sixteenth of an ounce and usually about half of that. Experiments indicate that only enough lead should be used to get the fly down. The heavier it is, the more difficult it is to cast. Users are cautioned to use care in casting. A loaded fly on a careless forward cast can pack a dangerous wallop! The head is applied close to the eye because all the dressing is behind it. Bullet heads usually are finished in black, with a yellow eye and black pupil, but that is merely our preference.

The *Doll-head streamer-jig* requires a ball-shaped lead casting at the bend of the jig hook below the eye. Jig hooks are available commercially, such as Wright and McGill's Eagle Claw bronze-finished #630 in sizes from 8 to 4/0. Since these are rather short, except for pond fish, Loring Dodge prefers to bend 6X or 8X hooks to shape. Most wires are pliable enough

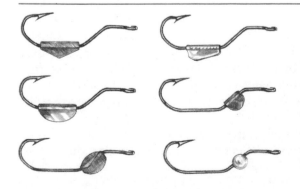

10–3 Various ways of weighting keel hooks. The split-shot method at lower right is the simplest. Note that the readily obtainable central draught hook —a worm hook—is similar to the keel hook and is preferred by some; it is shown in one of the Ballou Specials in Figure 10–4.

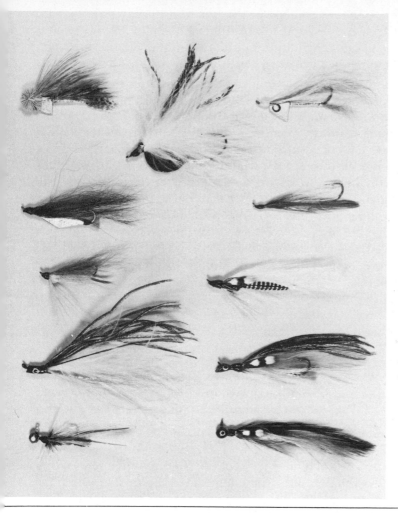

10–4 Typical streamer-jigs, weighted and dressed by Loring A. Dodge. At top, two Rudder heads (Muddler and Mickey Finn). Alone, below them, a Ballou Special on a central draught hook with a round lead weight of the Beer Belly type, five-eighths of an inch long and weighing a thirty-second of an ounce. Second row, keel heads (Black Nosed Dace and Sidewinder); third row, Shot heads (Warden's Worry and Black Ghost); fourth row, Bullet heads (Ballou Special and Supervisor); last row, Doll heads (Spruce and Nine-Three).

for this. After casting, the neck of the lead is removed; the head is trimmed or filed to proper ball shape and painted the desired color, and an eye with pupil is added. All dressing, of course, is behind the head.

Since most readers won't want to become involved with making molds, pouring castings, and finishing heads, this book won't discuss it. The few who do should contact Loring Dodge, who may provide a source for obtaining suitable molds or even the finished products.

As this is being written, a year and a half from the outset, the research on streamer-jigs is far from completed. Although it has been fun, readers who find the subject of interest owe a round of standing applause to Loring Dodge. I did this, in a way, with a nip from a flask of Jack Daniel's when I hooked my first trout on a streamer-jig on the East Branch of the Westfield River last fall.

I was testing various varieties of streamer-jigs in a backwater where their action could be seen, and was entranced by the way the Black Ghost worked head down while being twitched along the bottom over rocky weeds that failed to catch on the upturned hook. The action was that of a grubbing minnow, which was just what we wanted. The fly cast better than I thought it might, although it was inclined to hook if the cast was checked—a fault which can be used to advantage. Finally, in trying for distance, I dropped the fly behind a midstream rock and let it settle. At the first twitch a good trout had it. In these days of overfishing with worms, spoons, and spinners, good trout are rather hard to come by on the East Branch! Streamer-jigs have a lot going for them, and Loring and I hope that many readers will find them valuable.

Of course weighted flies are far from new, but styles in weighting change, as this chapter indicates. Two historic methods of weighting— equally good nowadays—were originated by two of the greatest old-time steelheaders that ever waded the riffles of famous streams in Oregon and northern California. One of them was C. Jim Pray, of Eureka, originator of the Optic Bucktails.

10–5 C. Jim Pray's Optic Bucktail, with clamped metal body.

The heads of Optic Bucktails are made from opened metal beads, available in one-eighth-, three-sixteenths-, and one-quarter-inch diameters, which can be clamped just behind the eye of the hook and painted as suits the angler. Nowadays Jim probably would have filled the cavity with Epoxy Plastic Steel. He preferred the quarter-inch size for his steelhead flies, applied usually to hooks No. 4 in length with a 1/0 bend, 4X strong, with hollow point and tapered eye in the Limerick pattern. These were made for him by Mustad. Here are his five favorite patterns, dressed in the style shown in Figure 10–5:

OWL EYED OPTIC
HEAD: Quarter-inch brass bead painted black, with yellow eye and black center
BODY: Oval silver tinsel
WING: Optionally, red, red and yellow, or red and white, or with the hair of squirrel, badger, or something similar

This was the first one, originated in the 1940s. From it, four more specific named patterns evolved, as follows.

BLACK OPTIC
HEAD: Quarter-inch brass bead painted black, with yellow eye and black center

BODY: Oval gold tinsel
THROAT: Black hackle, nearly to point of hook
WING: A moderate-sized bunch of black hair, extending well beyond bend of hook

RED OPTIC
HEAD: Quarter-inch brass bead painted black, with yellow eye and black center
BODY: Oval silver tinsel
THROAT: Red hackle, nearly to point of hook (optional)
WING: A small bunch of hair dyed red, over which is a smaller bunch of hair dyed yellow, both extending well beyond bend of hook

ORANGE OPTIC
HEAD: Quarter-inch brass bead painted black, with white eye and red center
BODY: Oval silver tinsel
THROAT: Red hackle, nearly to point of hook
WING: A moderate-sized bunch of orange hair, extending well beyond bend of hook

COCK ROBIN OPTIC
HEAD: Quarter-inch brass bead painted black, with yellow eye and black center
BODY: Oval silver tinsel
THROAT: Orange hackle, nearly to point of hook
WING: A moderate-sized bunch of ground squirrel or badger hair, extending well beyond bend of hook

Jim Pray often made bodies of radio pins, as the drawing shows, but he later preferred tinsel, and such pins are not now available. Styles in flies are more fickle than fishes' tastes for them. Optic patterns now are rarely used, perhaps because the bead heads are considered unnecessary and because they lacked sufficient weight to be effective. The bright color schemes in these historic patterns are as popular for steelhead in modern times as they always were.

Weighting streamer-fly bodies with wire is so common that it needs only a mention, plus the historic method of Peter J. Schwab, who lived in Yreka, and who was one of my fishing companions on several steelhead rivers in Oregon and northern California. During the middle of this century Pete Schwab was one of the greatest artists with the fly rod who ever lived, comparable only to such modern experts as Joe Brooks and Lefty Kreh. As a steelheader, Pete was the supreme regional oracle, and his ability in dressing superb steelhead flies was unsurpassed. His historic patterns included the Bellamy, Bobby Dunn, Brass Hat, Paint Brush, Princess, Queen Bess, Van Luven, and Wood Pussy, dressings for which are given in Part Four. Although these patterns are rarely used in modern times, many of the

143

modern ones have descended from them. The important thing, however, is to learn how to apply wire bodies properly. No one ever has exceeded Pete Schwab in this, so I describe his method as he wrote it down for me. His method provides the ideal amount of weight to sink flies in fast rivers, yet not to the excess that would make them lazy in action or difficult to cast. His flies were so well made that they were nearly indestructible:

"The importance of using the correct hook cannot be overemphasized. Hook and wing lengths must be correctly proportioned. The standard light wire hooks which answer so well for bass and minor trout have no place on a steelhead river, where they must be very strong. The Limerick bend, in the lengths and weights specified below, has the fewest faults, but even here I should like to see the depth of penetration increased on all sizes smaller than the No. 2.

"For the two-winged bucktails I use the following: size 1/0 Limerick, standard wire; size 2 Limerick, 2X strong; size 4 Limerick, 3X strong; and, rarely, size 6 Limerick, 3X long and 3X strong. For three-winged bucktails (and often for two-winged) I use 1/0 Limerick, standard wire and shank; size 2 Limerick, 3X long and 2X strong; size 4 Limerick, 3X long and 3X strong. Ball-eyed hooks are better for bucktails and streamers than tapered-eye hooks because they are heavier, stronger, and larger, sinking better and allowing better knotting to the leaders. Get them TDE (turned-down eye), of course.

"In the all-wire-bodied flies, the bodies are made of copper, brass, silver, or gold wires, in diameters to match size of hook—i.e., .018-inch wire for size 6 hooks, .023-inch wire for size 4 hooks, and .028-inch wire for sizes 2 and 1/0 hooks. All wires must be soft. Where the pattern calls for tinsel-, wool-, or floss-covered bodies over wire cores, use the next-size-smaller wire. Otherwise the fly will be too fat to be pleasing and too heavy for nice casting.

"Prepare the hook with a tightly spaced winding of size A sewing silk as shown in sketch 1 in Figure 10–6. (The 00 and smaller sizes of tying silks are too small.) Finish with whip fastening. Lacquer and dry for at least half an hour while you prepare additional hooks. This preparation is necessary to prevent slippage of the wire body.

"Grasp end of wire with small pliers or fingers of left hand, bend over hook at *A* in sketch 1, and pull tightly with right hand which is holding spool of wire. Wind forward in close, tight coils, starting on the bare hook, three-sixteenths inch above the bend and going forward over the lacquered foundation and over the bare hook again to within one-quarter inch of the eye. You won't think these minute details redundant after you have tied a few!

144

"Use small cutting pliers to cut off surplus wire. Press loose ends into close contact with body coils and with an ignition file (or other small file having rounded, smooth edges) file the burrs and rough ends of the wire down to a slight taper as shown in sketch 2 of Figure 10-6. Burnish the body

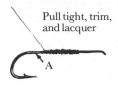

Pull tight, trim, and lacquer

1. Preparing the hook

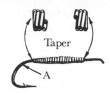

Taper

2. Applying wire body and tapering ends

A   B

3. Making silk winding for rear wing of three-wing fly

4. Method of raising wing on two-wing and three-wing flies

5. Completed three-wing (note "spike-type" throat)

6. Completed two-wing fly (both are Brass Hat pattern)

10–6 Dressing Peter J. Schwab's wire-bodied bucktails.

with any convenient tool. Wipe body with clean cloth. Flow with thin water-clear lacquer to prevent tarnish with age. Dry.

"Make a few turns with size A sewing silk over bare hook at *A* in sketch 2. Make half hitch. Lacquer. Attach tail and wind tightly with enough silk to build up to diameter of wire body. Saturate with lacquer.

"For three-winged bucktails only, first apply close winding of silk thread over center of body, making a band about one-eighth inch wide as shown at *A* in sketch 3. Lacquer. Tie on the rear wing, trimming butts of hair closely with curved manicure scissors. Saturate butts with lacquer and finish with a narrow band of windings as in sketch 4. Lacquer, dry, and proceed as in next paragraph.

"For both two-winged and three-winged bucktails, prepare end of hook, using enough size A sewing silk to close eye of hook at one end and to pull a tapered jam against wire body at other end as shown at *B* in sketch 3. Lacquer copiously.

"Tie in hackle (throat) if called for by pattern. If no hackle is wanted, proceed as in next paragraph. Where hackle is required, fasten in by butt

145

end; run silk back to thread clip at *left* of hook; wind hackle back toward bend in close coils, catch with thread, break off hackle tip, then wind thread forward *through* the hackles and fasten at front with half hitch, thus securing a hackle tie which will stand much rough usage and chawing by the fish before it will come loose. Lacquer.

"Tie in base color of hair, always the *lightest* of the several colors to be used. To prevent matting of hair in a solid bunch flat against body of fly, after first catching the hair in position, take a turn of silk around the hair alone as shown in sketch 4 of Figure 10–6. Now pull the thread tightly forward, thus raising the hair until it stands in a round tuft at an angle of nearly forty-five degrees above the hook. Holding the thread tightly, start the next turn diagonally over butts of hair to keep the wing elevated while you complete the winding. After another turn or two of silk, make a couple of tight half hitches, trim off butts of hair, saturate with lacquer, and finish the tie. Lacquer and allow to dry before applying final top wing. (If a spike is to be used, lacquer and tie the spike in while lacquer is still wet; finish off with whip tie, lacquer again, and dry. The spike is tied in in the same way as the base color of hair.)

"Tie in top color of wings. To prevent the two colors from blending, make the same kind of turn around the top hair by itself as was suggested for the base color of hair. This time, however, you will find that after fastening the hairs of the top wing your left fingers will be unable to raise the top wing hairs without also lifting a few of the base hairs beneath. It looks like a tangled mess but it isn't. The colors still are separated at their bottoms.

"Tilt the wing forward with your left fingers; poke a needle into the bottom open spaces between the two colors and hold it there. Now open your left fingers, releasing the hair. Pass the needle upward and presto! the wing colors are separated again.

"Tie in jungle cock, kingfisher, or other overlays to suit your taste, or tie off without them. Lacquer. The fly is finished."

In addition to Mr. Schwab's instructions as given above and the instructions for dressing each individual fly as explained in Part Four, the following comments are contained in letters he has written me:

"The only significant change [in this series of bucktails] has been the substitution of hair tails for feather tails, using gray squirrel in the Queen Bess, black hair or skunk in the Wood Pussy, and dyed polar bear hair of proper color in all other patterns. The hairs named outlast feathers and are equally effective.

"Originally, only the Paint Brush was tied in the three-winged style, followed by the Brass Hat and others, but during the past three seasons [this letter was written in 1949] *all* patterns are tied in *both* two-wing and three-wing styles. A simplified Paint Brush in the two-wing style, with the rear bright red wing eliminated, has been popular.

"The most popular three-wing patterns are the Queen Bess, Brass Hat,

146

and Paint Brush. For steelhead I only use them myself after the season is well under way, when big fish have arrived and the water is high, cold, and often clouded. For the most part, during early and mid-season and in high altitudes or some distance from salt water, the two-wing patterns are much more used and more easily cast.

"It is important that all wire-bodied bucktails should be polished with liquid metal polish immediately after tying, as even polished wires lose their luster by opening of the surface as they are wound around the small shank of the hook. A powdered cleanser on a piece of wet Turkish toweling is excellent and is easily scrubbed off in running water. Without scrubbing, some of the abrasive will remain between the coils of wire and is sure to cloud the finish after lacquering. After polishing, scrubbing, and drying over heat, the wire bodies are lacquered with thin, colorless lacquer or head cement to prevent tarnish. This is all done, of course, before tails and wings are added.

"Unquestionably, the most *killing* material is the crinkly hair of eastern white-tailed deer in natural and dyed shades, gray squirrel, or black bear. Unfortunately, deer hair doesn't last long (in steelhead fishing). The most *lasting* flies, though lacking in much of the lively action of those tied with deer tail hair, are tied with gray squirrel, polar bear, and black bear hair. Long, thin polar bear hair has a *much* better action than the short, thick polar bear hair used by most professionals for production reasons.

"The most effective bucktails are those tied with long, rakish, lightly dressed wings. They are far more effective than when tied with short wings in the orthodox 'hair-fly' style.

"Spikes (beards, pectoral fins, or torn gills—call them what you will) are usually omitted. They have a tendency to spoil the swimming action, particularly in the two-wing patterns, and if the fly shows the slightest tendency to swim sideways instead of on an even keel, the spikes are promptly snipped off or are thinned to a very few hairs.

"Historically, with the single exception of the Princess, I have been using all of these patterns and many, many more since about 1926 but always with unweighted bodies, usually of tinsel. The only *new* things about the patterns are the wire bodies, the tying technique, and the careful selection of the *best* patterns, involving the elimination of the unnecessary patterns, however beautiful or effective they might be at times when the fish would grab anything thrown at them. This work was done on the Klamath River in 1945 and 1946, where it is imperative to use flies that will sink well, excel in swimming action, and cast easily. The first flies were of tinsel, floss, or dubbing, dressed over wire cores. The fish soon tore the coverings off, whereupon the plain, uncovered wire proved to be more effective than the covered wire on all three of the counts just given. I had the help of George Bellamy and Bobby Dunn, with whom I fished every day for not less than three months in 1945 and through most of 1946.

"I have a seemingly uncontrollable habit of tying my wings a trifle

147

shorter than they should be for greatest effectiveness. The wings should always extend beyond the bend one-half the length of the shank. These bucktails are tied to imitate minnow action, not insects.

"Don't be fooled by the apparent uprightness of the wings. In water, under the influence of the current, or manipulation of the angler, the wings quickly fall down and the bucktail assumes the slender, rakish form of a minnow. The wings are tied upright in the first place so they won't later fall so low as to mask the glitter of the body. Every effort has been made to secure greatest visibility."

While uncovered wire bodies have given way to ones of weighted Mylar tubing, and other such practices, the excellence of Pete Schwab's method should provide valuable suggestions, and it is worthy of preservation.

Weighting with lead wire is simpler. A strip bound on under the hook's shank may suffice, with the body dressed over it. We can wind as much of the body as we wish with .020- or .040-diameter lead wire, either a few turns in the middle of the shank or as much as all along it, binding it down with thread, as just described, and then covering it with the final body. As expedients, lead shot can be crimped or strip lead ("Twiston") can be wound on the leader a foot or so ahead of the fly, or a few turns of wire can be made around the bend of large hooks—a last resort because the fly sinks tailfirst, unless retrieved rapidly.

An idea I like better with unweighted streamers when they should drag bottom is to tie a tippet to the leader with a blood knot, leaving one of the ends which protrude from the knot about a foot long. Crimp a split shot to the end of this. It won't pull off as easily if the end of the monofilament is touched to a flame to melt it into a small ball. With the right weighting in suitable currents the shot will drag bottom, fishing the streamer right over it. If the shot snags between rocks, all that should happen is losing it when pulling loose. This connection, of course, is merely a dropper such as would be used when fishing two flies. The idea works particularly well when a streamer which wants to float, such as a Muddler with a head of hollow deer hair, is used. The weight fishes the fly within inches of the

148

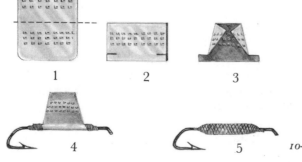

10–7 *Weighting bodies with dental lead.*

bottom, where it should be, but not on the bottom, where it would be less visible and could snag more often.

Finally, let's get a bit of added value from the family dentist by asking him for some rectangles of lead, which he usually discards after taking dental X-rays. These very thin lead sheets measure (in various sizes) about one inch by one and a half inches, and are useful in making underbodies for weighted streamer flies.

Following Figure 10–7, (1) fold a sheet in half. (2) Cut above the fold on both sides inward about an eighth of an inch and an eighth of an inch above it. (3) Fold the two sides inward, leaving two tabs for attachment and the sides slanted so the top of the sheet measures about half an inch. (4) Wind the hook with close coils of thread, lacquer it, and attach both tabs of the lead to the hook with a few turns of thread. (5) Now, carefully wrap the lead tightly around the hook and secure it in place by tightly crisscrossing the thread over it. The thread should bite into the lead. Lacquer this underbody, and it is ready for dressing.

Loring Dodge recommends these reclaimed lead rectangles for making Rudder heads and Keels, but since the lead is so thin, two or more rectangles must be cemented together with epoxy and allowed to dry before use.

11

Tandem Flies for Casting and Trolling

AMERICA'S REVERED Carrie Stevens, queen of the streamer fly, tied many of her feathered confections for trolling dressed on abnormally long-shanked hooks with feathers about four inches in length. Their slim, side-dressed style was so appropriate that they were famous fish takers, but the long hooks produced a sawing effect that sometimes allowed the quarry to work loose. This problem is solved by tandem-hooked patterns, usually of about the same length, but often quite a bit longer or shorter.

Tandem-hooked flies have an important place in trolling, and the trolling of flies has an important place in angling, whether or not we care to consider it fly fishing. Purism in angling can have a snobbish element when overdone. Trolling with flies can be much more successful than trolling with bait partly because we don't need inspections or changes so often. Thus, the fly is in the water more of the time, only needing occasional checking for weeds.

Trolling flies is a pleasant change from constant casting, particularly on windy days. It is the best way to locate fish when they are scattered. It is a necessary method of exploration when fish are deep. A big fly simulates more of a meal than a smaller one, and therefore usually tempts larger prizes more often. Fish, regardless of size, may take bigger streamers (which can't be cast well) when they refuse smaller castable ones. Tandem flies are better hookers when fish are striking short. When oversized patterns are used, a forward hook is of advantage because we know that fish often hit baits, lures, or flies sideways and thus, with long singles, often miss the hook. Do you remember the many hits you have had without hooking anything? Strikes at the head of a fly often cause this.

Thus, we seem to have a pretty good case in favor of tandem-hooked trolling flies, even if they are a second choice to casting smaller ones. Having learned the elements of trolling in Chapter 4, let's see how various experts prepare trolling flies. In explaining this I am indebted to advice from two famous anglers who are top tandem-fly trollers: Ray Salminen and Paul Kukonen, from Massachusetts. To theirs I have added some comments of my own.

Three methods should cover the subject: (1) a tandem-hooked fly with a changeable rear element, (2) a tandem-hooked fly with a fixed trailer, and (3) a tandem-hooked fly with a monofilament connection. This latter one is an expedient when we lack nylon-coated twisted wire, such as Seven-strand or Mason's Nylostrand. These are not liable to kink or warp, as plastic line or leader materials often do, thus making the fly useless. The nylon-coated twisted wire should be in smallest diameters, testing from thirty to sixty pounds. It won't rust, due to the coating.

There is a choice of hooks for these three methods. If the front one is size 2, such as Mustad #9575, the rear hook should be size 4, such as Mustad #3399A—this for hooks and connector measuring three inches or longer for a fly four inches or longer. The forward hook is always larger than the rear one, and both are usually singles. Some anglers prefer a double salmon hook in front and a single to the rear or vice versa. Others have different ideas. The trailer hook can be applied either up or down. The down position balances the fly better and resists any tendency to spin. The only value of the up position seems to be in resisting weeds, in which case the dressings of both hooks could be applied in the upside-down position described in Chapter 9.

British anglers tie their Demons and Terrors with three hooks—a single in front and rear pointing downward, with the one in the middle pointing up. These flies usually are quite small, two or three inches long. The three hooks of the Terror are silver-bodied with red wool tails. The forward hook (only) has blue neck hackles extending to the end of the rear hook and fairly long and wide shoulders of teal. Demons are dressed in various ways—for example, rear hook silver-bodied with red wool tail, middle hook silver-bodied (only), forward hook dressed with a bunch of peacock fibers extending to end of rear hook, and a medium blue hackle throat. Another pattern is the same except that the forward hook has a wing of badger or furnace hackles and a red throat.

Before discussing basic dressings of tandem flies, two points of caution should be mentioned. First, regional fishing laws may regulate the number of hooks permitted. Second, big flies may be no problem for heavy rods, but can strain lighter ones; this can be avoided by using smaller flies tied on smaller hooks. Since trolling flies get thoroughly soaked it is well to dry them before storage to avoid rusting and rotting.

Let's first look at a *tandem fly with a changeable rear hook,* shown in Figure 11–1. Cut a piece of wire (as previously described) about three and a half

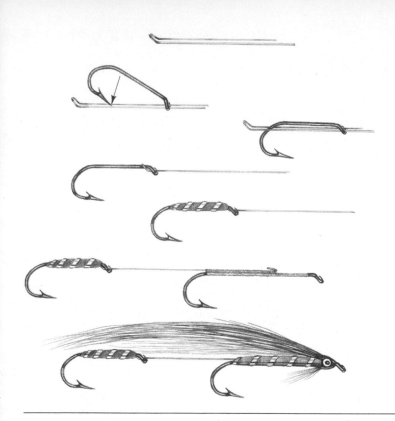

11–1 Tandem fly with
changeable rear hook.

or four inches long. Fold it, leaving one end about a quarter of an inch longer than the other. Pass the open ends through the eye of the rear (dressed or undressed) hook from the rear and loop the wire over the hook shank. Pull the wire tight and wind the hook behind the eye with tying thread of the same color as the body, thus tightly securing the hook in place on the looped wire.

Make a thread body on the forward hook by winding the thread closely from front to rear. Apply lacquer. Lay the doubled wire on the hook and wind closely and tightly forward until the shorter of the two lengths is covered. This should be about a quarter of an inch from the eye. Bend back the single wire tightly toward the rear and tie it down firmly with close windings backward and forward. Apply lacquer. It now is impossible to pull the hooks apart. Proceed to dress the fly as usual.

If the rearward hook needs replacing for any reason, merely cut the windings of thread which lash it down and push the looped wire back and around the hook, thus freeing the hook from the loop. Attach a new dressed or undressed hook in the reverse manner.

The changeable rear hook gives this tandem troller considerable versatility. The rear hook or fly can be changed in a minute or so and the new one can be lashed in place without a vise. Try trailer hooks dressed with fluorescent materials or with marabou. If the forward fly has no red in it, add some to the trailer.

152

Ray Salminen, who conducts fly-tying classes as a hobby and specializes in trolling with flies, has a favorite way of dressing *tandems with fixed rear hooks.* He says, "I use 3/0 silk thread instead of floss, although, if one wishes to attain perfection, the silk thread can be covered with flat nymph thread, which is almost a fine floss. I always use the lightest possible tying thread that is practical for a specific job. Unwaxed thread is used because the bodies are covered with cement. I use Ambroid cement, not lacquer. The cement loses some of its thinner and becomes thick when it gets about halfway down in the bottle. This is what I prefer for coating the inside of bodies."

As indicated by the sketches in Figure 11–2, let's tie a tandem with the hooks and connector totaling three and a half inches long. Insert a size 4 hook (such as Mustad #3399A) in the vise. Start the thread about an eighth of an inch back from the eye and wind down the shank to where it starts to bend, and then wind it over itself back again to the eye.

With a pair of light wire cutters cut two and five-eighths inches of Mason Nylostrand (or equivalent) from the coil. This will have a slight curve. Run the wire through the eye of the hook with the arc of wire curving upward and bind it to the hook on the underside by crisscrossing back and forth with thread along the shank. Apply thick cement to windings, making sure there is still an eighth of an inch of space left behind the hook's eye. Now tie in a strip of tinsel on the side at the very rear end of the wire.

Build up the body with the tying thread (or something else) evenly and smoothly and make a half hitch in the front. Wind the tinsel forward in even spirals. (If the body is made with tying thread, use, for example, orange for the Gray Ghost, black for the Black Ghost, and so on.)

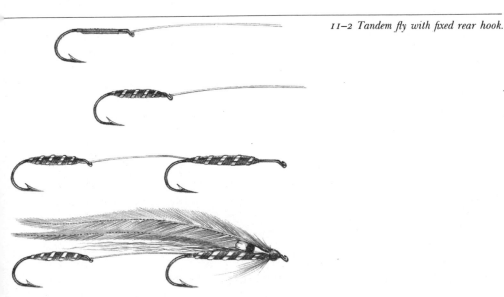

11–2 *Tandem fly with fixed rear hook.*

153

Now build up the eighth-of-an-inch space left at front with the tying thread until it is of the same thickness as the body. Tie off, and coat the entire body with a layer of thin cement, which the thread will absorb.

Remove the rear hook and connector from the vise and in its place fasten a size 2 hook (such as Mustad #9575, which is about one and three-quarters inches long). Starting about half an inch back from the eye, wind the thread back about three-quarters of an inch and then to the point of beginning. Now bend down the Nylostrand at eye of rear hook so that it is reasonably parallel with shank of hook, placing same in slit in vise and a material clip *over* the hook to keep it in place.

The front end of the connecting wire should now be at the point where the thread was started on the front hook, half an inch back of the eye. Take a couple of turns of thread to secure the wire on top of the shank, and apply cement.

Continue winding the thread up the shank until the wire is bound down firmly. Now come back down the shank with the thread and tie in a length of tinsel about an eighth of an inch forward from the extreme rear of the thread on the front hook. (If the tinsel were tied in at the rear and wrapped there it could cause the connector to break the tinsel on the front hook. For this reason thread is left behind the starting point of the tinsel.)

Place the tinsel in the material clip to keep it out of the way and wrap a nicely tapered body with the thread (or other material). Wind on the tinsel and cement several times.

Leaving a half-inch space behind the front hook eye provides sufficient room for completing the wing, throat, etc. On a tandem hookup the body is thinner in the front half due to lack of the connecting wire. This allows adding a small amount of hair on top of the fly before the wing is applied. This method provides a support to attain a better silhouette. When tying tandems with all-tinsel bodies, use white thread. As in the method just described, permit about an eighth of an inch of thread to be exposed before covering the body with tinsel.

Mylar-bodied tandem flies are excellent attractors because the silver Mylar tubing very closely imitates the shiny underbody of a large bait fish. My experience leads me to prefer them, and most of my trolling flies are made that way. The method is simple.

Tie a tandem linkage as has just been described except that it is unnecessary to dress the fly bodies. Lead weighting can be applied to the front hook or to both, if desired. Cut a section of tubing the exact distance from behind the eye of the front hook to the bend of the rear hook. After removing the core, slip the tubing over the front hook. Bend the linkage so it conforms to the bend of the front hook (which puts it in a U position) and work the tubing over the bend and barb of the front hook, over the connector, and over the shank of the rear hook to its bend. The front end of the tubing then should be a quarter of an inch or so behind the eye of the front hook.

Push the barb and bend of the front hook through the tubing and straighten the linkage.

When straightened, the tubing should extend from the bend of the rear hook to enough behind the eye of the front hook to allow the wing, etc., to be dressed without the Mylar interfering with it. If not, trim the Mylar to proper length. Lash down both ends of the tubing as previously described. At this point the tubing can be colored in whole or in part with a felt-tip waterproof marker before applying two or more coats of cement to the body. Then dress the fly as desired.

Some fishermen disapprove of twisted wire on the theory that it weights the fly too much and that weighted trolling flies lack the natural action of bait fish. If weight is necessary they like it on leader or line, not on the fly itself. These men use *spinner-shaft wire* in the same ways discussed above. Those of this opinion may find that spinner-shaft wire kinks a bit more, but that such bending usually can be straightened.

Monofilament is another alternative, but not a very good one because it kinks more than other connectors and may twist the trail hook out of alignment. To use it, cut a section to proper length and hold each tip against the side of a flame until the ends melt into small nubs or balls. This keeps the linkage from slipping. Then dress the fly as has been described.

Finally, for freshwater trolling, it may help to comment on spinners, because they often are used as attractors ahead of the flies. Admittedly, this isn't a proper method of fly fishing, but it is a valuable adjunct to trolling when fish are deep. Few fishermen recognize the differences in spinners, so let's look at four very different types as examples. Some provide more flash, others more attracting vibrations. None have an abundance of both.

The *Williams Firefly Spinner,* available in gold and silver finishes, single and tandem blades, and several sizes, is an oval flat blade which spins at nearly a right angle to its shaft. It is an exceptionally high-speed blade that slices through the water in such a manner as to create steady high-pitched vibrations that attract fish from a distance. It has little flashing value.

With suitable sinking lines the Williams Spinner is a great favorite for attracting denizens of the deep, such as lake trout, to large streamers and bucktails. A good fly is one predominantly yellow, with a touch of red, such as an oversized Dark Edson Tiger.

The *Colorado blade* spins at nearly forty-five degrees from the shaft and vibrates about half as much as the Williams. What it lacks in attracting vibrations is made up for in flash. It is of teardrop design and more dished in shape. It spins wide and slowly and is least popular for use with flies, most popular when used alone with a bare hook attached.

The *Indiana blade* revolves at an angle of only about fifteen degrees and therefore offers less vibration and more flash. It is a dished oval design and primarily a flasher. Like the Colorado blade, it is most popular in silver finish. A tiny blade, about half an inch long, in connection with a small

155

sparse bucktail or streamer can be cast easily with a fly rod and will attract big fish, especially when sputtered across current.

The *Willowleaf blade* is a pointed elongated oval design only slightly dished. It spins close and fast to its shaft and therefore offers less resistance to water than any of the others. It provides almost no vibration, but a maximum of flash. It gives more of an illusion of a bait fish than any of the others. Very small Willowleafs are great attractors with small flies.

Thus, spinners, as adjuncts to streamers and bucktails, offer in varying degree the qualities of flash, vibration, and motion. Of these four the Williams and the Willowleaf are opposites, the former being primarily a vibrator and the latter a flasher. Vibrators are favored for very deep fishing or for action in discolored water. Water is a better sound conductor than air, and fish can find a vibrator long before they can see it. Flashers are superior nearer the surface.

Tube flies in Iceland—How to make a simple tube fly—Advantages of color interchangeability—Plastic and metal tubes—Quill tubes—Two ways of rigging tubes—Notes on hooks—Tiny tubes—Color suggestions—Comments and history of tubes

12

The Versatility of Tube Flies

THE CLEAR, COLD WATERS of southwestern Iceland's small Laxá and Bugdá rivers merge amid lush meadowland a mile above the volcanic waterfalls which dump the combined streams into an estuary of the sea. They meet in a large pool marked from the point of land by a visible edge of currents sometimes made more obvious by the muddying of one stream or the other after rains. Salmon seasonally lie in large numbers hidden in the depths along the edge, one or another often firing the angler's adrenalin by lazy rolls or splashing jumps. When extending casts toward and beyond the merging currents swing the fly deeply downstream, the drift often is interrupted by a strong pull. The angler is fast to a bright Atlantic salmon which may race about the big pool, taking the line deeply into its backing, or which may flash down fast water toward the falls before breaking loose or finally giving up and being led gently but firmly onto the beach.

Such fishing can be a feast or a famine, and this was an hour of famine. Repeated casts with flies changed from large to small and from bright to dark brought no response. No technique worked. As I was changing to still another pattern my guide, who had been dividing his time with a rod upstream, waded out and offered me something new.

"Try this tube fly," he invited. "They often do well when usual patterns fail."

I looked at the fly with concealed distaste. I had read about tube flies, principally in British angling periodicals, and had used them a few times where legality permitted, but had dismissed them as being rather outlandish and unsporting.

The short metal tube of this one was dressed bucktail-fashion with long, soft black hair. A plastic bit of tube had been pushed far enough onto the rear of the metal one to hold firmly. I strung this onto the leader and tied the leader's end to a No. 8 treble hook, the eye of which then was pushed into the rear of the plastic tube. The connection of hook to fly was flexible,

157

so less leverage was available for the fish to try to free itself, as it often can from standard long-shanked bucktails.

The unusual fly cast well and quickly submerged close to the edge of the current. I watched the white fly line as it veered while the current took the tube fly downstream. It had made only slight progress when the rod tip snapped down with a jolt. I was fast to a salmon, which, when beached, weighed fourteen pounds. During that hour I hooked and landed two more bright and lusty large Atlantic salmon on the tube fly.

As Olé, the guide, and I rested against a rock at stream's edge, I looked at the tube fly with renewed interest. Olé produced a little box which contained many more tube-fly components in a variety of dark, medium, and bright colors. The tubes mostly were tiny and not over half an inch long. Two tubes could be strung on the leader, providing a variety of color combinations. Some of the hooks were bare, some lightly hackled, and some had had their shanks dipped in fluorescent paint. If an angler had only six forward tubes and six rear ones he would have a combination of three dozen color possibilities, with others provided by dressed or painted hooks. Forward tubes often merely are hackled collars, or hair splayed backward on each side, like a jet's wings. Others can be dressed like the wings of bucktails or streamers. Rear tubes can have their bodies dressed in tinsel and/or floss and can contain a secondary wing or tail. The possibilities are infinite.

"Iceland permits treble hooks," I remarked rather needlessly to Olé, "because fish taken are expected to be kept. In America we wouldn't use trebles for trout because they usually are illegal and because trout usually should be released. Regardless of that, tube flies should be excellent for bass and various pond fish, and they could be adapted to saltwater fly fishing."

"Treble hooks allow the fly to swim best," Olé answered, "but we often use double hooks with tube flies, and they even work all right with singles. A great advantage is that much smaller and shorter hooks can be used because they are not related to the size of the body. These lighter hooks make the fly cast better, and they will hold at least as well.

"Another advantage," he continued, "is that the plastic body of an unweighted tube fly is soft. It may be a personal opinion of mine, but I'm sure fish will hold onto the soft body longer, without spitting it out, so hooking possibilities are increased. This is one of the reasons why your plastic worms are so successful."

As I lighted my pipe I looked at the three beautiful salmon lying in the grass and thought of all the fruitless casting I had done before trying the tube fly.

"Tube flies must have some quality that appeals to salmon when they won't take anything else," I thought, and then said to Olé, "I recollect what Charlie Ritz said in his book *A Fly Fisher's Life*; it was to the effect that in the three years before he wrote the book he used nothing but tube flies for

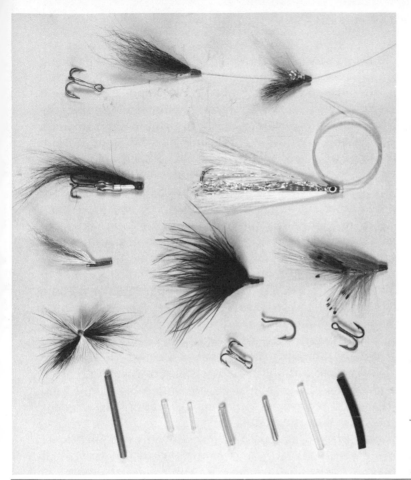

12–1 Tube flies and components. At top, a freshwater, nonrigid tube fly strung on monofilament with parts separated. Next, a black bucktail tube fly with flexible plastic tube linkage and a typical saltwater tube fly. In the three bottom rows, miscellaneous dressed and undressed tubes and suitable hooks.

salmon and took more than one hundred and fifty in that time, while his friends took several hundred more. He said that he preferred tube flies to all flies used for salmon. But what makes tube flies so effective in themselves or as a change-of-pace fly?"

Olé glanced at his watch and began to pack our gear for the jeep ride back to the lodge for lunch. "Who knows why salmon do things?" he said. "Some say it's the flow of water and oxygen through the tube that adds to action, but the tube is so small, with the leader passing through it, that I doubt it. It may be the different action of the tube body or because the fly reacts better to the varying flows of river currents. I like to use conventional flies first but, when they don't get results, I always change to tube flies, and they usually improve the score."

This conversation happened on my first trip to Iceland, several years ago. Since then I have become convinced that tube flies with single hooks are very effective for trout when dressed streamer fashion as well as when made for fishing in the surface film or as nymphs. They should do well for steelhead, midwest and Pacific salmon, and in fly rodding for bass and pond

159

fishes. They should be effective in salt water, although, as this is being written, there are no documented experiences to relate.

This versatility is because of the wide range in colors and sizes of tubes; their availability in all weights from surface fishing to bottom bumping; the interchangeability of a complete variety of color combinations in hair, feathers, flosses, and tinsels; and the fact that they can be made in sizes from very tiny to the largest that can be cast. Fly tyers with even elementary ability can make them, and if any are discarded later for one reason or another, we haven't wasted hooks. Let's make one with materials all fly tyers have on hand in order to learn the basics. Then we can see how to do a wealth of others which may be more suitable.

Cut the cylindrical part of the metal filler of a ball-point pen into four equal sections, each of which will then be about an inch long. If wire cutters are used, or the cutting jaws of fisherman's pliers, we'll need a reamer to restore ends to a cylindrical shape. If the reamer can flare out each end a bit this will help to prevent tying thread from slipping off. Also deburr both ends, if possible, to smooth them and prevent fraying the leader. Now we need something to hold the little tube securely in the vise. Try a tapered darning needle, or something similar, clamping its end in the vise. The tube should slip securely over this, without its holder's end protruding. Fasten the tying thread at the head of the tube, as in dressing a hook, and wind the thread to the rear end. Secure with a half hitch and apply lacquer for a good base on which to make the body.

Dress the body with floss and/or tinsel as in dressing any streamer body, securing this covering with a few windings of the thread (or with a half hitch) which has been brought forward. Now for the wings, in a choice of two ways. For the first way, take a small bunch of bucktail or other hair (about thirty hairs) and tie it on top of the tube so that it flares out slightly. Turn the tube halfway around and do the same on the opposite side of the head. The tube will look something like an aircraft with the two bunches of hair representing backswept wings. For the second way, apply a little more hair all around the head of the tube—not too much, because the body should show through. Wind on part of a hackle as a collar, if you wish, but this isn't necessary. Finish and varnish the head to complete the tube fly. Slide this onto the leader and fasten on the hook, preferably a treble one in size 6 or 8. This part of the tackle is now ready for fishing.

How can we improve on this experiment?

In the first place, pen refill tubes are a bit large in diameter for small tube flies. Second, the cut ends of metal can chafe the leader. Chafing is prevented by inserting a piece of plastic tubing that will comfortably fit the bore of the metal tube. Cut it so it protrudes not more than an eighth of an inch on both ends. Apply lacquer (cement) to the outside of the plastic tube so it won't slip in the metal one. Slightly flared lips can be made on the ends of the plastic by holding it momentarily against a flame such as a cigarette lighter. This flaring smooths the tube ends to prevent chafing of the leader, and also helps keep tying thread from slipping. Many of these tubes can be made at one time, ready for dressing when desired.

Now, let's discuss other tubes and where to get them. There are plastic tubes for unweighted lures and for liners, aluminum tubes for lightly weighted lures, and copper or brass tubes for deeper fishing. All of these come in various small sizes suitable for making tube flies.

Plastic tubing can be bought from hobby shops such as those that sell materials for making model airplanes, etc. If you know a doctor or nurse, ask for a few feet of surgical tubing in whatever small sizes are available. If you know a telephone repairman or anyone else who works for Ma Bell, ask for a foot or two of telephone cable. This is a bunch of plastic-coated wires in many colors of plastic to distinguish one wire from others. Pull out the wires to obtain the fine tubing in so many colors that you won't have to bother to dress the bodies! This tubing is fairly flexible and should be stored straight; lengths can be fastened to a straight stick with rubber bands.

Tubes with the smallest diameter which will accommodate the leader are preferable for most freshwater fishing. A great favorite is made from tubular lead solder about a sixteenth of an inch in diameter with flux in the core. Cut this to proper length and soak it in acetone to remove the flux. After the fly is tied and *before* the cement has set, insert a .020-to-.025-inch-diameter wire into the tube, or when the cement dries it will shrink the tube to such an extent that the leader can't be run through it. This lead tubing will not fray the leader, and its minimal weight hardly compensates for the buoyancy of the dressing.

Remember that tubes made from harder metals such as brass must be deburred and the ends must be flared, or they will fray the leader. Connoisseurs of tube flies often think that plastic tubing is too thick and doesn't make a very neat job.

Metal tubing can be obtained from hobby shops. A doctor can save used hypodermic needles for you, which can be cut into small tubes. Soft-metal tubes in many diameters are used for crimping trolling leaders usually used in saltwater fishing. These are made by the Sevenstrand Tackle Manufacturing Company, of Westminster, California, and are available at tackle shops dealing in such equipment. The four smallest sizes are best for tube flies.

Quills of feathers can be cleaned and cut for very light tube flies. By the time this book sees the light of day, many tackle dealers should be selling tubes of all types. Tube flies are well established in the United Kingdom, and one can send $2 to get by air mail Veniard's 140-page catalog of fly-dressing materials. (Part of this cost is refunded on your first order.) John Veniard, of E. Veniard (Retail) Ltd., is active in British fly-fishing circles and runs the largest fly-dressing-materials firm in Great Britain. Address: 138 Northwood Road, Thornton Heath, Surrey, England.

Veniard offers four types of tubes in seven sizes ranging between half

161

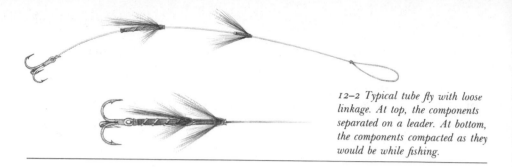

12–2 Typical tube fly with loose linkage. At top, the components separated on a leader. At bottom, the components compacted as they would be while fishing.

an inch and two inches in length. One type is a plastic tube with rounded ends; another is a stronger plastic one with a cavity for the hook's eye. Veniard also offers a plastic-lined aluminum tube for lightweight fishing and a plastic-lined brass tube for deeper water. I have found that some of Veniard's tubes can be cut in two, with the rounded end at the head, so that the two-inch tube, for example, can be made into two one-inch ones.

When dressing tubes I like them as short as possible so that more than one can be put on the leader, if desired, without making the lure too long. The front tube, which often has hackle wound on as a collar, need not be more than half an inch long, just enough to hold the dressing. The rear tube need be no longer than an inch, often shorter. Very small tubes, both in diameter and length, make better tube flies than thicker and longer ones, and they cast better with the smaller hooks, which are as efficient as larger ones.

There are two ways of rigging tube flies: with a loose hook and with a hook whose eye is secured in the rear end of a plastic sleeve. In the former method one or more components, such as a short hackled tube and a longer body tube, are strung on the leader before tying on the hook. These components, of course, can slide up the leader when a fish is hooked. The short-shanked hook provides little or no leverage, so the fish can't wear a hole where the barb is and thus work the hook loose, as it sometimes can with longer ones.

In the latter method the tube is of metal and a very short end is left undressed so a short plastic tube of slightly larger diameter can be pushed over it far enough to hold the plastic tube securely. This plastic tube normally is not over three-quarters of an inch long. The hook, attached to the leader, then is pushed into the plastic tube far enough to cover the hook's eye. This linkage can bend enough to prevent the hook from wearing loose. Experienced anglers seem to favor the latter method, perhaps only because we have had better success with it.

162 In selecting treble hooks for tube flies, use the smallest that seem practical and insist on those with straight eyes (turned neither up nor down). The eyes of many brands can be bent straight without snapping, but this is a remedy of last resort. The eyes of straight-eyed treble hooks should be pear-shaped rather than rounded, so that they can be pushed into the plastic sleeves more easily. Most treble hooks have rounded eyes, but they

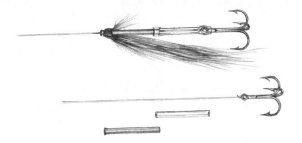

12–3 Typical tube fly with fixed linkage. Both the metal and the plastic tubes can be only about half as long as shown—just long enough so they and the hook can be joined together.

can be crimped into pear shape. Try this carefully with fisherman's pliers. We often do it on streamside by holding the hook's bend with pliers, laying the eye vertically against a large rock, and tapping it into oval shape with a small one.

Double hooks can be adjusted in the same ways when necessary.

Single hooks, which often would be proper or required for trout fishing, can be of the short-shank salmon-egg type. These usually come either with turned-up or turned-down eyes. It is easy to straighten most brands with pliers, and the small eyes should fit into the plastic sleeves without difficulty.

My early aversion to tube flies turned to admiration when I realized how delicate they could be and how sensible they are for trout fishing even on streams where all fish must be released. Tiny tube flies with very small short-shanked single hooks are fun to fish with and can be lighter than other types tied on standard single or double hooks. The tubes of these tiny flies can have bores so small that heavy leaders won't pass through them. They can be made weightless enough to float or can be weighted as much as necessary. Whether or not the combinations seem to the angler to imitate anything in particular, success with them indicates they are attractive to fish.

Any pattern combinations that could be suggested would vary with where we are fishing and what we are fishing for, so everyone should plan his own set. The following six rear-tube and forward-tube combinations might do for a start. The feather wings or bucktail wings of the forward tubes should be long enough to cover the rear tubes. The collars should be long enough to partly mask the rear tubes. Of course, collars or throats can be added to the winged tubes if desired. These six rear and forward tubes offer three dozen combinations, and all can be carried, with an assortment of hooks, in a container about as small as a matchbox.

Rear Tube	Forward Tube
Silver with red tail	Badger or furnace hackles
White with silver rib	Grizzly hackles
Yellow with gold rib	Peacock over brown bucktail
Black with silver rib	Black over yellow bucktail
Red with silver rib	Gray squirrel as collar
Red with peacock tail	Yellow hackle as collar

163

Tube flies have been popular in European countries for more than a quarter of a century, but American anglers have failed to recognize their effectiveness. An author in the September 1959 issue of *Trout and Salmon* says, "Perhaps the most important advance which has occurred in salmon fly fishing since Wood introduced the greased-line method is the appearance of the tube fly. Armed with a treble hook it swims better, casts better, and hooks far better than the traditional fly."

While the above author is an Atlantic salmon specialist, he could have said the same about tube flies with respect to other species, and he need not have confined his remarks to the use of treble hooks. Tube flies open another avenue of fun and experimentation in fly tying and in fly fishing, even though they may not be suitable or permissible everywhere. Luckily, in angling, no one method or type of tackle is the answer to every need.

Who started all this? Historically it is verified that tube flies were originated about 1945 by the noted fly dresser Mrs. Minnie Morawski, when she was working for the tackle firm of Charles Playfair & Company, of Aberdeen, Scotland. At first she used sections of turkey wing quills with the pith scraped out and with the shanks of the strung treble hooks inside the quill sections. She dressed orthodox flies (body dressing, wing, hackle, etc.) on these. A doctor named William Michie, when visiting the shop, suggested using sections of surgical tubing instead. Later the treble hook was left on the outside so the tube could travel up the leader, out of harm's way, when a fish was hooked. Also the wing later was dressed around the tube, instead of in only one place. We now do these things both ways, according to individual choice.

13

Those Marvelous Matukus, and Other Fixed-Wing Patterns

While in the South Pacific during World War II, I met Australian and New Zealand anglers-turned-soldiers who showed me a fly type which we, more or less in error, call the Matuka: a fixed-wing streamer in which the forward part of the wing is laced to the body by ribbing, thus preventing the tendency of the wing to foul itself in casting by catching under the bend of the hook.

In spite of this advantage I rejected the fixed-wing concept as lacking in adequate action, and forgot about it. After all, who wants to dampen wing action by tying it down? Or so I thought, forgetting a statement by one of my college professors to the effect that every idea should be given a fair chance.

Soon after returning home I began correspondence with a prominent New Zealand angler named Hector Sodersten, of Rotorua, who sent me a beautiful set of several dozen New Zealand flies, including many of the fixed-wing type. After considerable admiration I put them away and later gave them to a collector who wanted to frame them for museum exhibition. I remember asking friend Hector why New Zealand anglers didn't use our free-wing streamers and bucktails. He showed the letter to members of his angling club. The verdict was to "tell that Yank, Bates, not to knock a deadly type of fly until he gives it a few swims." New Zealanders *have* used our free-wings, but they think their fixed-wings are more effective, and they have submitted many photographs of giant rainbows to prove the point.

165

It was a decade or two later before New Zealand's fixed-wing flies became recognized in North America, helped along by anglers with more perception than I exhibited—for example, famous angling artist and fly dresser Dave Whitlock, who wrote about them in *Field & Stream* magazine. So, at long last, I tried fixed-wings, found them effective, renewed my correspondence with New Zealand anglers such as Hector Sodersten, and concluded that fixed-wing streamers (which we now call Matukas) are well worth using and writing about. However, there are some misconceptions remaining to be cleared up. There is much more to be said about them and how to dress and fish them, as this chapter will reveal.

First, the proper name is Matuk*u*, rather than Matuk*a*. *Matuku* is the Maori word for a bird similar to what we know as a bittern, as respected in New Zealand as the American eagle is over here. The name is improperly applied because bitterns are on the protected list, and their feathers no longer are used in flies. No matter. Others are just as good, or better. In New Zealand, Australia, and elsewhere, fixed-wing streamers no longer are called Matukus. Except for one or two specific patterns, all fixed-wing streamers are called what they are—fixed-wing streamers. In North America we now call them Matukas, and the name, although incorrect, probably will stick. We note that the word is used elsewhere also. For example, these flies were called Matukas in Hardy Brothers catalogs back in the 1930s. In this book let's properly call them fixed-wing streamers except in the rare case or two when they are properly called Matukus. Let's start with their New Zealand background, and then see what we can add to it. We'll learn herein a lot more about an unusual and highly effective fly type that should add greatly to fishing fun and success.

Fixed-wing streamers are effective not only because the laced-down wing prevents its fouling under the hook's bend. The wing barbules still provide a lot of action, and the lacing down presents a slim silhouette, more like a natural bait fish. The fly's body and wing do not separate into a V as too often happens with free-wing streamers. Shorter hooks can be used, thus reducing leverage. Weighted or unweighted, we arrive at an entirely different action. Under varying conditions one type or the other may be more effective. That is for each of us to decide. Incidentally, if we should think that fixed-wing streamers lack sufficient action, we should remember that New Zealanders think that American flies "have movement to excess."

New Zealand was, and still is to an extent, a trout fisher's paradise. Rainbow trout were introduced there between 1883 and 1884. They were first liberated in tremendous Lake Taupo in 1903. There they reached phenomenal weights, large numbers exceeding twenty-five pounds. Originally, they overtook the food supply, and recourse to large-scale netting was employed to prevent deterioration. Recent reports indicate excellent lake and stream fishing, but in smaller sizes and quantities. Brown trout also had been introduced, and they proliferated to such an extent that many anglers (preferring the rainbows) considered them a pest.

166

It is not recorded who took the first trout on a fly in New Zealand, although many have claimed the distinction. Even as far back as the early 1880s there were many anglers there. Strangely enough, however, it was not a white man but a native Maori who first developed the fixed-wing or Matuku type of fly. This seems particularly strange because the Maoris fished for food rather than for sport. Any method that took the most fish the quickest was the popular one, regardless of fishing regulations, unless the authorities were looking on.

Under the glut of good fishing that existed in New Zealand in these early years, why should the native meat fishermen bother with nets or bait when even the crudest form of fly would take fish on cast after cast merely by tossing a line in the water?

No one really knows where the Maoris got the idea of using artificial flies with their crude tackle, but it may have been a hand-me-down from some of the Atlantic salmon patterns the first British settlers brought with them under the impression that they might be useful. Anyway, the Maoris were noted as fly fishermen, albeit with what we would call crude tackle; in fact, they were, and still are, renowned as great fishermen for any type of fish.

The first New Zealand Matuku evidently consisted of a single hackle bound to the body of the fly to provide a long, thin silhouette intended to resemble a smelt. We could presume they did it that way because it was sturdy as well as easy for tyers lacking cement and much knowledge of knots. It would appear that the Maori type of fly was evolved soon after rainbow trout became prolific during the first years of this century.

The faint cream to dull black feathers of the *matuku* bird were great favorites with the Maoris for their fishing, perhaps due to superstition or respect for the bird, or because they considered it lucky. The brown bittern (called by the Maoris *matuku-kurepo*) has the Latin name *Botaurus poiciloptilus*. As I have said, its feathers no longer are legally used for fly dressing because it is on the protected list.

The use of *matuku* feathers became prohibited gradually. Letters from the New Zealand Wildlife Service (1977) say that the bittern was first protected by legislation in the Animals Protection Act of 1907, which made it an offense to "take or kill," but not to possess. It would therefore not have been illegal under this act to have bittern feathers and to use them in fly tying.

The Animals Protection Act of 1922 made it illegal to have such feathers in possession. In 1950 this was specifically brought into the Rotorua and Taupo Regulations because a number of birds still were being shot for the feathers despite the fact that since the 1920s a considerable number of skins were being imported into New Zealand from Australia. The Australian bird was so similar to the New Zealand one that it was virtually impossible to tell the difference. In the early 1960s the Australians made it illegal to export bittern feathers or skins, or to have them in possession. Consequently the true Matuku, or bittern, fly has disappeared and, over the years,

167

imitations have been developed. This protection of the bittern more largely was due to the fact that, in addition to the use of the feathers in New Zealand, great quantities of skins were being exported to Europe and elsewhere.

In New Zealand anyone now found in possession of *matuku* feathers in any form is dealt with severely by the courts. Bittern (or *matuku*) plumage is virtually unobtainable, and the name has passed out of New Zealand fly dressing and angling to the extent that it is all but unknown to the younger generation there.

While all this may or may not be of interest to readers, the background of Matuku flies never before to my knowledge has been explained in any book on angling. Let's now ignore the bird and its feathers and consider how this type of fly can be used to improve our fishing. For that, *matuku* feathers may not be even as good as those of many other birds. New Zealanders and Australians now use substitutes such as the plumage of the soft flank feathers of the hen ringneck pheasant, feathers from the German owl, the light hawk, or the well-barred ones from a bird they call the grizzel, etc. I have two New Zealand flies with genuine *matuku* feathers dressed in the early 1920s. The feathers have soft, wide spade hackles, slightly barred in a gray-brown color. If such were to be selected from the flank of a hen pheasant, I doubt that anyone could tell the difference.

Since the flies on which these substitutes (and others such as barnyard-fowl hackles) are used are given different names from Matuku, this name has been forgotten to the extent that if anyone asked for Matuku flies in a New Zealand tackle shop he would be met by a blank stare. We can call them Matukus or Matukas if we wish, but back in their home territory they are referred to as fixed-wing streamers, or, more easily, "longtails."

Author Keith Draper, of Tackle House, Ltd., Taupo, in his *Trout Flies of New Zealand* lists only one fly under the name of Matuku. This, on long-shanked hooks in sizes 2 through 8, has a yellow or orange wool or chenille body and a wing of two soft hen pheasant flank feathers tied on back to back and bound to the body with oval gold or silver tinsel ribbing taken through the wings.

The two genuine Matukus lent to me are tied on regular Limerick TDE trout hooks in size 6. One body is of red wool with fine gold tinsel ribbing (five turns) and a sparse brown hackle collar. The other has a yellow wool body with a red tag (or butt) and fine gold tinsel ribbing (four turns) plus a sparse brown hackle collar. Each has a wing of two *matuku* feathers about twice the length of the hook. The flies are rather crudely tied. They are shown in Color Plate V.

168

Hector Sodersten, who located these old and rare examples, comments: "One has a yellow body and it is easily seen how it became the prototype of the Parsons' Glory. Resemblance is apparent. The other has a red body and it is easily seen where our Hawk and Red evolved. Lengths overall are two inches and one and a half inches respectively. These two flies were tied by a white angler. So far as I can ascertain there was no appreciable difference between the Maori and the white methods of tying."

New Zealand writers who describe the original Matuku flies say the wool or chenille body can be of any color the angler fancies. Usually the barbules of that part of the two wing feathers contacting the hook's shank are stripped off on their lower sides so their spines can be laid directly on the shank. Otherwise, the Matuku types are dressed in the same way as free-wing streamers except that the ribbing, tied in securely at the tail, is wound on after the wing is applied, so that it can be wound in between the upper barbules of the wing feathers in four or five turns, then tied in at the head. The upper barbules which have become crushed down in doing this can be picked out with a pointed instrument such as a pin or a bodkin. The optional addition of a collar or throat is a later development (since 1920). The part of the wing which extends beyond the bend of the hook is not stripped and is about as long as the body. This free part of the wing provides most of the action, although the barbules over the shank of the hook also contribute to it.

The red-bodied fly in Color Plate V is the *only one* named Matuku that is sold commercially in New Zealand as this is being written. It was provided by Pakes Sports Store in Rotorua.

The Taupo area of New Zealand, with its big lake of that name and its many streams, is one of the best rainbow trout regions in the islands. Keith Draper, previously mentioned, the prominent angling authority and fly dresser, is the author of several valuable booklets on New Zealand fly patterns. He was kind enough to provide a list of his "ten best" and to give their dressing instructions. These follow, and some are shown in Color Plate V. Descriptions in his words are included.

GREY GHOST
HOOK SIZE: 2 to 10
RIBBING: Oval silver tinsel
BODY: Flat silver tinsel
WING: Two cock's hackles dyed gray
HACKLE: Two or three turns of a gray hackle

"The most effective sizes are 8 and 10. We like the head painted grey, with a small white eye and black pupil because this enhances the likeness to a smelt. Different-colored bodies can be turned out, the most popular being green. The hackle adds to the fly but can be dispensed with. This is a very useful fly for smelting fish and, in the larger sizes, real good as a trolling lure." Carrie Stevens' most famous pattern roams far afield! Why not dress it as she did, adding shoulders and cheeks after the wing has been tied down?

169

RABBIT FLY
HOOK SIZE: 2 to 10
TAG: A few whisks of red or yellow hackle
RIBBING: Oval silver or gold tinsel
BODY: Wool or chenille, color to suit
WING: A strip of rabbit pelt with ends nicely tapered
HACKLE: To suit, but usually tied to match the body color. For yellow- or orange-bodied flies a pale hackle is used, whereas for night patterns a black or claret hackle does well.

"This popular and effective fly was originated in the 1930s mostly as a night fly using black rabbit fur. Grey fur was used with equal success. It is a great fly in rivers for lake-run fish. The skin softens and the fur works and ripples with every movement of current. Tied on size 8 or even on 10 hooks it makes a good smelt fly. In the larger sizes, with two cheeks of hen pheasant feathers tied in alongside the body, it can be employed usefully where larger bait fish abound." Of course this is a *type* rather than a specific pattern, and is one that we should find very useful. With the rabbit skin fur side down, use a straightedge and razor blade to cut very narrow (one-eighth inch) strips with the grain of the fur. Cut the strips a bit longer than twice the length of the hook's shank, and taper each end to a narrow V, stripping the front end slightly. Tie in the forward point as with any streamer wing. Then run the ribbing in three or four turns through the separated fur and pick out with a pointed instrument the fur which has become crushed down by the ribbing. Properly done, the fur shows no separations where the ribbing has passed through it. Color combinations are the angler's choice, and any soft fur can be used, such as possum, squirrel or fox.

Here are two popular New Zealand rabbit-fur patterns, both using a wing of fairly long gray rabbit fur. One has a red hackle tail, a black wool body, oval silver ribbing, and a black hackle collar. The other has a white hackle tail, a red wool body, oval silver ribbing, and a white hackle collar. American designs could resemble any of our imitator or attractor patterns with the advantages of having a fixed-wing "longtail" with a fluffy, action-filled wing not unlike a combination of marabou and hackles.

DOROTHY (RED)
HOOK SIZE: 2 to 8
TAIL: Red wool (or hackle)
RIBBING: Oval silver tinsel
BODY: Red wool (or chenille)
WING: Two well-barred grizzly hackles
COLLAR: Two turns of above

"Tied as above, it can take its place with the best. A popular variation is the Yellow Dorothy. This is the same except that it has a yellow body. In New Zealand it is particularly effective on dull days, in the evening, or during a change of light. As in all these flies, the wing is bound on Matuku-style."

HAWK
HOOK SIZE: 2 to 10
TAIL: A very small bunch of red hackle fibers
RIBBING: Oval silver tinsel
BODY: Yellow wool or chenille
WING: Two flank feathers of the harrier hawk tied in Matuku-style

"A variation of this pattern is the same except that it has no tail and has a body of embossed flat silver tinsel. In the past this was a most popular fly but is seldom in use these days, due no doubt to the scarcity of good skins. The paler the bird, the better the fly. This is a good killer when the trout are in a taking mood." The soft, marabou-like very light gray or very light brown flank feathers of a hen pheasant or white turkey can substitute for hawk. The proper feathers are very light and fluffy with tips of the neck-hackle type.

BLACK PRINCE
HOOK SIZE: 2 to 8
TAG: Red wool or hackle fibers
RIBBING: Oval silver tinsel
BODY: Black wool or chenille
WING: Two black cock's hackles
COLLAR: Two turns of a black hackle

"A variation of this is the same except that it has no tail and has a body of red wool or chenille. It is a good night fly much in evidence in the Rotorua district in years past. It is always worth a 'swim' fished by the usual nightly methods and will take its toll with the best."

PARSONS' GLORY
HOOK SIZES: 2 to 10
TAIL: A small bunch of red or orange hackle fibers
RIBBING: Oval silver tinsel
BODY: Yellow chenille or wool
WING: Two well-marked honey grizzly neck hackles
COLLAR: Two turns of above (optional)

171

"This undoubtedly is New Zealand's favorite daytime lure. It was evolved many years ago by Philip Parsons, a farmer who fished the Taupo area during the heyday of New Zealand's trouting. Much of its success depends on the well-marked honey grizzly feathers used for the wing, representing the markings of the sides of fingerling trout. Wing colors can vary from pale buff to ginger.''

TAUPO TIGER (or TIGER ROSS)
HOOK SIZE: 2 to 8
HEAD: Red
TAIL: A small bunch of red hackle fibers
RIBBING: Oval silver tinsel
BODY: Yellow chenille or wool
WING: Two badger hackles with pronounced black centers
COLLAR: Two turns of a badger hackle (optional)

"This fly ranks high in popularity and was originated about 1930 by James Ross. Being in the tackle business he tried to keep retail rights to himself. Although he could not patent the dressing he was able to register Tiger Ross as the trade name, so others called it the Taupo Tiger. It is a consistent taker, in large sizes for trolling and in small sizes for casting when trout are smelting. The Tiger is readily identified as being the only fly featuring a red head. A variation is the same, but with a grass-green body.''

GINGER MICK
HOOK SIZE: 2 to 8
TAIL: A small bunch of yellow hackle fibers
RIBBING: Oval silver tinsel
BODY: Red chenille or wool
WING: Two ginger cock hackles with black centers
COLLAR: Two turns of a ginger cock hackle

"While a close relative to the Parsons' Glory this fly doesn't enjoy the latter's popularity, although it has its adherents, particularly among trollers. Otherwise it is a useful standby. Other body colors are yellow and green.''

HOPE'S SILVERY
HOOK SIZE: 2 to 8
TAIL: The tip of a barred rock feather, bunched
RIBBING: Oval silver tinsel
BODY: White wool or chenille
WING: A strip of pale blue silk floss tied in along each side and extending slightly beyond the bend of the hook, over which are tied down two pale buff or palest honey grizzly hackles. Over this, as a topping and not tied down, are from six to eight green peacock sword fibers.

172

"This more elaborate southern New Zealand pattern is particularly popular in the Canterbury area. It is intended to simulate the features of a smelt; hence the strips of floss which impart a bluish tinge along the sides. It is a lovely pattern and swims most realistically. Primarily it is a daytime fly with a reputation of appealing to brown trout, but it also is considered valuable on moonlight nights."

JACK'S SPRAT
HOOK SIZE: 2 to 8
RIBBING: Oval silver tinsel
BODY: Oval silver tinsel
WING: Two badger hackles
COLLAR: Two turns of a badger hackle (optional)

"This pattern was designed by Jack England, a onetime tackle dealer on the Tongariro River. It is a first-rate smelt fly in the smaller sizes. If jungle cock is available, a pair of cheeks add to effectiveness. It is considered a 'must' when fish are on the smelt."

In commenting on these patterns of fixed-wing or longtail flies selected by Keith Draper, we note a pronounced similarity in the shapes of most of them. Americans will think the idea is more important than the patterns because the idea can be applied to many feather-winged streamers which we consider important. Since the ribbing holds the wing down it should be tightly anchored with thread. While most of these patterns call for two wing feathers, four often are used.

In addition to the above Matuku, Matuka, fixed-wing, or longtail patterns—whatever we wish to call them—there are several other New Zealand types which may present creative ideas to other fly dressers.

The Fuzzy Wuzzy is a type one of which includes black squirrel tail, red chenille, and large black cock's hackles. The small bunch of squirrel tail is fairly long. Midway along the chenille body are several turns of black hackle slanting about forty-five degrees backward. This is repeated at the head. This is a crayfish imitation and should be fished very slow and deep.

Sometimes soft fur, such as opossum, is substituted for the hackle and is applied as a double wing tied in both at the midsection and at the head. For example, the Yellow Fuzz has a tail of opossum tail, a body of yellow chenille, and a double wing of two bunches of opossum tail fur tied in at the top of the body.

13–1 The Fuzzy Wuzzy.

173

13–2 *The Killer.*

The <u>Killer</u> style includes several patterns such as the Mrs. Simpson, Lord's Killer, Hamill's Killer, Barred Killer, and Leslie's Lure. All have a squirrel's tail tail and the "cased" body feathers of a bird, often of a hen pheasant. Apply a small bunch of squirrel for the tail without flaring it out. Tie in a body feather on each side of this to encase the base of the tail. Build the body with a strand of wool. Midway along the body tie in two body feathers on each side to slightly overlap those at the tail. Do the same at the head, so there are five body feathers on each side, with the middle pairs slightly larger than the others. The body feathers "case" the body of the fly, meeting above and below, so little of the body can be seen.

Dressed as above, the <u>Mrs. Simpson</u> has a tail of black squirrel, a body of red wool or chenille, and side feathers of the brownish-black rump feathers of a male ringneck pheasant.

Also dressed as above, the <u>Hamill's Killer</u> has a tail of black squirrel, a body of red wool or chenille, and side feathers of gray partridge dyed pale green. Both of these flies are very famous patterns fished sunken and retrieved in slow jerks a few inches at a time.

Another type is the <u>Split Partridge</u>, which employs a bird's middle tail feather (both sides matched), such as a partridge or grouse. Split a section of this feather carefully with a razor blade and match the two parts, back to back. Tie this in as a wing in the same manner that the previously described fixed-wing patterns are dressed, separating the barbules with a bodkin to accommodate the ribbing. In this case there could be a tail of some sort, such as hair, and probably a collar or throat, tied over any suitable body material. The spine of the split wing extends slightly beyond the bend of the hook.

Readers or dealers who desire authentic New Zealand patterns can obtain them by mail order from Tackle House, Ltd., Heu Heu Street, Taupo, New Zealand. Keith Draper is the managing director of this reliable establishment, and as I have noted he has written several valuable booklets

13–3 *The Split Partridge.*

on dressing all types of flies used in Australia, New Zealand, and Tasmania.

American free-wing patterns have made no more of an impression in those countries than their fixed wings have over here. To each his own! I hope that this chapter will spread some of the news about what anglers under the Southern Cross are doing and that we under the North Star will profit by it. We still may prefer our own patterns, as they prefer theirs, but many of their ideas can be converted to our own uses—and vice versa.

Anglers in New Zealand mention several basic principles which we can compare with ours:

"Size, shape, and color are conveyed by the type of feathers used; and especially entry, which means a streamed effect when drawn through the water, leaving no unnatural wake."

"When using longtails certainly the most important factor is the way the fly is manipulated in the water. Other factors contributing to success are the color of the fly, its makeup, and the size chosen."

"Streamers should be retrieved in longer jerks than wet flies, to imitate the darting motions of a small fish trying to flee from a larger one."

"When retrieving the streamer, the rod must be kept pointing at the fly so that the strike will be more direct, but the tip of the rod should be at forty-five degrees or so above the water so the bend of the rod can cushion the shock of a hard strike."

"In the stripping retrieve, a big variety of movements can be imparted to the fly by varying the speed of the strip and the time between each strip."

"Keep experimenting with different speeds and fishing the fly at different depths. The bigger the streamer used, the faster should be the retrieving speed."

"Matukus are fished in precisely the same manner as is employed in your streamers; upstream on a tight or a slack line, or downstream on a tight line."

"In lakes they should be worked in short jerks in imitation of the bait fish, and the leader should be long and fine."

"When fish are obviously smelting, the fly should be retrieved fast, at times nearly skittering it along the top."

"If nothing is showing and fishing on the blind is called for, a slow-sinking line is used when water is comparatively shallow and the usual hand-twist retrieve is used with rod-tip lifts of short jerks. A 'palsy-like' shake of the rod hand is a good method of manipulation because it imparts a quivering movement to the fly."

"In deep water a fast-sinking (high-density) line is often called for and a slow retrieve with jerks is usually employed."

"Where smelt are prevalent a green fixed-wing fly is good, and in the deeper lake parts a red-and-black will often bring results."

Correspondence with New Zealand anglers indicates that their fixed-wing patterns always are tied with the two wing feathers back to back—in other words, not splayed. I asked why, commenting that I thought tying

175

down their fixed wings reduced action, which could be intensified by narrow splaying in flies for use in lakes and wider splaying for use in currents. No clear response was received, but perhaps some are experimenting with the suggestion.

Having noticed no evidence of the use of tandem trolling streamers in New Zealand, I inquired why this was so. Comments were that the fishing was so good that trolling was unnecessary, and that anglers there looked down on the practice, which older anglers call "harling," a word which was used for trolling in many countries but now is passing out of usage. The story goes in New Zealand that one angler asked another how he caught his fish.

"I got them harloting."

"You mean harling, don't you?"

"Hell, that's worse!"

Here are some comments of other writers on angling about this interesting subject of Matukus and other fixed-wing flies.

Alfred H. Chaytor, a prominent English angling author, evidently visited New Zealand in the 1930s, and says:

"We favored a fly with a thin red body with a long overhanging wing of mottled buff-brown bittern's feathers. The body is thin and can be either red or light blue, dressed on a [Limerick] hook about an inch long. The wing is very narrow, and about an inch and a half long. There is no hackle; merely body and wing. The long, thin mottled buff wing of bittern's feather is supposed to represent the 'inanga' [a small prevalent bait fish now called the smelt].

"The fly that they [rainbow trout] took was a fancy one, a blue wool body with silver tinsel rib, and for wings a couple of red-brown whole feathers from the breast of a cock pheasant.

"The Maori favor a huge fly, two and a half to three inches long, very roughly made with a black or dark body, with or without tinsel ribbing, and with a long straggling wing lying along the body and made of the dusty black hairy feathers of the kiwi. Trout take it for the koura." (The kiwi is a native bird of New Zealand and the national emblem. Like the bittern, it now is on the protected list, and therefore its feathers no longer are used in flies. *Koura* is the Maori name for the freshwater crayfish.)

Rodger Hungerford, in his *Guide to Trout Angling* (Australia: Pollard Publishing Company, 1971) lists Matukus and streamers in the same category. He says:

"In the construction of these flies long hackle feathers are used for wings, and they are often tied with four feathers placed in such a manner that the two on either side of the fly face outwards, which brings the natural curve of the feathers together, so the wing, when tied on the top of the hook (which usually is the long-shank type), looks as one feather.

"The wing is the most important part of the fly as it is the action of its

176

PLATE V Matukus, and Other New Zealand Originations

1. & 2. Two original Matukus, c. 1922 *(with real Bittern feathers)*

3. The only pattern now called "Matuku"

4. Grey Ghost

5. Rabbit Fly

6. Dorothy (Red)

7. Hawk

8. Black Prince

9. Parson's Glory

10. Taupo Tiger

11. Ginger Mick

12. Hope's Silvery

13. Jack's Sprat

14. Yellow Fuzz

15. Mrs. Simpson

16. Craig's Nighttime

17., 18., & 19. Three typical Australian "Longtails"

20. American Rabbit Fly *(Oliver's Orvis Shop)*

21. Muddler *(Oliver's Orvis Shop)*

22. Silver Spruce *Dressed by Dave Whitlock*

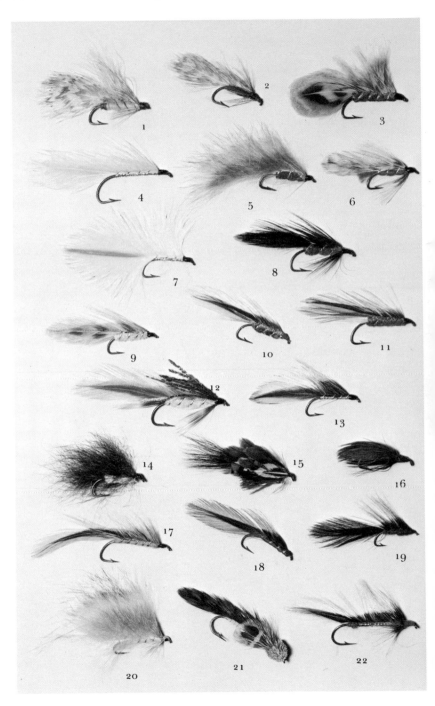

All patterns except bottom row are courtesy of Hector Sodersten (Rotorua) and Keith Draper (Taupo), New Zealand

PLATE VI Muddlers, and Other Prominent Sculpin Imitations

1. Missoulian Spook
Dressed by Dan Bailey

2. Spuddler
Dressed by Bud Lilly

3. Marabou Muddler
Dressed by Dan Bailey

4. Miller's Thumb
Dressed by George F. Grant

5. Flathead Sculpin
Dressed by George F. Grant

6. Sharptail Goby
Dressed by Loring D. Wilson

7. Whitlock Sculpin
Dressed by Dave Whitlock

8. Whitlock Marabou Muddler
Dressed by Dave Whitlock

9. Troth Bullhead
Dressed by Al Troth

10. Muddler Keel-Fly
Dressed by Don Brown

weaving through the water, when fished with small jerks, that represents the movement of a small fish.

"A very popular type of Matuku has a body constructed of red wool, with a black hackle feather bound to it with a gold rib.

"It is a common practice with this type of fly to incorporate an 'eye' at the side of the head."

Hungerford also writes of a <u>Mini-Matuku</u>, or <u>Tadpole Matuku</u>:

"It is made of black neck feathers of a hen or young rooster. The feathers must be soft and are bound to a number 12 hook over a red wool body with silver fuse wire. Bodies can vary, but red and black are very effective; the light colored of red bound by silver and half concealed by black hackles.

"Take a number 12 downturned-eye hook. Tie one end of a four-inch-long piece of wool or silk to the head of the hook; then, as you bind this down the hook shank, put a quarter-inch end of a two-inch piece of fuse wire under it; bind tight, and tie it off.

"Take a neck feather of three inches or longer and, leaving half an inch at the end of the feather, cut [strip] the hackles off one side and lay it on the wool body clipped side down. Then begin binding it on to the wool body with the projecting piece of fuse wire, leaving the half-inch tail of the feather projecting at the rear of the hook. About five or six turns should do.

"Twist off the fuse wire from the hook eye. This leaves about two inches of feather out. With this you wind it around to form the hackle, making sure the hackle is lying close to the body. Wind your hackle till about half an inch remains, then tie it off with black cotton and whip."

North American critics may think that many of the patterns provided thus far are not as suitable to our fishing as our own. Nevertheless, after absorbing what our friends way down under are doing, we can benefit by some of their ideas, as they can from ours. So, what are ours?

Harry Darbee, the noted Catskill angler and fly dresser, spends summers fishing for Atlantic salmon in Nova Scotia. In his excellent book *Catskill Fly Tyer* (New York: Lippincott, 1977) he describes a pattern he calls the <u>Horrible Matuka</u> and says he has found it a good high-water salmon and trout pattern. "Use a size 1 or 2 long-shanked salmon hook and wind a silk foundation back to the tail, tying in a ribbing of medium oval silver, then a body of fluorescent pink chenille. After wrapping the body take two badger saddle hackles dyed fluorescent orange. Strip the fibers off one side of the quills [as has been described for fixed-wing patterns] and tie them in as wings, with the fibers up and the [unstripped] tips of the hackles extending past the hook as long again as the hook shank. Make two or three turns of the tinsel under the tail for a tag and then wind the tinsel, spaced about one to three, tinsel to chenille, binding down the wings as you go. Take another badger hackle of the same color; fold it to get the barbs lying

177

in the same direction, tie it in by the tip at the head of the fly, and wind four to six turns as hackle [collar]. Then wind the thread for the head, crowding the hackle, giving it a slight backward slant, streamer-fashion. Lacquer the head black. That's it—a very simple salmon fly."

Dave Whitlock, who has many claims to fame, including being one of the world's most innovative fly dressers, describes Matuka streamers in his outstanding book (a "must" volume for fly tyers) *The Fly-Tyer's Almanac* (New York: Crown, 1975) as being "one of the most dynamic styles of streamers ever conceived but which has too long waxed and waned between obscurity and popularity." He also says, "Besides being *the* streamer style for trout, I consider them even more effective for bass and saltwater species."

Dave was kind enough to send me several of his famous patterns for this book. The first of his three Matuku patterns which I have the honor to include here, the Green Wing Matuku, is called by him "the most popular in the United States of all Matukus."

GREEN WING MATUKU
HOOK SIZE: Mustad #79580, 1/0 through 12, 6X long, or any 4X
   long streamer hook
THREAD: Black
RIBBING: Gold wire or small gold tinsel
BODY: Dark olive green seal's fur or dark green Orlon wool dubbing
   and seal's fur over eight to fifteen turns of lead wire (optional)

13-4 Dave Whitlock's Matuku patterns, dressed by him. At left, the Marabou Matuku Minnow; at right, the Green Wing Matuku; and below, the Matuku Sculpin.

WING: Four or six badger hackles dyed dark olive (or dyed black or orange)

THROAT: Two or three turns of red wool (to provide a gill effect), forward of which are one or two turns of the same color of hackle as the wing

Another of Dave Whitlock's innovations which no one should miss is a marabou minnow tied Matuku-style. This vertically deep-bodied fixed-wing streamer imitates such bait fish as alewives, herring, shiners, and gizzard or threadfin shad. It has earned many good reports in both freshwater and saltwater fishing, such as for salmon off the Pacific Coast and in estuaries of the Great Lakes, as well as a general fly for bass, pike, etc. It can be tied normally (vertically) or with the wing on the sides of the hook, but side-tying more realistically represents a crippled bait fish. The pattern (or type) can be dressed in various colors, usually with white nylon thread, or with fluorescent yellow for discolored water. If the fly isn't weighted a heavy wire streamer hook of any suitable size is recommended. Given below is a mainly white version, which can be varied in coloration as desired.

MARABOU MATUKU MINNOW

RIBBING: Silver wire or oval silver tinsel

BODY: White seal's fur or Orlon wool dubbing, fairly thick

WING: Two white (turkey) marabou feathers tied down Matuku-style plus six very thin silver Mylar strips tied in at head only

THROAT: Two or three turns of red wool (to provide a gill effect)

OVERWING: A few strands of white ostrich herl, with a few strands of green peacock herl as a topping

CHEEKS: A barred mallard flight or breast feather on each side extending to bend of hook. On each of these is painted a very large white eye with black pupil. Another black dot as large as the pupil can be placed back and upward of the eye.

Finally, among these American adaptations of fixed-wing streamers let us particularly note the Whitlock Sculpin in Chapter 14 and dress it as a Matuku Sculpin. This is dressed the same as the Whitlock Sculpin except that, in Matuku style, there is no underwing of squirrel hair. The wing is tied down with gold oval tinsel. Hook sizes are large, from 2/0 to 4, 3X long, with turned-up or ringed eye.

Let's note particularly in Dave Whitlock's Sculpin pattern that the roundish concave cheeks, which imitate pectoral fins, are tied in with the concave side *outward,* rather than pressing inward, as is customary in all of our streamer patterns calling for cheeks. This impresses me as a rather striking innovation which could be applied to many American streamer patterns with the result that the outwardly splayed cheeks would add greatly to the lifelike action of such flies.

179

Another idea in dressing fixed-wings is to tie in a large butt, such as red fluorescent wool, before winding in the ribbing. (The ribbing is not wound over the butt.) This cocks the tail of the fly up, adding to its action. New Zealanders prefer this type for use "in early floodwater fishing for mooching trout among the backwaters." A famous fly of this type is called Migram's Robin, named for Richard Migram, a noted Tasmanian angling author. Tie in the salmon-egg-type fluorescent red wool butt first, then the gold oval ribbing. The body is black seal's fur, with four black dense spade hen hackles tied in at the neck. The hackles are tied down with the gold ribbing in front of the fluorescent wool, thus cocking the tail up at a slight angle. Jungle cock cheeks of moderate length are used if available.

A noted New Zealand scientist observes, "Trout need *cold* water. They *must* have it. They're comfortable up to 60° F. At 65° they turn sluggish. At 75° their metabolism is so slow they cease to feed. This dependence on temperature is absolute; in water above 80° a ravenously hungry trout will starve with food all around him.

"This puts the trout in a dilemma. The New Zealand trout's main food —whitebait, smelt, bullies, and crayfish—are most plentiful in summer. But this is the time of maximum temperatures, often above the trout's feeding threshold. The impasse is most acute in our lakes, where such foods are produced in abundance, but are concentrated in the warmer surface waters.

"In the shallower lakes the trout overcome this by feeding at *night*, when water temperatures fall. In the deeper lakes their problem is solved by the existence of a thermocline in summer. The temperature transition caused by this may occur in a zone only a few feet in depth. Under such conditions a trout can live comfortably in the deep, cool water, make brief forays into the rich harvests in the warm surface waters, and return to his comfortable depths to digest at leisure."

This explains why fishing for big trout in New Zealand is very productive at night, and it gives us a clue often very valuable over here. Keith Draper, the noted Taupo tackle dealer, explains how they do it:

"Briefly, the most popular way is around stream and river mouths after dark—where they flow into lakes as a rule, although some of our salmon rivers flowing into the sea have good night fly fishing for sea trout after dark.

"We normally use a big fly of dark color, such as the Black Phantom, Fuzzy Wuzzy, Craig's Nighttime, Mrs. Simpson, etc., in sizes 2, 4, and 6 and occasionally size 8. We use floating or sinking lines according to the geographical features of the water being fished; the double-taper or weight-forward floating line for shallow water and the sinking line for deeper drop-offs. It's exactly the same as fishing during the day except you need to know your water well. It's bad practice to walk off into deep holes!

"We work our flies to simulate bait fish, bullies [a sculpinlike bottom dweller], and freshwater crayfish and shrimps. We wade or fish from the edge according to the current flow. Sometimes we are out into the lake above our waists; at other times we seldom go above the ankles. This is a very successful way of fishing as, especially during the summer, it can be very hard during the day. After dark it becomes much easier.

"You may get a bit of a flurry at sunset; then it goes quiet for an hour or more before the action really starts. We fish a lot according to the phases of the moon. Generally it's not so good during moonlit nights, although a large cloud cover will help. Best of all are really dark nights from the period of about five or six nights after full moon to the first quarter. The darker the night, the better.

"Some nights we fish our flies slowly; other times fast. The weather, waves, etc. don't affect them too much as long as you can still cast a line. It's also very good during the winter when, after a long period of frosts, a period of rain arrives. The trout are ready to run the streams and hang around the mouths and are of a very snappy state of mind. They are waiting for that fresh, discolored water to come down the streams. Some of these are small creeks you can jump across; others are large rivers."

To sum up, Matuku and other fixed-wing patterns from "way down under" are rather simple and seem more like attractors than imitators. Regardless of what we may think of the patterns themselves, the fixed-wing method of dressing has much to recommend it. When adapted to almost any of our popular streamer patterns, this method may result in more effective flies than we ever had before.

14

The Adaptable Muddler Minnow and Its Potent Progeny

In about the year 1950, Don Gapen, of the Gapen Fly Company, Anoka, Minnesota, originated the Muddler Minnow, usually considered to be the most versatile streamer fly ever conceived. He tried to represent the cockatush minnow, sometimes called a muddler, which is very prevalent along the Nippigon watershed as well as elsewhere. This is a flathead type that lives under rocks in stream water, and is one of more than a hundred varieties of the sculpin family.

Don didn't imitate a sculpin very well, but he was the first to try it. We now can do better, as we shall see. He did, however, create an all-purpose fly that can work bottom as a nymph, range midwater as a streamer or wet fly, or glide the surface as a terrestrial (such as a grasshopper) or a dry fly (such as an emerging Gray Drake). Because of this versatility we should become very well acquainted with the famous Muddler Minnow and its variations. It will help fishing success immeasurably.

To lay a solid basis for this fishing success, let's learn more about what Don Gapen was trying to represent. Sculpins, in over a hundred varieties from tiny to eating sizes, are bottom feeders that vaguely resemble bullheads, with very large pectoral fins, a head usually large and depressed, and eyes set high and close together. Colors range from olive, gray, or green to dark brown on top, cream or faint green below, and dark saddles across the back. These fishes are chameleonlike; they quickly change colors to those of their surroundings. Since sculpins have no swim bladders they remain on the bottom, more like lizards than fish. They hide under rock edges to dart out for prey, but they can only swim a few yards before tiring. Thus, when a big trout, for example, can get a sculpin out from under a rock, it can exhaust it easily and with little pursuit, taking this tasty mouthful with minimal effort.

Since sculpins spend most of their time in hiding, we seldom notice them. However, they are widely prevalent in both fresh and salt water, and are substantial and favored food for game fish everywhere.

Don Gapen (not his son, Dan) knew that he had conceived a very adaptable pattern, because he wrote to me:

"When the Muddler Minnow is fished underwater, it represents a minnow. In the smaller sizes and fished very slowly, it represents a nymph very well. In the grasshopper season you can float it to represent this trout food. I have used them during mayfly time with great success. I have caught the following fish with them: all trout, all bass, crappies, sunfish, snook, bonefish, and redfish (channel bass). Also, at times, I have taken walleyes, pike, grayling, bonito, jacks, and even sharks."

When Don mentioned using his streamer as a mayfly, he meant as a spent one, drifting on the surface in the current. I used it once as an emerging mayfly, with great success.

My wife and I were fishing Pierce's Pond, in Maine, during blackfly time when surface water was too warm for trout and landlocked salmon. In the evening, however, just before dark, these fish came into the shallows, amid clusters of great rocks, to feed. Since we did not care to fish deep, our fishing during the day was casual, but at dusk we anchored near shore outskirting the big rocks and noticed the dimpling of brook trout or salmon. We were laden with boxes of streamers and small dry flies, but none we tried proved very effective.

Then, as shadows deepened, a hatch came on. Here and there big nymphs bobbed up. As we watched, their cases split and a fly from each

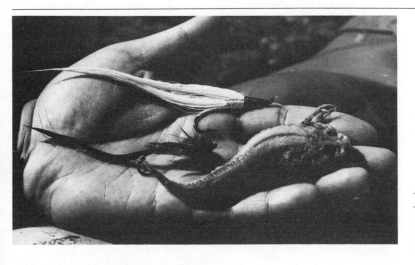

14–1 A large sculpin taken from the stomach of a five-and-a-half-pound trout, shown with Platinum Blonde and Troth Bullhead streamers. (Photo: Alfred C. Troth)

emerged. These were Gray Drakes, or something similar, about two inches long—the biggest I ever have noticed. Some of the Drakes, resting on their floating casings until their wings spread, hardened, and could support flying, soon took to the air. Others disappeared amid small swirls as they were sipped in by fish.

Dammit! All these boxes of flies, and none the right thing! As I hurriedly pawed through the collection, I noticed a Muddler Minnow. Suitably gray, and of about the right size, it was, however, minnow-shaped and lacked the large cocked wings of the naturals. A stray thought made me push the wing upright, and, with pressure, it stayed that way. I carefully fanned it out— a pretty good imitation of the natural. I sprayed it with flotant, tied it on, and cast it out. It looked good. Nearby another natural emerged, and, as I watched the natural and the imitation, a swirl engulfed the latter. I was fast to a small salmon. It had taken the imitation in preference to the real one! During the short time before blackness I hooked several more trout and salmon, carefully releasing all of them. Experimentation sometimes pays off, and I wish Don Gapen had been around to see it! The remodeled Muddler proved to be the hottest dry fly of the week for late-evening dry-fly fishing.

With these bits of background it seems quite obvious that the Muddler Minnow is not a very good representation of the sculpin it is supposed to copy, and it rarely is fished on the bottom where the sculpin makes its home. No matter. The fly is a versatile winner, and we'll come to much better representations later on. First, however, let's see what Don Gapen's original looks like, and then see some of the many variations which have evolved from it. Choose them and use them as you will.

MUDDLER MINNOW (original)

HOOK SIZE: 1/0 to 10, 3X long

THREAD: Black (red, for weighted flies)

TAIL: A strip of mottled brown (oak) natural turkey wing feather, quite wide and about half as long as the body (two strips are sometimes used)

BODY: Wound with medium flat gold tinsel, well lacquered

WING: A moderately large bunch of gray squirrel tail hair, on each side of which, and partly as an overwing, is a fairly large section of mottled turkey wing feather (as above) tied on nearly as long as the hair, extending to the end of the tail and cocked upward at about a thirty-degree angle

SHOULDERS (AND HEAD): Natural deer body hair, spun on to surround the hook, flattened and clipped short at front and tapered longer backward, leaving a small part as long as possible. (Use care when applying the wing to leave room at the head for the clipped deer-hair shoulders. This can be dressed rather heavily, perhaps packing on two or three spinnings of the hair.)

184

Gapen's original version, as shown in Color Plate I, called for using wolf's hair in the wing, but that is harder to come by and no more efficient. Dan Bailey, who has done much to develop the Muddler series, prefers to use brown calf tail under white calf tail. Before spinning the deer body hair for the clipped head and the throat (the hackle), be sure to remove all underhair and fluff, or the hair won't spin on correctly. Use a good deal of varnish for a secure head.

The success of the Muddler Minnow influenced the development of a darker version called the Thief, which also has influenced many variations. This hasn't become as popular as the original, but is well worth trying:

THIEF
HOOK SIZE: 2 to 12, 3X or 4X long
HEAD: Covered with several turns of black chenille
TAIL: A small section of red duck wing feather, as long as the gap of the hook, and tied in upright
BODY: Wound with silver tinsel, well lacquered
WING: A bunch of gray squirrel tail hair extending slightly beyond the tail. Over this on each side is a fairly wide section of mottled (oak) turkey wing feather as long as the hair.

This Gapen fly can be varied by using an underwing of mixed black and white calf tail hair. The head can be of spun body hair from deer, antelope, caribou, or other animals. In this and in the Muddlers the hair tips should be evened off by shaking them in a small cup such as the cover of a lipstick container.

The Thief was designed to take crappies in lakes and streams in Minnesota where a slightly darker fly than the Muddler Minnow was needed. It was first used in the International Falls area of Minnesota for big black crappies, but was later found to be an excellent fly for all species of trout, especially rainbows. An original is shown in Color Plate X.

Another very prominent Muddler variation, which could be called a White Muddler, is named the Missoulian Spook:

MISSOULIAN SPOOK
HOOK SIZE: 6 to 12, 3X long
THREAD: Black (red for weighted flies)
TAIL: A strip of mottled brown (oak) natural turkey wing feather, quite wide and about half as long as the body (two strips sometimes are used)
BUTT: Two or three turns of medium red chenille
BODY: Wound with white wool
RIBBING: Three or four turns of medium silver tinsel
UNDERWING: White calf or bucktail extending to end of tail

185

MIDDLE WING: A small bunch of mallard breast fibers extending to
  end of tail
OVERWING: On each side and slightly higher a strip of turkey wing
  feather the same as the tail, extending to end of tail
SHOULDERS (AND HEAD): Natural deer body hair (as in the Muddler)
  spun on in front of the wing and clipped closely at the head,
  leaving some of the fibers extending over the wing and as a throat.
  (The clipped part of the shoulders, or head, should be about a
  quarter of an inch in diameter and rounded into oval or ball shape.
  This is for a No. 6 hook, and is larger or smaller in proportion for
  other sizes.)

The Missoulian Spook has been widely promoted by Dan Bailey, famous
fly dresser and tackle dealer of Livingston, Montana, and has won prizes
for its ability to hook big fish, especially rainbows, brown trout, and cutthroats. In the Rocky Mountain area it is tied with a light shade of turkey
feather, or white turkey or goose, and the head is of white deer hair.

John Searcy, a California angler and fly tyer, was dissatisfied with results
obtained from the original Muddler, so he developed his own version,
which was found to produce better in his own area, as well as in other parts
of the country. This is a very interesting and unusual variation of the
original pattern and is particularly effective on big streams during low
water. The delicate dressing of the fly suggests its use dry when hoppers,
caddis flies, or stoneflies are on the water, but when fished wet it serves well
as an imitation of a small minnow. Here is the correct dressing:

SEARCY MUDDLER
TAIL: A small bunch of fibers from a teal's flank feather
BODY: Spun tan otter fur
RIBBING: Fine oval gold tinsel
WING: A well-barred teal flank feather tied on flat over the body
HACKLE: Deer body hair
HEAD: Deer body hair clipped quite small, as in usual Muddler
  patterns

The broad teal side feather used as a wing in place of the usual turkey
feather is thought to provide a dark mottled back more like the natural
sculpin.

Now let's look at another prize-winning sculpin imitation whose name
is a combination of the Spruce and Muddler because the pattern contains
elements of both of these flies:

SPUDDLER
HOOK SIZE: 1/0 to 8 (usually 2), 3X long
THREAD: Cream or white

TAIL: A small bunch of brown bucktail or calf tail

BODY: Dubbed badger underfur or cream angora yarn

WING: Brown bucktail or brown calf tail as long as the tail. Over this are four grizzly or Plymouth Rock hackles dyed brown and set on edgewise as is usual with streamers. Let the two inner hackles extend only to the bend of the hook (to give more body and to help prevent twisting) and extend the two outer hackles to the end of the tail.

GILLS: A few turns of red wool

SHOULDERS (AND HEAD): A bunch of fox squirrel tail tied on top but flared to sides. Forward of this is brown antelope or brown deer body hair spun on and clipped closely as with other Muddler types. If natural deer hair is used it can be stained a darker brown with waterproof ink applied with a felt-tip pen.

Many of these sculpin imitations are weighted, because, properly, they should be fished as close to the bottom as possible, that being where the sculpin is found. Weight also is necessary to counteract the natural buoyancy of the hair. We have the choice of weighting the body or weighting the head. In the latter case working the fly gives it a diving or grubbing motion more like a small fish foraging on the bottom, as has been discussed in Chapter 11.

Now let's turn to several variations of the Muddler with marabou wings. Dan Bailey says about these: "The Marabou Muddlers have become our best producers for very large trout. They are also very effective for bass and saltwater game fish. They have the clipped deer-hair heads of the regular Muddlers and long marabou streamer feathers which give them a wonderful action in the water. The tinsel chenille bodies add to the attractiveness of these flies."

George Grant, the renowned Montana expert, says: "The Muddler Minnow is considered to be the most widely used and effective streamer type on our large western rivers. One of its variations, generally credited to Dan Bailey, is used to a great extent by boat fishermen and is called the Marabou Muddler. It is used throughout the season, but it is particularly useful and effective during periods of high, roily water in June and then later when the water is discolored by irrigation releases from water-storage dams. The Marabou Muddler is often tied with a white wing that is from three to four inches long and is intended to be an attractor pattern that is most often fished close to the surface."

Dan Bailey, of Livingston, Montana, one of the great Rocky Mountain area experts, recommends in his tackle catalog five variations of the Marabou Muddler. All are dressed the same except for the color of the marabou wing, which can be either white, brown, yellow, black, or gray. These flies are big ones and need a weight-forward line to cast them to reasonable distances.

187

MARABOU MUDDLER

HOOK SIZE: 1/0 to 10, 3X long

THREAD: White (or any color, because the head actually is of clipped
deer hair, and the thread shows almost not at all)

TAIL: A small bunch of red hackle fibers

BODY: Silver tinsel chenille (gold-on-yellow version)

WING: Marabou, in the choice of colors, extending slightly beyond
end of tail

TOPPING: About nine peacock herl fibers, as long as the wing

SHOULDERS (OR HEAD): Deer body hair, spun on as usual with
Muddlers, clipped to a rounded head in front, with a fringe behind
left uncut, like a collar

Whether or not these five colors are varied by substituting others or
combinations is, of course, optional. For example, Ed Oliver (Oliver's Orvis
Shop, Clinton, New Jersey) favors a tandem trolling Muddler with olive
over white marabou. The trail hook is dressed with silver tinsel and has a
tail of a few red hackle fibers. Otherwise, the pattern is the same as above.
Except when trolling or near-surface fishing the flies usually should be
fished on or near bottom, where what they are supposed to represent
actually lives, but these fly types are surprisingly adaptable to a wide variety
of circumstances.

Alfred C. Troth, of Dillon, Montana, developed a sculpin variation that
many anglers call deadly:

TROTH BULLHEAD

HOOK SIZE: 3/0 to 1/0 (such as Mustad #36890)

THREAD: Black (Monocord)

TAIL: A small bunch of mostly cream-colored skunk tail hair

BODY: Wound fairly full with white floss or cream angora yarn

TOPPING (AND UPPER TAIL): A large bunch of black ostrich herl (*not*
peacock). Tie this in at the head (like a wing) and bind it down at
bend of hook, letting it extend to the end of the skunk tail hair.
The combined tail is as long again as the hook.

SHOULDERS (AND HEAD): Natural deer body hair left unclipped (as a
collar) mostly on top and sides. Spin on enough to also provide a
clipped head, as on all Muddlers.

The Troth Bullhead was originated on Montana's Madison River about
1960 and has become a standard sculpin imitation on Rocky Mountain
rivers. The clipped deer-hair head should be trimmed flat on top for more
lifelike appearance, and it should be blackened with a waterproof felt-tip
marking pen.

Alfred C. Troth says about it: "The stomach contents of all the big trout
I examined were full of sculpins, or bullheads, as they are referred to in the

1. Tie in tail of skunk tail fibers, cream angora body, and black ostrich topping. ◄

2. Tie down herl at bend of hook with size D black nylon thread. Whip and lacquer. ►

3. Tie in collar of natural deer flank hair, complete, and clip head to Muddler shape. ◄

4. The clipped deer-hair head and shoulder (collar) should look like this. ►

5. Blacken the top of the head with a waterproof felt-tip marking pen. ◄

6. The finished fly when wet. Note that bend of hook is weighted with wire. ►

14-2 The Troth Bullhead. (Photos: Alfred C. Troth)

west. I had my pickup camper parked beside the river and I was working on a sculpin imitation. This is the fly that evolved. I have kept the dressing the same for my own use ever since. I stepped out of the camper just to make a few casts to see how the big fly would look and act in the water. On the first cast a dandy brown trout latched on and took off down the river. I called to my wife in the camper to come out and hold the rod while I slipped into a pair of waders. Following the fish about two hundred yards downriver I finally beached him; a beautiful fish of over four pounds. Inside the stomach were seven sculpins. It is strictly a big fish fly. I rarely catch fish under two and a half pounds and once killed four trout that weighed thirteen and a half pounds after they were dressed.

"In heavy water I usually add a couple of turns of heavy lead wire around the bend of the hook. I feel this gives the fly a little more keel, keeping it swimming upright. I like to cast the fly upstream, on an OX tippet, fishing it dead drift, or once in a while lifting it slowly off the bottom and then letting it settle back down. Make it behave like a real sculpin. A nine-foot rod handling a 9- or 10-weight line helps in controlling the fly. Some people look amazed at the large hook, but it doesn't look too big in the mouth of a five-pounder!"

In a later letter Al Troth discusses his Baby Bullhead as follows: "As fishing pressure increased on the Madison River there were not enough big fish to make fishing the big bullhead worthwhile. I scaled the fly down to fit hook sizes 2, 4, and 6 and substituted marabou for the ostrich herl. The large, buoyant heads of the Bullhead and the Baby Bullhead were OK for shallow waters such as the Madison, but I wanted a fly that I could fish in the deeper holes of the Beaverhead and the Big Hole rivers. Instead of using a clipped-hair type of head I just tied in a hair collar. The head is then

14–3 This big brown trout took a jigged Troth Bullhead. (Photo: Alfred C. Troth)

wound with lead fuse wire and covered with a material called art foam. I soak the varnish into the foam and then I spin dyed olive rabbit fur in a loop and form the head. I trim the bottom flat and pick out the fur on the sides and top.

"A jigging action is very deadly when imitating sculpins. Casting the fly upstream and letting it settle to the bottom and then lifting it slowly and allowing it to swim to the bottom again is very effective. I always use a lead shot at the head of the fly, right against the eye, often in addition to making a few turns of lead wire around the bend to offer a better keel. Sculpin imitations seem to be excellent choices for high, muddy waters or at night when the sculpins are most active—and so are big trout!"

Since one of the best ways to fish Muddlers is on or near bottom, where sculpins should be, we may need not only a weighted pattern but also one that won't hang up often. We can make them weedless, as discussed in Chapter 9, we can use weighted up-turned jig flies, as discussed in Chapter 10, or we can dress flies on weighted keel hooks. Below is a good sculpin imitation dressed on a keel hook, but, before giving the pattern, let's operate on the hook to make it more effective. The keel hook is hard to hang up, and is therefore good for bottom-bumping or for casting close to brush where big fish often are. However, some of us think it has failings as a sure hooker. To remedy this, open the gape to put the barb at about a thirty-degree angle with the shank. Then bend up the eye to the same angle. It should hook much better that way. Set the hook bend down in the vise until the body is completed. Then turn it bend up to dress the wing. Wrap the shank of the hook with between fifteen and twenty turns of one- or two-amp lead fuse wire, depending on depth of water or swiftness of current.

KEEL MUDDLER
HOOK SIZE: 2 (Eagle Claw #1213)
THREAD: Yellow
BODY: Light olive angora yarn
RIBBING: Gold oval tinsel
WING: A moderate-sized bunch of the dark part of bucktail dyed
      yellow or olive, extending to bend of hook. On each side, partly
      covering the hair, tie in two olive hackles and a grizzly hackle dyed
      brown, with the grizzly hackles outermost. These extend to cover
      the bend of the hook and, with bend up, they rest tent-style over
      and partly covering the hair part of the wing.
SHOULDERS (AND HEAD): Deer body hair dyed olive brown and spun
      on like other Muddlers, with the head clipped close, ball-shaped
      and the rear part unclipped, as a throat or collar

191

In all the Muddler patterns given so far you may have noted an omission in that the very large pectoral fins of the sculpin are not adequately represented. This omission was solved by Dave Whitlock, the famous artist and fly dresser who also is the co-author of *The Fly-Tyer's Almanac* (New York: Crown, 1975) a practical and highly instructive text that no angler or fly dresser should be without. Dave Whitlock's sculpin imitation is so lifelike that, as I look at it on my desk, it all but wiggles away. I don't see how big fish can resist it, and, according to reports, they don't! Fly dressers will enjoy copying it. It is both a conversation piece and a masterpiece. See it in Color Plate VI and observe that, lengthwise, it divides itself into four equal parts. The first is the abnormally large clipped deer-hair head. The second quarter is occupied by the representation of the sculpin's very large pectoral fins, imitated by roundish or fan-shaped barred back feathers of pheasant, chicken, or grouse. The third quarter shows the end of the body and the bend and point of the hook. The last quarter is the end of the wing. These proportions are important.

WHITLOCK SCULPIN

HOOK SIZE: 2/0 to 4, 3X long, turned-down or ringed eye
THREAD: Strong yellow or orange nylon
BODY: Yellow or cream-colored Orlon or seal's fur, moderately
    dressed. Before winding this on add between ten and twenty-five
    turns of lead fuse wire to offset buoyancy of the fly.
RIBBING: Fine gold oval tinsel
UNDERWING: A moderate-sized bunch of red or gray fox squirrel
    extending just beyond bend of hook
OVERWING: Two golden brown Cree or grizzly hackles, tied on flat
    and extending a quarter again as long as the hook
CHEEKS: A pair of the brown-barred stiff fan- or spade-shaped back
    feathers of prairie grouse, pheasant, or chicken. These feathers,
    one on each side, are tied in with concave sides outward, set in
    midway of the shank of the hook, in imitation of the large pectoral
    fins of the sculpin.
THROAT: A few turns of red Orlon or red seal's fur (this is intended
    to represent a wounded fish, and is nearly concealed by the head)
HEAD: Alternating dark and light spinnings of deer body hair. The
    head is clipped very large and rounded at top and closely clipped
    flat underneath. The top of the head is marked with black bands,
    using a felt-tip pen. Some of the back hair is unclipped on top and
    sides.

Dave Whitlock thought that usual Muddlers failed to properly represent sculpins, and this is his most excellent answer to the problem. He reminds us that the fly can be varied in color scheme to match the chameleonlike changes of color of the sculpin, which vary in different rivers from olive to tan to dark gray to nearly black in combinations of light and dark tones. The golden brown one given above is one of the most prevalent. It is the basis of the Matuku Sculpin described in Chapter 13.

Dave Whitlock seems to agree with Dan Bailey that the fluffy undulations of marabou are effective in representing the swimming motions of sculpin. He was kind enough to present this book with three color schemes of his version of a Marabou Muddler, and I would bet on them, largely because the abnormally large head is more bullhead-like, and a better representation than the Marabou Muddlers previously described.

WHITLOCK'S MARABOU MUDDLER

HOOK SIZE: 2/0 to 4, 3X long, turned-down or ringed eye
THREAD: Fluorescent orange
BODY: Before applying the body wind on ten to fifteen turns of lead wire to offset buoyancy of the deer hair. Then slip on a body of gold Mylar tubing, tying it down at the rear with fluorescent orange thread, like a butt.
WING: White under yellow under brown under orange marabou, over which is a topping of six to eight peacock herls, all extending slightly beyond the bend of the hook
HEAD: Consecutive spinnings of deer body hair, white, yellow, brown, orange and black. As in the previous pattern, the head is clipped very large (nearly as wide and deep as one's index-finger nail), rounded spadelike at top and clipped flat underneath, with some of the rear hairs left uncut at top and sides. The middle of the top of the head is darkened with a waterproof felt-tip pen.

This provides an attractive streamer which is an excellent sculpin representation. Dave also suggests two others, which are the same except:

(#2) BODY: Silver Mylar tubing
WING: White under yellow under olive marabou, plus peacock
HEAD: White, yellow, olive and black deer body hair
(#3) BODY: Silver Mylar tubing
WING: Black over white marabou, plus peacock
HEAD: Black, white, and black deer body hair (nearly all black)

In color, this last pattern resembles Ted Trueblood's well-known Integration Streamer. The shape of the head and the action of the wing has a lot to do with the effectiveness of the patterns. They also imitate bullheads, chubs, and perhaps shiners, are good streamers for big fish in general, are excellent for steelhead, and are super-producers for bass.

In Terry Hellekson's book *Popular Fly Patterns* he notes that Paul Drake and George Bodmer, of Colorado Springs, Colorado, vary the standard Muddler pattern by weighting the head in one of the ways described in Chapter 10 of this book. They call this the <u>Bullet Head Muddler.</u> They prefer Mustad #79580 hooks and stop the dressing at the point of spinning on the deer-hair head. They crimp on a split shot behind the eye of the hook, leaving a small space between the eye and the split shot. They then spin on the deer hair in front of the shot and fold it back over the shot, forming both the head and the shoulders. A rod ferrule helps greatly in folding the hair back. They use red thread when tying this type of fly because the red band behind the head is suggestive of minnows' gills. This weight up front makes the fly dip and dart close to stream bottom when it is given rod action, as explained in more detail in Chapter 10.

In Chapter 6 it was noted that George F. Grant, who might rightfully be considered the most skillful and innovative angler and fly dresser that the Rocky Mountain area has ever produced, refers to sculpin imitations as "big fish flies" and thinks they are of primary importance in the field of flies which imitate bait fish. In his most essential book, *Montana Trout Flies,* * he refers to several sculpin imitations developed by him. These bear a strong resemblance to the Whitlock Sculpin, but their construction is quite different. In this privately printed book George says, in part:

"Practically everyone who fishes for trout in Montana waters is familiar with the Mottled sculpin (*Cottus bairdi*), usually called 'bullhead' by most fishermen. The average size is from two to three inches in length, although individual specimens up to six inches have been reported. The general color of the back, or top side, is dark gray to olive brown with brown or black splotches. The sides are slightly lighter, and the belly is whitish or cream. The back color will vary according to the surroundings and, in some cases, may be predominantly dark olive green with darker spots; in others, a mottled brown. The other distinctive features of the sculpin are the flat,

---

*George F. Grant is the author of *Montana Trout Flies* and *Weaving Hair Hackles.* The latter book explains how hair, instead of feathers, can be used for hackling, and gives the advantages of the method. Address: George F. Grant, 2215 North Drive, Butte, Montana 59701.

14–4 The proper way to trim a Muddler, top and side views. The head should be trimmed nearly flat underneath for minimum interference with the barb of the hook.

oversized head and the large, strong, spine-rayed pectoral fins with which it propels itself from rock to rock across the stream bottom.

"The Mottled sculpin is found in practically all of the fast-flowing rivers of western Montana. In those rivers where it is found it is very abundant, and is an exceedingly important food source for trout, particularly large trout. These small sculpins spend their entire lives on the stream bottom, either hiding beneath the rocks or hovering just above them as they move about in search of food. They are not strong, swift swimmers like minnows or the young of game fish and are often captured by large trout, as even casual examination of their stomach contents will reveal. It is evident that, as a trout grows larger and less inclined to exert himself unnecessarily, the availability and good size of the average sculpin affords a substantial meal. It could well be compared to the main portion of our own dinner, or, in other words, the 'meat and potatoes.'

"As time went on I gave considerable thought and time to the development of an artificial sculpin as it suggested itself to me as being the best possible way a fly fisherman could take big trout consistently. Long before the advent of the Muddler Minnow I worked out two patterns that took good-sized trout but not any better than large nymphs, and it was impossible to determine if they were actually taken as bullhead.

"The success of the Muddler Minnow gave impetus to the idea that the sculpin could actually be imitated and used successfully by the fly fisherman, and since that time quite a few fly-tying anglers have applied themselves to the interesting possibility of taking big trout with such flies. There are now several patterns which I believe to be superior to the Muddler for the specific purpose of imitating the sculpin. [See Color Plate VI.]

"In addition to the excellent patterns that have been developed, the high-density sinking line is an equally important factor in making artificial bullhead fishing more logical. My early efforts in this type of fishing were always partially defeated by the necessity of fishing the artificial near the bottom, which was required if we were to present the sculpin where the big trout would be searching for them. A fly of more than fifteen grains is difficult to cast, and even this weight is not adequate to attain proper depth quickly. If weight in the form of sinkers is placed on the leader, casting is made even more difficult and there is also a feeling that you are not truly fly fishing. The combination of a weighted artificial and a high-density sinking line now gives the angler some better working tools, although much is still to be learned."

George Grant achieved such great success with his sculpin imitations that they have to be seen to be believed. Other fly dressers would have to study his books to even come close. If any of them want to answer the supreme challenge, this is it! The printed dressings can only hint at the results achieved by this peerless artist in his chosen areas of fly dressing, but we offer the following two.

FLATHEAD SCULPIN
TAIL: Brown-olive marabou fluff
BODY: Shaped with brass pins and wound closely with dead soft brass
wire (.018), or nylon-covered wire-core trolling line
PECTORAL FINS: Greenish pheasant fibers from a cock pheasant rump
feather
HEAD: Compressed deer hair as in other Muddlers, but trimmed flat.
Natural gray deer body hair may be used and then colored with
brown and green marking pens. Eyes are formed with thick
lacquer.

The original pattern for this mottled sculpin (*Cottus bairdi*) was tied with
a body shaped with common straight brass pins in the same manner as
George Grant's large stonefly nymphs, but in this instance the outer covering is closely wound soft brass wire, a feature inspired by the Brass Hat and
other Pete Schwab wire-bodied steelhead patterns. A large, well-marked
green-black-tan cock pheasant body feather glued to the back of the brass
body lends a good suggestion of the mottled back of the natural sculpin.
The body is beetlelike in shape, a cross section representing a horizontal
oval.

The following variation of the Flathead Sculpin is intended for fishing
in shallow streams for brook trout, or for late-season use on big rivers. The
shape of the pattern is similar to the one above.

MILLER'S THUMB
TAIL: Greenish fibers from a large cock pheasant rump feather
BODY: Wound with nylon-covered wire-core trolling line or plain flat
monofilament
PECTORAL FINS: Greenish fibers from a large cock pheasant rump
feather, or whole green-black-tan small hackle feathers
HEAD: Mixed yellow and green deer body hair woven onto thread in
the form of a hackle and applied to the hook shank, then trimmed
to shape

In this pattern the brass wire is replaced by nylon-covered trolling wire,
or even by flat monofilament if less weight is desired. George Grant forms
the head by his weaving process, which produces a large sculpinlike head
which is not nearly as buoyant as compressed deer hair. This head can also
be woven from badger or squirrel hair, neither of which is nearly as buoyant
as deer body hair. A realistic effect is obtained by gluing small pheasant
feathers along the back of the preformed body.

In one of his letters to me, George Grant offers the following comments
on tackle and fishing practices for sculpin imitations. If there is any repetition of previous remarks, it is intended for emphasis:
"Just as there is a similarity and yet a difference between orthodox

196

streamers and sculpin imitations there are also some distinct differences in the manner in which such artificials are fished on large western rivers.

"The streamer is often fished 'dead drift' and then retrieved in a series of jerks designed to imitate the quick erratic movements of small fish. The sculpin imitation is most often fished 'dead drift' throughout in order to gain and maintain maximum depth and because the sculpin is not ordinarily a 'free' swimmer.

"Both of these types can be most effectively used in late summer or fall when the rivers are comparatively shallow—most western rivers such as the Madison, Big Hole, or even the Yellowstone are not deep rivers at this time of the year.

"The streamer fly does not require a full-sinking line, but can be weighted in tying and used on a floating line if desired, or it can be left unweighted and used with a wet-tip line.

"Whereas minnows may be found at varying depths, the sculpin spends its entire life on or near bottom, and it is necessary to fish the artificial at similar depths. A high-density, full sinking line is better than using lures so heavily weighted that they are entirely devoid of buoyancy and difficult to cast. The combination of an extra-fast-sinking line and a lightly weighted lure is more likely to be successful.

"Regardless of whether a line is floating, wet-tip, or full-sinking, it is best to use the weight-forward design with monofilament shooting line in order to achieve long casts and deal effectively with the ever-present strong winds.

"Leaders six to seven feet in length are adequate and need to be no lighter than .011 at the tip end. Using longer or lighter leaders with these large flies, often weighted, will not increase their effectiveness, but will, as a matter of fact, create many problems for the caster."

In summary, what are the best ways to fish Muddlers and what types should be selected for each? There are five basic ways and, in suitable water, it is possible to use more than one, or even all five, during the same cast!

For example, cast the original type of Muddler upstream and across. Let it drift on the surface, dry-fly style, until it starts to sink, mending the line as necessary to provide a free float. It then imitates a spent insect or a terrestrial such as a grasshopper. When it begins to sink, continue the drift. It then represents a drowned fly, or a spent terrestrial. After a bit of that let it continue to sink while working it very, very slowly to simulate a nymph. Bring it to life and start the retrieve, using long and fast strips. This fishes it as a streamer in imitation of a frantic bait fish. When the fly's swing is completed let it drop back and sink to the bottom (if water depth allows) while raising and lowering the rod tip to simulate the darting of a sculpin. Finally, retrieve it jerkily, close to deep banks and obstructions that offer cover, thus fishing it as a streamer again.

Let's discuss these five ways in greater detail. When using the Muddler

197

as a dry fly or as a submerged spent one it should be in one of the smaller sizes of the Gapen type. While it floats, use the slack-line method, mending the line as necessary, to present the fly broadside to the current so its silhouette can be seen more clearly by fish. While it floats it can be worked very slightly, like a live grasshopper trying to swim. A floating line is best here, or even one with a sinking tip, although the latter of course will pull the fly under quicker.

When the fly sinks, continue the drift on the slack but controlled line to give the impression of an insect being carried by the current. Avoid letting the line and current pull the fly because we want a free drift.

When this fly has sunk close to bottom let it drift near it, perhaps working it very slightly. The Muddler now simulates a nymph, and we must be alert to strike on the slightest pretext, because fish usually take nymphs very delicately, although they often hook themselves. An angler once told me that when fishing a stream with a gravel bottom, he left his line, leader, and nymph in the water while having lunch in order to keep the leader wet. The current worked the more or less stationary nymph enough for a large trout to take it.

On this same cast, or a new one, try fishing the Muddler as a streamer. Many of us like to retrieve with long and sharp pulls, especially for brown trout, because they seem to like it that way. Special attention, of course, is paid to working the fly close to good holding positions such as around rocks, along the edges of divided currents, near blowdowns, close to under-cut banks or near brush along the shoreline. A larger-sized Gapen Muddler might be preferable in wider and deeper water, and this would be ideal also for a Marabou Muddler, a Spuddler, or the Spook.

Finally, using a sinking line unless the water is very thin, fish the fly as close to the bottom as possible to imitate a sculpin in its natural habitat, just over the rocky bottom. Western anglers on their big rivers probably would use a fast-sinking (high-density) shooting head with monofilament backing in order to make longer casts and to get the fly down deeper. Make the retrieve in short jerks, as a sculpin would swim. This can be varied by raising and lowering the rod tip. Big fish often take sculpin imitations on the drift-back. Fishing close to bottom calls for one of the more lifelike representations rather than the impressionistic Gapen type of fly. Ideal ones would be one of the Whitlock or Grant patterns previously described, or perhaps the Troth Bullhead. In order to work the bottom on some streams these patterns may need to be weighted.

We note that Muddler patterns are favored in brighter colors such as white and yellow, as well as in gray, brown, and black. All experienced anglers have color preferences, and their own reasons for them. The following are rules which are accepted by the majority.

On a bright day try a bright fly, or one with more tinsel. This also is good when the fish is between the fly and the sun, because fish then can see detail and flash better. Such a fly is preferred in discolored water.

As light decreases, use less silver and try a darker fly, such as a gray one. On very overcast days try flies with brown or orange in them. When there is very little light, or when the fly is between the fish and the sun, a darker fly should be better because it gives a better silhouette. Near dark or after dark is the time when a black fly should do best.

Another part of the general rule concerns selecting flies for size. If an impressionistic pattern such as one of the Gapen type is used to simulate a dry fly or a nymph, we usually would prefer small sizes, even as small as size 10. We imitate in size what we are trying to represent, and we know that this applies to bait-fish imitations. These smaller sizes should be preferable in thin or placid water, particularly when it is clear. As water becomes darker, deeper, or heavier we should switch to larger sizes, and often brighter ones, because of the flies' better visibility.

Although sculpins don't exist everywhere, the multitude of their varieties and their abundance recommend that their imitations should enjoy wide use. The original Muddler is the most versatile of flies, and the improved sculpin representations simulate the "meat and potatoes" of the underwater larder—the big fish food.

Vacationers staying most anywhere along both oceans can enjoy fly-rod fun and fish for dinner without the expense of hiring boats or patronizing specialized angling resorts. Drive along the nearby coast and look for streams flowing from salt ponds, estuaries of small rivers, and other likely spots such as potholes amid rocks at low tide. Many of these places hold sporty fish, and the fact one doesn't see them doesn't mean they aren't there!

While walking a beach on Cape Cod we came to a brooklike stream placidly flowing from a marsh. It looked inviting where it widened into the sea, but no fish were showing. I returned with a fly rod fitted with a floating line with sinking tip, cast a streamer into the current, and worked it slightly while it swung downstream. There was an immediate hit and I beached a baby bluefish weighing not over a pound. Nearly every cast hooked another. Admittedly, this isn't the peak of the sport, but it is fly-rod fun.

On another of many similar occasions we waded along a channel of a harbor on an emptying tide and hooked striped bass—big ones resting in the depths of the channel until the tide turned. A sandy beach looked inviting at another time, when a weighted fly cast far out and dragged in over the sand hooked as many flounders as we could carry. We didn't patronize expensive fish markets very much that summer.

Many types of saltwater streamers are suitable for such blind fishing— even freshwater patterns if we don't mind ruining them with rust. Such fishing isn't always blind. Tackle dealers can tip off patrons by suggesting specific locations for sport fish such as steelhead and salmon. In selecting fly types, don't ignore sculpin imitations, because there are many small species of sculpins which are very prevalent in salt water, as well as in fresh.

199

A major experimenter with such patterns is Loring D. Wilson, of Edgewater, Maryland, who described this in an article in *The Flyfisher* magazine. The remainder of this chapter is quoted from it with permission. Note his recommendation (useful in many of the preceding patterns) to firm the representations of the large pectoral fins by stroking the hackles lightly with rubber cement or lacquer smeared between thumb and forefinger before tying them in.

"For years people have known of the effectiveness of sculpin minnow imitations in fresh water. Such patterns as Don Gapen's Muddler Minnow, Dave Whitlock's Sculpin, the Spuddler, and other ties have been cleaning up on trout, bass, and many other freshwater species, and have been recognized for almost a decade as among the most effective freshwater flies available. However, little had been done to imitate the sculpin effectively in salt water, where it provides for a greater variety of fish than in all the fresh waters of the world. Admittedly, some people tried the Muddler and its offshoots in bays, rivers, and estuaries, but success was limited and most fly fishermen returned to the Blonde patterns and other saltwater standards.

"For several years I felt that fly fishermen were missing something by overlooking the sculpin, but I did nothing about it. It was only after a trip to Hatteras, where the most popular live bait at the time happened to be a little fish called the goby, that I finally decided to try to work out a sculpin

14–5 Loring D. Wilson's Goby patterns, dressed by him. At left, Longjaw Goby; at right, Naked Goby; and below, Sharpta Goby. (Photo: Loring D. Wilson)

imitation that would be as effective in the salt as the standard patterns were in fresh water.

"The first step in the process was to study the sculpin. There are a number of saltwater sculpins, but a quick glance at the size of some of them shows there would be little point in imitating them.

"There are other saltwater species with the same characteristics, even though they are not technically sculpins. Most important of these are the gobies, and it was these fish that I finally chose as a model for a saltwater sculpin pattern. Gobies are frequently used as live bait for bottom fishing, and their resemblance to the true sculpins is close.

"The gobies constitute a relatively large family of small fishes which are quite common along beaches and in the shallow waters of tidal estuaries. Gobies are found all along the coasts of North America, although they are more common from New Jersey south on the East Coast and from northern California south in the west. They are related to the clingfishes, and so they have modified sucking discs, large heads, shortened bodies, and the large pectoral fins of the true sculpins (to which they are not related).

"The most prevalent goby on the East Coast of the United States is the naked goby (*Gobiosoma bosci*), found in great numbers all the way from Cape Cod to Florida. It has a tendency to frequent empty shells (which is the reason it turns up so often in oyster dredges) and reaches a length of about three inches.

"Because I live on Chesapeake Bay in Maryland, the Naked Goby was the first pattern I attempted to develop. Later I refined the pattern into two others, one representing the sharptail goby (*Gobionellus hastatus*) of the Gulf Coast, and the longjaw goby (*Gillichthys mirabilis*), a plentiful, hardy goby of the Pacific Ocean which has long been greatly in demand as a bait fish. For purposes of saltwater fishermen on both coasts, I will include the description of all three patterns.

"Developing the proper shape and color combinations for the various goby imitations took more than a year of experimentation, but the results were well worth the work involved. If you follow the tying instructions, I believe you will find the saltwater sculpins most productive.

NAKED GOBY

HOOK: Mustad #9672, size 4
THREAD: White
TAIL: Two pale blue hackle feathers one and a half times as long as the hook
BODY: Light gray chenille over five turns solder
PECTORAL FINS: Two partridge hackle feathers
HACKLE: Reddish orange
HEAD: Natural deer hair, tied full and trimmed to shape

"Place the hook in the vise and tie in the white thread approximately one-half inch back from the eye. Wind the thread evenly back to a point just opposite the barb of the hook and half-hitch.

"Now take the two pale blue hackles and tie them in opposite the barb of the hook, with the glossy sides together so that the two hackles flare outward away from the hook. At the same time, tie in a length of pale gray chenille, the largest size available (small chenille may be used, but the larger size gives a softer feel to the finished fly and also saves work in the wrapping). Wind the thread back to the point at which it was first tied on and bind in a length of fine-diameter solder of the sort used in electrical work (if all you have available is the acid-core variety, push the core out of the length of solder with a needle; otherwise the acid in the core will adversely affect the other materials). You may wonder at my recommendation of solder rather than standard lead wire. The fact is that solder is more easily obtainable than lead wire and the greater diameter is of advantage in a fly with the natural buoyancy this one will have when it is finished. In addition, if the solder is used with the core removed, the walls of the solder will collapse during the winding to provide a flatter body.

"The solder should be tied over the thread and wound toward the rear of the hook, allowing the forward third of the hook to remain free of any materials. Wind the thread back over the lead to secure it to the hook and then back to its original point and secure the thread with a half hitch.

"Now wind the chenille up to the thread and back and forth until you have formed a cone-shaped tapered body, with the shoulder being quite thick. Tie it off and trim away the surplus.

"Tie in the partridge hackles on each side of the shoulder so that they bend away from the body of the fly. The partridge hackle is extremely effective because its barred coloration gives an excellent representation of the rayed pectoral fins of the actual bait fish. If you don't happen to have any on hand and find it unavailable, pale barred mallard or teal flank feathers with a pronounced curve can be used as a substitute. Whichever one you use, firm them up by stroking them lightly with rubber cement or lacquer smeared between your thumb and forefinger. *Without this reinforcement the feathers will pull together, streamer fashion, in the water, and destroy the effect of the pectoral fins.* **

"Apply three turns of the reddish orange hackle in front of the pectoral

---

*In a later letter Loring Wilson says, "When I was developing the goby patterns, I tried the rubber-cement-stroke method and it does make them more durable, but it also narrows and stiffens them. I developed my patterns by watching the real gobies in an aquarium I set up for the purpose, and their pectoral fins are very soft and fluid in motion. A cemented feather won't duplicate that motion. I sometimes spray the partridge hackle with Clear Cote, a flexible acrylic coating used in art. It dries in just a few minutes and doesn't matt the feathers as much as does the stroking method." However, I have found that if one strokes the feathers outward on both sides of the spine while coating them with rubber cement this narrowing is reduced. A feather larger than necessary can be coated and trimmed to size to maintain width. If rubber cement overly stiffens them this could be an advantage in all but the slowest currents.

fins and tie it off. This hackle will simulate the blood-charged gills of the goby as it opens and closes its gill covers. Use a relatively soft hackle to create the proper appearance and fluctuations as the fly is pulled through the water.

"Now it's time to tie on the head. Take a small bunch of natural gray deer hair and lay it across the top of the forward (bare) third of the hook shank, pinching it to the shank between your thumb and forefinger. Loop the tying thread over the center of the hair and pull down firmly. As the hair begins to flare, release your grip and allow the hair to spin around the shank of the hook. With the fingernails of your forefinger and thumb, shove the deer hair back firmly against the shoulder of the body chenille. Continue this process until the forward third of the hook shank is packed with the deer hair. Tie it off, whip-finish the head, and apply thinned head cement so that it will penetrate not only the thread but the head of the fly as well, cementing the hairs firmly to the thread. Now trim the deer-hair head to provide a nice, large rounded head, and the fly is finished.

"The instructions make it sound as if there is a lot of work involved, but once the technique is mastered the fly shouldn't take more than ten minutes to complete.

"The patterns for the other two species of gobies, using the same tying instructions, are as follows:

SHARPTAIL GOBY

HOOK: Mustad #9672, sizes 4, 2, 1/0
THREAD: Yellow
TAIL: Two cream hackle feathers, one and a quarter times as long as the hook
BODY: Yellow, gold, or pale tan chenille over solder (five turns for size 4, six for size 2, eight for size 1/0)
PECTORAL FINS: Two partridge hackle feathers
HACKLE: Reddish orange
HEAD: Yellow deer hair, tied full and trimmed to shape

"The sharptail goby reaches a length of six inches, which accounts for the greater range in hook sizes. Carry a few of each size. Although larger fish are more willing to take the smaller sizes, the greater strength of the larger hooks will be of advantage in fighting and landing the fish you hook. The sharptail imitation is especially effective on river tarpon on the Gulf Coast of Florida, and when the tarpon are cruising the shallows it outfishes the old standby cockroach pattern unbelievably.

203

LONGJAW GOBY

HOOK: Mustad #9672, size 4
THREAD: Brown
TAIL: Two dark olive hackle feathers, one and a half times as long as the hook

BODY: Two strands of chenille, one olive, one brown, twisted together
  and wrapped as one, over five turns of solder
PECTORAL FINS: Two grouse body feathers
HACKLE: Reddish orange
HEAD: Green deer hair, tied full and trimmed to shape

"The techniques involved in fishing the saltwater sculpins are quite simple. Admittedly, the action comes much faster when you have spotted feeding fish, but the goby imitations also serve as superb searching flies. I have located many a cruising fish when there was no outward sign of its presence by using the gobies, and whether the flies are cast blind or to a fish whose position is known, the techniques are the same.

"The fly should be cast as far as possible to provide maximum opportunity for a fish to see it on the retrieve—unless, of course, a fish already has been sighted and you are casting directly to it. The fly is allowed to sink, the deer-hair head counteracting the lead wire to give it a slow, realistic float to the bottom. The flared feathers serving as the pectoral fins also contribute to the natural-looking descent, causing the fly to coast first to one side and then the other, and this action in turn causes the streamer feather tail to undulate back and forth like a real fish's tail.

"The retrieve is made in short twitches, no more than six inches at a time. Again, the stiff pectoral fins cause a sway in the forward motion of the fly, and this sway coupled with the resulting undulations of the tail is quite realistic. Retrieve the fly as close as possible because some fish will follow the sculpin a great distance before finally taking it. When the strike comes, it generally is hard and fast with little need to set the hook, except in cases of hard-mouthed fish such as bluefish, tarpon, and the like.

"If the sculpin is excellent as a searching fly, it is devastating when a feeding school has been located. That was proved to me beyond all shadow of doubt on a trip last year to Cape Cod. I was fishing the shallow waters of the southern portion of Cape Cod Bay, out of Cummaquid, with only sporadic success on undersized stripers. Suddenly, about forty feet away, the water exploded almost as if there had been a minor volcanic eruption beneath the surface. I was using an Argentine Blonde at the time and the first two casts were futile. With shaking hands I hastily snipped off the Blonde and tied on a Naked Goby. All the while the school of feeding fish was moving closer to the boat.

"The first cast with the Goby brought a quick strike and a few minutes later, after several short, hard runs, I boated a half-pound Boston mackerel. From that point the action was fast and furious. The mackerel didn't even wait for the fly to sink, with some taking it the moment it hit the water. In no case did the fly sink more than a foot before a fish fell upon it.

"If you are fishing over a rough bottom, or where there are pilings or snags, I strongly recommend the flies be tied on keel-type hooks, which will keep the point of the hook elevated and relatively free of snags. Stainless-steel hooks may be used for all patterns, whether Keel flies or not, but the fact is that the fish are so hard on the flies they may never have a chance to rust.

"Tie a few saltwater sculpins and try them. The pattern is not difficult and the results may astound you. You won't be throwing your other saltwater flies away, but you may find yourself using them less and less."

Part Three

Saltwater Streamer Flies and Fishing

Harold Gibbs and striped bass—The Gibbs Striper, and variations—Woolner's Sand Eel
—Percy's Sand Eel—Bluefish Bucktail—Katydid Blonde—Irish Blonde—Silver Blonde—
Tips on fishing for stripers and bluefish—Notes on weakfish—Sea trout—Silversides—Brown's Sand Eel—Silver Minnow—Copper Demon—Fly fishing for
pollock

15

Northeastern Saltwater Flies and Fishing

Fond MEMORIES often return to remind us of important days spent with one
noteworthy person or another, partly because of the fun wc had, and partly
because of facts we learned, to be stored away and drawn upon in the
future, like money in the bank.

One of several such treasured occasions happened many years ago,
when Harold Gibbs asked me to fish Rhode Island's Warren River with him
for striped bass. To call Harold "noteworthy" is an understatement. He
was, for many years, commissioner of fisheries for the state of Rhode
Island, a renowned angler with the fly rod, a marine-research specialist, an
unexcelled artist at carving miniature wildfowl, and the originator of the
famous Gibbs Striper Bucktail. With this fly he is reputed to be the first man
ever to take a striped bass with a fly rod.

"You'd best show up at my place early afternoon next Wednesday,"
Harold said over the phone. "The moon then will be full, and the tide will
be high by dark. We'll get in a few hours of late-afternoon fishing, and we
can try it again after dinner, if you've a mind to. Bring a fly rod that could
handle a long line in the wind. I'll have enough flies."

Harold's place was a small and comfortable farmhouse on a broad bluff
of land overlooking the river just upward of its estuary. His wife answered
my tap on the door. "He's downstairs," she smiled, "doing the usual. Why
don't you go on down."

Ducking my head to miss the rafters, I stumbled down the steep stairs
to the stone-lined cellar, where, close by the furnace, amid a clutter of
shavings and bits of wood, Harold sat under a light in a comfortable arm-

209

chair, delicately sanding what was to become a wood duck, so small that it could be hidden in the palm of a hand. On a bench nearby were several other tiny miniatures of ducks, geese, and upland birds, some beautifully painted, and others, mounted on bits of driftwood, awaiting their final colors. I wish I had bought more of them, because they are treasured collector's items today.

Harold's infectious grin wreathed his tanned and weatherbeaten face as he pushed his carving tools aside. "I've been waiting for this," he said, "because this full moon means a higher tide, and it's high at just the right time to bring stripers into the shallows. The crabs are shedding in the marsh grass. The bass know it, and they'll be working close in. We'll have some tea, pull on our waders, and go try for them. Here's some flies I tied for you." He handed me several of his favorite pattern, dubbed by others the Gibbs Striper, and as famous a fish-taker now as it was many years ago, back when all this happened.

Parking the car not far from the bridge, we crossed the lawn of an estate bordering the placid stream where it widened into the estuary. Marsh grass grew abundantly into the shallows near shore, its tips farther out now scarcely showing with the rising tide. As we waded outward Harold pointed to several small crabs, disturbed by our progress, as they scuttled away to bury themselves again in the sand.

"Some of these are shedding their shells, so, for protection, they hide, with only eyes showing, until the new shells become hard," he said. "Bass love to grub for them between the low and high tide levels, where most are found. They shed during the full or dark of the moon. Full-moon tides are higher ones, so provide better fishing. That's why I wanted you to come today. From now on, with the waning moon, fishing will drop off until the dark of the moon. After that evening fishing improves more and more again to the full-moon period.

"You'll also notice many bait fish here, feeding on things in the grasses," he went on. "Now, wade out beyond the grass line until you can't see bottom. Cast across, or up and across, and let the fly swing, gradually increasing casting distance. Your floating line with sinking tip should work the fly deep enough. No need to move around much. A school of bass should find your fly sooner or later. I'll be in sight, downstream a bit."

Wading out to hip depth, I tried a few practice casts nearby and, when fly and leader seemed to sink properly, cast quartering upstream to let the fly swim deep. A plop and a strong swirl caused me to glance downstream, where, in an open spot amid the grasses, another swirl occurred. Harold and I exchanged glances. Too separated for conversation, he held up thumb and forefinger touching in the OK sign to indicate that bass were coming in on the flooding tide.

During this interruption my Gibbs Striper 2/o bucktail had been swinging in the mild current of the wide, brackish river. As it started to hang at the end of the drift a strong yank pulled the rod tip down. As I twitched

210

A

B

Bank

Salt creek

15–1 Fishing a tidal current. The angler should cast upcurrent to point A, allowing fly to sink and swing, and then fish the fly most intensively at point B, where strikes are most apt to occur.

upward the bass made a sizzling run downstream, where it swirled in a wide boil. The fast run had taken out all the fly line and much of the twenty-pound-test Dacron backing. Palming the reel as a brake caused enough tension to induce the fish to return upstream, where it flashed nearby, defiantly shaking its head in a perplexed effort to free the hook. Nearer, it noticed the cause of its predicament and sped doggedly away again, but not as far. After two or three shorter runs it lay exhausted on the surface, shimmering in fresh silver and marked with the dark lateral stripes which sometimes cause its species to be termed "linesides." I put it on the stringer and hurriedly cast again.

211

This time a striper snatched the fly as soon as it touched the water. After a battle similar to the first it was added to the stringer. These were "school bass" of between six and ten pounds, far smaller than those taken over reefs or near rocks at sea, where they may average in the twenty-to-fifty-pound class. These big ones usually are taken in the surf, sometimes with bait, or by casting or trolling big plugs, heavy squids, colorful jigs, or rigged eels with much stronger gear.

As I secured the second striper, I glanced at Harold, whose rod was bowed. He released the fish. The tide now was nearing its high. Bass were showing everywhere, arching in the current and wallowing in the grasses. A profusion of gulls and terns excitedly skimmed and dove over the action, weirdly crying and clucking as they swooped to pick up bits of bait fish discarded by the feeding bass. My rod arm ached as bass after bass was subdued, all but three being released. Harold had done at least as well. As the sun's golden disc nestled into its crimson bed low in the west, he approached slowly along the bank while I waded ashore to join him.

"I'm not as young as I used to be, and I can't take too much of this anymore," he said, grinning at the three striped bass I carried. "Let's go home for dinner. We can try some night fishing later, if you've a mind to.

15–2 Harold Gibbs nets a striped bass for outdoor writer George Heinold. (Photo: Earl Appleton)

My guess is that with this high tide and full moon, the bass will be hitting all night. I've seen similar action when bluefish come in, using similar tackle but with six inches of wire between fly and leader."

Striped bass and bluefish are two of the North Atlantic saltwater fishermen's "favorite four," the others being weakfish (squeteague) and channel bass (red drum, or "redfish"), the latter predominating farther to the south. Mackerel also provide fast and furious sport when boats find them schooling near the surface so anglers can cast into the school. Light tackle is appropriate, with any small fly containing a lot of flash.

The northeast is much less noted for named fly patterns or definite types than the southeast and the west, perhaps because the latter areas boast more species suitable for fly fishing. The famous Gibbs Striper long has been paramount among the very few named streamers with acknowledged popularity and value. It is a prime taker of the species just noted, as well as others. Here is the correct dressing and some useful facts about it:

GIBBS STRIPER BUCKTAIL
HOOK SIZE: 1/0 to 3/0, regular, noncorrosive
HEAD: Black, with yellow eyes and red pupils
BODY: Narrow flat silver tinsel
THROAT: A small bunch of red hackle fibers, rather long
WING: A bunch of capra (Asiatic goat) hair with some of the underfur
   left in (white bucktail may be substituted)
SHOULDERS: A section of dark blue nazurias (swan wing feather) half
   as long as the wing. This should be tied in so it will lie midway of
   the wing to make a stripe down the middle of the wing.
CHEEKS: Each a short barred teal body feather, one-third as long as
   the shoulder (Bali duck or guinea hen breast feathers may be
   substituted)

Harold N. Gibbs, of Barrington, Rhode Island, originated this fly to represent a silverside, which is a forage fish of the smelt family. In addition to saltwater fish it is successful for smallmouth bass, landlocked salmon, and other freshwater species. In 1965 Harold Gibbs gave me an improved version, saying, "After a bass or two had been taken on the old Gibbs Striper the blue swan shoulders were reduced to only four or five blue hairs, so we replaced this with blue capra or bucktail to form a triple wing of white over blue over white. The bright hooks don't need to be bound with tinsel, but we do put a silver-tinsel body on black or bronzed hooks. We prefer short-shanked hooks and rather short wings, about twice as long as the hook."

213

Harold also sent me a similar version tied by Al Brewster, a professional fly dresser of Riverside, Rhode Island. In this one the upper white of the wing is eliminated to provide blue over white. The head has yellow painted eyes with red pupils. Shoulders are jungle cock breast feathers (the long oval black ones with a white stripe along the quill). The throat is red, as before. Brewster says, "This variation is intended to imitate bait fish such as shad, white perch, butterfish, pogies, and alewives. Flies used here in July have wings two and a half inches long. By October they are increased to a full five inches. This is an extremely successful fly."

Another adaptation, unnamed as far as I know, has a silver body, a long white bucktail wing, and shoulders of violet hair half as long as the wing, over which are barred teal body feathers half as long as the shoulder. This fly has no throat, but has a black head with white eye and red pupil. The silver body is of Mylar tubing slipped on over the shank. An alternative way to apply Mylar tubing for a body is to remove the core, flatten the Mylar, and wind it in close coils to the bend of the hook and then back to the eye, where it is tied down.

Frank Woolner, the affable editor of *Salt Water Sportsman* magazine and by my vote the most knowledgeable of northeastern anglers who prefer the briny, maintains that there are no named saltwater patterns, as such, but only types, and he gave me a good one:

WOOLNER'S SAND EEL
HOOK SIZE: 4/0, regular, stainless steel
HEAD: Green, with white eye and black pupil
BODY: Silver Mylar tubing three and a half inches long
TAIL: A green neck hackle with tip removed, inserted in the tubing so the spine protrudes half an inch
WING: A small bunch of green bucktail as long as the tubing, with a few hairs of black bucktail on top
CHEEKS: Jungle cock

This fly could be called a type because it can be dressed in different ways. This one represents the sand eel, or American sand launce (or lance), which is a small, slender, silvery fish slightly resembling an eel. It is found in shallow water along both coasts, where it grows to about six inches. It is a favorite food for salmon, mackerel, bass, bluefish, and other marine sport fish.

To dress this fly, remove the core from a three-and-a-half-inch length of silver Mylar tubing (piping). Dip the end of the green neck hackle in cement and insert all but half an inch into the tubing, lashing it in place with black thread. Push the barb and bend of the hook through the other end of the tubing until nearly an inch is threaded on; then push the hook through the tubing and push the tubing on the shank of the hook, where it is tied down behind the eye. The tubing now should be straight. Dress the fly as usual. Optionally, the Mylar core can be left in except for about a quarter-inch at the tail and the forward ends. Mylar tubing is available in three sizes—small, medium, and large—and in diameters of one-sixteenth, one-eighth, and three-sixteenths of an inch. The medium size is recom-

214

mended here. This fly of course also can be made with tandem hooks, as discussed in Chapter 11, but the above dressing is intended for casting. Several variations can be made in the tail, such as using two neck hackle tips splayed outward. Dyed or natural badger or furnace hackle tips are attractive. To avoid a bulky head, secure and cement the front of the tubing so it ends about three-eighths of an inch behind the eye of the hook. The wing is applied here.

The sand eel, or sand launce, more properly named the eulachon, also is known as the needlefish, or candlefish on the West Coast, where it ranges from northern California to northwestern Alaska. It enters rivers to spawn and apparently dies afterward. It is, or was, used by the Indians extensively for food and for making cooking oil. The term "candlefish" comes from the fact that the Indians dried the fish and fitted them with wicks to serve as candles because of the large amount of oil they contain. A Candlefish Bucktail pattern is given in Part Four.

The importance of this common bait fish along both coasts, along with the fact that there are other forage fishes quite similar to it, recommends another imitation originated by Peter B. Sang, president of the ancient Percy Tackle Company, of Portland, Maine. The fly is made in various color combinations and utilizes the plastic-coated copper wires that come in telephone cable for bodies. The cable contains many fine wires in a variety of colors, and as stated earlier, a foot or so of cable, available as scrap from a telephone installer, can make hundreds of bodies.

PERCY'S SAND EEL

HOOK SIZE: 2 to 2/0, regular, stainless-steel or chrome finish
HEAD: Same as body color
TAIL: A small bunch of straight bucktail between two and three inches
　long
BODY: Wound in touching coils with plastic-coated (insulated)
　telephone wire
RIBBING: Fine silver wire or oval tinsel wound on between the body
　windings and lacquered twice

This simple fly can be dressed in any color; the most popular are black, white, yellow, and red. If black is desired, for example, use black thread, black bucktail (or synthetic hair), and black-coated wire. About four strips of the finest (sixty-fourth of an inch) Mylar tinsel could be mixed with the tail, although the pattern doesn't call for it. The fly imitates the sand eel more in shape than in color. My color preference is black.

215

When bluefish are in a taking mood, which is most always, they aren't fussy about fly patterns. Since their teeth ruin flies quickly, simple and securely dressed ones are most practical. The one that follows is an old standby in New England, albeit a bit fancier than need be.

15–3 *Fly patterns popular in one area usually work well in others. (Photo: Larry Green)*

BLUEFISH BUCKTAIL

HOOK SIZE: 4/0, Eagle Claw #66SS*
HEAD: Black, with white painted eye and red pupil
BODY: Medium flat silver Mylar, lacquered
THROAT: A few strands of red hackle fibers
WING: A bunch of light blue capra (Asiatic goat) hair with some of the underfur left in. Bucktail or artificial hair can be substituted. The wing is very long.
SHOULDERS: Jungle cock breast feathers, one-fourth as long as the wing

216   This pattern was originated by Frank B. Gibbs, of Rumford, Rhode Island, and should be fished very slowly. Current action is all that is needed. The fly is tied with the head an inch or more back on the shank of the hook

*Or use special bluefish hooks, if they can be obtained, or the longest, strongest ringed-eye noncorrosive hooks available.

to make it less likely that the sharp teeth of the bluefish will contact the leader. Those who have seen the big mouths of bluefish will want a little more protection, and it has been noted that about six inches of wire leader is advisable.

A wire leader used by many of us is made with about eight inches of nylon-coated braided wire of about thirty pounds test. Double one end through the fly's eye so the double part is an inch long. Using pliers to hold the two wires together, touch the forward half-inch of the double part over a flame to fuse the nylon coatings to each other. Wrap the completed bond with monofilament of about six pounds test, wrapping one end over itself and binding the other with half hitches or a whip finish. Coat this with Pliobond. A small black swivel can be attached to the other end in the same way. These rigs can be made up in advance, or materials can be carried in the tackle box to do the job quickly whenever needed.

The fact that a fly pattern or type was originated and is popular in one area doesn't mean that it won't work in others. Types like Lefty Kreh's Deceiver and Dan Blanton's Whistler (discussed in the following chapters) are famous respectively in Florida and on the West Coast, but that doesn't mean they won't do well in the northeast; in fact, the reverse is true. About three such types, offering varied actions and in a few different color combinations and sizes, should be sufficient to take any saltwater fish anywhere. One of paramount importance is the Blonde series discussed in Chapter 8. Let's add three color combinations to those already given, because they do excellently in the northeast. The first two were developed in 1967 by Joe Brooks and Tom Cooney in Baltimore, Maryland.

Joe Brooks reported that these flies were very effective in the Caribbean area, perhaps because their colorations resembled species of bait fish there. The third is a favorite of my own which provides the flash of a squid without the weight.

KATYDID BLONDE
HOOK SIZE: 1/0 to 3/0, regular, stainless steel
TAIL: White or pink bucktail (if pink is used add a sparse throat of white)
BODY: Silver tinsel or Mylar
WING: Medium green bucktail over four doubled strips of finest Mylar, very long

IRISH BLONDE
HOOK SIZE: 1/0 to 3/0, regular, stainless steel
TAIL: Light green bucktail
BODY: Silver tinsel or Mylar
WING: Very dark green bucktail

217

SILVER BLONDE

HOOK SIZE: 1/0 to 3/0, regular, stainless steel

HEAD: White, with painted eye and pupil optional

TAIL AND BODY: Cut about two inches of silver Mylar tubing; remove core, and work the tubing over barb and bend of hook until it can be tied down behind the eye. Push hook point through Mylar and tie it down at end of shank. Pick apart the rest of the tubing to form a fairly long tail.

WING: About eight (or more) doubled strands of finest Mylar tinsel, trimmed to be a bit longer than the tail

When this fly is weighted enough to drag bottom it will take flounders in sandy areas if retrieved with small, slow spurts to make it kick up a little sand. In small sizes it is one of the best for mackerel, snapper blues, and other diminutive types. In the above sizes it is as good as the best for the big ones.

The big ones are where one finds them, which is where the bait is. This may be in the surf, where powerful spinning gear and big plugs are the rule. The surf rarely is ideal for fly fishing, but days come when it is mild, the breeze is on our backs, and the fish are herding bait close in. Close in often means an easy cast of not over thirty feet! Fly-rodders must choose more fun rather than more fish, but they sometimes enjoy both, much to the envy of others using more orthodox gear. Take along a fly rod, rigged for instant use. It can make a good day a super one.

Few strikes will be missed if hooks are sharp—a precaution too often ignored. Before tying on the fly, test its point for sharpness. The best honing instrument is a Red Devil wood scraper's file, No. 15 or smaller. Use the triangulation method to get three cutting edges: flat on the bottom and sloping to a point on the sides.

Fly-rodders in the surf find fish by following the crowd, by watching bird action, or by learning the habits of fish, which means studying books on such subjects. On a falling tide, look for sand bars not too far out, with deeper water in between. Bait often becomes penned in such places, and big fish remain to feed. On falling tides, salt ponds and creeks partially empty, washing bait with the flow. Knowing this, big fish wait in deeper water close by and hungrily take many types and colors of flies.

The seaward sides of breakwaters harbor stripers and bluefish in season because they rest there or can find bait in fissures amid the great rocks. Move the boat slowly a moderate cast away. Look for holes and put the fly close in with an incoming wave. School stripers often inhabit small coves in bays. Chesapeake Bay, for example, has many such places. We use the hunting method, anchoring or drifting in one spot and moving to another when that seems barren. One good spot may be enough, because bass in the five-pound range or bigger can be hooked cast after cast.

There is nothing weak about weakfish except for their mouths, which are soft, like shads'. Northern weakfish usually are called "squeteague," or "squets," and are distant cousins of the more spotted southern variety referred to as "trout." The northern weakfish is a beauty, with a dark spotted back, iridescent sides, and a white belly; it usually weighs not over five pounds. Its range extends from Massachusetts to Florida, with greatest concentrations between New Jersey and Chesapeake Bay.

Weakfish nearly became extinct in Atlantic waters in the 1960s, but now are rather common, so their value to fly fishermen should be stressed. They are schooling fish, preferring shallow, sandy bottom areas near the protection of rocks. Since their diet is of wide variety the same tackle and flies used for school striped bass is adequate. In the Chesapeake Bay area they are most abundant between April and November and take flies best under varying conditions, but ordinarily before and after high tides.

Sea trout, or sea-run brown trout, too often are ignored by saltwater fly-rodders, either because they run in relatively few rivers or because anglers don't realize they are there. One of my introductions to them was under the guidance of Don Brown, of Kingston, Massachusetts, a professional fly dresser and a specialist on sea trout. We fished several Cape Cod streams—trout-stream-like graveled-bottom ones in view of their estuaries, deep but narrow and sinuous salt marsh rivers where holding water was far from obvious, and fast flows under bridges into salt ponds.

The sea trout is to the brown trout as the steelhead is to the rainbow, sheathed in shining silver and a robust fighter on light fly tackle, but rarely exceeding five pounds in size. In addition to the Cape Cod fishery some are found in the lower reaches and estuaries of rivers in Connecticut, on the north shore of Long Island, in a few rivers in Maine, and in northeastern Canadian waters, where Atlantic salmon anglers consider them something of a nuisance because they are out for bigger game.

Sea trout often live and thrive in the sea in or near estuaries, running up and down the lower reaches of their rivers with the tides, but some have been known, like Pacific salmon, to roam far afield. Brook trout with the same habits are known as "coasters," usually using big lakes, such as Lake Superior, as their oceans, and traveling into rivers in the same manner.

Small streamers and bucktails such as are used for inland trout are excellent for sea trout and coasters—preferably patterns containing some silver, in sizes between 4 and 12, of which size 6 is a good average. Favorite flies in New England include the hair-wing Gray Ghost, Green Ghost, and Muddler plus the dressings given below and various tan shrimp imitations.

SILVERSIDES

HOOK SIZE: 4, 6X long, Mustad #3665A or #9575
HEAD: White, with black eye and yellow pupil
TAIL: A small bunch of white goat hair about as long as the body

BODY: Small or medium silver Mylar piping bound at rear with white
   thread
WING: Sparse white goat hair, under which is an equal amount of
   peacock herl from the eye of the feather, both extending to end of
   tail

This fly was originated about 1970 by Don Brown of Kingston, Massachusetts, and has been very effective as an imitation of the bait fish of the
same name not only for sea trout but also for striped bass, pollock, mackerel, and landlocked salmon.

BROWN'S SAND EEL
HOOK SIZE: 4 to 6, 8X long, Mustad #94720
HEAD: White, with black eye and white pupil
BODY: Small (sixteenth of an inch) silver Mylar piping bound at rear
   with white thread
THROAT: A very small bunch of white calf tail extending into gap of
   hook
WING: A sparse bunch of pale green calf tail extending slightly
   beyond bend of hook

This sand eel imitation is named for one of its originators to differenti-
ate it from the two sand eel patterns previously mentioned (pages 214–15).
The pattern was developed about 1970 by Don Brown and Jeff Wyman and
is especially effective in areas where sand eels are present for sea trout,
striped bass, pollock, and mackerel.

SILVER MINNOW
HOOK SIZE: 2/0 to 6, regular, stainless steel
HEAD: White
BODY: Silver tinsel or Mylar tubing
THROAT: A sparse and fairly short bunch of red hackle fibers
WING: A bunch of white bucktail, over which is a small bunch of
   peacock herl fibers

This pattern is made by many dressers with variations such as using long
white nylon fibers or other artificial hair for the wing, mixing the narrowest
Mylar flat tinsel into it, and/or adding two or four pale blue hackles under
the peacock herl. Wings are dressed in various lengths, depending on
bait-fish sizes.

220

COPPER DEMON
HOOK SIZE: 8 to 12, 1X short
HEAD: Black
TAIL: A very short bunch of hot orange marabou
BODY: Wide oval copper tinsel over an orange floss core

THROAT: A small bunch of hot orange hackle, which also may be
  applied as a collar
WING: A bunch of hot orange hair extending to end of tail

This fly, usually in larger sizes, is a steelhead pattern, used for sea trout in murky water or as an attractor when the usual ones, as given above, seem to be ineffective. It may be taken by fish as a shrimp, and is included as a change-of-pace fly.

Saltwater anglers often find schools of pollock, which, although related to the lowly cod, are reasonably sporty as fly-rod fare when better game is lacking. I never seek them, but when striped bass fishing was in the doldrums have had fun with them, using flies such as given above. Schools of pollock often come close inshore, some being in the ten-pound range, or bigger, and can be taken on cast after cast. On one day we found big ones boiling in a sandy cove near Point Judith, Rhode Island. On another one when my wife and I were prospecting for mackerel near the bridge between Bailey's Island and Orr's Island, in Maine, we found small pollock which took readily on bucktails swinging in the flow over a grassy area. Their affinity for relatively shallow water helps the fly-rodder.

Pollock are rather pretty, shaped somewhat like striped bass or bluefish, but with backs of olive to brownish green over a yellowish lateral band blending into silver gray below. Schools can be found by trolling. Since they are common commercially they may be underestimated by anglers.

Last, but not least, among the northeastern saltwater fly fishermen's "favorite four" and lesser species is the channel bass, or "redfish." Although its range extends to Massachusetts its value to the fly-rodder mainly is from New Jersey southward, so we'll become acquainted with it in the next chapter.

16

Southeastern Saltwater Flies and Fishing

As you fish southward from Chesapeake Bay, the striped bass gradually gives way to the channel bass, regionally also termed "red drum," "redfish," or "spottail," the last because this coppery-hued fighter can most easily be identified by one or more round black spots on each side of the base of the tail. Shaped much like the striped bass, and fished for similarly, the drum is a member of the croaker family which has a reddish copper-colored back shading to silvery white along the lower sides and belly. It is not a true bass and often makes an audible drumming or croaking sound when feeding or alarmed.

Redfish taken in the surf usually range from twenty to fifty pounds. Fly rods are inadequate weapons except under rare circumstances, so fly fishing for this quarry is more common in inlets, backwaters, sloughs, and other calmer areas. In such spots they run smaller and are called "puppy drum"—exciting fly-rod fare.

A typical day's fishing for puppy drum may consist of towing a skiff behind an outboard until mudding fish or schools are sighted; the latter are sometimes indicated by a bronze-pink coloration in the water. Then, angler and guide or companion transfer to the skiff and stalk the fish by quiet poling. Since drum are very nearsighted, the bright fly must be placed or fished closely in front of one when it raises its head from grubbing on the bottom and starts to move forward. If the cast is clumsy, the fish may flush, but there are others to try for. When the fly is correctly presented, the redfish will smash it and put up a battle similar to that of a striped bass. Any fly the fish can see easily is appropriate. Fish it slowly, striking only when sure the fish has the lure. Much of this is done in sloughs with very shallow water, sometimes hardly enough to float the fish. Therefore, slow-sinking breather-type flies or upside-down weedless ones are popular.

Redfish are less migratory than stripers and bluefish and are available in some Virginia and Carolina areas year-round. Stripers, redfish, and the small puppy drum are found in January along beaches in the Willmington-Southport area, and through April in Roanoke Sound, Oregon Inlet, and other North Carolina hot spots. Fishing falls off in summer and late winter. Seasonal conditions and the long and varied coastline make it important to seek regional advice on where and when to go.

While experts can become rather dogmatic in preferences about saltwater tackle, those less skilled should find that equipment proper for striped bass, bluefish, or Atlantic salmon should do nicely for most saltwater fishing situations all along the Atlantic Coast and around the Gulf. This would be a fiberglass or graphite rod between eight and a half and nine and a half feet long handling a size 9, 10, or 11 standard forward-taper or saltwater-taper fly line, plus 150 to 200 yards of twenty-pound-test braided Dacron backing on a controllable reel such as the economical and efficient Medalist 1495 or 1498. The longer rod helps in lifting line from the water and in properly manipulating the fly. My favorites are an eight-and-a-half-foot Scientific Anglers graphite and a nine-foot graphite made by Cortland, with Scientific Anglers reels because they can be controlled by palming. Resident experts along the coast prefer more expensive precision reels, mainly for their added efficiency in handling record and near-record fish.

If one has trouble getting the line on the reel with this amount of backing, the backing should not be decreased. Instead, cut back on the running line (from the reel end). Tapered leaders to about fifteen pounds test need be no longer than the rod, and may require about ten inches of shock tippet of forty-pound-test monofilament for fish with sharp gill covers such as tarpon and snook.

Hunting tarpon, both big and small, becomes an obsession with many of us. Fish of a hundred pounds and bigger are more suitable for skilled specialists. Those in the fifty-pound class and smaller provide enough sport for me.

The fun for visiting anglers, such as myself, is in the hunting and the hooking, rather than in the size. I remember a wide ditch along the road to Flamingo, on the northern tip of mainland Florida, where tiny tarpon no more than a foot long were boiling and bubbling. At first, a tiny fly and small rod tempted no takes, but later experimentation brought hits and jumps from several, all of which were released.

Small resident tarpon inhabit many parts of canals within sight of Route 1 down the Florida Keys. While such canals usually are lined with houses, a polite request to owners normally gains permission to cast from

223

16–1 Small tarpon amid the mangroves.

their lawns. Look for fish first. Their presence often is indicated by bubbles, and they sometimes can be seen cruising—some rolling, others sunning near the surface. Place the fly ahead of and beyond a selected fish and work the lure before it. The solid take and the somersaulting jumps provide thrills never forgotten. Breather-type flies on hooks about 2/o, about four inches long, in most any color combinations, should be successful.

This urban fishing is a pleasant interlude during a drive along the Keys, but it is more fun to hunt small tarpon out of sight of civilization, in coves and ponds among the mangrove islands. The fish here often are plentiful and in the ten-to-thirty-pound class—great fly-rod fun. Go with someone familiar with the area, because he should know where the fish are and how to find the way back to the dock.

This fishing often is done by poling a small powered skiff or by quietly prospecting with an auxiliary electric motor. Look for showing fish or for bubbles indicating they are below. Watch lanes going into the mangroves, because processions of tarpon often school from them. Cast to selected fish and enjoy their exciting takes and spectacular jumps. These jumps often enable the fish to throw the fly, but the fun is in the hooking and in the jumping. All should be released, anyway.

Working up to the big ones, let's take a cruise into the "back country" —the vast island-dotted area of Everglades Park northwest of the route down the Keys. The skiff, with a competent guide to take you there and get you back, is equipped with a powerful motor for fast traveling, because the trip to selected hot spots can be a long one. The guide takes pride in speed, rooster-tailing the fast boat through narrow waterways between mud flats skirting mangrove islands until, except for him, there seems no way to find the route back home.

On a pleasant, windless day the trip alone is worth the cost. The water from shallow to deep varies from off-tints of white to pale and deeper greens and all shades of blue. The emerald green of the dense mangrove islands erupts with flights of birds, while others unconcernedly tend their young in their big nests. Brown pelicans predominate, but there are pinkish white flocks of roseated spoonbills and other exotic species, all protected in the sanctuary of the great park.

Objects under the surface claim equal interest. The slowly moving boat startles three great rays, which flop through the thin water like migrating geese, clouding the marled bottom. Behind them may be a permit or small shark looking for uncovered crustaceans. The tropic sun beats down on languid activity. A giant turtle swims stolidly by.

Suddenly the guide stops the motor and peers ahead intently. "Three tarpon," he says quietly, pointing. "Big ones!" I grab the fly rod, pulling off line, which trails behind, ready for a cast.

In a division of the channel forming a small darker pool in the thin aquamarine of the flats, four great torpedolike shapes show blacker, quietly cruising.

225

16–2 Stu Apte lip-gaffs a tarp *for Lefty Kreh. The fish was* *released. (Photo: Stu Apte)*

"Try the leading one," the guide murmurs. "Put the fly a few feet ahead and beyond. Let it sink a bit and work it near his nose."

The fly is a yellow-hackled red splay-wing streamer about five inches long on a 4/o stainless-steel hook, carefully sharpened by triangulation. The cast is an easy forty-footer.

A sweep of the rod puts the trailing fly into the air and drops it properly. As the hook's weight gently drifts it downward the big fish leisurely cruise forward. I twitch it slightly and can see the bright wings open and shut enticingly with each short motion. All is deathly quiet. The boat is motionless, anchored securely by the pole, held by the guide, its tip solid in the marl.

226

The fly flutters forward. The leading tarpon sees it. It increases its pace, great jaws gaping expectantly. Will the fish take, or refuse? As its mouth draws near, the fly seems to sweep quickly into it. Loose line is put quickly on the reel as I tighten on the fish, feel the contact, and set the hook hard into the bone and gristle.

Then all hell seems to break loose.

The great fish, feeling the prick of the steel, erupts into the air. Black-backed and armor-clad in shining silver, great mouth distended and gill covers rattling, it cartwheels above us, six feet of shimmering savage power. Its head and tail wave frantically, sometimes seeming to meet, as it falls to the water with a giant splash.

"Wow!" exhales the guide, as he pushes the boat backward swiftly. The fish is too close. Jumps of a giant tarpon can land it in a boat, doing very serious damage to everything.

I don't reply, being for the moment speechless.

The fish doesn't run much, and quickly leaps again, like a pole vaulter without a pole. It lands near where the boat was before the guide had backed us away to a safer distance. Motion pictures of the powerful leaps of big tarpon have awed audiences, but the real thing still has to be seen to be believed.

On the fourth jump the tarpon manages to throw the hook. The fly flutters abjectly down. The great fish flashes away. The others are nowhere to be seen.

"No matter," shrugs the guide consolingly. "Of the many hooked, few are conquered. All you lost was a scale for a souvenir!"

A stiff breeze is building up. The day is ending, and it is at least an hour's fast ride to the dock. We skim the whitecaps home. It is a teeth-rattling, bone-jarring ride.

This latest trip to the Florida Keys and other places south was partly to learn the latest fashions in flies so they could be described in this book. Barton Foth, the renowned angler and distance-casting expert, came to call, gave me samples, and helped fill several pages of notes. Captain Dick Williams, famous fishing guide of Islamorada, took us out for tarpon and bonefish. Later, over a drink or two in his trophy room, we discussed fly patterns on a what-to-use-and-when basis. Lefty Kreh, one of the most affable and helpful angling experts I have ever known, contributed samples of his secret weapons. No, not "secret." Lefty retains no secrets. He gladly shares his profound knowledge with everyone. This book also contains the patterns of other southern experts, some of whom will be noted from time to time as we go along.

Let's start this discussion of southeastern saltwater patterns with a few general observations. These patterns are useful everywhere, along both coasts. Most of them are "types" and can be dressed in all desired sizes and color combinations. Learn how to do each type so you will have a size and color design for all game fish anywhere in the briny. All represent bait fish in silhouettes and in actions of various sorts, so a type and size is selected according to the discretion of each individual angler. We don't select a certain type or pattern for tarpon and a different one for snook, for example. We select it to imitate the shape, size, and action, under varying water depths and conditions, of whatever the game fish seem to be feeding on.

227

Color is a minor consideration except that those on the red end of the scale may do better on top, while those on the green-blue end may be better deeper. Yellow and orange are very visible in discolored water, just as they are most noticeable on the clothing of hunters. White is a good general day color, with black when visibility is poor. There are no very definite rules. As Bart Foth says, "If one doesn't work, try another."

Also, in introduction to these patterns, some words from Charlie Waterman should be helpful. Charlie spends a lot of time fishing, and his regular columns in *Salt Water Sportsman* and other publications are accepted as gospel.

"In recent years I've been concerned with the illusion of length in saltwater streamers. Whereas in some kinds of fly fishing the problem is in getting a small silhouette, the exact opposite is frequently true in the salt. Since really bulky lures simply don't work with fly rods, the object becomes one of giving an illusion of length and keeping a streamlined form that will cast satisfactorily.

"We have used a great deal of peacock herl, the strands left quite long, giving many streamers an illusion of extra length and also resembling the dark lateral line and dark backs so often found in bait fish. We like to add a few strands of very dark bucktail to many patterns, along the sides or on the top. I have felt that the peacock herl is a key to the success of the Silver Outcast, a streamer given to me many years ago by Dr. Ralph Daugherty of McKeesport, Pennsylvania. There have been many times when that pattern has displayed superiority in both fresh and salt water.

"Another suggestion along the same line is the longnose patterns. That began with saltwater anglers tying extremely long 'heads' of thread in order to keep the feathers or hair from fouling on the hook. The heads in themselves gave an illusion of extra length.

"George Radel, a master streamer fly tyer, has come up with some extremely long noses on 6X long hooks. With painted eyes they give the impression of sizable bait fish, and still don't kill the cast. George's longnose flies are more extreme than the ones we've been using but, when I tried them, I was delighted with their performance on tarpon and snook."

SILVER OUTCAST

HOOK: Any size, regular, stainless steel
HEAD: Black
BODY: Flat silver tinsel or Mylar (optional)
WING: White under yellow under medium green bucktail, of any
  desired length, but usually very long
TOPPING: A few peacock herl fibers; usually the longest, but at least as
  long as the wing

This sample given to me by Charlie Waterman is on a 4/0 stainless-steel hook of regular length (one and three-quarters inches) with each succession of hair a bit longer than the one below and with the peacock extending four and a half inches from the eye of the hook.

Since longnose streamers are a comprehensive type that is excellent in various sizes and colors for all saltwater game fish everywhere, and because they deserve more attention in freshwater patterns as well, let's understand their importance by starting at the beginning and tracing their development from then to now.

While saltwater fly fishing had been enjoying slow development all during this century, the budding sport burst into flower because of concentrated experiments by Joe Brooks and a few other expert fly-rodders soon after World War II when towns like Islamorada and Marathon on the Florida Keys were only wide places in the island-hopping road to Key West —a far cry from the congested urbanization found now. Among the other anglers the names of Homer Rhode, Jr., and Lee Cuddy stand out.

Homer and Joe, both noted experts, developed an innovation in saltwater types then called the <u>Homer Rhode, Jr., Tarpon Streamer,</u> which was featured in my first book on this subject, published in 1950, very soon after all this began. Its purpose was twofold: to provide a fly with a longer silhouette and to prevent the wing from fouling itself around the hook. Homer, Joe, Lee, baseball's Ted Williams, and several others fished together. We compared notes, wrote about our little discoveries, worked on and gave away developing fly patterns, and gossiped with all who wanted to listen—all this probably forming the bedrock of modern saltwater fly fishing. I think the Homer Rhode, Jr., Tarpon Streamer was the first established type, or pattern, and this is the way it was dressed, as Homer gave it to me over a quarter of a century ago:

Put a hook in the vise, such as a 3/0 regular stainless-steel or plated one, and tie in four saddle hackles at the end of the shank where the tail usually would be. The two inside hackles can be different in color than the outside ones and can be tied in compressed (each set, concave sides together) or splayed (each set, back to back). The splayed version most often was used.

Now take two or more hackles of any desired color(s) and tie them in over the windings of the wing (tail), palmering them forward fairly thickly to the eye, where they are tied off to finish the head. This palmering (hackling) is, of course, as long as the body of the fly, and constitutes it.

This is the forerunner of all tarpon streamers, dressed in a great variety of colors, as we shall see. Readers will ask why saddle hackles are mentioned

16-3 The Homer Rhode, Jr., Tarpon Streamer.

229

for some flies, and neck hackles for others. The use of either is optional. The stiffer neck hackles, particularly when they are splayed, provide more pulsating action, while the softer shoulder ones wiggle or undulate more. They are equally popular but one kind often works better on a certain pattern or type than the other. If there is a choice, it is specified. The hackling (or palmering) over the body can be made as desired with stiff neck hackles or soft saddle ones, even including the bases of saddle hackles containing marabou-like fluff.

While this type was developed mainly for tarpon, it was found equally effective in smaller or larger (longer) sizes for most other species, including, in later adaptations to be discussed, sailfish.

There was one problem with it that later was solved in two ways, or by a combination of them. The heavy body hackling caused the fly to sink very slowly—a desirable quality under some conditions, but a nuisance in others.

The first solution was to decrease the hackling, which resulted in the beaked versions—the half-beak and the longnose, or full-beak. This in-

16–4 At top, a full-beak (longnose) fly dressed by George Radel. Below are less extreme half-beak flies. (Photo: Charles Waterman)

creased the rate of sinking, but perhaps not enough. In the latter case, bead chain or glass eyes were included to add a bit more weight at the head and to give the fly a diving motion. Understanding these basics is important, because they open the door to a great wealth of very effective saltwater patterns, as we shall see.

First, let's do a full-beak, or longnose, a fly appearing very similar to beaked bait fish such as the balao, usually called the "ballyhoo," a great trolling bait, particularly for sailfish and dolphin along the Gulf Stream.

Using a regular-shank hook about 3/0 in size, tie in four saddle or neck hackles, compressed or splayed, at the tail, as was done previously, such as two grizzly hackles inside two orange ones. In this case, use red thread. Take two defluffed hackles (one of each of these two colors) and make three or four turns to mix each of the two hackles over the tying thread which secured the hackles at the tail. Wind the thread in close coils to the eye of the hook and then back and forth to make a "beak" which tapers from the collar to the eye. Apply cement during these stages of dressing. Paint or varnish the beak, as desired, and add eyes and pupils optionally.

This particular dressing was given to me by Lefty Kreh, and the red beak merely was varnished. Stu Apte's Tarpon Fly, very similar, has a wing (tail) of yellow hackles outside orange ones, with a hackling of the same two colors and a fluorescent orange beak. These flies are between four and five inches long, including a beak of an inch or slightly less. They are for clear water and normally are on 3/0 hooks, which have been found to cast and hook better than larger sizes, even on tarpon over one hundred pounds.

Longnoses favored by George Radel are on 6X long, 3/0 hooks and extend a full seven inches, almost three inches of which is the beak. Some, however, are smaller and/or shorter, and all often have a topping of peacock herl, with painted beak, eye, and pupil.

Half-beaks are longnoses with beaks about half as long. These are made either by applying the wing (tail) a bit more forward on the shank or by stopping the winding on the shank halfway to the eye, so the beak is half as long as a full-beak, the rest being the bare hook behind the eye. This seems to be a shortcut to avoid some of the windings, and is less popular.

Longnose patterns are favorites all along the Atlantic. They also are finding popularity on the West Coast, as will be noted in the next chapter in the description of the Janssen Half-Beak. Length is the answer for the light-tackle fisherman who wants to represent big bait fish. As Charlie Waterman says, "You can't produce a big, fat bait without bogging down the casting. What's needed is a long, slender item with good planing qualities. It slides through the air easily and through the water the same way."

231

Thus, the longnose full-beak or half-beak streamers are the next generation in descent from the early tarpon fly which seems to have been originated by Homer Rhode, Jr., who lived in southern Florida and who was a noted angler, writer, and guide. In a box or two of these given to me by various angling experts, I note the following color combinations:

WING	COLLAR
Red	Orange
Red and yellow	Yellow
Pink	Pink
Pink	Blue (dark)
Orange	Orange and red
Orange and yellow	Yellow
Yellow	Red
Green (light)	Orange
Blue (dark)	Orange
Grizzly	Grizzly

No one has been able to provide tangible reasons for these color combinations, and the absence of white and black is noted. These may be omissions, because we will see that a somewhat similar origination of Lefty Kreh's is all white with fine Mylar strips included for flash.

In clear-water situations such as along the Keys and in the Caribbean, short flies four or five inches long are much preferred, despite whatever some writers say about it. When dark or dirty water is encountered the favorite flies for big tarpon are twice as big and as bulky. For example, Lefty Kreh sent me one popular at a tarpon camp on the Colorado River in Costa Rica. Such jungle rivers are roiled and dark. Bulky flies are easier to see and produce more strikes.

This particular 4/o pattern was named by Dan Blanton the Harold's Tiger, after one of the guides there. The wing has six chartreuse saddle hackles, on each side of which is a grizzly hackle. The collar is wound with an inch of hackles from wing to eye consisting of half black, a quarter chartreuse, and a quarter black at the head, where there are two medium-sized bead-chain eyes. From eyes to end of hackles the fly is five inches long.

Old patterns often bob up under new names to add to confusion and to deprive originators of their discoveries. Although the new names aren't worth recording, later comments affirm the values of the originals. Several of these purloined patterns are copies of Homer Rhode's Tarpon Streamer, about which it is said: "It is a killer in very shallow water, especially for sharks and puppy drum, because it sinks very slowly due to the palmered body; also giving maximum action." "Favorite color combinations are red tail and white body, red tail and orange body, red tail and yellow body, and combinations of these with grizzly hackles. Red and orange does well for puppy drum and for dolphin around weed lines along the edge of the Gulf Stream." (This "dolphin" isn't the mammal also called the porpoise. It is the dolphin fish.) "Try red and yellow for snook and red and white for sharks." Sharks offer fun on light tackle when better game is scarce. To the above colors I would add all black and all white, or a combination of the two.

Another very popular type no saltwater fly fisherman should ignore is the famous Deceiver, now called <u>Lefty's Deceiver</u>, originated by Lefty Kreh to provide a slim streamer, easy to cast, that would swim and give the appearance of usual forms of bait fish. He produced one of the best all-around flies ever to come out of a vise, tied small (inverted) for bonefish, large for sailfish, and in sizes in between for the basses, tarpon, snook, and other species that will take a fly.

Use any hook of average shank length, such as Mustad's #34007. Monocord 3/0 thread is good for small sizes and Nymo or any size A flat thread for hooks 2/0 or larger, in black or red. Let's try a white Deceiver (Lefty's favorite) with red thread. Use soft white saddle hackles that, when tied in, will be as long as the hook for small flies (such as sizes 1 and 2) and one and a half times as long as the hook for larger ones (such as 1/0 to 4/0). These lengths aren't mandatory because Lefty sent me a Deceiver he dressed himself which has a wing (tail) three times as long as the hook, this fly being for tarpon. Flies for snook and many other species would be shorter.

Select six white saddle hackles of the same size and tie them splayed to the end of the shank. Also, double about six strands of one-sixty-fourth-inch-wide Mylar and tie them in so six strands will be on each side of the feathers. These are nearly as long as the wing. Cement the base.

Wrap the body with eighth-inch-wide Mylar nearly to the eye of the hook, and apply head cement. Lead wire can be used to weight the body, which also can be made of floss, yarn, chenille, monofilament, Mylar tubing, etc.

The wings of the Deceiver are usually bucktail, taken from the middle underside for best breathing action. Arctic fox is excellent for small sizes, and other natural or synthetic hairs can be used, either by themselves or mixed. A good artificial is called FisHair, sold by mail by Fly Fisherman's Tackle Service. This comes in twenty-four colors and various lengths.

Take a moderate bunch of the selected hair and spin it around the hook as a collar just behind the eye, or apply it in two bunches, over and under the shank, so the two bunches meet. This hair is nearly twice as long as the hook. Lefty says, "Too many people don't tie the collar on properly. It should flow back over the feathers of the wing to form a bait-fish body shape."

Finally, apply a small bunch of hair on top to improve the silhouette and to help the fly to ride upright. This can be of a different color, or of peacock herl, etc. Cement the hair, complete the head, and apply several coats of lacquer. A Deceiver is shown in Figure 16-5.

233

This type also is recommended for big freshwater fish such as large-mouth, smallmouth, and landlocked striped bass, trout, salmon, etc. A wide

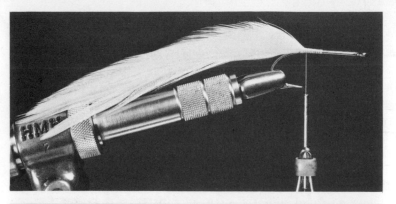

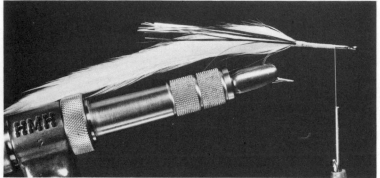

16–5 *Steps in tying Lefty's*
Deceiver. (Photos: Lefty Kreh)

range of color schemes is obvious. For example, dress the fly with a yellow or green wing, white collar, brown or black topping, and some strands of peacock as long as the wing over that.

Another excellent now-standard pattern similar to the Deceiver is the Cockroach—a fly quick and easy to tie, and named perhaps because of its dark colors. Using a regular 2/0 saltwater hook, tie in with black thread six grizzly neck hackles near the end of the shank so the two sets of three splay outward slightly. For this size of hook the feathers are three inches long. At the head, using red thread, spin on a bunch of white-tipped black to brown gray squirrel tail hair. The amount should be enough to conceal the hook and should be slightly longer than it. No body and other embellishments are necessary. Lefty Kreh recommends this pattern particularly for tarpon and doesn't mention its being dressed in other color combinations, but there is no reason why it shouldn't be. It looks like a good all-purpose freshwater streamer as well as a saltwater type for many species. This size is just under four inches long.

A brownish fly like this does well when fished over a white sandy bottom, probably because it shows better there.

An unnamed variation of the above pattern calls for four saddle hackles applied near the end of the shank, with a marabou tip on each side at the head. A large bunch (fifteen or so) of finest (sixty-fourth-inch-wide) Mylar strips are applied on each side as shoulders, and they are clipped to various lengths averaging about as long as the hook. The wing is twice the length of the hook and the marabou extends to the hook's bend. All white, with a white head, is popular, but this variation is made in many colors and combinations.

Tarpon flies nearly always are feather-winged because this gives more breathing action. Smaller patterns for snook are about equally divided between bucktails and streamers. Although options of anglers vary widely, this chapter provides a more than sufficient selection for all saltwater fish that can be enticed to take artificials. Bonefish patterns are rather unique and will be discussed later.

Dressing *bucktails with multiple wings* is far from new and evidently began with the work of a Wisconsin lady fly dresser who started at the bend of the hook to tie in alternating bunches of two colors of hair to form a large, flat wing covering the shank from bend to eye. This resulted in a popular pattern called the Ozark Weedless Bucktail and containing six or more

16–6 Stroud's Ozark Weedless Bucktail.

235

wings tied upside down to make it weedless, featured by the Stroud Fly Company, of Arlington Heights, Illinois. The pattern is shown in Figure 16-6. The fly, in sizes from 8 to 8/0, took all types of game fish, from bluegills to tarpon.

Credit evidently goes to Barton H. Foth, of Islamorada, Florida, for converting the idea into the multiple-winged Bart Foth Bucktail, as shown in Figure 16–7. The type affords a much longer wing than conventional bucktails, with a very bait-fish-like narrow and high silhouette, and avoids tying on too much hair at one time, which would make the head too bulky and insecure. The secret is in tying in small bunches of hair, one after the other, starting at the end of the shank and continuing to the eye with about five separated bunches.

Let's tie this as a large tarpon fly in yellow and red to make a fly five inches long. Put a 2/0 to 4/0 regular-shank saltwater hook in the vise and use strong red thread, winding in touching coils from head to bend. Lacquer the windings. Wind forward over the windings about six turns and tie in a small bunch of the longest yellow bucktail available, lashing it down with about six turns of thread. Clip off excess hair closely, slanting forward, and cement the windings. Make six more turns of thread and do the same again, and once more until three bunches of very long yellow hair have been applied. Then apply a bunch of red hair, and follow this by another bunch of yellow hair. Five bunches of hair have been applied, all of the same longest length. This should bring the applications to the head, which then can be finished and tied off. Five applications should be enough, but more or fewer can be used, according to the length of the hook's shank. The preliminary step of winding down the body can be dispensed with, but it makes a more secure fly.

16–7 The Bart Foth Bucktail, dressed by Bart Foth.

236

The Bart Foth Bucktail is dressed in a great variety of color combinations, and in all sizes. For example, starting from the rear, and using red thread:

All light blue

White, with last application light blue

Orange, with next to last application yellow
All pink
Pink, with next to last application orange
Pink, with last application light blue
All orange

Color selections depend mainly on water conditions. Try orange-yel-low-red patterns for clear water and blue-white ones for turbid.

It is difficult to find bucktail long enough for the big flies, but it is available. Smaller sizes for smaller tarpon, snook, dolphin, redfish, kingfish, mackerel, cobia, amberjack, etc. are effective in the above patterns or types, as well as in others that follow.

In Florida, chickens with grizzly (gray-barred) feathers are called Domi-nicks, and a fly using such is called a <u>Dominicker</u>, favored in small sizes for baby tarpon, bonefish, small dolphin, and other species. Secure white thread at the head of the fly and tie in a small bunch of orange hair, with a small bunch of white hair over it, both slightly longer than the undressed hook. On each side splay a grizzly neck hackle as long as the hair.

Dominickers are tied in other variations. For example, make a wing of orange bucktail and splay a dull orange grizzly hackle on each side, adding a collar of a grizzly hackle dyed yellow.

Chenille bodies are easy and effective in relatively small flies, and such types hook all but the biggest species—those too, on occasion.

Try a thick white chenille body with a fairly long wing of brown over white bucktail to which fine Mylar strips are added. Or try a white chenille body with a wing of long white bucktail, with very large glass eyes or ones of bead chain. Or a thick yellow or white chenille body with a bucktail wing of the opposite of these colors and a collar of red, grizzly, or black hackle. All combinations of red, orange, yellow, and white are effective, with wings of hair or splayed hackles. Some of these flies sport weighted bead heads; others, bead-chain or glass eyes. All do well at one time or another, and the sky's the limit.

Apply weed guards for grassy areas or for casting close to mangroves, but avoid them unless necessary.

While color selection isn't of major importance (and we have observed slight differences of opinion), many anglers go by the rule "The brighter the water and weather, the brighter the fly," and vice versa. Orange and yellow are good colors under all conditions, since they are midway between the whites and reds on one hand and the grizzlies and blacks on the other.

After I thought I had originated the Silver Blonde mentioned in Chapter 15, I was given a very similar sample, also dressed entirely in sixty-fourth-inch-wide Mylar. This one is done by the Deceiver method, rather than the Blonde one, and usually is tied on hooks from sizes 2 to 3/0; the fly is from two to about four inches long and is called the <u>Mylar Streamer</u>. Tie in a fairly large bunch of the fine Mylar near the end of the shank as a tail. Tie in other small bunches around the head, a bit longer than the hook and concealing it. The Blonde or the Deceiver method should be equally effective. In southern waters the pattern does well on bluefish, Spanish or king mackerel, and all other species that feed on bright, silvery bait fish.

Another fly which could be called a "type" because it can be dressed in various ways is the Glass Minnow. Make a short tail of anything desired, such as a bit of red marabou. Wrap the body in Mylar, varnish it, and then overwrap it with tight coils of monofilament. Fluorescent yellow Stren is good. This body represents a small semitranslucent bait fish, and any color(s) of hair wing can be used, with or without a throat. White, yellow, or green wings are effective; also the colors used in Candlefish, Herring, and Coronation bucktails.

Also, try this body with the wing dressed in the semiweedless upside-down method, for bonefish. The inverted version is popular in three sizes: on a No. 4 hook for tailing fish, on a No. 2 hook for fish cruising in shallow water, and on a No. 1 or 2 weighted hook for water over two feet deep.

Tarpon flies in 1/0 to 4/0 sizes are effective with the same body. Apply the long hackle tail, the body as above, and a small and narrow hackle collar. When wings (tail) of yellow and orange saddle hackles are used with a yellow hackle collar, the fly is called the Tarpon Special Streamer. Fluorescent yellow Stren is favored for the body.

Anglers visiting Florida waters usually have bonefish in mind, and the sizzling first long run of this "silvery ghost of the flats" has to be experienced to be believed. Big bonefish often make fast runs of about 175 yards. They do it in speed-record time.

Beginners usually try it first with bait, often placed before cruising fish by a guide using spinning tackle. A fish may pass by the bait without seeing it, but it often will smell it in the current and return to pick it up. When this happens, and the angler strikes, the reel drag had better have been set to only moderate tension.

Bonefish come up on the flats with the rising tide, slowly cruising forward in water only about a foot deep. Schools can be seen by looking for waving tails and dorsal fins, and by observing small light spots that suddenly appear as the fish muddy the marl while grubbing for crustaceans and other food.

Experienced anglers stalk bonefish by wading with fly rod and fly. They usually travel to bonefish flats in power boats towing skiffs or in small power boats that can be poled. They look for single fish or a few instead of a school, because the lone ones usually are bigger, and those of ten pounds or better are the quarry. Seeing these, the angler usually leaves the boat and quietly wades to put himself in a position well in front of the oncoming fish. As they approach, quick motion or a sloppy cast will flush them, sending them streaking for the sanctuary of deep water.

Ideally, the angler quietly casts the fly beyond and ahead of the slowly moving fish, which may stop from time to time to poke around in the chalky marl. Meanwhile, the fly slowly settles and is twitched in front of the fish

238

8 *An angler quietly casts beyond and ahead of a bonefish. (Photo: Orvis Co.)*

as it raises its head and moves forward. The bonefish should take it quickly if it hasn't been frightened. If it doesn't, the idea is to let the fly settle for only a second or two, and then to continue stripping it in.

When the hook has been set the fish will flash into a long run, the direction usually being predictable because it is back toward deeper water. The angler holds his rod as high as possible to try to keep the line clear of obstructions, such as mangrove shoots. If there are many of these, and the fish zigzags between them, it must be followed to try to free the line. Usually the run is unimpeded, and the fish finally will stop. Then tension can be applied to lead it back.

When the fish sees the angler it usually will make a shorter run or two; then, exhausted, it will slowly circle until it can be brought close enough to free the hook. Bonefish are poor as table fare, and those not desired for mounting as trophies should be released. Artificial resuscitation may be necessary if the freed fish can't depart upright. Hold it by the tail and slowly move it backward and forward until it regains enough strength to swim away.

Barracuda often are interested spectators, and seem to sense what's going on. One or more may lie in the thin water, malevolently eyeing the contest in the hope of attacking the tired bonefish. Under such conditions it is well to break loose and go somewhere else.

The Frankee-Belle Bonefish Fly has been popular on the Keys for more than a quarter of a century, and it still is. It was named for Frankee Albright

239

and Belle Mathers, relatives and highly competent guides. George M. L. La Branche spent many winters in Florida, and often fished with Frankee, who now raises orchids.

Hook sizes are 2 to 8, the smaller range being better for the flats. As Figure 16-9 shows, make a short body of medium-width yellow chenille and put on a throat of white bucktail extending a bit beyond the bend of the hook. The wing, a bit longer than the hook, consists of two splayed white hackles outside of which is a splayed grizzly hackle on each side, all of the same length. The head is red.

16–9 The Frankee-Belle Bonefish Fly.

This is a pattern which is varied by many color combinations of white, brown, black, or gray wings, green or yellow bodies, and white or yellow throats. A red or orange and yellow combination is good for discolored water. The previously mentioned Dominicker is one of these. Splayed-wing patterns settle slowly, provide excellent action, and are less inclined to pick up grass. Faster-sinking bucktails are made in the same sizes merely by tying a fairly long tail of one or more colors of hair on a hook and adding a body of any kind desired in color combinations already mentioned.

Bonefish flies usually are tied upside down, or on keel hooks, to make them more nearly weedless. Try the Frankee-Belle and similar versions on keel hooks, and also in the upside-down version. In the latter try polypropylene yarn instead of hair. This modern synthetic product is a twisted yarn of fine fibers that can be stroked straight easily. Since it is so buoyant that it actually is lighter than water, it helps greatly in making upside-down flies swim that way. Many fly dressers tie flies upside down and don't realize they don't ride with the hook's bend upward unless tied very heavily with extremely buoyant hair. Polypropylene actually forces the hook to turn over. Try swimming a few dressed both ways, as a test.

This substance is available in many colors and is excellent for very small flies, in both fresh and salt water, when used in weedy areas, such as in certain kinds of pond fishing as well as in bonefishing. Dress regular-shank hooks with flat Mylar and tie on polypropylene yarn under the head, as a thick throat, clipped off just beyond the bend. Add two or three doubled strips of finest Mylar in the same length as an attractor. This makes the hook turn over, so the throat becomes a wing. Try Poul Jorgensen's "Seal-Ex" for a buggy-looking body material. When using small stainless-steel hooks, many experts prefer Mustad's #34007 because of its very fine wire diameter.

Three combinations of these small polypropylene-winged upside-down flies are recommended for bonefishing, dressed on the above hook in size 4, 6 or 8:

Silver body with grass-green poly and Mylar strips
Brown body with brown poly with or without Mylar strips
Black body with black poly and Mylar strips

These three patterns were sent to me by the noted expert Lefty Kreh, whose proper first name (Bernard) he considers needless. With reference to the black pattern above and my wonder why black hasn't been used more in Florida and Gulf Coast patterns, Lefty says, "This is my personal favorite among all bonefish flies. I have had tremendous success with it. I am using more all-black flies. I started using all-black streamers for tarpon in the late 1960s and find them to outfish many other colors."

On an early spring day while visiting in Miami the report came in that it was too windy for good fishing on the Keys, so we decided to go to a recommended canal on the Tamiami Trail near Naples in search of snook. Snook are where you find them, and the best ways for visitors to do so is to take advice from local authorities, preferably hiring a guide until you get the hang of things.

Generally, around islands, high tide is best with flowing water. A run-out tide is good in creeks or rivers. Although snook are available year-round, fishing for them is best on the eastern side from early November past the middle of March. They frequent island areas on the Gulf side in warm weather, and big ones can be found in coastal passes during late spring and early summer. Excellent spots are close to deep mangrove banks where there is a moderate to strong tidal flow, such as among the Ten Thousand Islands from November to late March. Water is only a few feet deep, making a floating line with sinking tip appropriate. Cast close in, using a slow-sinking streamer such as the Homer Rhode, the Deceiver, or the Silver Outcast in sizes 3/0 or 4/0. Big tarpon streamers are appropriate, as well as the chenille-bodied patterns mentioned above.

Since snook aren't fussy about what they eat, presentation is more important than pattern. A twenty-to-forty-pound-test shock tippet is recommended because the snook's gills are sharp. When hooked, small fish usually head for the mangrove roots, and of course the trick is to power them out into deeper water, if possible. The big ones are more inclined to argue in the open. Many anglers favor popping bugs, but most experts will say that streamers usually are more successful—though not always.

Tamiami Trail's canals have drainage ditches running into the Gulf, like teeth on a comb. Locations are identified by the numbers on the many bridges. The recommended canal we visited was the color of coffee with cream, and looked rather hopeless. A white Deceiver did the trick, however, and we caught snook until we were tired of it, including a few big ones in the fifteen-pound range. Casts were made close to the opposite bank, but hookups usually occurred when the fly was invisible, deep in the dark water. When hooked, the fish would make a few runs, favor us with several jumps,

241

16–10 *Paul Crum releases a snook he took on a Lefty's Deceiver. (Photo: Lefty Kreh)*

and then try bulldog tactics until subdued. These often took the fish so close to one bank or the other that lines became entangled in saw grass or the fronds of jack palms, requiring us to reel in while working the tackle free, meanwhile keeping a cautious eye out for snakes.

If anglers in Florida should select from their many popular species a "favorite four," as we do in the north, snook surely would be one of them.

To end this wealth of popular southern patterns let's look at an unusual one recommended particularly for big barracuda but excellent for offshore game fish as well. It is made of a straight hairlike synthetic called Dynel, which comes in many colors. Called the Cuda Fly, it was originated by George Cornish and Ray Donnersberger. It is tied on a bare regular-length saltwater hook in sizes about 2/o with three small bunches of Dynel strands, dark blue over light green over white. These strands are nine inches long, or more, and make a bunch less than a quarter of an inch in diameter, secured and cemented behind the eye of the hook with red thread.

This streamer is not difficult to cast and works with a streamy eel-like effect. Big barracuda presumably take it for an eel. Having seen them take fish whole which are much longer than this, I don't doubt that they can inhale this length without effort. A trouble with it was that the rear of the fly would open, or "blossom," during pauses in the retrieve. Lefty Kreh remedied this by sealing the rear half-inch of the fibers together with rubber-based Pliobond cement. Now, someone up here in the north will get the idea of doing the Cuda Fly in *black* Dynel. I suspect it will be a killer

242

for striped bass, but the name will have to be changed!

Charlie Waterman says about the Cuda Fly, "Long things aren't hard to throw with light gear. A prime example is the foot-long (or even longer) Dynel streamers used for big offshore fish and extremely deadly on barracuda. Dynel, often called 'doll hair,' sheds water and remains light. Casting is no problem, and a foot of it glides through the water like a gaudy snake. It is the fly fisherman's answer to surgical-tubing lures."

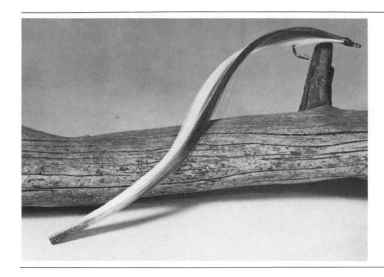

16–11 The Cuda Fly, originated by George Cornish and Ray Donnersberger and dressed by Lefty Kreh.

Patterns which have originated in one area often are equally effective in others, but may not be popular because they are unknown or untried. Bait fish are quite similar up and down both coasts, and game fish strike at size and action more than at color or pattern. Patterns and types provide varieties of action, which is why so many are so useful. In the next chapter, for example, we'll discuss Dan Blanton's Whistler, a West Coast origination very popular also in Florida and Gulf waters, and one which northeasterners should look at carefully.

17

Western Saltwater Flies and Fishing

Anyone writing on this subject should be awed by its scope, because the versatility and abundance of estuarial, coastal, and offshore game fish from Vancouver to Baja is almost beyond comprehension—coho and Chinook salmon, among others; cutthroat trout and steelhead; and shad, striped bass, bonito, mackerel, and yellowtail and a wealth of other offshore species, to mention some of the stars in the cast. Knowledgeable angler-writers could do complete books about several of them, and some have done so.

A book, or even a chapter such as this, on how to hook any of these fish with a fly rod really should not come from an eastern writer. Experts like Larry Green and Hal Janssen should do it. My excuse, as an infrequent visitor to the West Coast, is that the background of the earlier fly types and patterns can be presented, as well as over a dozen modern ones with which even some of the western addicts may not be familiar.

Under the shelter of such a leaky apology, let's take a quick trip down the coast to see what manner of furs and feathers fish are fond of.

Before the 1950s, most fishermen thought that winter steelhead, as well as coho and Chinook salmon, couldn't be coaxed to take flies. Under proper conditions, fly fishermen now are successfully taking winter sea-run rainbows in most of the coastal streams and estuaries of the northwest. Anglers who used to troll for big Chinooks with hardware now find it more fun, and just as productive, to prospect for these lunkers from prams and to hook them with flies wherever they are showing.

244

During the 1950s a few explorers working the late steelhead runs on California's Eel and Klamath rivers began hooking Chinooks (also known as king, spring, or tyee salmon). During this period great advances were being made in rods, lines, and fly types or patterns, not only making this possible, but also making it a standard way of life. If the fish were holding deep they could be reached with fast-sinking or high-density shooting heads, or lead-core ones for the very deep spots. These, when they were necessary, brought the flies to the fish, and excellent fly types and patterns began to burgeon, as we shall see.

A few bits of the background may be of interest, as they apply to the two most popular species of Pacific salmon—the Chinooks and the silver salmon (also called the coho, or cohoe), found principally inshore and offshore from the estuaries of river systems such as the Columbia, Willamette, Rogue, and Umpqua.

Silver salmon make very limited migrations from northern Pacific rivers into the sea, and often grow to full maturity within a relatively small area. They migrate to salt water as yearlings. At this time they frequently are caught and referred to as "sea trout." Upon reaching adulthood in their third year they return to their rivers to spawn, usually doing this on the gravel bottoms of very small creeks far up in the source waters of the rivers. In the Puget Sound area, fishing starts about the middle of June, with catches averaging between three and five pounds. Their growth continues at such an amazing rate that, by the middle of September, they reach a weight of ten or twelve pounds, with many much heavier. In this area September is the peak fishing month, because the salmon will usually have traveled up the streams to consummate their spawning activities by October and November.

During the 1950s flies for silver salmon became standardized to a considerable extent. A group of anglers including William Lohrer, George McLeod, Letcher Lambuth, Zell Parkhurst, and Roy Patrick concluded that the most successful flies were those of the bucktail type which represented in color and shape the two principal bait fishes of the area, the candlefish and the herring.

Bucktails imitating these have become standard patterns, with silver bodies and white polar bear (or substitute) wings shading to greens, blues, and other colors above. Three examples of these, as good now as they were then, are the Candlefish, Coronation, and Herring bucktails, whose descriptions are included in Part Four.

Roy A. Patrick, who will be remembered as a famous Seattle fly dresser, described to me the general color schemes and sizes of Pacific salmon flies in a letter from which the following quotation is taken:

"In my mind the person who has done the most toward the original standardization of both the Candlefish and the Herring bucktails is Mr. Letcher Lambuth, although it has been my pleasure to keep a finger on all the alterations and groups of patterns which have been fishably effective

245

since these two flies were originated. Changes made by fishermen, simplifi-
cations in dressing, and experiences in fishing have resulted in a flood of
color combinations, some of which have been found to be very good while
others have been discarded. The preferred combinations are as follows
(dressed on silver tinsel bodies with polar bear hair unless especially
noted):

Green over white
Blue over white
Orange over white
Brown (bucktail) over white
Green over yellow over white
Blue over green over white
Blue over red over white (Coronation pattern)
Green over red over white
Gun-metal gray over medium green over fuchsia over white
Blue over green over yellow over white
Gray over green over peach over white

"You will note that embossed tinsel has been used on some of these
flies. My inclination is to the pastel shades rather than the bright ones. We

*17–1 Famous western angler-writer
Larry Green admires a twelve-pound
Chinook taken on a simple bucktail.
(Photo: Larry Green)*

prefer long-shanked hooks in sizes 2/0 and 3/0. Sometimes a tandem or trailer hook is snelled to a lead hook of a larger size by a very short piece of fifteen- or eighteen-pound nylon monofilament. In recent years the trend has been to more or less do away with tandem hooks in favor of a single hook with an overall length of approximately two and a half inches, ranging in size from 3/0 to 5/0. This hook has a looped or ringed eye so that a spinner may be attached. A great deal of success has been obtained with the fly and spinner tactics."

While the use of fly and spinner does multiply hookups when trolling in or near estuaries, anglers devoted to fly fishing prefer casting for Chinooks as well as for silvers. Both species are found in the same places from time to time, usually by driving along the river while looking for surface action. When one or more Chinooks are seen rolling, small boats such as eight-foot car-top prams are launched. Casts usually are made quartering downcurrent, or crosscurrent to sink flies deeper. There is no mistaking the deep, head-shaking action of a big fish. It may bolt and take the line well into the backing, requiring the angler to pull anchor and allow the fish to tow the little craft until line is regained and the salmon has become exhausted enough to allow it to be tailed or beached. Upstream of estuaries the rivers usually become a series of definable pools whose flow still is influenced by the tide. Fish collect in such places, waiting for a rise of water to induce them to start for their spawning grounds.

Since bait fish haven't changed after this short account of the earlier beginnings, there is no reason for the flies to have changed either, but they have, to a certain extent. Usually they now are smaller, even down to size 8, and shorter, as in the Comet patterns described in Chapter 7. Each area has its favorites, and even these change from time to time, so regional authorities should be consulted.

Cutthroat trout in estuarial waters are relatively neglected because anglers usually are in search of the bigger game. Having caught cutthroats in the two-pound range (which is considered about average) and having found them to be tough little adversaries on light tackle, an easterner may be rather envious of this disinterest in them in the west.

The migratory cutthroat trout commutes so frequently between salt water and fresh water that, like the anadromous rainbow called the steelhead, it only partially belongs in a chapter on saltwater fishing. Like its landlocked counterpart, it is marked by a V-shaped red line between jaw and gills, this marking often being concealed unless the gills are spread. Unlike its freshwater brother, it is silvery of side and dark of back, very similar in appearance to the salmons and the steelhead. In Oregon it is called the "blueback" and in other places is known as the "harvest trout," "Rocky Mountain spotted trout," or by several other names. It rarely grows to a great size and is most often caught weighing in the vicinity of two pounds.

247

The sea-run cutthroat differs from the steelhead and the salmons in that, rather than traveling into fresh water only for the purpose of spawning, it travels often between salt water and fresh in search of food. Usually it spends its first two years of growth in the river and then travels to the sea for another two years, during which it lives in the estuary of its river and makes frequent trips into the fresh water for a change in diet. When it is three or four years old, it is an adult fish. At this stage of life it usually will go into its river in the early fall and travel to the source waters to spawn in the late winter or early spring, after which it returns to the estuary again. During this annual migratory season many young cutthroats and some adult fish will remain in tidewater.

The travels of the cutthroat are of interest to the fly fisherman because they indicate when and where fly fishing will be best. Fly fishing in the rivers is best in the fall and early winter, when the greatest number of cutthroats are in the streams. Fly fishing in bays and estuaries is best in the late spring and through the summer until the fall migration begins.

The cutthroat come into the rivers to follow the migrations of the several species of salmon and to feed on salmon fry when they are making their trip to the sea. Thus there are several minor migrations of cutthroat trout, but these vary so widely because of conditions of temperature, food, and the river itself that it would be dangerous and misleading to attempt to draw specific general conclusions.

Saltwater fishing for cutthroats in the late spring and summer is dictated largely by the actions of the tides. The fish travel into the estuary on the outgoing tide and return up the mouth of the river during the flood. It is easiest for the fly fisherman to locate them during the last of the ebb and the beginning of the flood tide, when many fish should be concentrated in the pools of the channel. In some places wading is possible, but in others a boat must be used if one is not to get caught far out on the flats and risk a ducking.

Favorite cutthroat water is not unlike what the eastern brook trout prefers: rocky, gradually sloping bottom so shallow it usually can be seen; pockets of quiet water, rather than fast currents; places near rip-rap or in the shade of overhanging foliage or sunken logs. Long casts rarely are needed. Fish often follow flies and take them so close that little more than the leader is off the rod.

Cutthroat flies usually are on size 6 or 8 hooks and are of two general types—those that imitate bait fish, as given above, and attractors such as the Royal Coachman bucktail or Mickey Finn and also the type used for steelhead, in reds, yellows, oranges, and whites, like the Skykomish Sunrise and Umpqua Special, which evidently imitate nothing. Bright flies aren't mandatory, however, because cutthroats feed on most anything they can find. A Muddler Minnow can be a good change of pace.

What has been said of the cutthroat trout applies to a large degree to

248

the steelhead as it exists in the estuaries and tidewater areas of northwestern rivers. Unlike the cutthroat, the steelhead makes a single annual upriver run, usually coming into tidewater from the sea in the late summer, fall, or early winter. Like the salmon, it waits in the estuary until rains swell the river and make travel upstream safe and easy. In its journey, and during its resting periods in eddies and pools, it keeps to the well-scoured main channel and shuns the silt-laden, weedy places. Its usual holding position is in the protection of rocks or below sand bars near the bottom of the channel, so the fly must be fished deep to enable the fish to see and take it. In such places one can fish for the steelhead either from a boat or by wading, as conditions allow. Boat fishing is more popular in most locations because few estuary and tidewater areas offer the opportunity for wading that would make it possible for the caster to reach the fish, even during the most favorable time of the tide.

When the fish are in the estuaries many steelhead are caught while casting for cutthroat trout or for silver salmon. Estuaries, of course, are a kind of boundary between salt water and fresh, so comments on these fish in this saltwater chapter overlap those in Chapter 7 on freshwater tactics, where more has been said about steelhead and the salmon, and flies recommended for them.

Another great game fish, which I think was introduced to the West Coast from the Atlantic in the form of fertilized eggs, is the striped bass, a very formidable adversary on a fly rod. Since the eastern and western fish are the same, the comments on the species in Chapter 15 apply here too. Anglers on both coasts have developed exceptional fly patterns, or types, for stripers. Regardless of which ocean (or lake) we fish in, it helps to be acquainted with them all.

One of the most outstanding western types is the Whistler series, originated about 1966 by Dan Blanton, of San Jose, California, for striped bass in San Francisco Bay. It is dressed in over a dozen color combinations and is amazingly successful as a general oceanic type for such gamesters as Pacific yellowtail and rockfish, groupers, cabrillo, jack crevalle, bonito, dolphin (fish), oceanic skipjack, and many others.

Killing patterns such as this don't happen by chance. In this case an expert angler had an idea which he developed through trial and error until he had perfected a fly acknowledged by others generally to be one of the best ever devised. This started with the fact that fishermen using spinning tackle were reaping amazing harvests with a beanhead jig dressed with white bucktail topped with red and a red chenille collar. This, partly because of its weight-forward diving action and pulsating retrieve, was beating anything fly-rodders could use by about ten to one.

249

To make a long story short, several months of experimentation perfected the Whistler, which eventually produced better than the jig. This was accomplished by using a 3X short, 3X strong live-bait hook in about size

17–2 Noted angler Dan Blanton shows a twenty-nine-pound striped bass that took his famous Black Whistler in San Francisco Bay. (Photo: Dan Blanton)

4/0, such as Eagle Claw's #318-N, and by tying in the tail at the end of the very short shank. In addition, a few wraps of lead wire were put around the shank and a pair of medium-sized bead-chain eyes were added for additional forward weight, thus giving the fly the necessary frontal heft to cause it to dip and dive nicely upon retrieval. Also, a large, broad saddle-hackle collar was added to provide the illusion of bulk and to make the fly undulate enticingly with every pull and pause. The chenille collar found on the jig suggested the red gills of a bait fish, so was included as a small but thick butt between the hackled collar and the tail. The white hackles closed around the red collar when it was pulled through the water, then would open again during the pause to provide a good imitation of a bait fish pulsating its gill plates.

The dressing of the White Whistler (Figure 17–3) should be tried first.

250

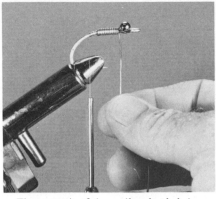 

1. Tie on a pair of size 3 silver bead-chain eyes and wrap several turns of No. 2 lead fuse wire around the shank. Use red thread.

2. Secure the wire with thread and tie on the white bucktail in three separate medium bunches, stacking hair for a high, vertical triangular wing.

3. Clip hair stubs to taper, cement, bind down, and apply a thin stripe of no more than ten red bucktail hairs midway of the wing.

4. Build a body just in front of the wing, using two close turns of medium red chenille. Tie off.

5. Select two or three long, webby white saddle hackles and spirally wrap, one at a time, to collar the gap between body and eyes.

6. The finished fly should have a full collar which does not obscure the red chenille body. See text for other patterns.

17–3 How to tie the White Whistler. Use a 3X short, 3X strong hook such as Eagle Claw #318-N or Mustad #9175 in size from 1/0 to 4/0, with size A Nymo thread or equivalent. (Photos: Dan Blanton)

Of course it also is made in other color combinations, of which the yellow is one of the best. Two hackled bucktail variations are given below. From these three, anglers can devise any others they wish.

BLACK WHISTLER
HEAD: Two medium-sized silver bead-chain eyes wrapped on figure-eight fashion with black thread. Weight shank with fuse wire.
WING: As a tail, stack three medium bunches of long black bucktail. On each side of this, flaring outward, are two natural grizzly hackles, one tilting upward, the other downward, to mask the top and bottom of the flaring black bucktail. Tail and hackles are of same length.
BODY: As a butt, two turns of medium black chenille to make a short but thick body
THROAT: Several turns of two or three of the widest and most fluffy marabou-like black hackles to fill the gap between body and bead eyes

WHITE WHISTLER, RED AND GRIZZLY (RG)
HEAD: Two medium-sized silver bead-chain eyes wrapped on figure-eight fashion with red thread. Weight shank with fuse wire.
WING: As a tail, stack three medium bunches of long white bucktail. On each side of this, flaring outward, are two natural grizzly hackles, one tilting upward, the other downward, to mask the top and bottom of the flaring white bucktail. Tail and hackles are of same length.
BODY: As a butt, two turns of medium red chenille to make a short but thick body
THROAT: Several turns of two or three of the widest and most fluffy marabou-like red hackles to fill the gap between body and bead eyes

The Whistler series is one of the greatest, if not *the* greatest, of developments in saltwater fly construction ever originated. Dan Blanton says about it:

"I fish the Whistlers as I would any saltwater fly, using whatever line is suitable to water conditions. Sinking lines carry the fly better because it is easier to maintain good line speed. An erratic retrieve with one-to-two-foot-long pulls, pausing occasionally to let the fly sink a bit, works well for me.

"I personally favor the White Whistler, White Whistler RG (red collar and grizzly hackles), Yellow Whistler, Yellow Whistler RG, and Black Whistler Grizzly, yet at times another will be the better producer, such as the Yellow Whistler Black. I tie the series on hooks from 1/0 through 4/0 to make flies from three to four and a half inches in length, but the 4/0 hook is the best all-round size.

"Many beginners find Whistlers easy to cast in comparison to others. The Black Whistler Grizzly is productive anytime, but best in hours of darkness. How did the fly get its name? When you cast one it will be quite obvious, as the holes in the chain beads cause it to whistle loudly while being cast."

Another type, sort of first cousin to the Whistlers, is <u>Given's Barred n' Black</u>, developed by Ed Given, of Salinas, California, in early 1970. It is a much fuller fly and especially effective when the quarry is feeding on large bait fish. In addition to the black dressing described below, it also is tied in white and in yellow.

Use a regular Mustad #3407 hook, such as size 4/0 or smaller, and tie in a pair of medium-sized silver bead-chain eyes at the head with black thread. On the shank above the point of the hook tie in six black saddle hackles, the pairs of three splayed. These are about four inches long for a 4/0 hook. Just forward of these tie in a bunch of very long crinkly black bucktail on each side so the bunches are quite wide vertically. (This best can be done with two smaller bunches tied on each side so one tilts up and the other down, meeting in the middle.) Just forward of this, tie in a pair of natural grizzly hackles on each side, splayed outward, one pair covering the top of the hair on each side, and the other pair covering the bend of the hook on each side, so the pair on each side is well separated. These are as long as the bucktail and nearly two inches shorter than the black hackles.

Over the last windings of thread tie in two very wide and webby black saddle hackles by their butts and take about two turns with each to make a moderately thick collar. This should bring the dressing to about a quarter of an inch from the bead-chain eyes. Fill this space in with a large head of the black thread, tapered down around the eyes to the eye of the hook. The fly, on a 4/0 hook, measures five inches from eye to end of wing, with the black bucktail and grizzly cheeks measuring a little over three inches.

Now, let's turn to a longer and slimmer black-and-grizzly pattern dressed to imitate a small eel. This is another origination of Dan Blanton's, for river fishing during striped bass spawning runs. It has been "a hell of a fly" since its birth in 1970 for both fresh and salt water wherever eels are found. Pacific Coast anglers call it the <u>Bay Delta Eelet</u> and tie it on regular Mustad #3407 hooks, usually in size about 4/0. In this size the fly is nearly seven inches long.

About a quarter of an inch behind the hook's eye tie in a pair of medium-sized silver bead-chain eyes. On the shank above the point of the hook tie in a moderate-sized bunch of black horse mane or artificial hair about five inches long. (Other natural hair isn't long enough.) On each side of this tie in three black narrow saddle hackles of the same length, back to back (not splayed).

253

17–4 Dan Blanton's Bay Delta Eelet, dressed by him

Tie in a length of medium black chenille to cover these windings and wind it in close coils halfway down the body, tying it down there but not cutting off the rest. At this point tie in as a wing six more black narrow saddle hackles on each side of which is a natural grizzly hackle, the two groups of four back to back, all as long as the feathers tied in at the tail (about five inches). (These will cock up slightly because they have to ride over the chenille.)

Now continue winding the black chenille forward, covering the rest of the body in close coils, crisscrossing around the eyes, and winding forward until tied down at the head. The hump of the wing simulates an eel's dorsal fin, and the grizzly hackles provide the blotchy effect often noticed on the backs of eels. Altogether, this provides a very slim, slithery eel-like representation which freshwater anglers should find effective in smaller sizes.

The Sar-Mul-Mac is another Dan Blanton origination with a couple of variations, all of which are excellent imitations of the three types of bait fish one or more of which is found most everywhere—the sardine, the mullet, and the mackerel. By varying the dressings, as will be shown, other bait fish such as anchovies, herring, and the beaked and half-beaked species can be represented. Again, we prefer Mustad's #3407 hook in 4/0 or whatever other size is desired. Use white tying thread.

Starting at the middle of the hook's shank, tie in a moderate bunch of white bucktail about three times as long as the hook. On each side of the bucktail apply three splayed white saddle hackles as long as the longest ends of the hair. Cut ten one-sixty-fourth-inch-wide Mylar strips and tie in five on each side of the saddle hackles. These are about as long as the hair.

Turn the fly over in the vise and apply another medium bunch of white bucktail as a throat of the same length as the other bucktail. This application divides around the hook's shank. Turn the fly upright again and tie in a natural grizzly hackle on each side to "tent" as much as possible over the

254

17–5 Dan Blanton's
Sar-Mul-Mac, dressed by him.

wing. These hackles are a bit longer than the white ones.

Now tie in an underthroat of marabou fibers about as long as the hook. The color of the sample I have is white, but others are pink, red, or maroon, which may be preferable. Next, tie in a short teal flank feather on each side as shoulders and a fairly large bunch of gray or brown marabou of about the same length on top of the wing (as a short topping). These various applications have helped to build up the forward half of the hook, which now will be used to make a large chenille head with glass eyes.

Over the windings of the topping tie in a short length of fine red chenille and a longer length of white chenille. Let these hang out of the way for the moment while you tie in two large glass eyes, brown or yellow, with black pupils. These will come on wires. Bend the wire of each at a right angle about an eighth of an inch from the eye (don't leave too large a gap) and center the eyes midway on the undressed part of the shank. The eyes can be fastened on by the long wires attached, binding down one eye at a time and then wrapping the wires in a figure-eight between the eyes.

Now, use the white chenille to make a very large head. When this is partially applied, make one turn of the red chenille around the fly, as a collar, and tie it in, covering the tie-in by added windings of the white chenille. Figure-eight the white chenille around the eyes and continue winding until the entire head is shaped; then whip-finish the head with the white thread. Use a fine brown marking pen to make two parallel lines from hook eye to wing between the eyes. While this dressing is a bit complicated, it is easier than it sounds, and the fly often turns refusals into solid strikes.

255

Before I wrote *Streamer Fly Tying & Fishing* in 1966 an expert fly dresser named Bill Catherwood, of Tewksbury, Massachusetts, called to show me some very large beaked streamers he had originated and recommended for big saltwater game fish, including sailfish. I'm not aware that even one sailfish had been taken on a fly at that time, and Bill's big patterns seemed cumbersome and difficult to cast. If they were at that time, they aren't with the more powerful tackle now available.

While Bill Catherwood's innovations may have been a bit ahead of their time, they form the basis for the flies now being discussed, which later skilled innovators, such as Dan Blanton, readily acknowledge. The following two flies are variations of the Sar-Mul-Mac, but they also are variations of Bill Catherwood's original Needlefish, as illustrated in my previous book. In fact, all the modern beaked and half-beaked patterns, and some others, are direct descendants of Catherwood dressings, whether their "originators" realize this or not.

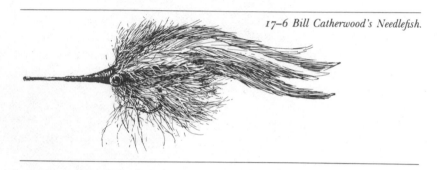

17–6 Bill Catherwood's Needlefish.

<u>Blanton's Green Needle</u> essentially is the Sar-Mul-Mac dressed on a longer hook to provide room for a beak (Eagle Claw #66SS in size 4/0). The dressing is the same to the point of applying the grizzly hackles, which are dyed green. The underthroat is white marabou. The shoulders are teal flank feathers dyed green, and the topping is green marabou. The white chenille-wrapped head with glass eye and red chenille collar is the same except that the large head begins two-thirds of the way back on the shank and tapers to a tapered beak wound with white tying thread which occupies the forward third of the shank. Use a green felt-tip pen to color the head between the eyes and the top of the beak.

<u>Blanton's Blue Needle</u> also is the same to the point of applying the grizzly hackles. Two slim natural hackles of darkest color are used on each side. The underthroat is white marabou. The shoulders are teal flank feathers dyed dark blue, and the topping is dark blue marabou. The white chenille-wrapped head with glass eye and red chenille collar is the same except that a dark blue felt-tip pen is used to color the head between the eyes and the top of the beak. Note that all three of these patterns are slim and have wings about five inches long when dressed on 4/0 hooks. We have seen that length and slimness are very important in flies that can be cast properly to interest big oceanic game fish.

One final example of the popular beaked or half-beaked types is worthy of interest because of its success and the method used to form an attractive and very durable beak. This is the <u>Janssen Half-Beak</u>, a favorite of expert angler Hal W. Janssen, of Petaluma, California, who says that the following

256

olive grizzly and antique gold color combination has been the most successful one for yellowtail directly on the surface when casting into feeding schools or to single fish. He says, "While this represents the balao, when tied with a darker brown saddle hackle wing it can also imitate the frequently occurring sand eels that are driven to the surface by the yellowtail. We also use a red-and-yellow version for fishing very deep with a lead-core (shooting-head) line."

The Janssen Half-Beak is dressed on a long-shank hook such as Eagle Claw #66SS in sizes from 2/0 to 4/0, wound with thread to the end of the shank. At this point secure white or yellow medium-sized chenille and build up a round ball directly above the barb. Just ahead of this tie in a medium amount of crinkly white bucktail on top of the hook and flare it to all sides evenly to form a veil over the chenille. This keeps the saddle hackles and other materials from being drawn tight to one another when pulled through the water. Over this tie on slim saddle hackles, backs to backs, from four to five inches long (depending on size of hook)—first, two white or cream ones, then two natural badger, two black, and six olive, each outside of the preceding ones. Apply a wide and thick collar of olive marabou and cheeks of gold (burnt orange) marabou. This occupies not more than half the length of the shank. The forward part of the shank is tapered with white floss to form a beak, into which small colorless glass eyes with black pupils are inserted. The top of the beak is colored gold-olive.

Hal Janssen explains, "The beak is just tapered floss which has been sealed with a clear model-airplane paint called Airogloss Enamel, which is

17-7 The Janssen Half-Beak, dressed by Hal W. Janssen.

a quick-drying paint. After it has been sealed, the Airogloss Enamel colors of a little yellow and green are mixed to match the wing colors, and just edged with yellow Airogloss paint. The beak then is epoxied with Elmer's epoxy, which usually takes overnight to set, but it provides a more durable body than some of the five-minute epoxies that are available."

While on the subject of long streamers for big oceanic fish such as albacore, yellowtail, and bonito, we come to one of the most beautiful and productive patterns—the Streaker Streamer, originated by Ned Grey, who started its fame by catching with it a fifty-pound roosterfish while on a trip to Baja. The fly is equally effective on the East Coast, where it has accounted for amberjack, snook, tarpon, wahoo, and sailfish, to mention only a partial list on both coasts. In the water its iridescent peacock herl and peacock sword wing looks so bait-fish-like that it is no wonder it is a winner. The dressing instructions include several suggestions useful in other patterns, so, before describing them, let's start with the basic formula:

STREAKER STREAMER
HOOK SIZE: 3/0, Mustad #3407 or Eagle Claw #254
HEAD: Color of body thread, prewaxed 4/0 monocord
TAIL: A small bunch of light crinkly white bucktail a little more than twice the length of the hook. Just forward of this is tied in about twenty strips of crinkled sixty-fourth-inch-wide Mylar about as long as the tail. Just forward of this is tied in a very small bunch of green bucktail.
BODY: Wound with green thread
THROAT: A small bunch of green bucktail nearly as long as the white
WING: About fifteen or twenty peacock herls, as long as possible (about five inches). Over these, as a topping, are two matched (a

17–8 Ned Grey's Streaker Streamer, dressed by Steve Fernandez.

right and a left) peacock swords tied in back to back and flue side
upward, as long as the peacock herls.
CHEEKS: A moderate bunch of green bucktail as long as the throat
and merging with it, but covering only the lower part of the wing

The Streaker Streamer is so named because it usually is fished in fast.
Select the peacock swords carefully to get dense ones with a high silhouette.
If tag ends are too long they can be burned off to proper length with a
cigarette, which is better than cutting them. Hair should be light and
crinkly. Use head cement liberally to secure all applications and to coat
body and head properly. Apply cement to hook shank before winding on
thread.

To crinkle Mylar, make the desired number of windings around the
extended fingers with it and then, holding the length at both ends, pull one
end until it crinkles properly. Then wind it back on the fingers, slide off the
coil, and tie it in over one end of the loops, binding these down with thread.
Cut the other end of the coil with scissors.

Unlike some of the previous patterns, this one has a high silhouette,
similar to certain kinds of bait fish. The secret of success is to select a
matched pair of peacock swords with the proper length, width, and density.
The Streaker also is dressed with blue thread and hair, instead of green,
and it sometimes has a white throat.

Inshore and offshore along the southern Pacific Coast, vast kelp beds
grow like forests in shallow parts of the sea, their rubbery pipelike stems
terminating in waving fronds covering or patching the surface. This is the
home of the kelp bass, and other fish more or less sporty, such as lingcod,
white seabass, and rockfish.

When these species can't be hooked on the surface with fly rods, they
usually can be coaxed into casting distance on top by chumming from an
anchored boat a good cast away from the edge of the kelp on the seaward
side. Sometimes kelp bass will take anything in a frenzy of feeding, but as
far as flies are concerned, some patterns and color schemes are better than
others. Larry Green, one of the leading anglers and writers of the West
Coast, recommends a pattern called the

WILD CANARY
HOOK SIZE: 1/o to 4/o, Eagle Claw #254 or Mustad #3407
HEAD: Red
TAIL: About six very long and slim saddle hackles of canary yellow,
tied in at the end of the shank. Over these on each side are about
six sixty-fourth-inch-wide Mylar strips about as long as the tail.
BODY: Silver, such as Mylar piping, wound on flat
COLLAR: Canary yellow hair, a moderate bunch on top and bottom,
tied in at the head, and a bit longer than the hook

259

WING: About twenty peacock herls as long as the wing. Over these, roofed and back to back, are two natural grizzly saddle hackles extending to the end of the tail. (On a 4/0 hook this fly is about five inches long.)

This fly represents a type, by now familiar to us, of the long, thin streamers which are so highly effective and which can be dressed in any color combinations anglers may consider to be effective.

Larry Green, who is an old hand at hooking every inshore and offshore game fish that California's coast affords, has this to say about bonito: "This particular fish captured my fancy so entirely that it changed my whole perspective on fly fishing. One small fish gifted with the speed of lightning and the grace of an angel, combined with cunningness and everlasting stamina, I found to be the greatest fly-fishing challenge I have ever encountered. I praise the California bonito as pound for pound one of the greatest game fish that swim. The bonito's eagerness to smash an artificial fly and the spectacular fight that follows offer stupendous sport for the adventurous fly-rodder."

If that isn't enough, schools of bonito (false albacore) are found in harbors all along the California coastline under warm-water conditions. They are small fish usually weighing only a few pounds, and rarely over ten, but they make up in spunk what they may lack in size. When Larry takes friends fishing he often stops near a bait boat in the harbor because bonito wait nearby for bait to be dropped over the side. If they aren't near surface they usually can be brought up by chumming, usually with anchovies, which are from two and a half inches to four inches long. The tricks are to match the size of the fly to the bait, to cast out, and to strip in fast. Sometimes, however, a fly sunk to ten or fifteen feet and worked in more slowly gets best results. Since bonito have sharp teeth, a shock tippet is advisable, but many anglers using strong tippets dispense with this and cut back frayed leaders. Flies on size 2 or 4 hooks, 4X or 5X strong, regular shank, are usual.

Bonito aren't fussy about fly patterns, but those with a lot of white seem most successful, such as the Platinum Blonde. Larry Green suggests two simple patterns. The Bonito Bandit is tied with white thread and a Mylar-piping body applied long to provide a Mylar tail at least as long as the body. Tie down the Mylar at the end of the shank and tie in on top of it a moderate-sized bunch of white marabou herl. Pick out the Mylar at the tail and trim both Mylar and marabou to a length a bit longer than the hook. Apply a white marabou wing at the head of the fly and tie over it a few crinkled Mylar strips. It is well to take along a few of these flies which are lightly weighted.

The second pattern also is dressed in the Blonde type and is called the Dunsmuir Dandy, originated by Joe Kimsey, of Dunsmuir, California. It has a tail of a small bunch of white bucktail about two inches long, a built-up body of black wool tied down with black thread, and a slightly cocked-up wing of white bucktail extending nearly to the end of the tail.

Larry Green also stalks saltwater flats for halibut, the big snowshoe flounders which, although not considered much as game fish, are big enough to give an angler a run for his money. I never tried to catch one, but have had fun raking the sand under mild surf for flounders with small weighted flies. If these little fellows can furnish fun and also provide a good dinner, maybe Larry's big halibut are underrated.

In any event, here is Larry's favorite fly for halibut, dressed on a 4/o short-shank live-bait hook. He calls it the <u>Sand Raker</u>, which indicates how it should be fished. Tie on over the hook three inches of Mylar piping and fray the length extending beyond the bend. Over this tie three colors of bucktail as long as the Mylar; white under pink under black. The head is black, with a pink eye. Larry doesn't explain the reason for the color combination, and I'm surprised that the fly isn't weighted. I'm sure he has reasons for this.

Many bucktails designed for specific species also are general-purpose flies good for many others, and they can be dressed in Beer Belly fashion to provide a keeled type with a deep silver or gold underbody extremely suggestive of the natural bait fish. Cut a fairly rigid wire such as stainless piano or leader wire a little longer than the hook's shank. Bend it into a low boat-shaped curve with short ends flat to fit under the front and rear of the shank. Cement and lash (or solder) one end under the extreme rear end of the shank and the other end where the head will be wound on. This makes a fishbelly-like frame over which Mylar piping can be stretched and secured at both ends as usual. Then apply dressing as desired.* Here are two examples:

<u>SILVER BEER BELLY</u>
HOOK: Any long-shank pattern
BODY: Silver Mylar piping applied over a stainless wire frame as above
TAIL: Yellow under red under blue bucktail, about as long as the
     hook
WING: Yellow under red under blue bucktail, extending to end of tail
HEAD: Black, with white eye and black-centered red pupil

<u>GOLDEN BEER BELLY</u>
HOOK: Any long-shank pattern
BODY: Gold Mylar piping applied over a stainless wire frame as above
TAIL: Pink or red and white bucktail, mixed, over which is blue or

261

---

*Also see the suggestion on page 138–39.

purple bucktail, all about as long as the hook
WING: Pink or red and white bucktail, mixed, over which is blue or
purple bucktail, all extending to end of tail
HEAD: Black, with white eye and black-centered red pupil

The Bonito Bandit can be dressed Beer Belly fashion, and usually is. An alternative to using wire reinforcement to make the boat-shaped body is to squeeze a piece of thin doubled metal (such as can be cut from an aluminum beer can) around the shank, cementing the double parts together to the hook's shank with epoxy. Then trim the keel to size to fit the Mylar piping. Keeled patterns such as this in various weights are described in Chapter 10.

This seems an appropriate place to recommend a likable general-purpose bucktail designed for striped bass in San Francisco Bay. It is one of Hal W. Janssen's well-known patterns and could be tied as a Beer Belly, but isn't. It is dressed on long-shanked hooks of many sizes and types for fresh and salt water.

JANSSEN STRIPER FLY
THREAD: White
BODY: Oval silver tinsel
THROAT: As an underbody, a small bunch of white polar bear hair or
bucktail half again as long as the hook
WING: Sparse bunches of white under blue under light green bucktail
half again as long as the hook
HEAD: See below

This fly carries its colors into the head, a suggestion generally useful. The underpart of the head is white and the top part is bluish-green, with a yellow eye and large black pupil. Hal says about it, "An interesting aspect is the continuation of the lateral line into the head and applying the eye with paint. The silver body material shows through the white underwing, which gives the fly a bait-fish translucence which is common when polar bear is used. Since this is scarce the white bucktail is tied very sparsely around the hook."

Finally, before going on to a very different and unusual type, here is the dressing for a Dan Blanton pattern called the

262   BAY DREDGER (GREEN)
HOOK: Any regular-length saltwater pattern
BODY: Gold Mylar piping wound on flat, like tinsel
WING: A fairly large bunch of white bucktail about twice as long as
the hook. Over this is a small bunch of bright green bucktail under
a small bunch of dark blue bucktail, with a topping of several

strands of peacock herl. The wing is more than half white, and all
components are of equal length.

HEAD: The head occupies the forward half or third of the shank,
wound very heavily with white thread, with two silver bead-chain
eyes just behind the hook's eye. Under the head are painted two
red gashes, like the gills of a cutthroat trout.

The Bay Dredger is a popular type done in various color combinations,
developed about 1966 when the Whistler series became prominent.

Unlike the vast variety of freshwater game-fish foods, those of salt water
could be reduced to four, of which only two are important to this book.
These are crustaceans such as shrimps and crabs; mollusks, including many
varieties of shellfish; and the two of major importance in the field of bucktails and streamers—the bait fishes, including eels, and the cephalopods,
which include octopus and squid. So far, we have been concerned with the
bait-fish imitations, which of course are of primary importance. Now, let's
see how to represent a squid.

Squids are free-swimming, active carnivores which roam the Atlantic
and Pacific in vast schools feeding ravenously on small fish, mollusks, and
crustaceans. They have large heads and eyes, eight arms, and two long,
grasping tentacles used to hold prey. Their bodies are long and cigar-
shaped, with a somewhat arrow-shaped fin on the anterior end. They can
change color rapidly from salt-and-pepper on off-white to iridescent hues
of blue, red, yellow, pink, or brown. They can swim forward or backward
by forcing jets of water from the mantle cavity.

The Atlantic and Pacific species are similar, ranging in size from about
an inch to a little over a foot. Most game fish favor squid over anything else
and will ignore other foods to get them. Thus, one type of streamer,
perhaps in a few color combinations, and in one size, should be sufficient
for fly-rod anglers. This oceanic "fly" is of major importance, fascinating,
and not difficult to dress.

The Sea Arrow Squid was developed about 1964 by Dan Blanton and
Bob Edgley of San Jose, California. It has been proved that it will take a
multitude of game fish from any sea in the world—a list too long to mention
here, including a few world's records.

Materials needed are: Hook, Mustad #79573-ST, 3X long, 3X strong,
size 2/0 or 3/0, or equal substitute; acrylic (decorative) fiber yarn (found
in variety stores); saddle hackles of proper color; large chenille; size A
Nymo tying thread the same color as the body; eight-millimeter amber glass
eyes (available from Herter's); and clear silicone rubber cement.

The following step-by-step directions and the accompanying illustrations should make dressings easy. This is a very interesting type to tie, and
one which will provoke the admiration of other fly dressers and provide a
new and different lure to ensure fishing success.

263

1

2

3

4

5

6
7
8
9

17–9 How to tie the Sea Arrow Squid. (Photos: Dan Blanton)

SEA ARROW SQUID (WHITE)

TIP: Gold Mylar piping wound like tinsel from halfway of bend of hook to end of shank

BUTT: Several turns of large white chenille in a ball—enough to make the hackles splay out (photo 1 of Figure 17-9)

TAIL: As a wing, eight white saddle hackles about three inches long, splaying in all directions (photo 2). Also, centered on each side, a white saddle hackle about five inches long, to simulate tentacles. Also, centered on each side, a few strands of coarse purple bucktail from two to three inches long to represent blood veins.

EYES: Bend the wire close to each eye to a ninety-degree angle and cut the wires just long enough to clear the eye of the hook by about a quarter of an inch (photo 3). Bind them down, one eye at a time.

TOPPING AND THROAT: Fill the gaps between the eyes, both above and below, with hackle fluff or marabou tufts of the same color as the hackles (photo 4).

WEIGHTING: Optional; wrap lead wire around hook shank, if desired

BODY: Pad the body with cotton or floss, tapered from eyes to head. Wrap on a body of medium to large chenille leaving about an eighth-inch gap between body and eye of hook (photo 5).

HEAD: Acrylic fiber yarn comes in a three-wrap strand. Cut two strands an inch and a half long and bind one strand on each side of the hook, by their middles. Secure tightly. Taking one side at a time, pull the strands out tightly at a ninety-degree angle to the hook shank, binding them at the base of the fibers by figure-eights around both sides (photo 6). A whip finish completes tying on materials.

Now pull the fibers out away from the hook shank tightly and cut each with a curved pair of scissors to about three-quarters of an inch long, using a circular cutting motion. The fibers will now have flared into a perfectly flat circle. Comb them to distribute them evenly, like spokes of a wheel (photo 7).

Using fingers for support, apply liberal amounts of GE rubber cement to both sides of the fibers (photo 8). Using fingers, apply pressure to the top and bottom of the fibers, working the cement into them by stroking from the center to the edges. This will taper the edges and encase the fibers in a flexible bond. Let the fibers set for about ten minutes. Then, with the fly turned over, trim them into an arrow shape (photo 9—note use of template), thus completing the simulation of the squid's anterior fin (photo 10).

This trimming is more like a pentagon than an arrow, with the point longer forward and the base, adhering to the forward part of the body, the shortest of the five sides. The hook's eye sticks out of the underside of the fin a bit forward of the center. The fin, of course, is flat on top, its rear

266

centered on the body, parallel to the point of the hook. The trimming should make the five-sided fin a bit smaller than a fifty-cent piece if the fly is about six and a half inches long.

Blanton and Edgley favor two other color combinations in addition to this white one. The Natural Sea Arrow Squid is white, as above, but tinted with dots of black and light brown with waterproof felt-tip pens. Before applying the hackles, polka-dot them quite heavily with mixed speckles. The body and head (or anterior fin) are similarly dotted so they contain about equal amounts of white, brown, and black.

The Pink Sea Arrow Squid is done in the same way, using a pink marker, so the effect is about half pink and half white.

The Histories and Dressings of Other Prominent Patterns

In PART FOUR of this book fly dressers will find accurate and detailed directions for dressing over three hundred historic and modern streamer and bucktail patterns exactly as their originators intended them to be. The patterns are in alphabetical order. These instructions are so meticulous that exact copies can be made without actual examples being seen, although about 174 originals and authentic copies are shown in faithful color in the twelve color plates.

For the angler who doesn't tie his own flies, these dressing instructions make clear what they should look like when he purchases them, and so help him to avoid accepting "variations" that may not be as effective as the correct forms.

Fly tyers who want to try something new will find basic ideas here. For example, it may be fun to locate an appealing formula and to tie a streamer as a bucktail, or vice versa, or to substitute marabou or synthetic materials for other furs or feathers. Thus, basic and successful color combinations and styles can be retained, at the same time affording latitude for ingenuity. Old hands at the game will, however, advise adhering to established patterns unless there are reasons for variation.

This book and its two predecessors are the only original repositories for authentic historic patterns, of which the most important have been retained here, with appropriate historical notes, because, as has been said, the old is the solid bedrock for the new. Patterns which have failed the tests of time have been eliminated. Many new and promising ones, by modern masters of the art, have been added, in addition to the many which it has seemed more appropriate to include in the preceding chapters. All this, then, is the up-to-date lore of streamer flies and bucktails from their early beginning to the present day.

Since there are already many excellent books on fly dressing, some of which are listed on page 109, this book assumes that its readers possess at least a basic knowledge of the art. Their authors, however, don't always agree on the nomenclature of fly parts, so an explanation of the terms used in this book may be helpful. Parts are explained in their order of application. These parts are pointed out in the accompanying drawing and are described as follows:

Hook sizes: These are given when the originators specify them. When not specified, an extra-long turned-down-eye Limerick or Sproat, as shown in Figure 8-2 on page 110, should be used in sizes from 4 to 10. Common sense dictates light wire for top water or low water, heavier wire for faster sinking or for handling strong fish, and stainless-steel or plated hooks for saltwater use. The longer the hook, the more torque is provided to help it work loose.

Head: This usually is listed first to indicate the color of thread to be used. When the head is dressed in an unusual manner it then is listed last, and the *thread* color takes its place. Thread color often is that which contrasts least with body color. While small and well-lacquered heads are a mark of excellence, the wings and other components behind the eye must be cemented and lashed down for security, even at the expense of head size. Some patterns call for heads with painted eyes, while others carry the body, throat, and wing colors into the head by application of paints. While not essential, such embellishments are necessary to conform to pattern.

Tag: This consists of a few turns of wire or tinsel around the upper bend of the hook just behind the tail. The tag should be lacquered before application of the tail. Sometimes there is a *tip* between tag and tail, common in Atlantic salmon flies,

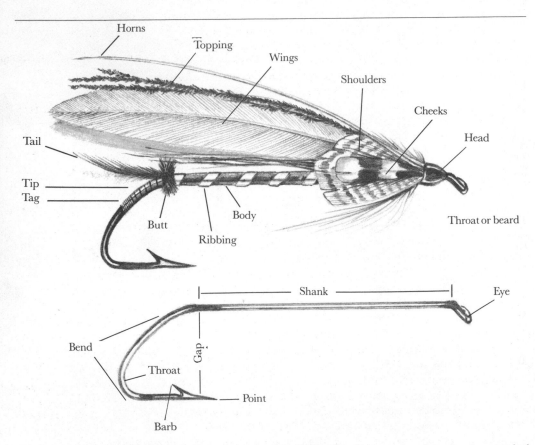

Parts of a streamer or bucktail and of a hook. The tip *is floss, held in place by a* tag *of oval tinsel or fine wire; both together are often referred to as a (mixed) tag. When no floss is used the tag can be flat tinsel. The* throat *or* beard *can be called a collar or hackle when the feather is wound around the shank.*

PLATE IX Flies Designed Primarily As Attractor Patterns

1. Alexandra
Of English origin. Dressed by Frier Gulline

2. Cains River Miramichi
Originated by Fred N. Peet. Dressed by C. Jim Pray

3. Parmachenee Beau
Originated by Henry P. Wells. Dressed by Fin, Fur & Feather, Ltd.

4. Harlequin
Originated and dressed by B.A. Gulline

5. Black & White
Originated and dressed by Austin S. Hogan

6. Sanborn
Originated by Fred Sanborn. Dressed by Gardner Percy

7. Rogan Royal Gray Ghost
Originated and dressed by Alex Rogan

8. Royal Coachman
Of English origin. Dressed by Fin, Fur & Feather, Ltd.

9. Binns
Originated and dressed by Frier Gulline

10. Dr. Burke
Originated and dressed by Dr. Edgar Burke

11. Golden Rogan
Originated and dressed by Alex Rogan

12. Gray Prince
Originated and dressed by B. A. Gulline

13. Bartlett's Special
Originated by Arthur Bartlett. Dressed by the Weber Tackle Company

14. Campeona
Of South American origin. Dressed by Mrs. Elizabeth Greig

15. Chief Needahbeh
Originated and dressed by Chief Needahbeh

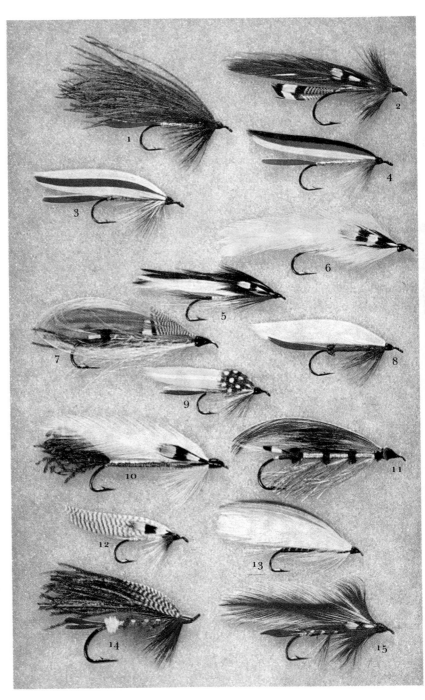

PLATE X Prominent Eastern Freshwater Patterns

1. Nine-Three
*Originated by Dr. J.H. Sanborn.
Dressed by Austin S. Hogan*

2. Grand Laker
*A development of the
"Rooster's Regret" type,
dressed by Benn Treadwell*

3. Trout Fin
*Originated by B.A. Gulline.
Dressed by Fin, Fur &
Feather, Ltd.*

4. Stewart's Hawk
*Originated and dressed by
Austin S. Hogan*

5. Satin Fin
*Originated and dressed by
Keith C. Fulsher*

6. Silver Tip
*Originated and dressed by
Keith C. Fulsher*

7. Miller's River Special
*Originated by Paul Kukonen
and Henry Scarborough.
Dressed by Mr. Kukonen*

8. Mascoma
*Origin unknown. Adapted and
dressed by Paul Kukonen*

9. Blue Marabou
*Originated and dressed by
Paul Kukonen*

10. Redhead
*Originated and dressed by
A. I. Alexander III*

11. Cock Robin
*Originated and dressed by
Joseph Kvitsky*

12. Governor Aiken
*Named for Senator George Aiken.
Dressed by the author*

13. The Thief
*Originated and dressed by
Dan Gapen*

14. Cosseboom Special
*Originated by John C. Cosseboom.
Dressed by Herbert L. Howard*

15. Cowee Special
*Originated and dressed by
Stanley Cowee*

16. Lady Ghost
*Originated and dressed by
Bert Quimby*

17. Spencer Bay Special
*Originated and dressed by
Horace P. Bond*

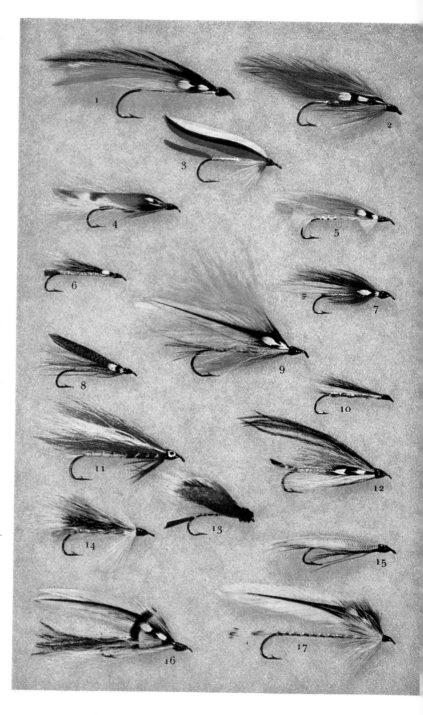

PLATE XI Imitator Patterns by Lew Oatman

1. Golden Shiner
2. Doctor Oatman
3. Red Fin
4. Silver Darter
5. Battenkill Shiner
6. Cut Lips
7. Brook Trout
8. Red Horse
9. Golden Smelt
10. Gray Smelt
11. Trout Perch
12. Male Dace
13. Yellow Perch
14. Golden Darter
15. Shushan Postmaster
16. Mad Tom
17. Ghost Shiner

The "Silver Darter" and the three flies below it are originals dressed by Lew Oatman. The surrounding patterns are exact copies of originals, dressed by Keith C. Fulsher from information provided to him and to the author by Mr. Oatman.

PLATE XII Historic Northeastern Streamers and Bucktails

1. **Warden's Worry**
Originated by Joseph S. Stickney and dressed for him by Gardner Percy

2. **Welch Rarebit**
Originated and dressed by Herbert L. Welch

3. **Bumblepuppy**
Originated by Theodore Gordon. Dressed by Herman Christian, one of Mr. Gordon's angling companions

4. **Parmachenee Belle**
Originated by Henry P. Wells Dressed by Fin, Fur & Feather, Ltd.

5. **Ballou Special**
Originated and dressed by A. W. Ballou

6. **Lord Iris**
Originated by Dr. Preston Jennings. Dressed by Fin, Fur & Feather, Ltd.

7. **Lady Doctor**
Originated by Joseph S. Stickney and dressed for him by Gardner Percy

8. **Mickey Finn (Streamer)**
Originated by John Alden Knight. Dressed by Fin, Fur & Feather, Ltd.

9. **Edson Dark Tiger**
Originated and dressed by William R. Edson

10. **Jane Craig**
Originated and dressed by Herbert L. Welch

11. **Edson Light Tiger**
Originated and dressed by William R. Edson

12. **Supervisor**
Originated by Joseph S. Stickney. Dressed by the author

13. **Black Ghost**
Originated and dressed by Herbert L. Welch

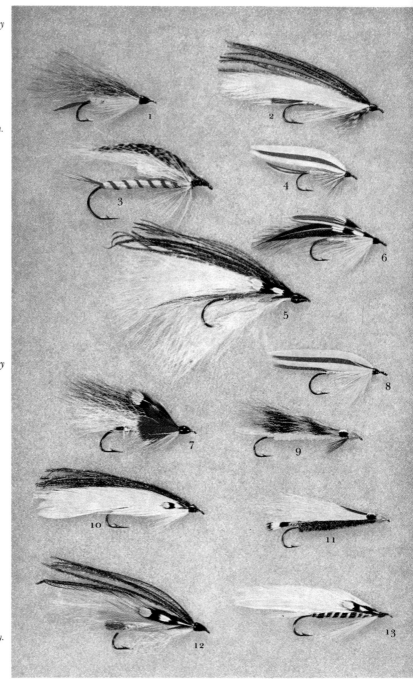

but rare in streamers. The tip is a few turns of colorful floss where the tag usually is, and there always is a tag below and touching it to hold the tip in position. Tag and tip are often given as the tag only, the tip being included, such as *"Tag:* fine oval silver tinsel and golden yellow floss."

Tail: This is a small bunch of hair or hackle fibers, or one or more parts of wing sections, applied at the end of the flat shank of the hook immediately forward of the tag. This book specifies amount and length of tail ingredients. If they are wing sections they usually should curve upward, so the tip of the tail touches the end of the wing. Tails of hair or hackle fibers can be cocked upward (if called for) by tightening a turn or two of thread under the tail while tying it down.

Butt: This is two or three (or perhaps more) turns of wool, silk, or herl (usually ostrich or peacock) around the base of the tail, concealing the windings there. The butt usually has the form of an egg sac, and it is intended to represent one. Thus, it has no place on bucktails or streamers except as a decoration. In applying a butt of herl the portion of the quill to which the "fluff" is attached is tied in to the left, pointing toward the tail. (Butts are borrowed from salmon flies, wherein a representation of an egg sac often was used because fly dressers of the Victorian era thought salmon fed on butterflies, so artificials then were dressed to imitate such colorful insects.)

Body: This covering of the hook's shank with tinsel, floss, herl, wool, or other substances is defined in the same way in all books on fly dressing. Tinsels are exactly wrapped in touching, but not overlapping, coils to conceal all winding threads; then they are varnished to prevent discoloration. Mylar is noncorrosive, but varnishing makes bodies more secure. Apply bodies as dressings dictate.

Ribbing: This also is standard, usually applied with various kinds of tinsel wound on from tail to head spirally, covering no more than half of the body, to provide flash. If the body is ribbed with flat tinsel, fancy dressings sometimes call for this to be followed by fine oval tinsel, or "twist," these windings touching those of the flat tinsel. Five turns are taken on hooks of average length, but this may vary depending on tinsel width and other components.

Throat: This is a bunch of hair or hackle usually applied under the shank at the head of the fly. It can be as long as the wing, and then may be termed an *underbody,* made to simulate the light underside of a bait fish. More usually the throat is quite short to represent the motions of pectoral fins or the reddish color of gills. When it is short it can be applied as a *beard* or as a *collar.* A beard is a throat consisting of a small bunch of hair or hackle (usually the latter, stripped from the quill) tied under or just behind the head of the fly. It can be made to flare, if desired, by carefully pulling the sides of the bunch sideways before cementing.

A collar is a throat made by taking one or more turns of one or two hackles around the shank of the hook a bit behind the eye. This is done before or after the wing is applied, as the instructions dictate. If it is done before the wing is applied, the top part of the circle of hackle is pulled aside and downward and tied in in this position, slanted backward slightly, to leave room for the wing. If it is done after the wing is applied, the hackle is merely slanted backward to conform with the angle of the front of the wing. These various ways of applying throats as underbodies, beards, or collars provide various attractive effects which impart added color and action to the fly. Hackle applied after the wing is tied in can provide a smaller and neater head.

273

In addition there is a throat called a *spike* which rarely is used, but is called for in a few of the steelhead patterns originated by Peter J. Schwab. It is a bunch of hair tied downward at a right angle to the hook and trimmed at the end, like a paintbrush. Even Peter Schwab thought it of so little value that it usually was omitted.

Wing: Since directions are so similar in all books on fly dressing, only two suggestions are offered. In applying hair wings, avoid tying in too much at once because it may pull out. Tie in a small bunch of hair, cement it solidly, and then, if necessary, tie in another bunch or two over or just ahead of the first bunch. In applying feather wings prepare the (usually four) feathers and pinch them together by their necks so the trimmed bare quills protrude side by side. Lay the bare quills on the tip of the other forefinger and use the thumbnail to score them at the base where they will be tied in so the scoring forms a slight angle. Pinching them the same way, set them on the shank and secure them with a few tight turns of thread. They then should ride together with no gaps, and can be slanted to the desired angle by winding backward with the thread.

Topping: This crowning touch on the wing of a streamer fly usually is a long golden pheasant tippet or a small bunch of peacock herl. If the former, the feather should curve close to the wing, roofing it, and extending to touch the end of the tail. This makes no difference to fish but it does add style to the dressing. Toppings in rare cases are of other feathers, and may be shorter, as instructions prescribe.

Shoulders: These usually are wide, spade-type body feathers normally applied on each side of the front of the wing to cover that part of it, as the dressing dictates.

Cheeks: These nearly always are of jungle cock, or its imitation, and are applied over the shoulders (if any) so the feathers center in the shoulders. (See the Carrie Stevens patterns in Color Plate II as good examples.)

Horns: These have no place in streamer flies and are used only in rare cases as decorations. They are common in classic Atlantic salmon flies to represent the "feelers" of a butterfly and are normally single fibers of blue-yellow macaw applied on each side nearly vertically along the top of the wing and fully as long as it.

With these comments to avoid misunderstandings, let's peruse the patterns which follow to learn the correct dressings and to adapt them to our uses.

ALASKA MARY ANN BUCKTAIL (Plate IV)　　　　*(As dressed by the originator)*
HEAD: Black
TAIL: A very small bunch of red hackle fibers or red hair
BODY: Dressed rather full with ivory or light tan silk
RIBBING: Medium flat silver tinsel (optional)
WING: A small bunch of white polar bear hair extending to the end of the tail
CHEEKS: Jungle cock, rather short

This Alaskan bucktail, originated by Frank Dufresne, well-known writer and former member of the U.S. Fish and Wildlife Service, had its beginning in a fishing lure used by the Kobuk Eskimos. Dufresne described it in a letter to me as follows: "I saw it first along the Kobuk River in Kotzebue Sound, Alaska, back in 1922. It was being used by the Eskimos, attached to a length of black whalebone line to haul out most anything in the river—Dolly Vardens, Arctic char, sheefish, pike, and grayling. They made it by carving a small piece of ivory roughly into the shape of a minnow, driving a cooper's nail through it, and bending the nail to form a

274

barbless hook. Then they tied on a smidgin of polar bear hair, and on the barbless hook they fastened a very small red corner from the mouth of the guillemot bird.

"That was the Kobuk Hook. I came down out of that country with several of them. They were killers, believe me. When I had lost all of them but one, I decided to tie another along more conventional lines. Using a No. 8 long-shanked hook I wound on some ivory-colored silk for a body, tied on a wing of polar bear hair, and added a wisp of red-dyed hair for the tail. To simulate the black whalebone eye, inset in some of the original Kobuk lures, I used jungle cock.

"The thing had no name until a friend of mine used it in southeastern Alaska in a stream where rainbows, cutthroats, Dolly Vardens, and salmon all abounded. He beat the heck out of me with my own creation, and when he said, 'Man, this catches 'em all; the whole Mary Ann of 'em,' the name was born.

"The Weber Tackle Company has been tying it for years and showing it in their catalog. It is tied in several different color combinations, but this is the correct one. Out west and in Alaska you see it all over the place. It's a bucktail, of course, and seems to work best when and where trout are hitting either whitefish or salmon fingerlings."

ALEXANDRA STREAMER (Plate IX)   *(As dressed by Fin, Fur and Feather, Ltd.)*
HEAD: Black
TAIL: A fairly long but rather narrow section of a red goose or swan wing feather
BODY: Medium embossed silver tinsel
RIBBING: Narrow oval silver tinsel
THROAT: A wide black saddle hackle wound on as a collar and separated at the top to accommodate the wing
WING: A fairly large bunch of bright green peacock herl. The herl should be so selected as to be very green and very fine. The wing extends beyond the tail of the fly.

Evidently this fly originated as a trout fly in England. In 1929, Frier Gulline, of Fin, Fur and Feather, Ltd., of Montreal, adapted it as a streamer fly. It has proved to be one of the best flies of this type for trout and bass in Canada. This pattern evidently was adapted from the Hardy Bros. Demon Streamer. The dressings are identical, except that the Demon has a throat of light blue hackle and the tail is red wool instead of a section of red feather. In England, this fly is favored for salmon, sea trout, and inland trout.

ALLAGASH AL   *(As dressed by the originator)*
HOOK SIZE: 2 to 8, 3X long
HEAD: Black
BODY: Flat silver tinsel
RIBBING: Oval silver tinsel (optional)
THROAT: A small bunch of fibers from a red golden pheasant body feather (the original pattern called for a bit of red marabou)
WING: A medium bunch of red bucktail extending slightly beyond the bend of the hook. Over this are four bronze or ginger well-marked furnace hackles, fairly thin.
CHEEKS: Jungle cock

275

Originated by Al Leibowitz, of the Percy Tackle Company, Portland, Maine, who says, "The fly is part of the regular Percy line and we sell it all over the country." It often is tied in tandem for trolling, using a trail hook dressed with silver tinsel.

ALLIE'S FAVORITE STREAMER (Plate II) *(As dressed by the originator)*

HEAD: Black, with red band
TAG: Three or four turns of narrow silver tinsel
BODY: Red silk, dressed very thin
RIBBING: Narrow flat silver tinsel
THROAT: A very small bunch of white bucktail extending beyond the bend of the hook, under which is a small bunch of orange hackle fibers, with a very small bunch of black hackle fibers under this
WING: Five or six strands of bright green peacock herl as long as the wing, over which are two orange saddle hackles with a black saddle hackle of the same length on both sides of these
CHEEKS: Jungle cock, fairly long

Originated by Carrie G. Stevens, of Madison, Maine, and named in honor of Allie W. French, of Willimantic, Connecticut, who preferred this fly for fishing in the famous Upper Dam Pool in the Rangeley section of Maine.

(Fly dressers are requested not to use Mrs. Stevens' trademark of the banded head because this confuses copies with the few remaining originals and is, in fact, *forgery*.)

ANSON SPECIAL BUCKTAIL *(As dressed by Herbert L. Howard)*

HEAD: Black
TAG: Three or four turns of medium flat silver tinsel
TAIL: A very small bunch of red hackle fibers
BODY: Wound with peacock herl, moderately thin
RIBBING: Medium flat silver tinsel
THROAT: A few turns of a red hackle, tied downward. The hackle is sparse and rather long.
WING: A small bunch of white bucktail, extending slightly beyond the tail
SHOULDERS: Each a whole tip of a barred black and white teal flank feather, one-third as long as the wing
CHEEKS: Jungle cock, two thirds as long as the shoulder

Originated by Anson Bell, an old-time logger in the lumber camps of Maine and particularly on the Magalloway River in Maine and New Hampshire. This dressing is copied from an original given by Bell to Howard. The fly is popular for all species of trout, particularly in New England and New York State.

276 ASHDOWN GREEN STREAMER (Plate IV) *(As dressed by Fin, Fur and Feather, Ltd.)*

HEAD: Black
TAIL: A section of red duck or goose wing feather, rather long and thin
BODY: Maroon wool, dressed medium heavy and picked out slightly
RIBBING: Narrow oval gold tinsel
THROAT: A maroon saddle hackle, tied on as a collar and then tied downward.

The hackle is rather long and enough turns are made to make it fairly heavy.
WING: Two matched sections of white goose or swan wing feathers, extending
slightly beyond the tail

This is an old West Coast pattern originated by Ashdown H. Green, a famous
ichthyologist of British Columbia. H. L. Gulline, of the famous tackle store of Fin,
Fur and Feather, Ltd., in Montreal, reports having used this as a trout fly as early
as 1889 on the Cowichan River in British Columbia. It was adapted as a streamer
in 1939 by Frier Gulline and as such is a popular trout streamer in eastern Canada.

ATOM BOMB (YELLOW) (Plate IV)   *(As dressed by E. H. Rosborough)*
HOOK SIZE: 1/0 to 6, 3X long
HEAD: Black, with white painted eye with red pupil with black dot in center
TAIL: The tips of two bright yellow saddle hackles, half the length of the hook,
   tied in upright
BODY: Silver Mylar piping
THROAT: A small bunch of brown hackle fibers, rather long
WING: Bright yellow marabou, over which is a very small bunch of white
   bucktail, over which are six fibers of peacock herl, all extending to the end
   of the tail

This is a prominent northwestern pattern evidently originated by George and
Helen Voss, of Portland, Oregon. The Atom Bomb can be dressed in several color
combinations. The Gray Atom Bomb differs from the above only in the wing and
tail. The tail is the tips of two brown hackles. The wing is a very small bunch of
brown bucktail, over which is gray marabou, over which is a very small bunch of
brown bucktail. All are of the same lengths as in the Yellow Atom Bomb.

AUNT IDER STREAMER   *(As dressed by Gardner Percy)*
HEAD: Black (sometimes with red painted eye with white center)
BODY: Medium flat silver tinsel
RIBBING: Narrow oval silver tinsel
THROAT: Five or six strands of peacock herl, under which is a small bunch of
   white bucktail, both nearly as long as the wing
WING: A small bunch of yellow bucktail, over which are four grizzly saddle
   hackles
SHOULDERS: Each a Ripon's silver pheasant body feather, not over one-third as
   long as the wing
CHEEKS: Jungle cock

Originated by Mr. Frank Congdon of Middletown, Connecticut, and named for
Mrs. Congdon.

BADGER STREAMER   *(As dressed by Poul Jorgensen)*   277
HOOK SIZE: 2 to 6, 3X long
HEAD: Black, with white pupil and black center
TAIL: A section of barred wood duck flank feather
BODY: Medium embossed silver tinsel
THROAT: A small bunch of white bucktail extending to end of tail

WING: A small bunch of white bucktail extending to end of tail. Over this are four badger hackles of same length or slightly longer.

SHOULDERS: On each side a section of barred wood duck flank feather laid on over the spines of the hackles

CHEEKS: Jungle cock, optional

Originated by William F. Blades, of Wilmette, Illinois, about 1950. Bill Blades is the author of *Fishing Flies & Fly Tying* (Harrisburg, Pa.: Stackpole, 1951).

BALI DUCK STREAMER   *(As dressed by Earl Leitz)*

HEAD: Black

TAG: Narrow flat gold tinsel. The tag is rather long, extending partway down the bend of the hook.

TAIL: Fifteen or twenty strands of a golden pheasant tippet. The tail is rather long.

BUTT: Two turns of black chenille

BODY: Medium embossed silver tinsel. Just behind the throat is a forward butt of about four turns of peacock herl.

RIBBING: Medium flat silver tinsel, extending between the two butts

THROAT: Two turns of a brown hackle, tied downward. The hackle should be very soft and the throat sparsely dressed.

WING: Two Bali duck feathers (sometimes called "Yanosh"), tied so that the bright and glossy surfaces are on the outside with the bends of the feathers exactly alike. The wing extends beyond the tail by a distance equal to the length of the tail.

CHEEKS: Jungle cock

Originated by Arthur Bates, of Sault Ste. Marie, Michigan, and named by Ray Bergman, who fished with Bates and Leitz in 1948. This is one of several flies designed for taking the large rainbows (called "Soo" trout) of the St. Mary's River at the outlet of Lake Superior. Since the trout in these rapids are large, these flies usually are dressed on No. 2 hooks.

BALLOU SPECIAL STREAMER (Plate XII)   *(As dressed by the originator)*

HEAD: Black

TAIL: One or two short golden pheasant crest feathers curving downward

BODY: Medium flat silver tinsel

WING: About a dozen hairs of red bucktail slightly longer than the tail, over which are two white marabou feathers of the same length tied on flat (at right angles with the hook)

TOPPING: About a dozen strands of peacock herl as long as the wing

CHEEKS: Jungle cock

Originated in 1921 by A. W. Ballou of Litchfield, Maine (formerly of North Dighton, Massachusetts), after several years of experimentation in attempting to find a type of feather which would give greater action than the hackles usually used on streamer flies. The fly first was used at the mouth of the Songo River on Sebago Lake, in Maine, to catch the landlocked salmon which run up the river in the spring to spawn. The Ballou Special, often called by other names, is considered by many anglers to be one of the best and most successful imitations of the smelt. Mr. Ballou

278

says: "When I first got it up they called it the Powder Puff. I tied hundreds, and I mean hundreds, of marabou streamers with all types of dressings, and I had my marabou feathers dyed all colors. Finally I got down to three: the one I call the Ballou Special, another one tied with a red tail and a special light blue-green bucktail in place of the red bucktail, and one tied with a yellow body and some light blue bucktail under the marabou, without a tail. All have peacock herl topping and jungle cock cheeks."

Mr. Ballou is given credit for having originated the marabou streamer. His first ones were dressed on long-shanked single hooks, and this form of dressing usually is preferred by other anglers. Later he dressed them on short-shanked double hooks. He prefers the first method for use when smelt are running upstream, and the second method when they are returning downstream after spawning. Smelt going upstream follow the banks, while on their return they form in schools and keep to the channel of the river. Thus, Mr. Ballou finds greatest success in fishing the fly in the direction in which the smelt are running, casting upstream with the double-hooked fly when the smelt are running downstream and allowing the fly to sink and work in the current as it is being retrieved. Anglers fishing for landlocked salmon in the spring and early summer when the smelt are running feel that the migrations of the smelt govern the location and activity of the salmon, just as surely as fly hatches govern the feeding habits of trout.

BARNES SPECIAL STREAMER   *(As dressed by Gardner Percy)*

HEAD: Red

TAIL: Two very short jungle cock body feather tips

BODY: Medium flat silver tinsel

RIBBING: Narrow oval silver tinsel

THROAT: Several turns of a white saddle hackle, tied on as a collar after the wing has been applied. The hackle is rather long and full.

WING: A small bunch of red bucktail, over which is a very small bunch of white bucktail, over which are two yellow saddle hackles flanked on each side by a barred gray Plymouth Rock saddle hackle. The bucktail is nearly as long as the hackles.

This fly was adapted from the Hurricane streamer by C. Lowell Barnes, a guide at Sebago Lake, Maine, who added the yellow hackles between the Plymouth Rock hackles. The fly is a favorite in the Sebago Lake area.

BARTLETT'S SPECIAL STREAMER (Plate IX)   *(As dressed by the Weber Tackle Company)*

HEAD: Black

TAIL: A very short golden pheasant crest feather, curving upward and clipped flat at the end

BODY: Black silk, dressed rather thinly and tapered at both ends

RIBBING: Narrow flat silver tinsel

THROAT: A small bunch of yellow hackle fibers

WING: Four white saddle hackles

TOPPING: A golden pheasant crest feather as long as the wing and following its curve. Over this is a very narrow section (about three fibers) of a dark blue swan tail or wing feather as long as the wing and so curved as to follow its conformation.

279

This fly was originated by Arthur Bartlett of Presque Isle, Maine. It is essentially a Black Ghost with the topping added. This dressing was obtained from Edward C. Wotruba, president of the Weber Tackle Company, of Stevens Point, Wisconsin, who obtained it from Bartlett.

BATTENKILL SHINER (Plate XI)   *(As dressed by Keith Fulsher)*
HOOK SIZE: 6 or 8, 6X long
HEAD: Black
TAIL: A very small bunch of gray hackle fibers
BUTT: A few turns of red floss
BODY: Tapered white floss
RIBBING: Flat silver tinsel, over body only
THROAT: A small bunch of gray hackle fibers
WING: Two medium blue saddle hackles on each side of which is a silver badger saddle hackle, all extending to the end of the tail
CHEEKS: Jungle cock, rather short

This fly is an imitation of shiners common to the Battenkill River, in Vermont. It was copied by Keith Fulsher from an original given to him by the famous angler and fly dresser Lew Oatman, of Shushan, New York, who originated the pattern.

BAUMAN BUCKTAIL   *(As dressed by the Weber Tackle Company)*
HEAD: Black (red painted eye with white center is optional)
TAIL: A section of a barred wood duck or mandarin duck feather
BODY: Orange silk, dressed thin (or gold tinsel)
RIBBING: Narrow flat gold tinsel (if a gold tinsel body is used, use oval gold tinsel)
THROAT: A bunch of red hackle fibers
WING: A small bunch of white bucktail over which is a small bunch of yellow bucktail
TOPPING: A bunch of six or eight peacock sword fibers, half as long as the wing
CHEEKS: Jungle cock

Originated by Arthur Bartlett, of Presque Isle, Maine, and named for Art Bauman of the Weber Tackle Company, of Stevens Point, Wisconsin.

BELKNAP   *(As dressed by the originator)*
HOOK SIZE: 8 (2811S Allcock)
HEAD: Yellow (ooo silk)
TAIL: A small bunch of crimson hackle fibers
BODY: Six layers of No. 14 flat narrow gold tinsel, lacquered
WING: A very small bunch of the white tip hair from a genuine calf or fox tail extending to the end of the tail, over which is a very small bunch of the same hair half as long as the first one
TOPPING: Two narrow sections of gray mottled mallard body feather, not quite as long as the wing
CHEEKS: Jungle cock, rather short

Originated by Ray Salminen, of West Acton, Massachusetts, to imitate minnows in the Sandwich, New Hampshire, area. This fly is popular for stream fishing for brook, brown, and rainbow trout.

BELL SPECIAL STREAMER   *(As dressed by Herbert L. Howard)*
HEAD: Black
BODY: Medium flat silver tinsel
THROAT: Three or four scarlet hackle tips of moderate length
WING: A small bunch of white ostrich herl, over which is a very small bunch of brown ostrich herl. Both are of the same length and the brown is half as much as the white.
TOPPING: Four or five strands of peacock herl (not called for in the original dressing but later added by Bell)
CHEEKS: Jungle cock (optional)

Originated by Anson Bell, of Pittsburg, New Hampshire, who was a logger in the lumber camps of Maine. The original sample of this pattern was obtained by Howard from Bell, and was used in the paintings of flies in Ray Bergman's book *Trout.* The fly is popular for taking all species of trout, particularly in New York State and New England.

BELLAMY BUCKTAIL (Plate IV)   *(As dressed by the originator)*
HEAD: Black
TAIL: A section of a red goose wing feather, wide and long. (Subsequently Mr. Schwab found that a tail of a small bunch of red polar bear hair, rather long, was superior to the feather tail because of its added permanence. This should now be considered the standard dressing.)
BODY: Wound with copper wire, as described in Chapter 10
WING: A small bunch of white bucktail, over which is a small bunch of brown hair from a bucktail dyed yellow. The wing extends to the end of the tail. In applying the two parts of the wing, turns of thread are taken under the bucktail to raise the wing to an angle of about forty degrees.
THROAT: Dressed as a "spike," as explained above on page 274. A small bunch of California gray squirrel (ground squirrel) tail hair. This is generally omitted. A brown hackle applied as a collar may be used, but this also is omitted from the latest versions of Mr. Schwab's dressing.

Originated by Peter J. Schwab, of Yreka, California, whose comments on this fly, as printed in the June 1946 issue of *Sports Afield* magazine, are: "This bucktail is the great favorite of George B. Bellamy, who was largely responsible for its creation. We had been using shot to get our light bucktails deep enough and were having the usual trouble with cut and snarled leaders, awkward, difficult casting, and poor action of the lures. George bemoaned the fact that we had no weighted flies. I agreed and, luckily having an ample stock of assorted wires, went to work. The first fly actually tied was a Van Luven, with red wool body over a copper wire core. I believe that all bucktails should have a darker topping over a lighter wing, and a yellow dyed bucktail happened to be before me. I cut a lock of hair from the dark portion of the yellow tail, topped it over the white hair of the Van Luven, and christened it the Bellamy. It was an instant success. Its action in the water was fascinating, and the steelhead jumped to the attack. Their sharp teeth soon tore

281

the red wool covering from the body, but they hit the bare copper wire just as eagerly. I tied up a few without the red wool, and the bucktail continued to be successful through September, October, November, and December. George likes it with the brown hackle. I like it better without. The fish don't care which way it is served just so they can get it."

Although the Bellamy was developed as a steelhead fly for the Klamath River, in California, it is equally good as a trout and bass fly in other parts of the country.

BI-BUCK BUCKTAIL   *(As dressed by Fin, Fur and Feather, Ltd.)*

HEAD: Black
TAIL: A small section of a red duck, goose, or swan wing feather
BODY: Medium flat silver tinsel
RIBBING: Narrow oval silver tinsel (optional)
WING: A small bunch of white bucktail, over which is a small bunch of brown bucktail
CHEEKS: Jungle cock

This fly is the always popular and easily dressed brown-and-white bucktail in its most accepted dressing. It is called the Bi-Buck in Canada. The wing can be of several other color combinations and in almost any variety of hair. Brown and yellow, red and yellow, yellow and white, black and white, or red and white are among the most popular combinations. The darker color in a two-color bucktail is dressed over the lighter color.

BIG DIAMOND STREAMER   *(As dressed by the Weber Tackle Company)*

HEAD: Black
TAIL: A narrow section of a red duck wing feather
BODY: Medium flat silver tinsel
RIBBING: Narrow oval silver tinsel (optional)
THROAT: A very small bunch of greenish-blue bucktail, nearly as long as the wing. Under this is a very small bunch of guinea hen body feather fibers, as long as the shoulder. (Another version of the dressing calls for a very small bunch of white bucktail, nearly as long as the wing, instead of the above.)
WING: Two bright yellow saddle hackles with a golden badger hackle of the same length on each side
HORNS: Each a section (two strands) of a red swan feather, nearly as long as the wing
SHOULDERS: Each the tip of a brown barred mandarin duck body feather, one-third as long as the wing
CHEEKS: Jungle cock (optional)

Originated by Frank Congdon of Middletown, Connecticut, and named for a section of the Connecticut Lakes country in northern New England. This dressing is as given to the Weber Tackle Company by Mr. Congdon.

282

BINNS STREAMER (Plate IX)   *(As dressed by the originator)*

HEAD: Black
TAIL: A section of a red and of a white duck or goose wing feather, rather long and thin

BODY: Medium flat silver tinsel (sometimes yellow wool is used)
RIBBING: Narrow oval silver tinsel
THROAT: Two or three turns of a red and a white saddle hackle, tied on mixed
together as a collar and then tied downward
WING: In a matched pair, each a section of a white goose wing married between
two sections of yellow goose wing, the three sections being equal in width.
The wing is slightly longer than the tail.
SHOULDERS: Guinea hen breast feathers, one-third as long as the wing

Originated by Frier Gulline, of Fin, Fur and Feather, Ltd., for J. Binns of
Montreal, in 1937. It was originally tied as a trout fly and was adapted as a streamer
in 1940.

BLACK AND WHITE STREAMER (Plate IX)   *(As dressed by the originator)*
HOOK SIZE: 6, 4X long
HEAD: Black
TAIL: A very small bunch of crimson hackle fibers
BODY: Narrow flat silver tinsel
THROAT: A few pink bucktail hairs slightly longer than the hook, mixed with a
very small bunch of crimson hackle fibers not over half as long as the hair
WING: Four white saddle hackles, on each side of which are two jet black saddle
hackles, all of the same length, about half again as long as the hook. All the
fibers on the bottom of the black hackles are stripped off to provide a black
upper half and a white lower half of the wing.
SHOULDERS: Jet black mallard body feather on each side, one-third as long as
the wing
CHEEKS: Jungle cock

This streamer was originated by Austin S. Hogan, of Cambridge, Massachusetts, to provide high contrast when viewed against dim evening light. It is a good
example of Austin Hogan's color-blending technique, in this case done by stripping the lower sides of outside hackles to allow the lower parts of the inside hackles
to show.

BLACKBIRD BUCKTAIL   *(As dressed by William Reynolds)*
HEAD: Black
TAG: A few turns of narrow flat gold tinsel
TAIL: A bunch of black saddle hackle fibers, rather long
BODY: Black wool, fairly fat
RIBBING: Narrow oval gold tinsel
THROAT: A bunch of black saddle hackle fibers, very long
WING: A bunch of the guard hairs from a black bear, extending to the end of
the tail
CHEEKS: Jungle cock, rather long

283

Adapted by William Reynolds of Sturbridge, Massachusetts, from the Shenandoah Fly, which is dressed in an identical manner, except that the body is tied with
black chenille, full and fat, and the gold tinsel and jungle cock are eliminated. A
wiggling disc or small spinner usually is used on the Shenandoah Fly, which is a
favorite for bass. The Blackbird Bucktail is well recommended for all species of

trout, particularly in the Pennsylvania and Ozark regions, where it seems to imitate the madtom or perhaps the polliwog. The madtom, or stonecat, is a food fish found under rocks in the fast water of large rivers, where it is the prey of bass and trout —big brown trout, particularly. Small sizes are preferable late in the season. (See Chapter 14 for detailed information on bottom-dwelling bait fish and their imitations.)

BLACK DEMON BUCKTAIL (Plate IV)   (As dressed by C. Jim Pray)
HEAD: Black
TAIL: Two medium-width sections of a barred wood duck or mandarin duck feather, both sections being matched to curve upward, and rather long
BODY: Thinly wound with narrow oval gold tinsel, several turns of which are taken below the tail to act as a tag. On extra-long-shanked hooks flat gold tinsel and gold ribbing may be used.
THROAT: Several turns of an orange saddle hackle, applied as a collar and tied back but not gathered downward. The hackle is glossy and stiff, and of moderate length.
WING: A medium-sized bunch of black bear hair, extending to the end of the tail. (A feather wing is less often used and usually then only on the short version of the fly. It is two strips of black goose wing curving upward. These may be splayed outward and extend between the end of the hook and the end of the tail.)

This is the steelhead dressing of the Black Demon. For additional information, see notes for (Cains River) Black Demon Streamer.

BLACK GHOST STREAMER (Plate XII)   (As dressed by the originator)
HEAD: Black
TAIL: A small bunch of yellow hackle fibers
BODY: Of black silk, dressed rather heavily and tapered slightly at both ends
RIBBING: Medium flat silver tinsel
THROAT: A small bunch of yellow hackle fibers
WING: Four white saddle hackles extending to end of tail
CHEEKS: Jungle cock

The Black Ghost is one of the relatively few Maine streamer flies which have enjoyed national acceptance by anglers throughout the United States. In Maine waters, nearly every fisherman will acknowledge it to be one of the most productive, especially for landlocked salmon and squaretail trout. Its popularity has caused its origination to be misunderstood and, in some cases, to be misrepresented.

The fly was originated by Herbert L. Welch, of Mooselookmeguntic, Maine, in 1927, and was first tied under his direction at the Boston Sportsmen's Show in the spring of that year by Nellie Newton, a fly dresser of the Percy Tackle Company, of Portland, Maine, which had an exhibit there. Its dressing of black and white makes the reason for its name rather obvious.

Evidently Nellie Newton took a great interest in promoting the fly, as this letter to the author from A. W. Ballou, one of Maine's expert and old-time anglers from

Litchfield, Maine, will testify. He says: "On my trips it was my custom to stop at the Percy Tackle Shop in Portland, and to spend several hours having dressed new types of streamer flies which I had developed during the winter. On one of these stops in 1927 Mr. Percy asked Nellie Newton, one of his fly dressers, to work with me. Nellie tied a fly with a black body and several white feathers and said it was called the Black Ghost. I didn't think much of it.

"I went on from Percy's to Thompson's Camps at the mouth of the Songo River (on Sebago Lake). I had been there ten or twelve days when one morning I pushed the boat out into the river and anchored it there. I hooked into a beautiful trout and had him up to the boat several times, but finally lost him. Just then a Mr. Merritt from Connecticut came along in his boat with his guide. He had seen me with the fish on and shouted that it looked like a Pierce Pond trout. Just then he cast his fly about three feet from my boat and hooked a large fish. When he landed it he pulled up to my boat to use my scales. It was a nice five and one-half pound trout and the fly was still in his mouth.

"When I stared at the fly, Mr. Merritt said, 'Do you want a copy of this fly, Mr. Ballou?' I said I didn't, but asked him where he got it. He said he stopped the day before at a place in Portland where they tied flies and bought half a dozen, but that he didn't think the fly had a name. I said it had a name all right and that it was a Black Ghost; the same fly that Nellie had tied for me. After telling her that I didn't think much of it, and then seeing Mr. Merritt catch a five and one-half pound trout right under my boat with it, I swore I never would use one of those darned Black Ghosts as long as I lived, and I never have.

"As you know, it turned out to be one of the best streamers that ever was developed. I think Mr. Merritt gave it a big start by giving samples away."

The evidence is that Nellie Newton also gave away many Black Ghosts that year. Guides and sportsmen duplicated them, which contributed to the erroneous impression that the fly was invented by several people at about the same time. In checking up on the matter, I wrote to Gardner Percy. He replied: "With regard to the Black Ghost streamer fly, Herbie Welch was the originator of the pattern. Nellie Newton tied the fly for Herb at the Boston Sportsmen's Show back in 1927 when we had a display booth there."

In addition to its success with other fish, the Black Ghost is an excellent pattern for spring salmon when tied with a white bucktail wing and a throat and tail of golden pheasant crest. Both the feathered original and the bucktail adaptation are favorite flies for landlocked salmon and for bass, as well as for most species of trout. Mr. Welch considers it to be most successful in the early spring or in the late fall.

The Phoenecia bucktail is an adaptation of the Black Ghost bucktail formerly popular among Catskill anglers who fished the Esopus River in New York State between the portal and Ashokan Dam. It is identical with the Black Ghost except that it is ribbed with gold tinsel, has a tail of a double section of dark yellow wool, and has no throat. This area produces brown and rainbow trout.

The Rogers Knight has enjoyed considerable editorial attention in the New England area. It was originated (if the word should be used in this case) by Edward W. Rogers of Manchester-by-the-Sea, Massachusetts, and differs from the Black Ghost only in having a wing of rusty bronze dun saddle hackles, preferably with very dark medial lines.

BLACK GORDON BUCKTAIL   *(As dressed by Don C. Harger)*
HEAD: Black
TAG: Thinly dressed with three or four turns of red silk
BODY: Black wool yarn thinly dressed at rear and shaped larger toward head
RIBBING: Narrow flat silver tinsel
THROAT: A medium-sized black hackle; three or four turns tied on as a collar
    and then tied downward
WING: A small bunch of black or dark brown bucktail tied on as a steelhead
    wing, rather high, on a large steelhead hook 2X long

This fly was originated by Clarence Gordon, a well-known guide and steelhead angler of the North Umpqua Lodge on the Umpqua River of Oregon. It is especially good for summer-run steelhead on the upper reaches of Oregon's coastal rivers.

BLACK LEECH STREAMER   *(As dressed by E. H. Rosborough)*
HOOK SIZE: 2 to 8, 3X to 6X long
HEAD: Black
TAIL: A very small bunch of scarlet hackle fibers, a little longer than the gap of
    the hook
BODY: Wound rather heavily with peacock herl
THROAT: A black saddle hackle wound on as a collar and tied downward
WING: Four jet black saddle hackles, the two on one side being back to back
    with the two on the other side, to provide a splayed wing slightly longer
    than the tail

This is a popular northwestern pattern which is especially productive for trout in lakes where leeches are present. This fly should not be confused with another called the Leech Streamer, which consists of a heavy maroon body and a throat of a small bunch of black hackle fibers. The wing is two maroon saddle hackles, over which are two black saddle hackles. All four feathers are tied on flat (at right angles to the hook) so that the two black hackles are on top. Also note the Wooly Leech, which many consider to be a better pattern.

BLACK NOSED DACE BUCKTAIL (Plate I)   *(As dressed by the originator)*
HEAD: Black
TAIL: A fine piece of red yarn, very short
BODY: Medium flat silver tinsel
RIBBING: Fine oval silver tinsel
WING: A small bunch of white polar bear hair or bucktail, over which is a small
    bunch of black bear hair or black hair from a skunk's tail, over which is a
    small bunch of brown bucktail. The black hair is a little shorter than the
    brown and the white. Care should be taken to use small bunches of hair so
    that the fly will not be overdressed.

286

Originated by Arthur B. Flick, of West Kill, New York, to imitate the bait fish commonly called the blacknose or black-nosed dace, as described in his book *Streamside Guide to Naturals and Their Imitations* (New York: G. P. Putnam's Sons). Flick advised that the fly be dressed on hook sizes 4, 6, 8, or 10, the smaller sizes being preferable late in the season. When the small sizes are tied, Chinese or

Mexican deer tails will be found suitable, because the hair is softer than the hair of the whitetail deer. Harold N. Gibbs, the noted saltwater fly fisherman of Barrington, Rhode Island, has found this fly, in larger sizes, with a red throat added, to be excellent for taking striped bass.

BLONDE PATTERNS (Plate VII)
(See Chapters 8 and 15)

BLOODSUCKER *(As dressed by the originator)*
HEAD: Black
TAIL: A black silver pheasant crest feather extending slightly beyond bend of hook
BODY: Thinly cover shank with black silk or cover with tying thread and lacquer
THROAT: A black silver pheasant crest feather curving upward into gap of hook
WING: Two black silver pheasant crest feathers (only one on No. 10 and No. 12 hooks) extending to tip of tail and curving downward

Originated by Don Brown, of Kingston, Massachusetts, about 1965, for trout. The fly is especially effective in summer when water warms and fish go deep. This also is a proven Atlantic salmon pattern.

BLUE DEVIL STREAMER (Plate II) *(As dressed by the originator)*
HEAD: Black, with red band
TAG: A few turns of narrow flat silver tinsel
BODY: Thinly dressed with black silk
RIBBING: Narrow flat silver tinsel
THROAT: A small bunch of white bucktail, extending beyond the bend of the hook, under which is a small bunch of orange hackle fibers
WING: Six or eight strands of bronze peacock herl, over which are two orange saddle hackles flanked on each side by a dark blue saddle hackle, slightly shorter. The peacock is as long as the orange hackles.
SHOULDERS: Light brownish gray feathers from the breast of a partridge
CHEEKS: Jungle cock, rather short

This is one of the earliest streamer fly patterns originated by Carrie G. Stevens, of Madison, Maine, for eastern brook trout and landlocked salmon. It was first used at Upper Dam Pool, in the Rangeley Lakes section of Maine, in 1923.

BLUE MARABOU STREAMER (Plate X) *(As dressed by the originator)*
HOOK SIZE: 8 to 1/0, 6X long
HEAD: Black
TAIL: A very small bunch of red-orange hackle the length of the gap of the hook
BODY: Wound with gray floss
RIBBING: Flat gold tinsel
THROAT: A small bunch of grass-green polar bear hair, as long as the hook
WING: A small bunch of white polar bear hair extending to end of tail. Over this are two light blue marabou feathers slightly longer than the polar bear hair.

287

SHOULDERS: On each side, a badger saddle hackle almost as long as the wing
CHEEKS: Jungle cock, short

This fly was originated by Paul Kukonen, expert professional fly dresser and casting champion of Worcester, Massachusetts, for landlocked salmon and brook trout. It is similar to the Supervisor and the Spencer Bay Special, except that Kukonen thinks the addition of marabou and polar bear hair makes it more effective. He has caught many hundreds of salmon and trout on the fly in New England, Canada, and Labrador, including a seven-and-a-half-pound brook trout in Pierce's Pond, Maine. The fly in smaller sizes is excellent for brown and rainbow trout. Dressed as a tandem fly, on 6X long No. 2 or No. 1 hooks, it is excellent for trolling on the surface or for deep (wire-line) trolling in summer.

BOB WILSON STREAMER   (As dressed by Herbert L. Howard)
HEAD: Yellow
TAIL: A very short golden pheasant crest feather, curving upward. The feather
    usually is trimmed to even the end.
BODY: Copper wire or embossed copper tinsel, dressed very thin
THROAT: A few turns of a black hackle wound on as a collar and tied
    downward. The throat is long and sparsely dressed.
WING: Two matching sections of barred wood duck or mandarin duck feathers,
    fairly narrow and long, extending just beyond the tail.

This pattern originated in Scotland as a wet fly in about the year 1890. It was first tied by Robert Wilson, who used it as a boy in Scotland. He later lived in Old Greenwich, Connecticut, where he adapted the fly to a streamer in the early 1920s. Wilson was a close friend of George Fraser and of Howard. He used this fly in lively competition with Fraser and his Fraser streamer, but neither could decide which was the better one.

BOBBY DUNN BUCKTAIL   (As dressed by the originator)
HEAD: Black
TAIL: A section of a red goose wing feather, wide and long. (Subsequently,
    Schwab found that a tail of a small bunch of red polar bear hair, rather long,
    was superior to the feather tail because of its added permanence. This
    should now be considered the standard dressing.)
BODY: Wound with copper wire, as described in Chapter 10
WING: A small bunch of white polar bear hair, over which is a small bunch of
    red polar bear hair. A few strands of dark brown bucktail may be put over
    this, but it is omitted on the standard pattern. The wing extends to the end
    of the tail. In applying the two parts of the wing, turns of thread are taken
    under the bucktail to raise the wing to an angle of about 40 degrees.
    Bucktail may be substituted for the polar bear if desired.
THROAT: Dressed as a "spike," as explained above on page 274. A small bunch
    of red polar bear hair; this is generally omitted.

288

This is one of a series of steelhead flies originated by Peter J. Schwab, of Yreka, California, principally for fishing on the Klamath River. It is primarily influenced by the nationally successful Parmachenee Belle colors, and was named for Bobby Dunn, a noted California angler and fishing companion of Schwab's.

BOLSHEVIK STREAMER
(As dressed by the originator)

HEAD: Black
TAIL: The tip of a golden yellow neck hackle
BODY: Medium flat silver tinsel
THROAT: A small bunch of light brown bucktail, nearly as long as the wing
WING: A red saddle hackle on each side of which are two dark ginger furnace
 hackles with a very pronounced black stripe
CHEEKS: Jungle cock

Originated by Fred B. Fowler of Oquossoc, Maine, in 1925. This fly is preferred for late-fall fishing for both squaretail trout and landlocked salmon in Maine.

BONBRIGHT STREAMER (Plate VII)
(As dressed for the originator)

HEAD: Black
TAIL: Two very narrow and rather long sections of a red and a white duck wing
 feather, the red and the white of each section being married together. The
 colors of each of the two sections are reversed. A very short golden pheasant
 crest feather is added. The two married sections and the golden pheasant
 crest feather are of the same length and all curve upward.
BODY: Of medium flat silver tinsel, built up slightly toward the head. (The
 freshwater version is thin and not built up.)
RIBBING: Fine oval silver tinsel
THROAT: A small bunch of white hackle fibers of medium length
WING: Four white neck hackles, rather long
HORNS: Each a single fiber from a blue macaw tail feather, two-thirds as long as
 the wing
SHOULDERS: Each a golden pheasant crest feather nearly as long as the wing.
 Outside of this is a red duck breast feather with a solid edge, one-fourth as
 long as the wing. The red shoulders are dressed high so as not to conceal
 the body and throat but to conceal all the front of the wing. The throat joins
 the underside of the red shoulder on both sides.
CHEEKS: Jungle cock, set in the center of the red shoulders

This fly is a development of the Colonel White Streamer. The augmented pattern was dressed about 1925 on the instructions of G. D. B. Bonbright, president of the Seaboard Airline Railway, to Steward Slosson, a fly dresser for Abercrombie & Fitch Company, of New York City. Mr. Bonbright used the fly for tarpon fishing in Florida and made it famous because of the large numbers of tarpon and other saltwater fish taken with it. He preferred 4/0 hooks for tarpon and insisted that the heads of the flies be soaked in Dupont cement and then lacquered black.

The Bonbright Streamer, which had its genesis as one of Maine's earliest landlocked salmon flies, was readapted to Maine fishing by L. Dana Chapman, a tackle dealer of Boston, who gave the Percy Tackle Company an order for some of these flies dressed for freshwater fishing. Percy renamed it the Dana. It also has been called the Ross McKenney, as discussed in Chapter 2.

289

BRASS HAT BUCKTAIL
(As dressed by the originator)

HEAD: Black
TAIL: A very small bunch of yellow-dyed polar bear hair, very long (yellow-dyed

bucktail may be substituted). Early dressings called for "yellow or red goose, preferably yellow." Mr. Schwab later preferred the hair tail.

BODY: Wound with yellow brass wire (see instructions in Chapter 10)

WING: A small bunch of white bucktail, over which is a small bunch of yellow bucktail topped with a very few hairs of black bucktail or skunk. The wing extends to the end of the tail. In applying the two parts of the wing, turns of thread are taken under both the white and the yellow bucktail to raise the wing to an angle of about forty degrees. In the three-winged pattern the rear wing is white bucktail (dressed on a very long-shanked hook) and the lower part of the front wing is yellow bucktail, dressed fairly full, with the upper wing brown bucktail dyed yellow or an extremely small bunch of black bucktail or skunk. The brown bucktail dyed yellow is Schwab's choice.

THROAT: Dressed as a "spike," as explained above on page 274. A small bunch of yellow bucktail. This is generally omitted, particularly in the two-wing dressing.

The weighted dressing, as explained in the above reference, is a later improvement, succeeding the unweighted gold tinsel version. Of this fly, Schwab says: "I would hate to go steelhead fishing without this pattern in both two-winged and three-winged versions. Its only rival is the Queen Bess. When the day is dark or the river is high or murky, I bend on a Brass Hat, knowing it will be seen.

"When the day is dark but the water is clear and low, I use the Brass Hat in the two-winged version, tied to sizes 2 or 4 Limerick hooks, 2X and 3X strong respectively, on the standard shank. When the day is dark and/or the river is high or murky, I try a three-winged Brass Hat, tied on a size 2 Limerick, 3X long and 2X heavy. As a three-winged bucktail it is the perfect companion to the deeper-hued Paint Brush. It has everything—flashing, swimming, darting action."

Schwab originated this fly for use on the Klamath River, in California, but it is an excellent bucktail for all freshwater game fish in other parts of the country. Its color scheme should recommend it for saltwater fishing also.

BROOK TROUT (Plate XI) *(As dressed by the originator)*

HEAD: Olive green, painted white underneath

TAIL: A very small bunch of white hackle, over which is a very small bunch of black hackle, over which is a larger bunch of rich orange hackle, all as long as the gap of the hook. The three colors should not be blended, and the orange should be as much as the black and white together. The three imitate the color scheme of a brook trout's fin.

BODY: The rear three-fourths is white floss, with the forward one-fourth salmon pink floss, tapered quite full

RIBBING: Medium flat gold tinsel

THROAT: The same as the tail, and of same length

WING: Two grizzly saddle hackles, on each side of which is an olive green hackle. The green hackles are painted with about six alternating very small yellow and scarlet dots along the quill.

CHEEKS: Jungle cock, eye only

This beautiful imitation of a small brook trout was originated by the famous angler Lew Oatman, of Shushan, New York, for use in waters where large brook trout are accustomed to feed on small ones. The fly has had outstanding success, especially in Quebec and in California lakes where eastern brook trout were planted. It is also effective for rainbow trout and other species. (An original of the fly, dressed by Oatman, is illustrated in Plate XI.)

BROWN FALCON BUCKTAIL   (*As dressed by Gardner Percy*)

HEAD: Black
TAG: Two turns of medium embossed silver tinsel
BUTT: Red silk, rather wide
BODY: Medium embossed silver tinsel, butted just behind the head with red silk
WING: A fairly large bunch of white bucktail, over which is a fairly large bunch of yellow bucktail
SHOULDERS: A brown saddle hackle on each side, nearly as long as the wing
CHEEKS: Jungle cock

This fly is one of the most popular for black salmon in New Brunswick. It is very similar to Hardy Brothers' Smelt, which was the original of the pattern. Since black salmon flies are usually fished in very high water, and since weighted flies are not allowed, streamers and bucktails for this type of fishing must be dressed on extra-strong hooks to make them sink. All black salmon streamers are dressed on size 2 or 4 long-shanked hooks. Black salmon, incidentally, are those that have been unable to return to sea because of winter ice. In the spring they are bloated, emaciated, and furiously hungry; unfit for food, and too easy to catch. Fishing for them is allowed in some areas only to augment tourist revenue. No Atlantic salmon angler worthy of the name would consider fishing for them.

BROWN HACKLE STREAMER   (*As dressed by Poul Jorgensen*)

HOOK SIZE: 2, salmon
HEAD: Red
TAIL: A very small bunch of red hackle fibers and two tips of peacock herl as long as the gap of the hook, over which are two red hackle tips twice as long as the gap of the hook
BODY: In five sections each of a substantial butt of peacock herl forward of which are three or four turns of Coch-y-Bondhu hackle. The front hackle is somewhat wider than the others.

This fly was originated by Poul Jorgensen, of Columbia, Maryland, and is featured in his book *Dressing Flies for Fresh and Salt Water* (Rockville Center, N.Y.: Freshet Press, 1973).

BUCKTAIL SILVER STREAMER   (*As dressed by the originator*)

HEAD: Black
BODY: Medium flat embossed silver tinsel
THROAT: The tip of a very short golden pheasant crest feather dyed red
WING: A very small bunch of white bucktail over which are two creamy white badger hackles of the same length as the bucktail
CHEEKS: Jungle cock, very short

This is one of a series of three streamers originated by Ray Bergman of Nyack, New York, in 1933. These flies should be dressed sparsely in small sizes. They are excellent for all species of trout. A popular adaptation of this fly is made by applying the bucktail as a throat and leaving off the throat called for above. In this adaptation, medium flat silver tinsel is used on the body, which is ribbed with oval silver tinsel.

BUMBLEPUPPY (Plate XII)   *(As dressed by Roy Steenrod and Herman Christian)*

This historic fly, originally tied both as a bucktail and as a streamer, evidently is the first of all the modern patterns of this type. Originated by the famous Theodore Gordon, creator of the popular Quill Gordon and father of the American dry fly, the Bumblepuppy actually is not one fly but rather several related patterns as developed by Gordon over many years prior to his death in 1915. As described on pages 16, 17, 40, 41, 42, and 331 of *The Complete Fly Fisherman (The Notes and Letters of Theodore Gordon)* by John McDonald (New York: Charles Scribner's Sons), the fly is dressed as follows:

HEAD: Red or yellow chenille, or black, plain varnished
TAG: Silver and red silk
TAIL: Scarlet ibis, two mated feathers, back to back and quite straight on hook
BUTT: Red or yellow chenille
BODY: White silk chenille dressed full; not thin
RIBBING: Medium flat silver tinsel
THROAT: Badger; large, long and lots of it
WING: White hair from deer, white bear or goat, over which are strips of white
    swan or goose
SHOULDERS: Widgeon feathers, as long or longer than the badger
CHEEKS: Jungle cock, tied low (in line with the hook)

In Gordon's letters he states that he has "used the Bumblepuppy most success-fully for pike, salmon, striped bass, and other game fish." Probably the rather elaborate dressing which Mr. McDonald quotes was not the one to which Mr. Gordon refers, because it certainly is not the final version as developed by Gordon over the years, as the following will show.

In a letter to me, Roy Steenrod, of Liberty, New York, game-warden friend and fishing companion of Gordon's, says, "The Bumblepuppy meant to Mr. Gordon any fly to which there was no name. He tied many of them. I called on Herman Christian, a fly tyer friend of Gordon's, and we are both of the opinion that the fly I have tied and am sending to you was the favorite and the one of which he often spoke as having taken so many fish with in the lakes of Rockland County, New York. I know that Gordon was tying these flies as early as 1880." Steenrod's version of Gordon's favorite Bumblepuppy is as follows:

292

HEAD: Black
TAIL: A dozen rather long fibers from a red hackle feather
BODY: White chenille
THROAT: About two turns of a red and a white neck hackle, to make a very long
    but not heavily dressed collar
WING: A very small bunch of white bucktail, extending slightly beyond the tail
    of the fly

SHOULDERS: Four sections of a brown turkey tail feather; two for each shoulder. Each two are matched with the concave sides together to give the appearance of a single feather. They are tied on rather high, like the wings of a wet fly, but the two shoulders splay out to make a V when viewed from the top. The shoulders are nearly as long as the bucktail.

Herman Christian, of Neversink, New York, who fished with Gordon over a long period of years, differs slightly with Steenrod in the dressing of the Bumblepuppy, particularly in the fact that the Christian version does not have splayed shoulders. Instead, the brown turkey feather is used as a wing, as described in the following dressing:

HEAD: Black
TAIL: A small bunch of red hackle fibers, rather long
BODY: White wool or chenille, rather heavy
RIBBING: A single strand of red wool yarn
THROAT: About two turns of a red and a white neck hackle, mixed to make a very long but not heavily dressed collar
WING: A bunch of white bucktail, extending slightly beyond the tail of the fly. The lower half of the bunch of bucktail is clipped off at about half its length after it has been tied in. Over the bucktail is a wing of two long but narrow matched sections of a brown turkey tail feather, extending as far as the beginning of the tail.
NOTE: The early Bumblepuppies were tied on regular wet-fly hooks, usually in size 4 or 6. This version is dressed on a long-shank streamer fly hook, size 2 or 4. Long hooks were not available during Mr. Gordon's lifetime.

The above evidently is the Bumblepuppy preferred by Theodore Gordon. In using it, Christian found that better results were obtained by dressing the body with white chenille, without the red wool ribbing. In letters to me he said:

"Mr. Gordon made me lots of flies and when he got sick I started to make them but never thought I would do so for the public. Mr. Gordon made me a lot of Bumblepuppies—perhaps twenty different kinds. But the one I made was the only one that was any good. It is a killer. A friend of mine was fishing in Moose River [Maine] a few years back and caught his limit of big native trout and [landlocked] salmon every day with the Bumblepuppy, while his friends didn't catch any. Another man caught a brown trout in the Delaware River on the Bumblepuppy while fishing for bass. It weighed thirteen pounds and nine ounces. I have caught many, many bass on it, so it is a real good fly for big fish. I have also caught walleyed pike on it. I am sending you a fly like Mr. Gordon made for me (with the red ribbing) and one like I make (with the white chenille but no ribbing). Mr. Gordon almost always put a stripe on the body, either gold, silver, or copper tinsel or some kind of wool. I don't like the stripe and never have had much luck with Mr. Gordon's Bumblepuppies which had stripes on them. I think my version is the best one. Of course, I made it for bass but there have been lots of big fish caught on it all over the country, including big trout of all kinds, and salmon."

293

Thus it would seem that the "twenty kinds of Bumblepuppies" tied from time to time by Theodore Gordon were a progressive attempt by him to arrive at what he thought was the ideal pattern. Since Gordon's research was cut short by his untimely death, evidently Christian's adaptation should be considered as the final version and as such it should be accepted. Quite obviously, Theodore Gordon was far in advance of his time in developing streamers and bucktails, since his early work compares favorably with that of others done decades later. Added to his fame as the father of the American dry fly should be equal fame for having originated the modern streamer fly and bucktail.

CAINS RIVER STREAMERS   *(As dressed by C. Jim Pray)*

The Cains River is a small one flowing into New Brunswick's Southwest Miramichi near the town of Blackville. This famous series of streamers is included here for their beauty and historic interest in spite of the fact that they were originated mainly to take black salmon, a practice now despised by Atlantic salmon anglers. As said before, black salmon, or kelts, are fished for in early spring after they have been stranded under ice during the winter, thus having been prevented from returning to sea. They have become bloated, emaciated, and so hungry that any bucktail or streamer wavering in the current will hook them. In New Brunswick, fishing for them only has been allowed to bolster tourist revenue, despite the fact that, if left alone and allowed to return to the sea, about one in ten would come back as bright and much bigger trophy fish. Salmon hooked and released in this condition rarely survive.

This series of flies is credited to Fred N. Peet, a famous amateur distance fly-casting champion and angler of Chicago, Illinois. While it is true that Peet originated several of these patterns, it also is true that he did not design all of them and that their rather individual style of dressing was in use several years before Peet tied the first of the series for use in New Brunswick's Cains River in 1924. It is also true that additional patterns have been developed in Cains River style by other anglers and have been included in this set. For example, in William Bayard Sturgis' book *Fly Tying* he includes the Gold Demon, Black Demon, and Demon, the first of which evidently was brought to this country from New Zealand in 1933 or 1934 by the great fly fisherman Fred Burnham. This fly gained much of its American popularity through the efforts of C. Jim Pray, of Eureka, California, generally conceded to be the greatest expert on steelhead flies who ever lived. The Black Demon and Silver Demon were originated by Pray to complete this set of three, and are discussed further under those flies. I shall include them in the Cains River series because they are frequently considered to belong there, although Pray also tied them as steelhead bucktails with a somewhat different dressing.

One of the best-informed authorities on the genesis of the Cains River patterns was Oscar Weber, of the Weber Tackle Company of Stevens Point, Wisconsin, who was a friend and angling companion of Peet's. Weber wrote me as follows: "Mr. Peet originated the Highlander, Kidder, Miramichi, Peet's Masterpiece, and the Cains River Streamer. Herman's Favorite was designed by Mr. Raymond E. Herman, of Chicago, Illinois. Roaring Rapids was designed by a Colorado angler whose name I am unable to supply. Allen's First Choice, Allen's Last Chance, Dunk's Special, Aleck's Wonder, and Wade's Choice were designed by myself. Allen's First Choice and Allen's Last Chance were named for Mr. Harry Allen, who used to lease the Cains River and who furnished equipment and guides for the Cains River trip. Aleck's Wonder, Wade's Choice, and Dunk's Special were named for three guides who worked for Mr. Allen."

Though originally tied for taking black Atlantic salmon, the Cains River series also is good for trout (including steelhead), bass, and many other species of fish. Since these famous and beautiful patterns are regarded by many anglers and fly dressers as being collectors' items I shall include the dressings of twenty-one of the most important patterns.

All these flies are distinguished by having barred mandarin or wood duck tails about three-eighths of an inch wide and three-fourths of an inch long, occasionally with other feathers added. All have double-wound medium flat tinsel bodies (which should be well lacquered). In connection with the bodies, Pray states: "Peter Schwab (who knew Fred Peet personally) contends, and I subscribe to the same theory, that Fred Peet did tie quite a few of these flies with bodies other than flat silver or gold tinsel. The Cains River Steelhead Streamer, for example, is tied with a chenille body, although the original might have had a beige or tan yarn or silk body. I can't say for sure."

In the Cains River patterns the wings usually are of four hackles, the two in the middle frequently being of a different color from the two on the outside. Jungle cock cheeks are used on all the flies. The jungle cock is rather long, about three-fourths of an inch on flies of conventional size (with two-and-a-half-inch wings). The shoulder hackles are added *last,* tied on as a collar *over* the butt of the wing and the jungle cock. The hackles are of moderate width, fairly heavily dressed, and usually are of two different colors, most often not mixed. The second color is wound toward the head and is concentrated at the head after the first color has been tied down.

The dressings given here are as tied by C. Jim Pray, taken from patterns tied by him especially for this book. I realize that there may be different conceptions of the proper dressings of the Cains River patterns but consider that these done by Pray's expert hand are as authoritative as any which can be obtained. Many of these patterns originally were tied for the Weber Tackle Company, whose founder, Oscar Weber, testified as to their correctness.

Proper colors are important if these flies are to be dressed as Peet liked them. In this regard, Peter Schwab writes: "The beautiful blue which Fred preferred can be easily described if you know artists' watercolor paints. It is the rich French blue, a very full color and warm for a blue. He never used the washed-out, cold (but purest of all blues) cobalt, similar to the Silver Doctor blue. Fred's red is hard to describe except that it is also full and rich, decidedly on the order of warm scarlet. Fred's yellow is a full rich golden yellow, glowing, on the order of cadmium yellow." These comments may indicate to fly dressers the tones preferred by Peet in other colors.

On all Cains River streamers all wing hackles are of the same length. When a two-color collar is called for, the rear color should be twice as heavily dressed as the forward color. Two or three turns of tinsel should be taken around the bend of the hook below where the tail is tied in. The heads are varnished black. Mr. Pray used regular No. 2 Sproat hooks, although the flies may be dressed on hooks 2X or 3X long. Nearly all in the series are similar in design. An example is included in Color Plate IX.

For simplicity, the above information will not be repeated in the dressings which follow.

(CAINS RIVER) ALECK'S WONDER STREAMER

TAIL: Two sections of a barred wood duck feather with a thin section of a French blue goose wing feather of the same length between
BODY: Medium flat gold tinsel
WING: A scarlet saddle hackle with a rich yellow saddle hackle on each side and a French blue saddle hackle on each side of this
CHEEKS: Jungle cock
COLLAR: A few turns of a scarlet saddle hackle with a few turns of a French blue saddle hackle ahead of this

(CAINS RIVER) ALLEN'S FIRST CHOICE STREAMER

TAIL: Two sections of a barred wood duck feather
BODY: Medium flat silver tinsel
WING: Two French blue saddle hackles with a cream badger saddle hackle on each side
CHEEKS: Jungle cock
COLLAR: A few turns of a scarlet saddle hackle with a few turns of a rich yellow saddle hackle ahead of this

(CAINS RIVER) ALLEN'S LAST CHANCE STREAMER

TAIL: Two sections of a barred wood duck feather
BODY: Medium flat silver tinsel
WING: Two French blue saddle hackles with a gray Plymouth Rock saddle hackle on each side
CHEEKS: Jungle cock
COLLAR: A few turns of a gray Plymouth Rock saddle hackle with a few turns of a French blue saddle hackle ahead of this

CAINS RIVER STREAMER

TAIL: Two sections of a barred wood duck feather
BODY: Medium flat silver tinsel
WING: Two French blue saddle hackles with a beige saddle hackle on each side
CHEEKS: Jungle cock
COLLAR: Several turns of a beige saddle hackle

CAINS RIVER STEELHEAD STREAMER

TAIL: Two sections of a barred wood duck feather
BODY: Dressed fairly heavily with a very pale gray or cream chenille
WING: Four golden badger neck hackles
CHEEKS: Jungle cock
COLLAR: A few turns of a rich yellow saddle hackle with a few turns of a scarlet saddle hackle ahead of this

NOTE: This dressing is an adaptation of C. Jim Pray's for steelhead fishing and should be dressed on a heavy No. 1 hook, very short. The fly is especially successful on California's Klamath River.

(CAINS RIVER) DUNK'S SPECIAL STREAMER

TAIL: Two sections of a barred wood duck feather
BODY: Medium flat silver tinsel
WING: Two magenta saddle hackles with a French blue saddle hackle on each
 side
CHEEKS: Jungle cock
COLLAR: A few turns of a magenta saddle hackle with a few turns of a French
 blue saddle hackle ahead of this

(CAINS RIVER) HERMAN'S FAVORITE STREAMER

TAIL: Two sections of a barred wood duck feather
BODY: Medium flat gold tinsel
WING: Two scarlet saddle hackles with a medium brown saddle hackle on each
 side
CHEEKS: Jungle cock
COLLAR: Several turns of a medium brown saddle hackle

(CAINS RIVER) HIGHLANDER STREAMER

TAIL: Two sections of a barred wood duck feather
BODY: Medium flat silver tinsel
WING: Two emerald (Highlander) green saddle hackles with a gray Plymouth
 Rock saddle hackle on each side
CHEEKS: Jungle cock
COLLAR: A few turns of an emerald green saddle hackle with a few turns of a
 gray Plymouth Rock saddle hackle ahead of this

(CAINS RIVER) KIDDER STREAMER

TAIL: Two sections of a barred wood duck feather
BODY: Medium flat gold tinsel
WING: Two dark chocolate brown saddle hackles with a gray Plymouth Rock
 saddle hackle on each side
CHEEKS: Jungle cock
COLLAR: Several turns of a dark chocolate brown saddle hackle

(CAINS RIVER) MIRAMICHI STREAMER (Plate IX)

TAIL: Two sections of a barred wood duck feather with a thin section of a
 medium blue goose wing feather of the same length between
BODY: Medium flat gold tinsel
WING: Two magenta saddle hackles with a medium blue saddle hackle on each
 side
CHEEKS: Jungle cock
COLLAR: A few turns of a magenta saddle hackle with a few turns of a medium
 blue saddle hackle ahead of this

297

(CAINS RIVER) PEET'S MASTERPIECE STREAMER

TAIL: Two sections of a barred wood duck feather with a thin tip section of a
 French blue goose feather half as long on each side

BODY: Medium flat gold tinsel

WING: Two French blue saddle hackles with a cream badger saddle hackle on each side

CHEEKS: Jungle cock

COLLAR: A few turns of a dark chocolate brown saddle hackle with a few turns of a French blue saddle hackle ahead of this

(CAINS RIVER) RAINBOW STREAMER

TAIL: Two sections of a barred wood duck feather

BODY: Medium flat gold tinsel

WING: Two French blue saddle hackles with a golden yellow saddle hackle on each side

CHEEKS: Jungle cock

COLLAR: A few turns of a rich yellow saddle hackle *mixed* with a few turns of a scarlet saddle hackle

(CAINS RIVER) ROARING RAPIDS STREAMER

TAIL: Two sections of a barred wood duck feather with a thin section of a scarlet goose wing feather of the same length between

BODY: Medium flat silver tinsel

WING: Two scarlet saddle hackles with a rich yellow saddle hackle on each side

CHEEKS: Jungle cock

COLLAR: Several turns of a French blue saddle hackle

(CAINS RIVER) SCOTCH LASSIE STREAMER

TAIL: Two sections of a barred wood duck feather

BODY: Medium flat silver tinsel

WING: Two French blue saddle hackles with a rich yellow saddle hackle on each side

CHEEKS: Jungle cock

COLLAR: A few turns of a magenta saddle hackle with a few turns of a French blue saddle hackle ahead of this

(CAINS RIVER) SILVER DOCTOR STREAMER

TAIL: Two sections of a barred wood duck feather

BODY: Medium flat silver tinsel

WING: Two medium brown saddle hackles with a gray Plymouth Rock saddle hackle on each side

CHEEKS: Jungle cock

COLLAR: A few turns of a French blue saddle hackle with a few turns of a gray Plymouth Rock saddle hackle ahead of this

298

(CAINS RIVER) SILVER GRAY STREAMER

TAIL: Two sections of a barred wood duck feather

BODY: Medium flat silver tinsel

WING: Two bright orange saddle hackles with a gray Plymouth Rock saddle hackle on each side

CHEEKS: Jungle cock
COLLAR: Several turns of a gray Plymouth Rock saddle hackle

(CAINS RIVER) WADE'S CHOICE STREAMER

TAIL: Two sections of a barred wood duck feather with a thin section of a
French blue goose wing feather of the same length between
BODY: Medium flat silver tinsel
WING: Two gray Plymouth Rock saddle hackles with a scarlet saddle hackle on
each side and a rich yellow saddle hackle on each side of this
CHEEKS: Jungle cock
COLLAR: A few turns of a gray Plymouth Rock saddle hackle *mixed* with a few
turns of a rich yellow saddle hackle

(CAINS RIVER) WILKINSON STREAMER

TAIL: Two sections of a barred wood duck feather
BODY: Medium flat silver tinsel
WING: Two medium brown saddle hackles with a gray Plymouth Rock saddle
hackle on each side
CHEEKS: Jungle cock
COLLAR: A few turns of a magenta saddle hackle with a few turns of a French
blue saddle hackle ahead of this

(CAINS RIVER) BLACK DEMON STREAMER

TAIL: Two sections of a barred wood duck feather
BODY: Medium flat gold tinsel
WING: Four jet black saddle hackles
CHEEKS: Jungle cock
COLLAR: Several turns of an orange saddle hackle

(CAINS RIVER) GOLD DEMON STREAMER

TAIL: Two sections of a barred wood duck feather
BODY: Medium flat gold tinsel
WING: Two medium brown saddle hackles with a gray Plymouth Rock saddle
hackle on each side
CHEEKS: Jungle cock
COLLAR: Several turns of an orange saddle hackle

(CAINS RIVER) SILVER DEMON STREAMER

TAIL: Two sections of a barred wood duck feather
BODY: Medium flat silver tinsel
WING: Four gray Plymouth Rock saddle hackles
CHEEKS: Jungle cock
COLLAR: Several turns of an orange saddle hackle

299

The three Demon streamers described above, as tied in the Cains River style,
were adapted or originated by C. Jim Pray, and the dressings are from originals
tied by him. Regarding them he wrote me: "At the time William Sturgis published

his book *Fly Tying* he included in the Cains River series three flies which of course Fred Peet never could have seen. He figured they would work up nicely in the Cains River style. Two of them were my own concoctions and one of them was the original Gold Demon. The Gold Demon was the original of the Demon flies, orange hackles seeming to suggest a demon. The original fly was usually a conventional size 6 with a flat gold body, yellow golden pheasant crest tail, brown barred mallard feathers for a wing, and with jungle cock cheeks and an orange throat. In streamers there have been many materials offered to take the place of the brown mallard feathers, which are not long enough for streamers. The Gold Demon was very popular during its early arrival here [in California] and in Oregon.

"Late in 1935 or 1936 I brought out the Silver Demon, with silver rope tinsel body, barred wood duck tail, orange throat, and a wing of barred gadwall feathers. This fly originally contained no jungle cock cheeks. In its first year on the Eel and Klamath rivers my shop records show that the Silver Demon outsold the Gold Demon by 1,300 to 300. It still is a very standard number for steelhead trout on all coast streams.

"Along in 1937 a black fly was popular in the Orleans area of the Klamath River, and about that time I brought out the Black Demon. Originally I tied it with a silver body, no tail, orange throat, and a black bucktail wing. Since that time other tyers have incorporated a wood duck tail, and some have used gold for the body, so you may find it with a gold body and a wood duck tail. Probably it is better that the tail is the same as the Silver Demon. I am merely giving you the correct history."

CAMPEONA STREAMER (Plate IX) *(As dressed by Elizabeth Greig)*
HEAD: Red
TAG: Four or five turns of narrow silver tinsel
TAIL: Two very narrow but rather long sections of a red duck wing feather
BUTT: Three turns of fine white chenille
BODY: Bright medium green wool, applied as dubbing, pulled out loosely, especially on the underside of the body, after the ribbing has been applied. The body is not heavily dressed.
RIBBING: Medium flat silver tinsel
THROAT: Three or four turns of a dark red hackle, rather long and gathered downward. The body is fuzzed out nearly to the tip of the throat.
WING: A fairly large bunch of peacock herls of equal length, extending slightly beyond the tail
SHOULDERS: Each the tip of a teal body feather, covering the peacock and about one-third as long as the wing

This fly originated in Chile and is widely used in South America. The pattern was sent to Mrs. Greig, famed New York City dresser of salmon flies, for duplication for South American customers. Mrs. Greig has found it successful on New York State streams for all trout.

300

CANDLEFISH BUCKTAIL (Plate VII) *(As dressed by Roy A. Patrick)*
HEAD: Black, usually with white painted eye and black pupil
BODY: Medium flat silver tinsel. (If no ribbing is used, embossed tinsel is preferable.)

RIBBING: Medium oval silver tinsel (optional)

WING: A very small bunch of white polar bear hair, over which is a very small bunch of pale green(*) polar bear hair, over which is a very small bunch of pale blue(*) polar bear hair. These three bunches make up the lower third of the wing. The middle third is a small bunch of medium red polar bear hair. Over this is a very small bunch of pale blue polar bear hair, over which is a very small bunch of pale green polar bear hair. As an optional topping a very small bunch of French blue (or violet) polar bear hair may be added. If this topping is not added, the two colors marked with an asterisk may also be eliminated. All the colors of hair are of the same length, extending well beyond the end of the hook.

This fly, which originated in the Puget Sound area of the Pacific northwest, was designed to imitate the candlefish, a prominent bait fish for coho (silver) salmon. It is the result of studies made by anglers there to obtain a combination of colors which would most closely approximate those of the candlefish. Prominent among these anglers were Roy A. Patrick, Letcher Lambuth, and Zell E. Parkhurst, all of Seattle, Washington. The fly is one of the few standard patterns, and one of the most successful, for fly fishing for coho salmon.

CARDINELLE   *(As dressed by Paul Kukonen)*

HOOK SIZE: 12 to 2/0, 4X or 5X long, Limerick
HEAD: Fluorescent orange thread
BODY: Red or orange fluorescent wool or yarn
RIBBING: Not called for; optional flat or oval gold
UNDERWING: A small bunch of bright orange fluorescent nylon hair a bit longer than the hook
OVERWING: A large bunch of bright red fluorescent marabou, to make a high wing, extending slightly beyond bend of hook
THROAT: A yellow hackle wound on as a collar

The head, of fluorescent orange thread or floss, is built up and coated with color preserver and epoxy. The underwing's purpose is to help prevent the marabou from wrapping around the hook's shank.

This attractor pattern was designed by Paul Kukonen and Bill Chiba, well-known New England anglers. It is a generally useful fly in fresh or salt water, particularly good for landlocked salmon and smallmouth bass.

CARTER FLY   *(As dressed by the originator)*

HEAD: Black
TAIL: About a dozen tips of polar bear hairs dyed bright golden yellow. The tail is rather long.
BODY: Wound with scarlet chenille of moderate thickness
RIBBING: Narrow oval gold tinsel
THROAT: Several turns of a scarlet saddle hackle, applied as a collar and tied back but not gathered downward. The hackle is stiff, glossy, and of moderate length.
WING: A medium-sized bunch of glossy black bear hair, extending to the end of the tail

301

Originated in the spring of 1938 by C. Jim Pray, of Eureka, California, and named in honor of Harley R. Carter, of Berkeley, California. The fly is especially popular on the Klamath and Rogue rivers for steelhead fishing. For additional notes on Carter, see following pattern.

CARTER'S DIXIE BUCKTAIL (Plate IV) *(As dressed by the originator)*

HEAD: Black

TAIL: About a dozen tips of polar bear hairs dyed bright golden yellow. The tail is rather long.

BODY: Wound thin with narrow oval gold tinsel. Several turns of tinsel are taken below the tail, around the bend of the hook, as a tag, before the tail is tied in.

THROAT: Several turns of a scarlet saddle hackle, applied as a collar and tied back but not gathered downward. The hackle is stiff, glossy, and rather long.

WING: A medium-sized bunch of white bucktail, extending to the end of the tail. White polar bear often is substituted, and two strips of white goose may be used if a feather wing is desired.

Originated by C. Jim Pray, of Eureka, California, who writes of the fly as follows: "I tried this first in 1934 and Harley R. Carter used it that year both on the Klamath, in the Orleans area, and on the Rogue River. Harley Carter played guard on the Stanford football team in the period of Andy Smith's California Wonder Team along in the 1920s. I believe he also was Intercollegiate Heavyweight Boxing Champion during that period. The first time I saw him was on the great Big Bar Riffle below Orleans. We were all using waders, except Harley, and I remember that it was chilly. Harley had sneaked up for a day's fishing on his way north and had forgotten his waders. When I first saw him he was up to his armpits in the cold water, fly-fishing with nothing on but a pair of pants, a shirt, and an ordinary pair of shoes. He stayed there for several hours until he had caught quite a few nice steelhead. I shivered in my waders watching him. Verily, he was quite a man! It was at this time that I christened this fly, which then had no name, in honor of Harley Carter. Along in 1938 Harley decided that he wanted a black hair fly of some sort and that was how the Carter Fly came into existence. Although Harley used both flies, he favored the Carter Fly much more than this earlier Carter's Dixie. Many other anglers have adopted the Carter's Dixie, and evidently it is here to stay."

CHAMP'S SPECIAL STREAMER *(As dressed by the Weber Tackle Company)*

HEAD: Black

TAIL: A short section of red wool or silk floss

BODY: Medium flat silver tinsel

RIBBING: Narrow oval silver tinsel (optional)

THROAT: A very small bunch of white bucktail, under which are four or five peacock herls, both as long as the wing

WING: An extremely small bunch of yellow bucktail (for which two golden pheasant crest feathers sometimes are substituted) as long as the hackles, over which are four grizzly saddle hackles

This fly was originated by Frank Congdon, of Middletown, Connecticut, and was named for his wife. The dressing is as given to the Weber Tackle Company, of Stevens Point, Wisconsin, by Congdon.

CHAPPIE STREAMER (Plate IV) *(As dressed by the originator)*
HEAD: Orange
TAIL: The tips of two long and narrow Plymouth Rock hackles. The hackles are as long as the body (dressed on a regular hook) and may be placed back to back if desired.
BODY: Medium thick, of orange wool
RIBBING: Orange silk thread (to make a smooth, tight body)
THROAT: Two or three turns of a Plymouth Rock hackle tied on as a collar and not tied downward. The throat is sparse but as long as the body.
WING: The tips of two long and narrow Plymouth Rock hackles. The wing extends nearly to the end of the tail and is dressed very high on the hook. The hackles may be placed back to back if desired.

The fly was originated by C. L. (Outdoor) Franklin, of Los Angeles, California, for steelhead and cutthroat trout fishing. It was described in the November 1949 issue of *Field & Stream,* which commented as follows:

"During the 1947 season Mr. Franklin nailed 163 steelhead of over three pounds and sixteen salmon of from fifteen to thirty-seven pounds using this mottled-wing streamer exclusively. To tie the Chappie properly, you have to select the right hackle feathers for the wing and tail. Unless they are long and narrow they won't flutter. Some tyers place the feathers back to back (turned out). In Los Angeles several fly merchants sell it with a money-back guarantee. If you fish it slow and deep with slight jerks and don't get a fish you get your money back. To date there have been no refunds. This is a very popular fly in the coastal states."

Franklin was a familiar figure on the steelhead riffles of the Klamath and was regarded as one of the West Coast's most experienced anglers. In a letter to me, he said:

"I have used the Chappie for over twenty-five years with unfailing success; in fact, it is the only fly in my fly box year after year and I believe Peter Schwab will bear me out when I say that I hook and land more fish with the Chappie than any other fisherman on the Klamath River.

"It was introduced to me by a small chap on the Snake River just outside of Yellowstone Park. This chap was catching two-and-a-half-to-three-pound cutthroats on almost every cast while I, with my expensive tackle, could not get a single one. Upon my asking what he called the fly, he replied that he didn't know the name and that it was 'just a bunch of feathers.' I went to my car, where I had a supply of materials, and improved the outline of the fly. I named it Chappie after the young chap who gave it to me. I have sent samples of it all over the country, and everywhere the result has been the same. It takes black bass, tarpon, salmon, steelhead, rainbow trout, and even bluegills and crappie. The method of use is to allow plenty of time for the fly to sink and then to retrieve it *very* slowly. This has worked even on the famous golden trout."

303

CHESAPEAKE BAY SHAD FLY (Plate VII) *(As dressed by Burt Dillon)*
HOOK SIZE: 2, regular, heavy wire
HEAD: White, with red painted eye

TAIL: A few fibers of a golden pheasant tippet
BODY: White yarn, very full and tapered
RIBBING: Silver tinsel
WING: White deer hair, extending slightly beyond tail

This one of many shad designs was originated by Burt Dillon, of Baltimore, Maryland.

CHIEF NEEDAHBEH STREAMER (Plate IX)   *(As dressed by the originator)*
HEAD: Black
TAG: Narrow flat silver tinsel
TAIL: A section of red duck or goose wing feather
BODY: Red silk. (The original version, as dressed by Chief Needahbeh, has a
     red hackle "throat" one-third of the way forward on the body. A similar
     effect could be obtained by palmering a red hackle, but it was not done in
     this case. The purpose of the "throat" evidently was to give greater action to
     the fly.)
RIBBING: Narrow flat silver tinsel
THROAT: A red saddle hackle tied on as a collar after the wing has been
     applied. It is dressed rather full.
WING: A red saddle hackle on each side of two yellow saddle hackles
CHEEKS: Jungle cock, rather short

Originated by Chief Needahbeh of the Penobscot tribe of Indians, of Greenville, Maine, who also dressed this fly without a tail or secondary throat, and with orange hackles in the wing instead of red. Chief Needahbeh says that this later version is especially good on dark days and that both flies are good for smallmouth and largemouth bass, as well as for the trout and landlocked salmon for which the fly originally was intended.

COCK-A-TOUCH STREAMER   *(As dressed by the originator)*
HOOK SIZE: 4, 3X long
HEAD: Red nylon nymph thread
TAIL: A very small bunch of red hackle fibers of moderate length topped with
     two peacock herl tips of same length, over which are two badger hackles as
     long as the body and flared (splayed) outward
BODY: In four sections, each of which is wound with peacock herl forward of
     which are about three turns of badger hackle. The front hackle is slightly
     longer than the others.

This pattern was originated by William F. Blades, author of *Fishing Flies & Fly Tying,* of Wilmette, Illinois. Bill Blades also dresses this fly with ginger hackle instead of the badger, and evidently eliminates the tail. The fly then represents a Wooly Worm.

304

COCK ROBIN BUCKTAIL (Plate X)   *(As dressed by Kenneth Botty)*
HOOK SIZE: All sizes, 5X long
HEAD: Black, with white eye and black pupil
TAIL: A very small and short bunch of mixed hairs of the wing colors

BODY: Rear half is yellow wool; forward half is red wool, slightly tapered
BUTT: Narrow flat silver tinsel
RIBBING: Narrow flat silver tinsel, continued from butt
THROAT: A small bunch of red hackle fibers or red hair, extending halfway to
barb of hook
WING: A very small bunch of orange-red hair (bucktail, polar bear, ringtail or
impala) over which is a very small bunch of white hair, over which is a very
small bunch of orange-red hair, to form a triple wing extending slightly
beyond the bend of the hook
CHEEKS: Jungle cock (on larger sizes only)

Paul Kukonen, who obtained this pattern from Joseph Kvitsky, of Westfield, Massachusetts, says: "Tapered bucktail or polar bear hair should be used in the larger sizes, and the short hairs in each bunch should not be pulled out. Ringtail or impala (calf) is better in the smaller sizes. The fly originally was tied for spring salmon, but we have found it extremely effective in many areas for brook trout, lake trout, and smallmouth bass."

COLONEL BATES STREAMER (Plate II)   *(As dressed by the originator)*
HEAD: Red, with black band
TAIL: A small section of a red duck or swan wing feather
BODY: Medium flat silver tinsel
THROAT: A small bunch of dark brown saddle hackle fibers
WING: Two yellow saddle hackle feathers with a slightly shorter white saddle
hackle feather on each side
SHOULDERS: Gray teal breast feathers, nearly half as long as the wing
CHEEKS: Jungle cock

Originated by Carrie G. Stevens, of Madison, Maine, during the Second World War and named for me. With regard to this fly, Mrs. Stevens wrote that it is second only to her famous Gray Ghost in popularity among her customers. It is highly favored for landlocked salmon and for smallmouth bass at all times, and for all species of trout, particularly under conditions of discolored water. Dressed on saltwater hooks, it is successful for striped bass, baby tarpon, bonefish, weakfish, and many other saltwater species.

Frank Mooney, of the Andover (Massachusetts) Fly Fishers Club, says: "This beautiful streamer has been so consistently successful for me that if I had to settle for one streamer pattern I would be content with the Colonel Bates. This confidence is shared by many good fishermen. We use it chiefly for trout and tie it in the smaller sizes, 10, 12, and 14. In these small sizes we make two small variations, using mallard breast feathers for the shoulders and a small bunch of red hackle fibers for the tail. We have difficulty finding teal in the smaller sizes, and we think mallard gives a nice appearance, being not so strongly marked as the teal. When we tie the larger sizes we stay with the original pattern."

305

Rex Gerlach, in his *Creative Fly Tying & Fly Fishing* (New York: Winchester Press, 1974), says, "This is a killing streamer in both east and west on landlocked salmon, bass, pike, panfish, and trout. It is also effective in saltwater versions. I am especially partial to it for brook trout in lakes and rivers."

COLONEL FULLER STREAMER   *(As dressed by Gardner Percy)*

HEAD: Black
BODY: Medium flat silver tinsel
RIBBING: Narrow oval silver tinsel
THROAT: A small bunch of golden yellow hackle fibers
WING: Four golden yellow saddle or neck hackles. Marabou of the same color is
     substituted in some versions of this fly. In this case, the two marabou tips
     may be applied flat on top of the hook or they may be placed back to back.
     Both of these methods of dressing give better action than tying them on with
     the concave sides together. The fly also may be dressed as a bucktail, using
     either polar bear hair or bucktail dyed golden yellow.
SHOULDERS: Each the tip of a red goose or turkey body feather extending
     one-third the length of the fly. These feathers should be very wide, and the
     outside edges should be a pronounced line, rather than fringed.

This fly was adapted to the streamer and bucktail family by Gardner Percy. It
was taken from the bass fly of the same name, originated by John Shields, of
Brookline, Massachusetts, in 1894, and named in honor of Colonel Charles E.
Fuller, of Boston, Massachusetts. Being predominantly yellow, it is an excellent
pattern for spring salmon, landlocked salmon, bass, and all species of trout, particularly under conditions of discolored water. Its brightness makes it less successful
in clear water, except for landlocked salmon and bass, when a fly of less pronounced yellow color, such as the Colonel Bates, usually is more productive. These
colors of yellow and red are among the best for saltwater game fish, as well as for
many freshwater species.

COLONEL WHITE STREAMER   *(As dressed by Gardner Percy)*

HEAD: Black
BODY: Medium flat silver tinsel
RIBBING: Narrow oval silver tinsel
THROAT: A small bunch of white hackle fibers
WING: Four white neck hackles
SHOULDERS: Each the tip of a red goose or turkey body feather, one-third as
     long as the wing and with a pronounced edge

This fly is nearly identical to the Ordway Streamer, except for the method of
applying the wing. (See notes for Ordway Streamer.) This adaptation of the several
red-and-white streamer flies is attributed to William Burgess of Maine, who called
it the Rooster's Regret, although it is not of the Rooster's Regret type. When it
was placed in the list of patterns of the Percy Tackle Company, of Portland, Maine,
it was renamed as above, evidently because of its similarity to the Colonel Fuller.
It is an excellent saltwater pattern.

306 ### CORONATION BUCKTAIL (Plate VII)   *(As dressed by Roy A. Patrick)*

HEAD: Black, usually with white painted eye with black pupil. (The heads on
     many coho flies are made purposely large to imitate the heads of bait fish.)
BODY: Medium flat silver tinsel
RIBBING: Medium oval or embossed silver tinsel. (This is optional but is
     preferred by many anglers in order to give greater light reflection.)

WING: A bunch of white polar bear hair, over which is a bunch of bright red polar bear hair, over which is a bunch of medium blue polar bear hair. The three bunches are of the same quantity and length, extending well beyond the end of the hook. Usually the fly is dressed rather heavily. Single-hook flies can be tied on No. 2/0 or 3/0 long-shanked hooks, usually with ringed eyes so that a spinner may be attached for trolling.

Few coho (or silver salmon) flies have become standardized in their dressings. In addition to this one, the Candlefish Bucktail and the Herring Bucktail are shown in this list of patterns. The Coronation Bucktail was originated for coho salmon fishing by a group of anglers in the Puget Sound area of the Pacific northwest and is one of the best-known patterns for that type of fishing.

COSSEBOOM SPECIAL BUCKTAIL (Plate X)   *(As dressed by Herbert L. Howard)*

HEAD: Red
TAG: Three or four turns of medium flat silver tinsel
TAIL: A small bunch of fibers of medium olive green silk, of moderate length, cut off flat
BODY: Medium olive green silk, dressed moderately thin
RIBBING: Medium flat silver tinsel
THROAT: A light greenish yellow hackle, wound on as a collar after the wing has been applied. The hackle is fairly long and medium-heavy, and is not tied downward.
WING: A small bunch of gray squirrel tail hair, slightly longer than the tail of the fly

Originated by John C. Cosseboom, the angler and poet from Providence, Rhode Island, while fishing on the Margaree River for bright salmon when they would not take other flies. At the time, this fly proved successful and later was famed as one of the best all-round flies for bright salmon, especially on Anticosti Island, in the St. Lawrence area. The fly is popular in Nova Scotia, Newfoundland, New Brunswick, and Quebec and also has been used successfully in Scotland, England, Norway, Finland, and Iceland. It is a favored trout fly in many other foreign countries, where it is dressed on long-shanked hooks in sizes from 5/0 to 12. The original had a body of green rayon.

COWEE SPECIAL STREAMER (Plate X)   *(As dressed by the originator)*

HEAD: Black
TAIL: A section of a red goose feather, wide, short, and pointing upward
BODY: Thinly wound with medium flat gold tinsel
THROAT: A wide and short section of a red goose feather, tied on vertically
WING: A very small bunch of yellow bucktail with a single pintail duck side feather on top. The pintail feather extends to the end of the tail and is tied roofed against the hook, horizontal rather than vertical, and curling downward slightly on each side. A good way to apply roofed feathers is to tie one in much larger than needed, taking two or three turns of thread to partially secure it. Then pull it forward by the end of the quill until it is the size desired, thus curving it downward equally on each side in the proper "roof" position.

307

This fly was originated in 1938 by Stanley Cowee of Springfield, Massachusetts, for brook trout and rainbow trout fishing in New England. The flat wing opens and shuts in action to imitate a swimming minnow. The fly is especially popular for rainbow trout and is a favorite of many New England anglers, including the author. Usually it is tied in the smaller sizes, particularly in sizes 6 and 8 on 3X long hooks.

CRANE PRAIRIE STREAMER   *(As dressed by the originator)*

HOOK SIZE: 2 to 12, 2X long
HEAD: Red, with white eye and black pupil
TAIL: A small bunch of golden olive calf tail
BUTT: About three turns of oval gold tinsel
BODY: Wound with peacock herl
WING: A small bunch of hair from the dark part of a bucktail dyed yellow, extending slightly beyond the bend of the hook. Over this are four grizzly saddle hackles of same length.

This streamer was originated by A. A. (Tony) Whitney for catching big brown trout in Oregon's Crane Prairie Reservoir. The underbody usually is weighted for fishing deep.

CRANE PRAIRIE SPECIAL STREAMER   *(As dressed by E. H. Rosborough)*

HOOK SIZES: This is a tandem fly with the No. 6, 3X long, trailer hook pointed upward and joined to the No. 2, 3X long, forward hook as closely as possible. It often is dressed on gold hooks.
HEAD: Black
TAIL: The tips of four grizzly hackles, long enough to cover the rear hook. (The dressing is on the forward hook only.)
BODY: Wound with heavy light orange chenille
RIBBING: Oval gold silver tinsel
THROAT: A very wide grizzly hackle wound on as a collar
WING: The tips of six large neck hackles, the three on each side applied back to back with the three on the other side to provide a splayed wing. The wing extends to the end of the tail.

This fly is popular in the Crane Prairie region of Oregon. (The vast Crane Prairie Reservoir empties into the Deschutes River and is famous for big brown trout.) There is an optional body dressing of peacock green chenille twisted together with peacock herl. This has no added ribbing.

CUPSUPTIC STREAMER   *(As dressed by the originator)*

HEAD: Black
TAIL: A small bunch of yellow hackle fibers
308   BODY: Made in three equal parts. The rear third has a butt of peacock herl on both ends, separated by white silk, the three components being of about equal width. The forward two-thirds is dressed with bright red silk. The white and red parts are not built up.
RIBBING: Narrow flat silver tinsel, over red silk only
THROAT: A small bunch of yellow hackle fibers

WING: Two dark red saddle hackles with a bronze furnace saddle hackle on
   each side
SHOULDERS: Each a gray saddle hackle, two-thirds as long as the wing
CHEEKS: Jungle cock

Originated by Herbert L. Welch, of Oquossoc, Maine, and named for Cupsuptic Stream, a famous trout water in the Rangeley section of Maine. (Herbie Welch, being an artist, enjoyed fancy patterns regardless of their effectiveness, his famous Black Ghost being the exception.)

CUT LIPS STREAMER (Plate XI)   *(As dressed by the originator)*

HOOK SIZE: 2 to 8, 4X long
HEAD: Black
TAIL: A small bunch of blue dun hackle fibers
BODY: Lavender floss or wool, slightly shaped
RIBBING: Medium narrow flat silver tinsel
THROAT: A small bunch of blue dun hackle fibers
WING: A pair of olive green saddle hackles, on each side of which is a dark blue
   dun saddle hackle, all extending slightly beyond the tail
CHEEKS: Jungle cock

This is one of the famous imitator patterns originated by the late Lew Oatman, of Shushan, New York. The fly imitates the cut lips minnow, a very dark one that is found on New York's Ausable River, some parts of Vermont's Battenkill, and in many other trout streams, especially around rapids and falls. Oatman liked it tied in the larger sizes.

DAMSEL STREAMER   *(As dressed by Fin, Fur and Feather, Ltd.)*

HEAD: Black
TAIL: The tips of three strands of peacock herl, of conventional length
BODY: Rear half, peacock herl; front half, bright red wool
RIBBING: Narrow oval gold tinsel, over the peacock half of the body only
WING: Two matched sections of metallic turkey wing feathers, extending as
   long as the tail
SHOULDERS: About six strands of a peacock sword feather on each side, half as
   long as the wing
THROAT: An English partridge hackle applied on as a collar

This fly was originated by Andrew Barr, of Montreal, about 1939. It is one of the most popular Canadian streamers for trout, bass, and landlocked salmon, especially very early in the season, as soon as the ice has left the lakes.

DAVE AND MIKE BUCKTAIL   *(As dressed by the originator)*

309

HOOK SIZE: 2 to 4, 4 XL
HEAD: Black
TAIL: A moderate-sized bunch of red hair of medium length
BODY: Gray chenille, medium, not built up
RIBBING: Embossed silver tinsel
THROAT: A moderate-sized bunch of yellow bucktail, extending to end of hook

WING: A moderate-sized bunch of white bucktail, extending to end of tail
CHEEKS: Jungle cock

This fly also is dressed with a body of silver Mylar tubing. It was first tied by Ray Salminen, of Acton, Massachusetts, from instructions given to him by an old angler who got the pattern from a Maine guide, who had had success with it on Moosehead Lake. It was popularized by a club of doctors and lawyers from Lynn, Massachusetts, and has been in tremendous demand. It is most successful heavily dressed on large hooks, and was named for the old angler's two sons. It primarily is a trout and landlocked salmon fly.

DICK'S KILLER BUCKTAIL   *(As dressed by the originator)*

HEAD: Black
TAG: Narrow flat gold tinsel, very wide
TAIL: About fifteen strands of a golden pheasant tippet, rather long
BODY: Wound fairly heavy with peacock herl
WING: A bunch of yellow bucktail, short enough so that it will not catch under the hook. An extra-long-shanked hook is used.
TOPPING: A very small bunch of strands from a wood duck or mandarin duck breast feather, nearly as long as the wing
SHOULDERS: Each a section of a red turkey feather, rather slim but nearly as long as the wing
CHEEKS: Jungle cock, two-thirds as long as the shoulders

Originated by Dick Eastman, of Groveton, New Hampshire, in 1928. Eastman wrote in a letter to me: "I started tying flies in 1928 when I was camp manager at Idlewild on Second Connecticut Lake. One fly I tied was a yellow bucktail like the one enclosed and it worked very well. Later in the summer some guests had a fly called the Lake George, which also proved to be a good fish taker, with peacock herl body and a red wing. I experimented by putting the best parts of the two flies together and got a fly with a peacock herl body, golden pheasant tippet tail and yellow bucktail wing topped with wood duck, red turkey shoulders, and jungle cock cheeks. This fly proved to be a real killer of trout, so I named it Dick's Killer and have tied more than a thousand of this pattern.

"Later on that year, Bill Edson, who was camping at First Connecticut Lake, came to Idlewild and I went fishing with him. When he left, I gave him a couple of Dick's Killers. Some time after, he wrote me a letter in which he said, 'Your Dick's Killer works as well on rainbows and brown trout on the Westfield River as it did around Second Connecticut Lake.' After that, Edson promoted and tied the Light Tiger. Then he originated the Dark Tiger.

"These flies work very well here and in the Laurentide Park and other sections of Canada. They take [landlocked] salmon on the Connecticut lakes. I have tied Dick's Killer with yellow, red, and black heads. Probably the ones I gave Edson had yellow heads." (See comments for Edson Light Tiger Bucktail and Edson Dark Tiger Bucktail.)

310

DR. BURKE STREAMER (Plate IX)   *(As dressed by the originator)*

HEAD: Black
TAIL: About fifteen peacock sword fibers, more bunchy and longer than usual

BODY: Medium flat silver tinsel, somewhat thicker than normal, since it must be built up to compensate for the bulge of the tail

RIBBING: Narrow oval silver tinsel

THROAT: A bunch of yellow hackle fibers, rather long

WING: Four white saddle hackles

CHEEKS: Jungle cock

This fly was originated by Edgar Burke, of Jersey City, New Jersey, who wrote to me that it was "first devised and used on Kennebago Stream, in northwestern Maine, in 1927. It was designed as a dusk fly for large squaretail trout, and proved highly effective. Its name was given to it by my then guide, Frank Savage, of Bemis, Maine."

Dr. Burke was as famous as an artist and an angler as he was as a surgeon. He enjoyed decades of fishing on Maine's famous trout and landlocked salmon waters, especially Kennebago Stream, in the Rangeley area. It was he who so beautifully illustrated the trout flies in Ray Bergman's well-known book *Trout.* Another of Dr. Burke's originations is the Family Secret Streamer.

DR. MILNE STREAMER *(As dressed by the originator)*

HEAD: Black

TAG: Four or five turns of narrow gold tinsel

TAIL: One or two very short golden pheasant crest feathers, curving upward

BODY: Wound with yellow chenille

WING: A very small bunch of black bear hair as long as the tail, over which are four gray neck hackles extending well beyond the tail

TOPPING: A thin section of red swan or goose wing feather as long as the jungle cock

SHOULDERS: Each a brown mallard breast feather, nearly two-thirds as long as the wing

CHEEKS: Jungle cock, of medium length

This historic Maine streamer fly is popular for taking landlocked salmon. It was originated by Bert Quimby, of South Windham, Maine, as the result of suggestions made to him by Dr. Douglas M. Milne of South Portland, Maine, for whom the fly was named.

DR. OATMAN (Plate XI) *(As dressed by the originator)*

HOOK SIZE: 2 to 6, 3X long

HEAD: Black

TAIL: A small bunch of white hackle fibers, as long as the gap of the hook

BODY: The rearward two-thirds is white floss; the forward one-third is red floss. The body is slightly tapered.

RIBBING: Narrow flat gold tinsel

THROAT: A small bunch of yellow hackle fibers, slightly longer than the red section of the body

WING: Four white saddle hackles, extending slightly beyond the tail

CHEEKS: Jungle cock, fairly short

311

This is one of the famous series originated by Lew Oatman of Shushan, New York, around 1953. It was named for his father, who was a country doctor.

DON'S DELIGHT STREAMER (Plate II)   *(As dressed by the originator)*
HEAD: Black, with red band
TAIL: A small bunch of red hackle fibers
BODY: Medium flat gold tinsel
THROAT: A small bunch of white hackle fibers
WING: Four white saddle hackles
SHOULDERS: Each a golden pheasant tippet, extending one-third as long as the
    wing
CHEEKS: Jungle cock

    Originated by Carrie G. Stevens, of Madison, Maine, and named for Donald
Bartlett of Willimantic, Connecticut. The fly for many years was a local favorite at
Upper Dam Pool, in Maine.

DOT EDSON STREAMER   *(As dressed by the originator)*
HEAD: Silver
BODY: Medium flat silver tinsel with two narrow strips of pale blue flat tinsel
    tied in, one on each side, before the body is wound. The two strips are
    pulled forward and are tied at the head after the body is wound, so that they
    extend along both sides of the body.
THROAT: White bucktail as long as the hook, with a very small bunch of red
    hackle fibers beneath, tied in very short
WING: Four slim silver gray neck hackles
SHOULDERS: Each a Ripon's silver pheasant body feather, one-fourth as long as
    the wing
CHEEKS: Jungle cock, very short

    Originated by William R. Edson of Portland, Maine, and named by him for his
wife. This fly was tied to imitate a smelt and should be dressed very sparsely.

DUSTY STREAMER   *(As dressed by the originator)*
HEAD: Black
TAG: Four or five turns of narrow flat silver tinsel
BODY: Black silk, dressed very thin (red silk was used on the original version)
RIBBING: Narrow flat silver tinsel
THROAT: Six strands of peacock herl, under which is a very small bunch of
    white bucktail, both as long as the wing. Under this is a short golden
    pheasant crest feather curving upward. (This has been eliminated in the
    most recent version.)
WING: Four barred Plymouth Rock neck or saddle hackles, with very
    pronounced black and white bars
CHEEKS: Jungle cock

    Originated by Bert Quimby, of South Windham, Maine, especially for taking
312   landlocked salmon in the spring. The fly first was used on Moosehead Lake, in
Maine.

EAST GRAND LAKE SPECIAL   *(Origin unknown)*
HOOK SIZE: 2 to 10, 3 XL
HEAD: Black, with white eye and red pupil

BODY: Flat or oval silver tinsel

WING: A very small bunch of white bucktail, over which is a very small bunch of orange bucktail, over which is a very small bunch of lavender bucktail. Over this are a few strands of peacock herl and two grizzly neck hackles.

This streamer is popular in Maine's East Grand Lake area for landlocked salmon and trout. Its dressing varies somewhat with different tyers. The dressing should be thin.

EDSON DARK TIGER BUCKTAIL (Plate XII)   *(As dressed by the originator)*

HEAD: Yellow

TAG: Three or four turns of narrow flat gold tinsel

TAIL: The tips of two extremely small yellow neck hackles, back to back

BODY: Wound with fine yellow chenille

THROAT: The tips of two extremely small red neck hackles (to simulate gills)

WING: A small bunch of the brown hair from a bucktail dyed yellow, extending just beyond the bend of the hook. (An important element in dressing this fly, which is often overlooked, is that the wing must be short enough so that it cannot catch under the bend of the hook.)

CHEEKS: Jungle cock, extremely short; use eye only

This is one of the most famous of all bucktail flies for trout, landlocked salmon, bass, and many other species of game fish. It was originated by William R. Edson, of Portland, Maine, in 1929 as a companion fly to the Edson Light Tiger Bucktail. An extra-long shank hook is used, usually 5X long. Mr. Edson preferred a Sproat in sizes from 4 to 10. Gold metal cheeks sometimes take the place of the jungle cock on flies which Mr. Edson has dressed. He considers that the gold eye gives a better flash in the water. Jungle cock often is used by other fly dressers because the gold eyes are difficult to obtain.

EDSON LIGHT TIGER BUCKTAIL (Plate XII)   *(As dressed by the originator)*

HEAD: Black. (This fly is tied with black thread rather than with yellow thread because the black does not show when applying the peacock body. Many of Edson's early versions were dressed with yellow lacquer over the black head, but this no longer is considered necessary.)

TAG: Three or four turns of narrow flat gold tinsel

TAIL: A section of a barred wood duck or mandarin duck feather long enough to show two black bars

BODY: Wound with peacock herl, several strands being twisted with the thread while they are being applied. The body is fairly full, the number of strands depending upon the size of the fly.

WING: Yellow bucktail, short enough so that it will not catch under the hook. The ends should be fairly even.

TOPPING: The tips of two extremely small red neck hackles, not over one-third as long as the wing. (A section of red duck wing feather was used in the early versions.)

CHEEKS: Jungle cock, extremely short; use eye only. (See notes for Edson Dark Tiger Bucktail on hooks and use of optional gold metal cheeks.)

313

This companion fly to the Edson Dark Tiger Bucktail was originated by William

R. Edson, of Portland, Maine, in 1929. Its origination possibly was influenced by the Dick's Killer Bucktail, as is noted in the comments on that fly. Both the Light and Dark Tigers generally are conceded to be among the most successful flies for all species of freshwater game fish, and particularly for trout and landlocked salmon. Care should be taken that the wing is not overdressed and that it is tied very close to the body to give maximum streamlined effect. I prefer to dress the topping with a section of red duck wing feather rather than with the two red hackle tips. If the hackle tips are used, they should be applied flat, one over the other, to form a narrow V on top of the fly.

EELWORM STREAMER (WHITLOCK)   *(As dressed by the originator)*

HOOK SIZE: 3/0 to 6, any extra-long heavy wire hook with turned-up eye

THREAD: Herb Howard's fluorescent orange

TAIL: Four grizzly hackles dyed red, three times as long as the hook, applied in two pairs over the rear of the hook's shank, plus another pair, one on each side, half as long. Hackles should be narrow, with very flexible stems. Before tying these in attach a section of monofilament (stiff, .018 to .025 inches, depending on size of hook) for a weed guard.

HEAD: Two bead-chain eyes, applied in the usual figure-eight manner, around which is applied in the same manner enough lead wire to fill the gap between the eyes

BODY: A blend of half Orlon wool and half rabbit or muskrat fur dyed same color as tail. Over this dubbing are palmered two soft, webby saddle hackles with bright sides out, of same color as tail. These are palmered from tail to eyes and optionally may be clipped a bit longer than the body. Tie in weed guard's forward end by passing it through hook's eye and lashing down on top before finishing the head. Cover the lead wire with body material.

This fly is a variable type which imitates the eelworm, and it is to the fly fisherman what the plastic worm is to others. As with the plastic worm, this streamer is dressed in many colors and combinations, such as brownish purple, black, white, blue, lavender, red, brown, yellow, and olive. The body and hackling usually are of the same colors as the tail. Three requisites for success are the long, thin-stemmed hackles for maximum pulsating action, the weed guard to allow use in grasses and brush, and the weighted head, which balances the fly and causes it to dive in jig fashion.

This is one of the innovations of Dave Whitlock, famous angler-artist, and author of the highly recommended *Fly-Tyer's Almanac.* The fly should be fished like a jig or plastic worm, slowly and erratically, close to bottom. It is very effective not only for bass but for pike, big brown trout, striped bass, and other saltwater game fish.

Use bead chain in one of the three sizes suitable to the size of the fly. Cement each part of the dressing thoroughly with Pliobond or a fast-setting epoxy. After covering the lead wire with the body material, lash it down with figure-eight turns of thread. The red head is tied over some of the front of the same color as the winding thread. The fluorescent red or orange head makes the fly easier to see in murky water.

EMERSON HOUGH BUCKTAIL   *(As dressed by Peter J. Schwab)*

HEAD: Black

TAIL: About fifteen tips of light reddish-brown bucktail hairs of various lengths, the longest being about an inch

BODY: Of brown deer body hair tied on as a hair body, loose and rough. The body is almost spherical in shape and is clipped to enhance its roughness.

WING: A bunch of dark brown bucktail not over one and a half times as long as the hook and not quite as long as the end of the tail. The width of the body will make the wing cock up at an angle of nearly forty-five degrees.

The Emerson Hough Bucktail was originated by Indian guides in the Canadian northwest. Samples of it were brought back from that territory just prior to 1920 by Hough, an accomplished angler and angling writer of Chicago, Illinois. This fly is unusual in its type of body dressing, being very similar to a deer-hair bass bug in appearance. In clipped-deer-hair-body flies of this type, such as the Algoma Bucktail,* the hair of the body should be loose and reasonably sparse. This dressing is from an original given by Hough to Peter J. Schwab, who writes about it as follows: "Emerson Hough and Fred Peet, who used the fly a great deal, insisted that the important thing, never to be overlooked, was to keep the fly looking *rough.* According to them it should never be tied with the solid fullness so often seen in lures with buckhair bodies, and in my limited experience with the fly I agree with them. I never thought it dainty enough to throw at such beautiful fish as trout, but I have used it a lot for bass and panfish, all of which seem to show a preference for the rough body." The fly usually is dressed on a regular-length hook, preferably in size 6.

ESOPUS BUCKTAIL   *(As dressed by William Mills and Son)*

HEAD: Black

TAIL: Of bright red bucktail, cut off sharply, one-third as long as the wing. A good-sized bunch of bucktail is used to give the effect of a paintbrush when cut off.

BODY: Medium gold or silver tinsel. The body is first filled in with wool to enlarge it before adding the tinsel. This fat body is designed to give a large, shiny area. Regular-length hooks are used, so that the body and the tail are of the same length.

WING: In any of the following color combinations: black over white bucktail; brown over white bucktail; red over white bucktail. The wing is one and a half times longer than the body and tail combined. It is raised to an angle of forty-five degrees from the body to show the body more clearly and to give more action in the water. The wing is rather fully dressed.

This fly is very similar in shape to western steelhead flies. It was originated by William Mills and Son, of New York City, and originally was tied with a yellow tail.

315

---

*The Algoma Bucktail has a trimmed body of gray caribou or deer hair, clipped to a uniform fat cigar shape. The tail is a long, thin section of a Lady Amherst pheasant tail feather curving upward. The throat is a small bunch of fibers from a fiery brown hackle, rather long. The wing is a bunch of mixed gray and brown bucktail over a smaller amount of white bucktail, both extending to the end of the tail.

Since 1935 the red tail has been standard. This fly has been very successful for large brown trout (and other species of trout) on the Esopus River of New York State, for which it is named. A more popular version of the Esopus Bucktail is given in this book as the Bi-Buck Bucktail.

FAMILY SECRET STREAMER   *(As dressed by the originator)*
HEAD: Black
TAIL: Between ten and twenty peacock sword fibers, depending on size of hook. The tail is long and very bunchy.
BODY: Medium flat silver tinsel. The body is somewhat thicker than normal since it must be built up to compensate for the bulge of the tail.
RIBBING: Narrow oval silver tinsel
THROAT: A bunch of guinea hen hackle fibers, rather thick and long
WING: Four white saddle hackles
CHEEKS: Jungle cock

Originated by Dr. Edgar Burke, of Jersey City, New Jersey, who wrote to me: "This is really a modification of the Dr. Burke Streamer and in my own opinion is a more universally useful pattern. First used in 1928 for landlocked salmon, it proved spectacularly successful and the best catches of big salmon and trout I have ever made were due to it. It is a good pattern for virtually all freshwater game fish, bass included, and it is particularly effective for large brown trout." (See notes for Dr. Burke Streamer.)

In explanation of its name, Dr. Burke says: "During a sterile spell on the upper Kennebago River [in Maine], when none of the rods then on the stream had been doing anything for days, I had enjoyed excellent fishing. I was fishing the famous Island Pool when another angler, accompanied by his guide, appeared on the footpath, obviously much disappointed to find the pool already occupied. The guide, whom I knew well, called out to me, 'Do you mind if we watch you fish for a while, Doctor?' I, of course, assented. I was taking one good fish after another. This, in view of the prevailing nonproductiveness of the river, was too much for the guide. Unable to contain himself, he yelled out, 'For Pete's sake, Doctor, what fly are you using?' In a bantering tone I called back, 'That's a family secret, Jim!' Whereupon my own guide, Dick Grant, seized my arm and said, *'There's* the name for your fly!' and so it has been, ever since. The little incident narrated above, to the best of my recollection, was in 1928."

FRASER STREAMER   *(As dressed by Herbert L. Howard)*
HEAD: Black
BUTT: Two turns of "dirty-orange" chenille, in imitation of an egg sac
BODY: Of bright green wool, medium thick, not shaped and not picked out
RIBBING: Very fine oval silver tinsel
WING: Four white neck or shoulder hackles
SHOULDERS: Each a narrow, short yellow neck hackle, extending two-thirds the length of the wing, dressed high to show the lower part of the wing
CHEEKS: Jungle cock

316

Originated by George Fraser, of Edinburgh, Scotland, who learned fly fishing by poaching on Scotch rivers, particularly on the waters of the Tay River on the estate of Lord Dewar. Later, Mr. Fraser fished all over the world and was partial to this fly for all types of game fish. He used it on the Esopus River, in New York State, and in many other states and countries. The dressing is from an original given to Mr. Howard by Mr. Fraser.

FURNACE FREY STREAMER   *(As dressed by Poul Jorgensen)*
HOOK SIZE: 2 to 8, 3X long
HEAD: Black
TAG: Gold tinsel
TAIL: Barred wood duck, fairly long
BODY: Embossed gold tinsel
RIBBING: Oval gold tinsel (if used, body can be flat gold tinsel)
THROAT: Yellow bucktail, extending to end of tail
WING: Sparse brown bucktail dyed yellow, over which are four furnace hackles.
  The bucktail extends to end of tail, with the hackles a bit longer.
CHEEKS: Jungle cock, quite long

Originated about 1950 by William F. Blades, author of *Fishing Flies & Fly Tying*, of Wilmette, Illinois. Two other flies in this series are the Ginger Furnace Frey, which is as above except that ginger furnace hackles are used in the wing, and the Badger Furnace Frey, which has a silver body, white bucktail, and wings of badger hackles. These flies usually have white eyes with black pupils.

GALLOPING GHOST STREAMER   *(As dressed by the originator)*
HEAD: Black
TAG: A few turns of medium embossed silver tinsel
TAIL: A section of a red duck or goose wing feather
BODY: Of orange silk, dressed fairly thin
RIBBING: Medium embossed silver tinsel
THROAT: A bunch of orange-red hackle fibers, rather long
WING: Two Bali duck (Yanosh) shoulder feathers, extending beyond the tail
CHEEKS: Jungle cock, fairly short

Originated by Bert Quimby, of South Windham, Maine. This fly is very similar to the Jesse Wood Streamer, which is a much older pattern.

GASPEREAU BUCKTAIL   *(As dressed by the originators)*
HEAD: Black
BODY: Medium embossed silver tinsel
RIBBING: Medium oval silver tinsel
WING: A bunch of yellow bucktail over which is a bunch of red bucktail
CHEEKS: Jungle cock

This fly is essentially a red-and-yellow bucktail. It was originated by George T. Richards and Charles M. Wetzel, entomologist and author of *Practical Fly Fishing*, who wrote me as follows: "This fly was designed while salmon fishing in New Brunswick with Julian Crandall, Bob Becker, and Nick Kahler. It is named 'Gaspereau' for the small bait fish of that name, similar to alewife, which inhabit the river. Everyone took many salmon on it and it proved to be the most popular fly on the stream."

317

GEES-BEAU STREAMER *(As dressed by the originator)*

HEAD: Black
TAIL: Two narrow sections of an orange swan or goose wing feather, curving upward
BODY: Yellow wool picked out to make it fuzzy
RIBBING: Narrow oval silver tinsel
THROAT: A bunch of yellow hackle fibers, rather long
WING: Four white saddle hackles
SHOULDERS: Two matched sections of orange swan or goose wing feathers, fairly wide, nearly half as long as the wing and dressed high curving downward and covering the tops of the wing hackles
CHEEKS: Jungle cock

Originated by Charles Phair, a famed angler and fly dresser of Presque Isle, Maine, and author of the classic *Atlantic Salmon Fishing* (New York: Derrydale Press, 1937). The fly often is misnamed Jazz-Boa or Jessabou, but several examples in my collection, all formerly owned by Charlie Phair, are essentially identical except that some have yellow shoulders instead of orange and one has a red hackle throat. Very probably the three names are phonetic variations of the same pattern, as given above.

GENERAL MacARTHUR STREAMER (Plate II) *(As dressed by the originator)*

HEAD: Red or blue. (Mrs. Stevens tied it with three bands of red, white, and blue thread, but this is more than most fly dressers will wish to attempt, and her "trademark" never should be copied.)
TAIL: A small bunch of red hackle fibers of medium length
BODY: Medium flat silver tinsel
THROAT: A very small bunch of dark blue hackle fibers, under which is a very small bunch of white hackle fibers, with a very small bunch of red hackle fibers under this; all of the same length
WING: Two white saddle hackles, on each side of which is a light blue saddle hackle, with a Plymouth Rock saddle hackle on each side of this. All six hackles are of the same length, reaching just beyond the tail.
CHEEKS: Jungle cock

Originated by Carrie G. Stevens, of Madison, Maine, during the Second World War and named in honor of General Douglas MacArthur. Although the fly was designed as a patriotic gesture, rather than because the colors suited accepted angling standards, it has proved very successful for trout and landlocked salmon in Maine waters. The colors resemble those in the famous Supervisor Streamer, and the fish evidently take the fly for a smelt.

318 GHOST SHINER (Plate XI) *(As dressed by the originator)*

HOOK SIZE: 8, 4X long
HEAD: Same color as wing
TAIL: A few fibers from a light green hackle
BODY: Wound with white floss, tapered
RIBBING: Medium flat silver tinsel

THROAT: A small bunch of fibers from a white hackle, as long as the gap of the hook

WING: A sparse bunch of summer (European) sable tail hair, as long as the tail. (This is quite a silky hair, very light brown or tan in color.)

CHEEKS: Jungle cock, tied in short

This is one of the natural-imitation patterns originated by the famous angler Lew Oatman, of Shushan, New York. It imitates the bait fish of the same name. It also is similar to the straw-colored minnow, the pearl minnow, and the emerald minnow. It is a clear-water fly and can be tied down to very small, sparse sizes. It is one of a group which has done well under difficult conditions in England. In the smaller sizes it may be fished to resemble a darting nymph, or small fry. (The dressing and comments are from notes given to me by Mr. Oatman.)

GOLDEN DARTER (Plate XI)   *(As dressed by the originator)*

HOOK SIZE: 6 to 10, 6X long

HEAD: Black

TAIL: A very small section of mottled turkey wing quill, no longer than the gap of the hook

BODY: Wound with clear yellow floss, slightly tapered

RIBBING: Medium narrow flat gold tinsel

THROAT: A very small tip of a jungle cock body feather, no longer than the gap of the hook, and pointed downward

WING: Two golden-edged badger saddle hackles, slightly longer than the tail. (Use four hackles on large sizes.)

CHEEKS: Jungle cock, rather short

This is another imitative pattern originated by Lew Oatman, of Shushan, New York. In sending me this authentic dressing, Mr. Oatman said, "This fly imitates the black-nosed dace in a spare pattern. It is a running mate to the Silver Darter, and I use it in water that is somewhat discolored. The Silver Darter is best in clear water."

GOLDEN ROGAN BUCKTAIL (Plate IX)   *(As dressed by the originator)*

HEAD: Black, with a painted red band, narrow, at the back of the head

TAG: Four or five turns of fine silver wire, begun at the bend of the hook, forward of which are several turns of red silk, dressed thin, about three times as long as the silver

TAIL: A golden pheasant crest feather, fairly long and curving upward. Above this is the tip of a section of a barred wood duck feather showing a black, white and black band only, very thin and half as long as the golden pheasant.

BUTT: Three or four turns of a black ostrich herl

BODY: Consists of four butts of black ostrich herl, including the one above, equally spaced with the forward butt at the head of the fly. The spaces between are wound thinly with fine gold wire. Just ahead of the rear butt, and just behind the three forward butts, is a "throat" of about twelve strands of fine gold wire or the finest oval gold tinsel (called "French twist"). The ends of these four "throats" are cut in a graduated manner so that the rear

319

"throat" extends to the barb of the hook and each forward "throat" is slightly longer.

WING: A small bunch of golden badger hair with the black band in the middle, as long as the tail of the fly

TOPPING: Two golden pheasant crest feathers, dyed red, curving downward to meet the tip of the tail

The Golden Rogan Bucktail is not to be confused with the Golden Rogan salmon fly, as illustrated in *Fortune* magazine for June 1948, since the two dressings are entirely different. Both flies were originated by Alex Rogan, formerly of New York City, who was before his retirement generally considered to be one of the two greatest American dressers of salmon patterns (the other having been Elizabeth Greig, also formerly of New York City). Alex Rogan came by his extraordinary ability naturally, since his father was a celebrated Irish fly dresser and his uncle, Michael Rogan, was one of the most influential salmon fly tyers in history. It is not unusual, therefore, that the Golden Rogan Bucktail (and the Rogan Royal Gray Ghost shown elsewhere in this book) should be influenced strongly by the artistry of salmon flies in the superbly delicate and detailed workmanship of its dressing. Few anglers will go to the expense, or the labor, of acquiring flies of this sort for fishing, but many will delight in owning them or in attempting to dress them because, like the more complicated salmon flies, they are the summit of perfection and beauty in the fly tyer's art.

GOLDEN SHINER (Plate XI)   *(As dressed by the originator)*

HOOK SIZE: 10 to 6, 6X long

HEAD: Black

TAIL: A very small bunch of orange fibers from the base of an orange hackle or from the base of an orange goose or swan nashua feather. The tail is as long as the gap of the hook.

BODY: Wound with white floss, slightly tapered

RIBBING: Medium flat gold tinsel

THROAT: A small bunch of white bucktail, below which is a wisp of the tail material

WING: A small bunch of clear yellow bucktail topped with four peacock herl tips, all slightly longer than the tail

SHOULDERS: On each side, a gray-blue dun saddle hackle, as long as the wing

CHEEKS: Jungle cock, rather short

This is one of the imitative patterns designed by the late Lew Oatman of Shushan, New York. In sending the dressing to me, Oatman said, "This fly is designed for largemouth bass in lakes where the golden shiners have these rich colors. In some waters the golden shiner has a washed-out faded appearance, but in some northern lakes they are brilliant. This is one of the best patterns for largemouths, in my experience. I have had good luck with this and with the Yellow Perch even when the lake was working by fishing the streamer two or three feet deep and moving it slowly so it sinks just below the concentration of pollen which occurs near the surface. At such times, the strike is very deliberate and may feel as though the hook had caught."

320

GOLDEN SMELT (Plate XI)   *(As dressed by the originator)*
HOOK SIZE: 2 to 6, 6X long
HEAD: Black
TAIL: A very few black-ended tippets from a golden pheasant body feather, as
    long as the gap of the hook
BODY: The rearward two-thirds is wound with yellow floss, and the forward
    one-third with pink floss. The body is slightly tapered.
RIBBING: Medium narrow flat gold tinsel
THROAT: A small bunch of yellow hackle fibers, tied in fairly short
WING: Two light green saddle hackles, on each side of which is a golden
    badger saddle hackle, all extending slightly beyond the tail
CHEEKS: Jungle cock, tied in fairly short

Originated by Lew Oatman, of Shushan, New York, about 1953, to imitate the
bait fish of the same name.

GOLDEN WITCH STREAMER (Plate II)   *(As dressed by the originator)*
HEAD: Black, with red band
TAG: Four or five turns of narrow flat silver tinsel, beginning over the point of
    the extra-long-shanked hook
BODY: Dressed very thin with orange silk
RIBBING: Narrow flat silver tinsel
THROAT: A very small bunch of white bucktail extending beyond the bend of
    the hook, under which is a small bunch of barred Plymouth Rock hackle
    fibers
WING: Four or five strands of peacock herl as long as the hackles, over which
    are four barred Plymouth Rock saddle hackles
SHOULDERS: Each a golden pheasant tippet, one-third as long as the wing
CHEEKS: Jungle cock, rather short

Originated by Carrie G. Stevens, for taking trout and landlocked salmon in
Maine lakes. This is one of the earliest of the Maine streamer flies and is one of
the popular patterns for casting and trolling.

GOVERNOR AIKEN BUCKTAIL (Plate X)   *(As dressed by Fin,*
HEAD: Black   *Fur and Feather, Ltd.)*
TAIL: A section of barred wood duck or mandarin duck body feather
BODY: Medium flat silver tinsel
RIBBING: Narrow oval silver tinsel
THROAT: A bunch of white bucktail extending just beyond the hook, under
    which is a small section of red swan or goose wing feather nearly half as
    long as the bucktail
WING: A bunch of lavender bucktail
TOPPING: Five or six strands of peacock herl, as long as the wing
CHEEKS: Jungle cock

321

This fly was named in honor of Governor (since Senator) George D. Aiken, of
Vermont. It is one of the favorite bucktails in New England and is very popular in

Canada for landlocked salmon and for rainbow trout, particularly in the Lake Memphremagog area, where it is called the Smelt Streamer, and is considered to imitate the coloration of a smelt very accurately. The Canadian dressing is the same as the American, except that the wing has a very small bunch of yellow bucktail under the lavender, with a small bunch of white bucktail under the yellow. A gray mallard shoulder is substituted for the jungle cock cheek. The fly often is tied in tandem.

GOVERNOR BRANN STREAMER   (*As dressed by the originator*)
HEAD: Black
TAIL: A narrow section of a red duck wing feather, rather long
BODY: Medium flat silver tinsel
RIBBING: Narrow oval silver tinsel
THROAT: A very small bunch of dark brown bucktail, nearly as long as the wing. (The throat is not used in the latest patterns tied by Mr. Quimby, but is used in the patterns of several other fly dressers.)
WING: Four olive green saddle hackles on each side of which is a brown game cock hackle having a black middle stripe. All six feathers are of the same length.
CHEEKS: Jungle cock

Originated by Bert Quimby, of South Windham, Maine, and named for a former governor of Maine. The fly originally was tied and presented to Governor Brann on the occasion of his visit to the Boston Sportsman's Show during his term of office. It is a popular pattern for trout and particularly for large brown trout.

GRAND LAKER STREAMER (Plate X)   (*As dressed by Benn Treadwell*)
HEAD: Black
TAG: Three or four turns of narrow flat gold tinsel
BODY: Medium thin, wound with black silk
RIBBING: Narrow flat gold tinsel; two pieces tied in together and wound in opposite directions to give a diamond effect
THROAT: A very small bunch of brown bucktail, nearly as long as the wing, or a small bunch of very long light brown hackle fibers
WING: Four medium brown saddle hackles. The outside two may be slightly shorter than the two in the center.
CHEEKS: Jungle cock

This fly is a development of the flies of the Rooster's Regret type discussed in Chapter 2. Flies of this type originated on Grand Lake Stream, in Maine, about 1910. In discussing the Grand Laker, Benn Treadwell, old-time guide of Grand Lake Stream, wrote: "I cannot claim to be the originator; in fact, I do not think any one person can claim that honor, since the Grand Laker is the result of the combined ideas of many of our guides. In its original form it was very crude, consisting of two brown hackles tied on a short hook with thread. As time passed, one guide and then another would add to the pattern. Then someone started using the long-shank hook and dressed the fly as it appears today. It is probably the first, and certainly the best known, of our local flies."

322

GRAY GHOST STREAMER (Plate II)   *(As dressed by the originator)*

HEAD: Black, with red band
TAG: Narrow flat silver tinsel
BODY: Dressed very thin with orange silk
RIBBING: Narrow flat silver tinsel
THROAT: Four or five strands of peacock herl, under which is a very small
  bunch of white bucktail, both extending beyond the bend of the hook. The
  peacock is as long as the wing and the bucktail only slighter shorter. Under
  these is a golden pheasant crest feather as long as the shoulder and curving
  upward.
WING: A golden pheasant crest feather curving downward, as long as the
  hackles. Over this are four olive gray saddle hackles.
SHOULDERS: Each a Ripon's silver pheasant body feather, one-third as long as
  the wing and very wide
CHEEKS: Jungle cock

This famous fly was originated by Carrie G. Stevens, who described its origination in a letter to me as follows: "At the time my Gray Ghost was originated,
Wallace Stevens (who is a fishing guide) and I were living at our camp at Upper
Dam, Maine (which is only a short distance from the famous Upper Dam Pool). On
the first day of July in 1924 I had the inspiration of dressing a streamer fly with
gray wings to imitate a smelt and I left my housework unfinished to develop the
new creation. It was a much cruder job than those I have tied since then, but it had
two hackle feathers for a wing and an underbody of white bucktail, to which I added
several other feathers which I thought enhanced its appearance and its resemblance to a bait fish.

"Then I felt impelled to try the new fly in the pool and soon was casting with
it from one of the aprons of the dam into the fast water. In less than an hour I
hooked and landed a six-pound, thirteen-ounce brook trout which I entered in the
Field & Stream Fishing Contest. The entry won for me second prize and a beautiful
oil painting by Lynn Bogue Hunt, awarded for showing the most sportsmanship
in landing a fish. Because the trout was such a nice one and was caught on a new
fly I had made, it caused much excitement and resulted in my receiving many
orders for flies. Soon I found I was in the fly-tying business. My first flies left much
to be desired. I found that with too much hair and only two feathers the fly would
ride bottom up in the water, but by using less hair and four feathers the trouble
was corrected. For want of something better I used chicken-breast plumage which
I dyed myself to make the shoulders. I used a small feather with black spots for
the cheeks because I did not know then about the beautiful jungle cock and other
imported feathers I am using today.

"The Gray Ghost was one of my early fancy patterns and is the most popular
streamer used today. My next most popular pattern was originated during the war.
It is the Colonel Bates and was named for you, as you know. The Gray Ghost was
designed to represent a smelt and is especially good for early-season fly fishing in   323
waters where fish feed on smelt and similar bait fish. Mr. Frank Bugbee, president
of a bank in Willimantic, Connecticut, named the fly. He made semiannual trips
to Upper Dam until his death several years ago. I suppose the reason the fly has
enjoyed so much popularity is that all the fly tyers are making it and it is used more
extensively than most other patterns.

"I have never used a vise; have never seen anyone tie a fly and no one has ever seen me tie one. I have never read or had any fly-tying instructions. I was several years perfecting my flies and was not satisfied until they were right in every detail. My first flies were tied on regular hooks. I did not use the extra-long-shanked hooks until a couple of years after the Gray Ghost was originated."

Mrs. Stevens' patterns have the feminine touch of being dressed more for beauty of color and detail than because the combinations are chosen for their allure to fish. Her Gray Ghost is conceded by nearly every fisherman to be one of the nation's first ten most productive streamer flies for taking trout or landlocked salmon. Her patterns are such exquisite examples of the fly dresser's art that more of them are retained as collector's items than are used for actual fishing. As an accomplished fly dresser who learned the art unaided, Mrs. Stevens is conceded to be one of the truly great in American fly tying. The Gray Ghost was the first of the several flies of the so-called "Ghost family" which followed it, such as the equally famous Black Ghost (which was a true origination, rather than an adaptation) and the Green Ghost, Lady Ghost, White Ghost, and several others of lesser importance.

Carrie Stevens passed away in the fall of 1970. The rest of the story of the Gray Ghost will be found in Chapter 5.

GRAY PRINCE STREAMER (Plate IX)   *(As dressed by the originator)*
HEAD: Black
TAIL: A short golden pheasant crest feather, curving upward
BODY: Medium flat embossed silver tinsel
RIBBING: Narrow oval silver tinsel
THROAT: A badger saddle hackle tied on as a collar and then tied downward
WING: Four matched sections of pearl mallard feathers, extending slightly
    longer than the tail
CHEEKS: Jungle cock

This fly was originated in 1947 by B. A. Gulline, of Fin, Fur and Feather, Ltd., of Montreal. It is popular in Canada as a trout and bass streamer.

GRAY SMELT (Plate XI)   *(As dressed by the originator)*
HOOK SIZE: All sizes, 6X long
HEAD: Gray
TAIL: A golden pheasant crest feather, about as long as the gap of the hook,
    and curving upward
BODY: Wound with white floss, slightly tapered
RIBBING: Medium flat silver tinsel
THROAT: None
WING: Two light green saddle hackles, outside of which are two blue dun
    saddle hackles, one on each side. The wing is half again as long as the hook.
CHEEKS: Jungle cock

324

Originated by Lew Oatman of Shushan, New York. In a letter to me about this fly, Oatman said, "This fly was designed to imitate the white and silver flash and gray-green of the natural smelt. It has been very effective for trout and in 1953 took one of the rare Marston trout in Quebec. When tying larger sizes for landlocked salmon, care should be taken to emphasize its slenderness. While a smelt may look quite dark to us viewing it from above, the paler colors of this pattern may look more natural to the salmon striking from an angle below the fly. It also is excellent when used as a trolling streamer."

GRAY SQUIRREL SILVER STREAMER   *(As dressed by the originator)*

HEAD: Black
BODY: Medium embossed silver tinsel
THROAT: The tip of a very short golden pheasant crest feather dyed red
WING: A very small bunch of gray squirrel tail hair over which are two gray
   Plymouth Rock saddle hackles of the same length as the squirrel hair
CHEEKS: Jungle cock, very short

This is one of a series of three squirrel-tail streamers originated by Ray Bergman of Nyack, New York, in 1933. These flies should be dressed sparsely in small sizes. They are excellent for all species of trout. When I visited the Gunnison River in Colorado in 1948, the most popular streamer fly on the stream was this one. There it is called the G. J. Streamer and is erroneously attributed to a local fisherman, who must have acquired it when Mr. Bergman visited the Gunnison. A well-known angler on the Gunnison River says of it: "We have found it best suited for rainbows early in the season. It is also good in high water or for an evening fly for all species of trout."

GREEN BEAUTY STREAMER (Plate II)   *(As dressed by the originator)*

HEAD: Black, with red band
TAG: Four or five turns of narrow flat silver tinsel
BODY: Dressed thin with orange silk
RIBBING: Narrow flat silver tinsel
THROAT: An extremely small bunch of white bucktail extending beyond the
   bend of the hook, under which is a golden pheasant crest feather as long as
   the shoulder and curving upward
WING: Five or six strands of bright green peacock herl, over which are four
   olive-green saddle hackles. The herl is as long as the hackles.
SHOULDERS: Wood duck or dyed mallard side feathers of a variegated brown
   color, one-third as long as the wing
CHEEKS: Jungle cock

Originated by Carrie G. Stevens, for taking trout and landlocked salmon in Maine waters. The fly also has been used successfully for Atlantic salmon.

GREEN DRAKE STREAMER   *(As dressed by the originator)*

HEAD: Black
TAG: Four or five turns of narrow flat gold tinsel
TAIL: A very small bunch of black hackle fibers
BUTT: Two or three turns of peacock herl (four or five strands twisted)
BODY: Dressed thin with yellowish-brown silk
RIBBING: Black silk thread
THROAT: A small bunch of light brown hackle fibers, as long as the shoulders

325

WING: Two olive green saddle hackles, outside of which are two medium brown saddle hackles, one on each side
SHOULDERS: Each a teal body feather dyed yellow, one-third as long as the wing
CHEEKS: Jungle cock, fairly long

This is one of several streamer patterns which were inspired by trout flies of the same name. This adaptation was originated by Gardner Percy of Portland, Maine.

GREEN GHOST STREAMER

(As dressed by the originator)

HEAD: Black
TAG: Three or four turns of narrow flat silver tinsel
BODY: Dressed thin with orange silk
RIBBING: Narrow flat silver tinsel
THROAT: Five or six strands of peacock herl, under which is a small bunch of white bucktail, both extending beyond the barb of the hook
WING: Six medium green saddle hackles
TOPPING: A golden pheasant crest feather, as long as the wing and following its curve. (This sometimes is omitted.)
SHOULDERS: Each a Ripon's silver pheasant body feather, one-third as long as the wing
CHEEKS: Jungle cock

This fly was originated by Bert Quimby, of South Windham, Maine, for taking trout and landlocked salmon in Maine lakes. Its origination was influenced by the popularity of the Gray Ghost Streamer, which it imitates very closely except for the color of the wing. Streamer flies with green wings (such as the Nine-Three Streamer) are very successful on Maine lakes, since their color is similar to that of smelt, which are widely taken by trout and salmon, especially during the spring migratory runs of this important bait fish.

GREEN KING STREAMER

(As dressed by the originator)

HEAD: Black
BODY: Medium flat silver tinsel
WING: A small bunch of white bucktail, over which are two olive green and two gray Plymouth Rock neck hackles, with the green hackles outside. The bucktail is as long as the hackles.
CHEEKS: Jungle cock

This fly is an adaptation of the better-known Nine-Three Streamer with the Plymouth Rock hackles used instead of the two black hackles. The adaptation was made by Gardner Percy in the belief that it more closely imitated the coloration of a smelt.

A streamer very similar to the Green King is the Green's Pot (often called the Green Spot), which is dressed with four dark green saddle hackles and a very small bunch of bright green bucktail over the white bucktail. The body usually is ribbed with narrow oval silver tinsel.

326

GREYHOUND STREAMER (Plate II)

(As dressed by the originator)

HEAD: Red, with black band

TAG: Four or five turns of narrow flat silver tinsel, beginning above the point of a 5X long hook

TAIL: A small bunch of red hackle fibers, extending only slightly beyond the bend of the hook

BODY: Dressed thin with red silk

RIBBING: Narrow flat silver tinsel

THROAT: Six or seven strands of peacock herl, under which is an extremely small bunch of white bucktail, both extending just beyond the bend of the hook. Under this is a small bunch of red hackle fibers.

WING: Four light gray saddle hackles

SHOULDERS: Each a jungle cock body feather extending one-third the length of the wing

CHEEKS: Jungle cock, fairly short

Originated by Carrie G. Stevens. This fly usually is dressed on an extremely long-shanked hook, or on tandem hooks, and ordinarily is used for trolling.

GRIZZLY KING STREAMER   *(As dressed by the originator)*

HEAD: Black

TAG: Three or four turns of narrow flat gold tinsel

TAIL: Two narrow sections of a red duck wing feather, matched and curving upward

BODY: Dressed thin of green silk

RIBBING: Narrow flat gold tinsel

THROAT: A small bunch of gray Plymouth Rock hackle fibers

WING: Four gray Plymouth Rock saddle hackles

SHOULDERS: Each a teal body feather, one-third as long as the wing

This fly was inspired by the trout fly of the same name and was originally dressed by Gardner Percy, of Portland, Maine.

GRIZZLY PRINCE (Plate I)   *(As dressed by the originator)*

HOOK SIZE: All sizes, 4X long

HEAD: Black

TAIL: A very small bunch of stripped orange hackle fibers

BODY: Wound with flat silver tinsel

THROAT: A very small bunch of white bucktail extending beyond the bend of the hook. Under this is a very small bunch of stripped orange hackle fibers as long as the gap of the hook.

WING: Select two pairs of white saddle hackles and lay them on the hook, extending to the end of the tail. Prepare four grizzly saddle hackles (two pairs) of the same size as the white hackles, selecting wide feathers for the purpose. Strip all fibers from the bottom halves of the grizzly hackles. Lay two of these stripped hackles on each side of the white hackles so as to cover the upper half of the white saddle hackles, thus allowing the bottom halves of the white hackles to show.

SHOULDERS: On each side, a wood duck body feather covering the forward third of the wing

CHEEKS: Jungle cock

327

Originated by Austin S. Hogan, of Cambridge, Massachusetts, famous for his art of color blending to obtain natural bait-fish effects. This fly is a general bait-fish imitation for waters with medium visibility. It is of special note as an example of the two-color effect obtainable by stripping the fibers from either the top or the bottom of hackles.

HAGEN SANDS BONEFISH FLY (Plate VII) *(As dressed by the originator)*

HOOK SIZE: 1/0 and 1, stainless steel or nickel
HEAD: Black, built up, with yellow eyes and black pupils
BODY: None
WING: A fairly large bunch of white bucktail with the under fur retained, tied on top of the hook and extending beyond the barb. Over this are two yellow neck hackles outside of which are two gray barred rock hackles, all of the same length, slightly longer than the hook. The feathers are tied in as splayed wings curving outward and upward for a "breather" effect.

This fly was originated in 1949 by Hagen R. Sands, of Key West, Florida, to imitate both a small minnow and a small mantis shrimp. With it, Mr. Sands took a record bonefish weighing fourteen pounds, four ounces. Mr. Sands wrote me: "This is a consistent producer on the bonefish flats and has been used to catch large tarpon, permit, and numerous other fish. The fly is best fished by holding the rod parallel with the water and using the strip and pause method. The line should be stripped in nearly two feet at a time."

HALF AND HALF *(As dressed by Larry A. Kahle)*

HOOK SIZE: 2 to 6, 3X long
HEAD: Black
TAIL: Very small bunches of red over yellow calf tail, a bit longer than gap of hook
RIBBING: Medium embossed silver tinsel
LATERAL STRIPE: About four inches of black crewel yarn, tied in middle at tail
BODY: Medium yellow chenille, tied in at head, wound to tail, and back to head
THROAT: A small bunch of orange calf tail under a small bunch of white calf tail. The white extends to bend of hook, with the orange half as long.
WING: A small bunch of red calf tail extending to bend of hook, over which are four grizzly neck hackles dyed yellow, slightly raised and extending to end of tail
CHEEKS: Jungle cock

This streamer was originated by Larry A. Kahle and Tim Sauerwein for bass fishing in the Susquehanna River near Williamsport, Pennsylvania, and is in imitation of a bluegill, sunfish, or perch. Most important, and usable in other dressings, is the black lateral stripe. This is tied in midway along the body before throat and wing are applied. It is bound down with the tinsel. The name indicates it is half an imitator and half an attractor.

328

Two other body designs use white chenille or olive green chenille; other parts of dressing are the same. The fly also is used in salt water dressed on stainless hooks as large as 6/0. A heavier stripe of black wool is used on larger sizes.

HARLEQUIN STREAMER (Plate IX)   *(As dressed by the originator)*
HEAD: Black
TAIL: A section of a red swan or goose wing, rather long and thin
BODY: Medium flat silver tinsel
RIBBING: Narrow oval silver tinsel
THROAT: A badger hackle tied on as a collar and then tied downward
WING: Two long matched sections of goose or swan wing feathers, each section being married from equal parts of black, dark blue and white, with the black at the top and the blue in the middle. The wing is slightly longer than the tail.

This fly was originated by B. A. Gulline, of Fin, Fur and Feather, Ltd., for W. A. Newman of Montreal, in 1932. It represents a chub minnow, which has a bluish stripe down its side. It is one of the popular flies for trout in Canada. It is a member of the famous Trout Fin series, the other two flies in the series being the Trout Fin in orange and in red.

HELEN BATES STREAMER   *(As dressed by the originator)*
HEAD: Black
TAG: Four or five turns of narrow flat gold tinsel
TAIL: A very short golden pheasant crest feather, curving upward
BUTT: Two or three turns of bright red silk
BODY: Narrow flat gold tinsel, palmered fairly thickly from butt to head with a brown saddle hackle, with which the fly is built up at the throat
WING: Four dark brown furnace hackles
TOPPING: A golden pheasant crest feather, as long as the wing and following its curve
CHEEKS: Jungle cock

This fly, originated by William Reynolds, of Sturbridge, Massachusetts, was named in honor of Helen Ellis Bates—Mrs. Joseph D. Bates, Jr.—of Longmeadow, Massachusetts. Originally dressed and named as a courtesy to my wife, it is retained in this edition because the many anglers who have tried it have reported such success that it is now regarded as a standard pattern. Like its namesake, it is very attractive and has an excellent silhouette, regardless of water conditions. It is a favorite for all species of trout in the eastern United States throughout the year, and especially for large brown trout.

HERB JOHNSON SPECIAL   *(As dressed by the originator)*
HOOK SIZE: 2 to 4, streamer hook
HEAD: Painted silver, with yellow eye and black pupil (the head is quite large)
BODY: Black wool, fairly full
RIBBING: Embossed flat silver tinsel (wound in reverse, toward tyer)
THROAT: White bucktail, as long as the wing
WING: A very small bunch of bright yellow bucktail, slightly longer than the hook; on each side of this two strands each of red and blue fluorescent nylon floss; on each side above the floss one strand of peacock herl; over this a rather sparse bunch of brown bucktail dyed yellow. (All components

329

are of same length, slightly longer than the hook. On a No. 2 long-shanked hook the dressing is two and three-quarters inches long.)

This interesting dressing was originated by Herbert Johnson, a well-known angler of Portland, Maine, about 1950. The fly is regionally famous for trout and landlocked salmon, and we have used it very successfully for Atlantic salmon.

HERRING BUCKTAIL (Plate VII)   *(As dressed by Roy A. Patrick)*
HEAD: Black, usually with white painted eye and black pupil
BODY: Medium flat silver tinsel. (If no ribbing is used, embossed tinsel is
   preferable.)
RIBBING: Medium oval silver tinsel (optional)
WING: A very small bunch of white polar bear hair, over which is a very small
   bunch of pale green polar bear hair, over which is a middle band of a bunch
   of polar bear hair of gun-metal gray. Over this is a very small bunch of dark
   green polar bear hair, with a very small bunch of dark blue polar bear hair
   over this.

This is a companion fly to the Candlefish Bucktail, and is a scientifically de-signed pattern made to imitate the herring, a common bait fish for coho (silver) salmon. The fly is used extensively in the Puget Sound area of the Pacific northwest and is one of the few standard patterns for coho fishing. It was designed from the angling experiments of a group of Puget Sound anglers, notably Roy A. Patrick, Zell E. Parkhurst, and Letcher Lambuth, all of Seattle, Washington. For hook sizes and other data on coho fly fishing, see Chapter 17.

HORNBERG SPECIAL STREAMER (Plate I)   *(As dressed by the*
HOOK SIZE: 6, regular   *Weber Tackle Company*
HEAD: Black
BODY: Wound with flat silver tinsel
WING: Two barred gray mallard breast feathers one and one-half inches long,
   between which are the very narrow tips of two yellow neck hackles as long as
   the mallard and nearly concealed by it. These cover the shank of the hook,
   and are stroked to a point at their ends by applying a small amount of
   lacquer to them, rubbed between thumb and forefinger. The width of the
   feathers (for above size of hook) is at least a quarter of an inch, with the
   yellow hackles narrower. (An easy way to apply the mallard is to strip the
   lower sides of the feathers from the quills.)
CHEEKS: Jungle cock, fairly long
THROAT: Four or five turns of a grizzly hen neck hackle wound on dry fly style
   as a collar after wing and cheeks have been applied. (This dressing should
   be fairly wide and heavy. The wing should not be applied too far forward, to
   accommodate it.)

330   Ed Wotruba, president of the Weber Tackle Company, Stevens Point, Wisconsin, wrote me: "This was the idea of retired conservation warden Frank Hornberg when he was on active duty in Portage County. We helped him develop it, and tied the first one for commercial sale. I think he had in mind to simulate a small minnow, which this fly does nicely when fished wet. It is also very effective when dressed

and fished dry. It is primarily a trout fly but takes panfish very readily. This is an authentic sample of the original pattern."

This fly, called the Hornberg in the east, is considered "a great new fly." In the eastern version no lacquer is added to the tips of the wing. Some variations use yellow hair instead of the yellow hackles and teal instead of the mallard. The fly often is fished dry until it sinks, whereupon it is fished as a streamer.

IMPROVED GOVERNOR STEELHEAD BUCKTAIL (Plate IV)   *(As dressed*
HEAD: Black   *by the originator)*
TAIL: A very small bunch of red hackle fibers, rather long, tied in forward of
   the red silk and gold ribbing, after they have been applied
BODY: Rear third is red silk, ribbed with narrow oval gold tinsel. (This is in
   effect a tag, since the tail is tied in forward of it. Mr. Pray prefers a heavy
   hook with a No. 1 bend, very short.) Front two-thirds is dark green chenille.
   (The usual dressing for the Improved Governor calls for peacock herl over
   padding, but the chenille gives the same effect and is more permanent, since
   steelhead tear peacock herl badly.)
THROAT: Mahogany (red-brown) hackle tied on as a collar, long, stiff, and full
WING: Dark brown wolverine hair, very long. (The regular dressing calls for a
   section of a dark mottled brown wing feather of a hen ringneck pheasant,
   woodcock, or turkey.) A hair wing is preferable in the steelhead version.
   Dark brown bear hair may be substituted if wolverine is not available.
CHEEKS: Jungle cock, dressed high and rather long. (This is not called for in
   the regular dressing.)

The Improved Governor is an adaptation of the Governor fly which originated in England prior to 1850. There are several variations of the fly, including the Improved Governor and the Governor Special. This steelhead version was originated by C. Jim Pray of Eureka, California, a famous fly dresser and steelhead angler. It is particularly effective on the Klamath and Eel rivers of California.

INTEGRATION BUCKTAIL   *(As dressed by the originator)*
HOOK SIZE: 2 to 8, 3X long
HEAD: Black
BODY: Medium oval silver tinsel wrapped to eye to prevent hair from flaring
THROAT: A small bunch of straight white bucktail extending slightly beyond
   bend of hook
WING: A small bunch of straight bucktail dyed black extending slightly beyond
   bend of hook

This simple pattern was originated by Ted Trueblood, for many years an editor of *Field & Stream* magazine. It is a good dark-day or evening fly both in fresh and salt water.

IRIS NO. 1 BUCKTAIL   *(As dressed by the originator)*   331
HEAD: Black, with painted red band at rear
BODY: Medium flat silver tinsel
RIBBING: Very fine oval silver tinsel or silver wire
WING: A very small bunch of dark red polar bear hair, over which is a very

small bunch of bright yellow polar bear hair, over which is a very small bunch of pale green polar bear hair, with a very small bunch of light blue polar bear hair over this. All bunches are of the same length and must be extremely small so that the fly will not be overdressed. (Bucktail may be substituted for the polar bear hair, if desired.)

CHEEKS: Jungle cock

This fly, originated by Preston J. Jennings, of Brooklyn, New York, is typical of a series devised by him on the theory that minnows best can be imitated with flies dressed in spectrum colors. Another of Jennings' flies, shown in this book, is the Lord Iris Streamer.

JANE CRAIG STREAMER (Plate XII) *(As dressed by the originator)*

HEAD: Black
BODY: Medium flat silver tinsel
THROAT: A small bunch of white hackle fibers
WING: Six white saddle hackles
TOPPING: Seven or eight strands of bright green peacock herl, as long as the wing
CHEEKS: Jungle cock

This is one of the earliest of the Maine streamers. It was originated by Herbert L. Welch, of Mooselookmeguntic, Maine, and named in honor of Jane Craig, a vaudeville actress of the team of Dalton and Craig, which toured the Keith Circuit when this fly was originated in about 1923. Mr. Welch later dressed the fly with yellow hackles and named it the Yellow Jane Craig. The white version was dressed to imitate a smelt. The yellow adaptation was designed to give the fly greater visibility on dark days or in discolored water. Mr. Welch considers saddle hackles vastly superior to the heavier neck or shoulder hackles because they make a more streamlined fly and give better action in the water.

JEAN BUCKTAIL *(As dressed by Herbert L. Howard)*

HEAD: Black
TAIL: A very small bunch of orange bucktail tips or orange hackle fibers
BODY: Medium flat gold tinsel
THROAT: Two or three turns of a yellow hackle, dressed downward, rather long and sparse
WING: A small bunch of blue-gray bucktail, over which is a small bunch of orange bucktail, with a small bunch of blue-gray bucktail over this. The bunches must be extremely small so that the fly will not be overdressed. They are of the same length and extend slightly beyond the tail.
SHOULDERS: Each a very small jungle cock body feather, one-third as long as the wing
CHEEKS: Jungle cock, half as long as the shoulder

332

This fly originated in British Columbia or in the northwestern United States, where it is popular for all species of trout. The dressing is from an original given to Herbert L. Howard, of New Rochelle, New York, who gave it to Ray Bergman for his popular book *Trout*.

JESSE WOOD STREAMER (Plate I) *(As dressed by Ray Bergman)*
HEAD: Black
TAIL: A narrow section of a red duck wing feather, rather long
BODY: Medium embossed or oval silver tinsel. (In the early versions, the body
  was wound with fine silver wire.)
THROAT: A furnace hackle tied around the hook and bunched downward. The
  hackle should be short and used only in part to make the throat thinly
  dressed. (In the earliest version of this fly, a sample of which was presented
  to me by Arthur C. Mills, Jr., of William Mills and Son, the throat is dressed
  much longer and heavier than recommended here, and the hackle is almost
  black at the front, shaded to dark brown at the rear.)
WING: Two Bali duck shoulder feathers, extending just beyond the tail. The
  upper halves of these feathers should be light brown in color, and the lower
  halves jet black.
CHEEKS: Jungle cock, fairly short

This fly was originated by Jesse Wood, of Warwick, New York, in 1926 to
imitate a minnow. As a customer, he worked with Ray Bergman in developing the
fly when Bergman was a salesman with William Mills and Son, of New York City.
This is the dressing which is personally approved by Bergman. Wood preferred the
tandem-hook dressing but the fly is correctly tied with either single or tandem
hooks. The fly also was dressed for Wood by Frier Gulline, of the firm of Fin, Fur
and Feather, Ltd., of Montreal, in 1929. The dressing is the same, but in Canada
the fly usually is known as the Demon Streamer.

JOSSY SPECIAL BUCKTAIL *(As dressed by E. H. Rosborough)*
HOOK SIZE: 8, 4X long
HEAD: Black
BODY: Wound with white chenille
RIBBING: Two or three twisted strands of peacock herl
WING: A fairly small bunch of brown bucktail half again as long as the hook.
  On each side of this is a white saddle hackle of the same length as the hair
  and applied to splay outward.

This pattern was originated by W. E. Jossy, of River Forest Place, Oregon. It
is especially popular on Oregon's Deschutes River, which is famous for steelhead
fishing. (In applying peacock herl wound on as a body or ribbing, twist the strands
of peacock herl with a section of similarly colored thread for added strength.)

KENNEBAGO STREAMER *(As dressed by the originator)*
HEAD: Black
TAIL: A small bunch of orange hackle fibers
BODY: Rear third: a butt of peacock herl followed by pale blue silk followed by
  another butt of peacock herl. The silk occupies half of this section. The
  forward two-thirds is dressed with medium flat gold tinsel.
RIBBING: Medium oval silver tinsel, over gold only
THROAT: A small bunch of orange hackle fibers
WING: Two dark red saddle hackles with a golden badger saddle hackle on each
  side
CHEEKS: Jungle cock

333

Originated by Herbert L. Welch, of Oquossoc, Maine, and named for Kennebago Stream, a famous trout and landlocked salmon water in the Rangeley section of Maine. This attractive pattern is important only because Herbie Welch did it.

KENNEBAGO SMELT STREAMER   *(As dressed by the originator)*
HOOK SIZE: 2 to 8, 4X long
HEAD: Black
BODY: Flat silver tinsel
RIBBING: Oval silver tinsel
THROAT: White bucktail, a bit longer than the hook, with a bit of yellow hackle
    applied as a beard
WING: Very small bunches of red and blue bucktail, mixed, with four black
    saddle hackles over this, all extending slightly beyond the bend of the hook
TOPPING: About six peacock herls, as long as the wing
CHEEKS: Jungle cock

This smelt imitation is best known as a landlocked salmon fly and is very popular in northern New England and southern Canada, either trolled near the surface or deeper when the salmon are deep. It was originated by Bud Wilcox, formerly a game warden and guide, of Rangeley, Maine.

LADY DOCTOR BUCKTAIL (Plate XII)   *(As dressed by the Percy Tackle Company)*
HEAD: Black
TAG: Three or four turns of narrow flat gold tinsel
TAIL: The tips of two moderately long and very small yellow neck hackles back
    to back
BUTT: Two or three turns of bright red silk
BODY: Thinly wound with bright yellow silk
RIBBING: Narrow flat gold tinsel. Just ahead of the tinsel is palmered a yellow
    hackle, tapering larger toward the head. The balance of the usable part is
    wound on as a throat.
THROAT: A small bunch of yellow hackle fibers, if the remainder of the
    palmered hackle (tied downward) is not sufficient
WING: A small bunch of white polar bear hair over which is a smaller bunch of
    black bear hair, both extending just beyond the tail
TOPPING: Two jungle cock feathers tied closely back to back over the wing.
    They should be half as long as the wing.
SHOULDERS: Each a red dyed breast feather with a sharp outside edge one-third
    as long as the wing and tied straight along hook

This beautiful and productive fly was originated in 1926 by Warden Supervisor Joseph S. Stickney, of Saco, Maine. Originally it was tied in small sizes to imitate a bee, but it now is more popular dressed as a bucktail, even though it seems to lack a logical reason for being such. The fly was named by Stickney for his wife, a well-known physician. Since Mr. Stickney did not dress his own flies, the majority of them were made for him by the Percy Tackle Company, of Portland, Maine. The dressing described here is from a fly presented to me by Stickney, who was one of my fishing companions for many years.

334

The Lady Doctor is famous as a trout, bass, and landlocked salmon fly under conditions when a bright pattern is needed. In 1934 Gardner Percy dressed a variation of it, called the Adeline, which is identical except that it lacks the black part of the wing and the red shoulders. This fly is included in the set of small trout bucktail patterns sponsored by the Cape Cod Trout Club, of Massachusetts. Both the Lady Doctor and the Adeline are excellent for all species of trout when tied as ordinary wet flies in small sizes. I have used them successfully for cutthroat trout, steelhead and Atlantic salmon.

LADY GHOST STREAMER (Plate X)   *(As dressed by the originator)*

HEAD: Black
BODY: Medium flat silver tinsel
RIBBING: Narrow oval silver tinsel
THROAT: Six or seven peacock herl fibers, under which is an extremely small
   bunch of white bucktail, both as long as the wing. Under this is a fairly short
   golden pheasant crest feather, curving upward.
WING: A golden pheasant crest feather, as long as the wing and curving
   upward, over which are four golden badger saddle hackles
SHOULDERS: Each a Reeves pheasant body feather, showing a golden-brown
   base and a black edge. The feathers are one-third as long as the wing.
CHEEKS: Jungle cock, long enough to touch the black outside band of the
   shoulder

This imitation of a minnow was originated by Bert Quimby, of South Windham, Maine, formerly one of his state's best-known and most experienced guides and fly dressers. The original version of the fly differs somewhat from this new dressing, in that it has a tail of a few strands of golden pheasant tippet and a body of red silk ribbed with narrow flat silver tinsel. In this dressing the two golden pheasant crest feathers are lacking and the Reeves pheasant shoulders have a white base and a wide dark red-brown outside band. Evidently Bert Quimby had the Gray Ghost in mind when he dressed this one!

LEECH STREAMER (Plate I)   *(As dressed by the originator)*

HEAD: Black
BODY: Dressed moderately heavily of maroon wool
THROAT: A bunch of black hackle fibers
WING: Two maroon saddle hackles over which are two black saddle hackles.
   The four feathers are tied on flat (at right angles to the hook) with the black
   feathers on top, and they are somewhat longer than usual.

This fly was originated by Frier Gulline, of Fin, Fur and Feather, Ltd., in the early 1930s. Since it is dressed to imitate a leech (commonly called a bloodsucker in many parts of the United States), the red feathers and wool must be a very dark blood red. The fly is very popular in Canada for both trout and bass, since the leech is a favorite item of their diet in many northern lakes. The fly must be fished very deep and very slowly, in the gradual undulating motion of a leech rather than with the darting motion of a minnow. It is especially productive early in the season. (Also see the Wooly Leech.)

335

LEITZ BUCKTAIL   *(As dressed by the originator)*

HEAD: Black

TAG: Narrow flat gold tinsel. The tag is rather long, extending partway around the bend of the hook.

TAIL: The tips of two red hackles, rather long and splayed outwardly

BUTT: Two turns of black chenille

BODY: Medium embossed silver tinsel. Just behind the throat is a forward butt of four turns of black chenille.

THROAT: Two turns of a red hackle, tied downward. The throat is rather sparsely dressed.

WING: A bunch of white bucktail, over which is a bunch of black and red bucktail mixed equally. The wing extends to the end of the tail and is rather fully dressed.

CHEEKS: Jungle cock, rather long

Originated by Earl Leitz, of Sault Ste. Marie, Michigan, and named in his honor by Dr. Marks of the same city, who took a prize rainbow trout on this fly in 1947. This is one of several flies which were originated for taking the large rainbows, or "Soo" trout, of the St. Mary's River at the outlet of Lake Superior. Since the trout in these rapids are large, these flies usually are dressed on No. 2 hooks.

LITTLE BROOK TROUT BUCKTAIL (Plate I)   *(As dressed by the originator)*

HOOK SIZE: 2 to 12, 6X long

HEAD: Black

TAIL: A very small bunch of bright green bucktail under or over which is a section cut from bright red floss, both slightly longer than the gap of the hook

BODY: Wound with cream-colored spun fur

RIBBING: Narrow flat silver tinsel

THROAT: A very small bunch of bright orange bucktail, the same length as the tail

WING: Of four very small separated bunches of hair, each extending slightly beyond the tail. A very small bunch of white bucktail over which and blending into it is a very small bunch of bright orange bucktail. Over this is a very small bunch of bright green bucktail, topped by a very small bunch of barred badger hair.

CHEEKS: Jungle cock

This fly and the two which follow were originated by Samuel R. Slaymaker II, of Gap, Pennsylvania, to imitate trout fry as mentioned in Chapter 5. The three flies originally were manufactured for sale by the Weber Tackle Company, of Stevens Point, Wisconsin, both in regular sizes and small "streamerette" size. They have exceptional records for taking trout in waters where trout fry exist, and are almost equally useful for many other species.

336

LITTLE BROWN TROUT BUCKTAIL (Plate I)   *(As dressed by the originator)*

HOOK SIZE: 2 to 12, 6X long

HEAD: Black

TAIL: A very small breast feather, with the dark center removed, from a ringneck pheasant. The feather is as long as the gap of the hook, and curves upward

BODY: Wound with white spun wool

RIBBING: Copper wire. (Narrow flat gold tinsel may be substituted.)

THROAT: None

WING: Of four very small separated bunches of hair, each extending slightly beyond the tail. A very small bunch of yellow bucktail over which is a very small bunch of reddish-orange bucktail, slightly blended. Over this is a very small bunch of medium dark squirrel tail topped and slightly blended with a very small bunch of dark brown squirrel tail.

CHEEKS: Jungle cock

Originated by Samuel R. Slaymaker II, of Gap, Pennsylvania, as described in the preceding pattern.

LITTLE RAINBOW TROUT BUCKTAIL (Plate I)   *(As dressed by the originator)*

HOOK SIZES: 2 to 12, 6X long

HEAD: Black

TAIL: A small bunch of bright green bucktail, slightly longer than the gap of the hook

BODY: Wound with pinkish-white fur

RIBBING: Narrow flat silver tinsel

THROAT: A very small bunch of pink bucktail, as long as the tail

WING: Of four very small separated bunches of hair, each extending slightly beyond the tail. A very small bunch of white bucktail over which is a very small bunch of pink bucktail, slightly blended. Over this is a very small bunch of bright green bucktail topped and slightly blended with a very small bunch of natural badger hair.

CHEEKS: Jungle cock

Originated by Samuel R. Slaymaker II, of Gap, Pennsylvania, as described in note for the Little Brook Trout.

LLAMA BUCKTAIL   *(As dressed by Oliver's Orvis Shop)*

HOOK SIZE: 6 to 10, length same as wing

HEAD: Black, with black dotted white pupil

TAIL: A small bunch of grizzly hackle

TAG: Flat gold tinsel

BODY: Red floss

RIBBING: Flat gold tinsel

WING: Woodchuck guard hairs

COLLAR: Two turns of a fairly narrow grizzly hackle

This bucktail was popularized by Eric Leiser, author of *The Complete Book of Fly Tying*. If it were given a red tail it would be the old Red Abbey Bucktail, which is popular as a hair-wing Atlantic salmon fly. The Llama is dressed in a choice of body colors: yellow, white, black, orange, or fluorescent pink or red. The wing should be of the same length as the hook to its bend. The approved woodchuck hair is white-tipped, with a black bar, a tan midsection, and a black base. The best comes from the lower neck just below the shoulder. Hook size 10, 3X long, is preferred,

337

which would have a tail three-quarters of an inch long and hackle fibers five-eighths of an inch long. The wing is quite sparse and is tipped upward at about a thirty-degree angle. Users say the Llama takes all varieties of trout "with regularity."

LORD DENBY STREAMER   *(As dressed by the originator)*

HEAD: Black

TAIL: About six or seven fibers from a golden pheasant tippet, medium long

BODY: Medium flat silver tinsel

THROAT: Two turns of a red saddle hackle mixed with one turn of a light blue saddle hackle, applied as a collar and then tied downward. The throat is dressed sparsely, with the hackles of medium length

WING: Two light blue saddle hackles between two Plymouth Rock saddle hackles, extending slightly beyond the tail

CHEEKS: Jungle cock, small and rather short

Originated by Robert E. Coulson, of Lyon and Coulson, Inc., of Buffalo, New York, in 1924. Coulson was an angling writer who used the pen name "Breems Forrest." The Lord Denby Streamer, as well as the Saguenay and St. Ignace, were designed for taking the large eastern brook trout on the Nipigon River in the Nipigon district of Ontario. It was named for Lord Denby, who fished the river with Coulson.

LORD IRIS STREAMER (Plate XII)   *(As dressed by Fin, Fur and Feather, Ltd.)*

HEAD: Black

TAIL: In two matched sections, each a married section of swan or goose wing feathers, red, blue, and yellow, with the red at the top. Each completed married section is narrow but rather long.

BODY: Medium flat silver tinsel

RIBBING: Narrow oval silver tinsel

THROAT: A yellow hackle tied on as a collar and then tied downward

WING: Four ginger furnace hackles

SHOULDERS: Each a matched section of red, blue and yellow swan or goose wing, married together with the red at the top. The shoulder is dressed along the top of the wing and is two-thirds as long, but rather narrow.

CHEEKS: Jungle cock

This fly is one of those originated by Preston Jennings, of Brooklyn, New York, supposedly to imitate the colors of minnows as they appear by the breaking down of light passing through a prism.

MAD TOM (Plate XI)   *(As dressed by the originator)*

HOOK SIZE: 2 or 4, regular

HEAD: Black

TAG: Several turns of medium flat silver tinsel

TAIL: Two bunches of marabou fibers. First, a small short bunch of white. Above that is a longer bunch of tobacco brown extending about an inch and a half beyond the bend of the hook.

BODY: First wrap the hook shank with white floss. Then, just ahead of where the tail is tied in, tie on a bunch of black marabou fibers which top the full length of the tail. Then tie in an end of large black chenille and wind back and forth, finally tying off at the head. This is built up to represent the thick shoulder of the natural catfish.

WING: None

THROAT: A black hackle with fibers about an inch long, wound on as a collar. These fibers should be coarse so that when wet and sticking together in clusters, they resemble the whiskers of a catfish.

This is an unusual pattern originated by the famous angler and fly dresser Lew Oatman, of Shushan, New York. The above dressing was sent to me by Oatman just before his death. In the accompanying letter he said, "This pattern is not intended to be an exact imitation of any one species of catfish, but rather a general pattern resembling several such as the mad tom, stone cat, tadpole cat, and all the little bullheads and cats having the characteristic thick shoulder, tapering body, and generally dark appearance."

MAGOG SMELT BUCKTAIL   *(As dressed by Harold N. Gibbs)*

HEAD: Black, with tiny yellow painted eye with black pupil

TAIL: A very small bunch of teal body feather fibers

BODY: Medium flat silver tinsel

THROAT: A very small bunch of red hackle fibers

WING: A very small bunch of white bucktail, over which is a very small bunch of yellow bucktail, over which is a very small bunch of violet bucktail

TOPPING: Five or six strands of peacock herl

SHOULDERS: Each a teal body feather, one-third as long as the wing

This fly was originated by Frier Gulline, of Fin, Fur and Feather, Ltd. It was first used for taking landlocked salmon in the Memphremagog Lake area near the border of Quebec Province and Vermont. Edward A. Materne, of East Providence, Rhode Island, obtained a sample and dressed duplicates on No. 1 hooks for striped bass. It is particularly successful for smallmouth bass, landlocked salmon, and striped bass, as well as for several other varieties of freshwater and saltwater game fish. Harold N. Gibbs, of Barrington, Rhode Island, and Materne, both famous saltwater fly fishermen, gave the fly its original popularity in the United States.

MALE DACE STREAMER (Plate XI)   *(As dressed by the originator)*

HOOK SIZE: 4 to 12, 4X long

HEAD: Black

BODY: Wound with very pale cream floss, slightly tapered

RIBBING: Medium narrow flat gold tinsel

THROAT: A very small bunch of rich orange hackle fibers, about as long as the gap of the hook

WING: Two olive green saddle hackles, on each side of which is a golden-edged badger hackle. All are of the same length, extending slightly beyond the bend of the hook, and all should be slender.

CHEEKS: Jungle cock, tied in short

339

This is another of the natural imitation patterns by Lew Oatman of Shushan, New York. In his notes he says, "This fly imitates the male black-nosed dace in spawning season. These little fellows are very common in our trout streams, and this pattern has just enough color under such conditions."

MARABOU PERCH STREAMER (Plate I)   *(As dressed by the originator)*
HEAD: Green, built up to match body, and painted with large yellow eyes with red pupils
BODY: Of silver Mylar tubular cord, painted on sides with green vertical bands and with a red band just behind the eye
THROAT: A bunch of white marabou fibers extending to barb of hook
WING: A yellow marabou feather, over which is an olive green marabou feather. Over this is a topping of several strands of peacock herl, all extending slightly beyond the bend of the hook.

Originated by Arthur Fusco of Medford, Massachusetts, to imitate a small yellow perch, which is a favorite food for game fish living in lakes and ponds. Fusco is an expert in dressing flies with Mylar bodies.

MASCOMA STREAMER (Plate X)   *(As dressed by Paul Kukonen)*
HOOK SIZE: 4 to 10, 4X long
HEAD: Black
TAIL: A very small golden pheasant crest feather, curving upward
BODY: Two or three layers of flat gold tinsel (to build up the body)
RIBBING: Oval gold tinsel
THROAT: A very small bunch of orange hackle fibers about half as long as the hook
WING: About seven hairs of polar bear or bucktail in each of the following colors: yellow, blue, and red. These can be mixed. Over this on each side is a section of bronze mallard wing with the tips curving slightly upward. All these elements are of the same length—slightly longer than the hook. (Teal or mallard can be substituted for the bronze mallard.)
CHEEKS: Jungle cock, preferably of light color and tied in very short

This pattern (of unknown origin) began as a salmon fly in New Brunswick and has been very successfully adapted as a trout streamer; it is especially productive with the mallard or teal wing in discolored water and with the bronze mallard wing in clear water.

MICKEY FINN BUCKTAIL (Illustrated as a streamer in Plate XII)
HEAD: Black   *(As dressed by John Alden Knight)*
BODY: Medium flat silver tinsel
RIBBING: Narrow oval silver tinsel
WING: A very small bunch of yellow bucktail, over which is a very small bunch of red bucktail, with a bunch of yellow bucktail equal in size to the first two bunches over this. (In dressing this fly correctly, it is important to note that the lower yellow band and the red band are of the same size, but that the upper yellow band is about twice the size of the lower.)

340

Jungle cock cheeks are not called for on the official version, although they frequently are used. In Canada, the fly is dressed with feathered wings, by adding to the tinseled body a long but narrow tail of a section of a red goose feather, a yellow hackle throat, and a wing, extending to the end of the tail, of married sections of yellow, red, and yellow goose wings. The wing is double and is long but narrow. The Mickey Finn also can be dressed as a marabou streamer by substituting for the wing two yellow marabou tips and by adding shoulders of red saddle hackles, as long as the marabou. Jungle cock cheeks also are added in this dressing.

This fly was an unnamed and relatively unknown pattern until John Alden Knight, angler and author, of Williamsport, Pennsylvania, popularized it in his writings. The story of its introduction is told in letters to me from the principals. Mr. Knight says: "In the spring of 1932, when I was living in Rye, New York, I was invited to fish the waters of a trout club a short distance out of Greenwich. My host, Junior Vanderhoff, gave me a small bucktail which he had found most effective for catching stocked squaretail trout from this little stream [the Mianus River]. It delivered the goods that day; in fact, it was the only fly that did so.

"I learned from Mr. Vanderhoff that this fly was one of a series of six small bucktails in various color combinations which were at one time put out by William Mills and Son. Then, the fly was known only as the Red and Yellow Bucktail. I used the fly for a couple of years quite successfully.

"In 1936 I had occasion to go to Toronto, Canada, on business, and there I met the late Frank Cooper, of the firm of Larway, Temple and Cooper, and his friend, Gregory Clark. Mr. Cooper and a friend of his took me as a guest to the Mad River Club, where we fished for native squaretail (by 'native' I mean the unstocked variety). The club members had been taking these fish, not without a little difficulty, by the greased-line method with small salmon flies. I showed them the one pattern of [what later was to be called] the Mickey Finn that I had with me but they were not impressed. Finally I prevailed on one of them to give the fly a trial.

"On the first cast I cautioned the angler to let the fly sink three or four feet below the surface before starting the retrieve. He did so, rather lackadaisically, and then started the fly across the pool in short, well-spaced jerks. On the second cast, fished in this way, he hooked a two-pounder. I used the fly on the Mad River that afternoon and with it managed to hook and release about seventy-five trout, a feat which was unheard of on the part of a guest in those waters.

"On the way home we christened the fly the Assassin. Later that year it was rechristened by Gregory Clark, noted feature writer and war correspondent who was with the *Toronto Star.* He called it the Mickey Finn.

"In the fall of 1937 I made an arrangement with *Hunting and Fishing* magazine and with the Weber Tackle Company to write a story about the Mickey Finn for *Hunting and Fishing.* The Weber Company took a full-column advertisement in that issue and featured the fly and yours truly in it. The magazine appeared on the newsstands when the Sportsmen's Show was on in New York. In the space of two days not a single copy of *Hunting and Fishing* magazine could be found on the New York newsstands. I suppose that the name and the flashy colors struck the public fancy. In any event the fly tyers at the show were busy for the entire week tying Mickey Finns. Each night bushel baskets of red and yellow bucktail clippings and silver tinsel were swept up by the cleaning crew at Grand Central Palace, and by Friday of that week not a single bit of red or yellow bucktail could be purchased from any of the New York supply houses. It was estimated that between a quarter

341

and a half million of these flies were dressed and distributed during the course of that show. How accurate that estimate is I have no way of knowing but I do know that almost everybody encountered in the aisles had a Mickey Finn stuck in his hatband.

"During the next few months the entire facilities of the Weber Company were stretched to the breaking point in their frantic efforts to keep up with Mickey Finn orders. One outfit in Westchester actually saved itself from bankruptcy proceedings by specializing intensively in the manufacture of Mickey Finns. As matters now stand, it is a difficult thing to find any angler on any stream anywhere who has not at least one Mickey Finn in his kit. The 'Mary Pickford Trophy' for the prize brook trout taken annually in Ontario was won for the next two consecutive seasons with Mickey Finn flies. I still use the fly and find it to be a consistent fish-getter."

Gregory Clark, mentioned by Knight in his letter above, adds this: "A day or two after I named the fly the Assassin I recollected a story that recently had been published in *Esquire* magazine about how Rudolph Valentino had been killed by Mickey Finns administered to him by the resentful waiters of New York and Hollywood, and I rechristened the fly the Mickey Finn. All we did up here was to make it respectable and legitimate and to give the nameless waif an honest name."

MILLER'S RIVER SPECIAL BUCKTAIL (Plate X)   *(As dressed by the originators)*
HOOK SIZE: 4 to 12, 4X long
HEAD: Black
TAIL: Five or six golden pheasant tippet fibers extending only slightly beyond bend of hook
BODY: Wide flat gold tinsel
RIBBING: Oval gold tinsel
WING: A very small bunch of yellow polar bear hair or bucktail, over which is a very small bunch of black polar bear hair or bucktail, both extending just beyond end of the tail
SHOULDERS: Each a golden pheasant red side feather extending half as long as the wing and tied in so the lower part acts as a throat, with the upper part no higher than the wing
CHEEKS: Jungle cock, light-colored and tied in short

This very attractive fly was originated by Paul Kukonen and the late Henry Scarborough of Worcester, Massachusetts, and is named for the river in the northern part of the state. While favored as a brook trout and landlocked salmon fly, it is especially suitable for brown trout in stream or river fishing. Mr. Kukonen (a famous fly dresser) says, "Select the brightest-colored shoulder feathers and peel the sides to the correct size. Tie both sides in together by making three turns of thread around the quills and pulling them into place until the feathers just start to crush. Tie the jungle cock in short if the fly is to be cast; long if to be trolled only." This fly is one of my favorites for brook trout.

MINNOW STREAMER   *(As dressed by E. H. Rosborough)*
HOOK SIZES: 6 to 10, 3X long
HEAD: Black
TAIL: A small bunch of fibers from a cock ring-necked pheasant's tail, half as long as the hook

BODY: Wound with magenta floss, slightly tapered

RIBBING: The ribbing is narrow flat silver tinsel, and is wound on starting at the middle of the body and going forward. (Thus, the ribbing should be tied in before the body is applied.)

WING: Two sections of fibers from a cock ring-necked pheasant tail, extending to the end of the tail

This is a popular northwestern pattern.

MIRACLE MARABOU STREAMERS (Plate I)   *(As dressed by the originators)*

This series of five imitative patterns was originated by Bob Zwirz, of Ridgefield, Connecticut, and by Kani Evans, of New York, over a period of several years prior to 1963 in an effort to copy closely the five most important species of minnows common to waters in the northern states. The use of Mylar is important in the series, to provide flash along the sides rather than along the belly of each pattern. The series was introduced by Zwirz in an article in the March 1963 issue of *Field & Stream* and in other publications.

The five flies are dressed, using size 000 white silk thread, on 4X long-shanked hooks in sizes from 8 to 2. All have fully built-up heads painted with clear lacquer and tinted with colors in the dressing instructions which follow. Rather large white or cream-colored eyes with black pupils are painted on the heads. Bodies are of spun fur in colors specified in the dressings, tapered full toward the head of the fly and picked out on the sides with a dubbing needle, the picked-out hairs then being stroked backward toward the tail.

The wings are of whole marabou feather tips in colors as noted. Each feather is moistened, preferably by running it through the lips before placing it on the shank of the hook. The Mylar is cut in strips slightly less than a quarter of an inch wide (depending on the size of the fly); it is tied in horizontally on each side of the wing, extending slightly beyond the bend of the hook and cut on the lower sides toward the ends to taper upward gradually to a point. Wings are slightly longer than the Mylar. Throats and tails are a small bunch of fibers stripped from saddle hackles, slightly longer than the gap of the hook. If the Mylar does not cling to the marabou wing, it can be brushed on the inside *lightly* with clear head cement. For purposes of simplicity these general instructions are given for all the flies and are not repeated in the individual dressings. The five patterns are as dressed by the originators.

(MIRACLE MARABOU) BLACKNOSE DACE

HEAD: Top half, brown; lower half, white

TAIL: Cream or very light ginger

BODY: Antique white

THROAT: Same as tail

WING: Two whole antique white marabou feathers, over which are two whole light drab (olive toward brown tone) marabou feathers

MYLAR: Silver, with upper third painted black, the paint extending from the tip to the painted eye. Use black Magic Marker or lay a narrow (wetted) strip of black saddle hackle just over the Mylar.

343

The blacknose dace is a small member of the dace family vitally imporant as a bait for trout. It is widely distributed from the St. Lawrence southward through

Georgia and westward to the Mississippi in the more northerly latitudes. It is exceedingly common in small, clear brooks and prefers moving water but avoids the very fast riffles which harbor its cousin, the longnose dace.

(MIRACLE MARABOU) BLUEBACK SHINER

HEAD: Top half, medium blue; lower half, white
TAIL: White
BODY: White angora
THROAT: Pale cream or very light ginger
WING: Two whole white marabou feathers, over which is a Silver Doctor blue marabou feather, over which is an American flag blue marabou feather. These are topped with a few short fibers of medium green marabou at the head of the fly.
MYLAR: Silver

This shiner is also known as river bait and spottail shiner. Two other members of the *Notropis* genus, the emerald shiner and the satin fin shiner, also have a good deal of blue coloring. Though these shiners are found mainly in lakes, and especially in the larger bodies of water, they spend enough time in rivers and streams to be of great importance to trout and salmon fishermen. Members of the blue-backed group are distributed widely from James Bay (in Canada) southward through the Great Lakes and the Mississippi River system down through South Carolina. They are abundant throughout their range and are of great value as natural forage for various freshwater game fish.

(MIRACLE MARABOU) GOLDEN SHINER

HEAD: Yellowish, painted with clear lacquer
TAIL: Pale yellow
BODY: Pale yellow angora
THROAT: Orange
WING: Two pale maize marabou feathers, over which are two medium olive marabou feathers, all extending to the end of the tail of the fly
MYLAR: Gold

This shiner is best known as a bait for largemouth and smallmouth bass and pickerel. Fundamentally it is a warm-water species inhabiting ponds, lakes, and slow-moving stretches of broad rivers. Occasionally it grows to lengths of ten or twelve inches. It is widely distributed from Manitoba eastward to New Brunswick and southward all the way to Florida.

(MIRACLE MARABOU) LONGNOSE DACE

HEAD: Top half, olive; lower half, white
TAIL: Cream or very light ginger
BODY: Palest green or antique white angora
THROAT: Orange
WING: Two whole pale maize marabou feathers, over which are two medium drab olive marabou feathers, all extending to the end of the tail
MYLAR: Gold, with the upper third painted black, as described in pattern for the blacknose dace imitation.

344

This minnow, called the rock minnow in some localities, is one of the most important of bait fish. It is a lover of fast water and usually is less than four inches in length, but sometimes grows to six inches. It is a relative of the blacknose dace (*Rhinichthys attratulus*), but likes faster water than the blacknose. The longnose dace is one of the most widely distributed minnows in North America, ranging from coast to coast in the latitude of the Great Lakes and southward through North Carolina and then down to northern Mexico.

(MIRACLE MARABOU) SILVER SHINER

HEAD: Top half, drab olive; lower half, white
TAIL: Two-thirds white and one-third pale olive, mixed
BODY: White angora
THROAT: Same as tail
WING: Two whole white marabou feathers, over which are two whole dark olive marabou feathers, all extending to the end of the tail of the fly
MYLAR: Silver

This shiner is a stream dweller requiring moving water. It is plentiful in most trout streams and sometimes is mistaken for brook silversides. It ranges widely from Quebec to Saskatchewan and southward to the Gulf of Mexico. There are several subspecies, but all with the same general coloration. Many of these subspecies move into clear lakes in large schools, but streams are their primary home.

MONTREAL STREAMER   *(As dressed by Gardner Percy)*

HEAD: Black
TAIL: A long and narrow section of a red duck wing feather
BODY: Medium flat silver tinsel
RIBBING: Narrow oval silver tinsel
THROAT: A bunch of magenta hackle fibers
WING: Four magenta saddle hackles
SHOULDERS: Each a section of a brown turkey tail feather, of medium width and one-third as long as the wing

This pattern was adapted from the trout fly of the same name. There are several accepted dressings for it, no one of which can be considered authentic. Another popular dressing is:

TAIL: Scarlet impala or a small bunch of scarlet hackle fibers
BODY: Scarlet silk, medium thick
RIBBING: Narrow oval silver tinsel
WING: Fox squirrel tail

MOOSE RIVER STREAMER   *(As dressed by the originator)*

HEAD: Black
BODY: Medium flat silver tinsel
WING: A very small bunch of white bucktail, nearly as long as the hackles, over which are four golden badger neck hackles
TOPPING: Six or seven strands of peacock herl, as long as the wing
SHOULDERS: Each a golden pheasant tippet, one-third as long as the wing

345

Originated by George Munster, of Rockwood Station, Maine, in 1932 and first used on the Moose River, in Maine. Although this is a standard Maine streamer pattern, its popularity has spread to the northwest, where it is one of the few Maine streamer patterns used for all species of western trout.

MORNING GLORY STREAMER (Plate II)   *(As dressed for the originator)*
HEAD: Red, with black band
BODY: Red silk, dressed thin
RIBBING: Narrow flat silver tinsel
THROAT: White bucktail extending just beyond bend of hook, beneath which is a black silver pheasant crest feather and then a very small bunch of blue hackle fibers, both as long as the shoulders
WING: A black silver pheasant crest feather as long as the saddle hackles and curving downward over which are four bright yellow saddle hackles
SHOULDERS: Each a red macaw body feather, one-third as long as the wing
CHEEKS: Jungle cock

Originated by Carrie G. Stevens, of Madison, Maine.

MUDDLER MINNOW (Plate I)
See Chapter 14.

MYLAR-BODIED BUCKTAILS (Plates I, IV, and VIII)
See Chapter 8.

NIMROD BUCKTAIL   *(As dressed for the originator)*
HEAD: Black
BODY: Medium flat silver tinsel
RIBBING: Narrow oval silver tinsel
THROAT: A very small bunch of yellow bucktail, as long as the wing
WING: A small bunch of medium green bucktail, over which is a small bunch of black bear hair or black bucktail of the same length
CHEEKS: Jungle cock

This bucktail was originated by Henry S. Beverage, former fishing editor of the Portland (Maine) *Press-Herald,* and was dressed for him by Bert Quimby, well-known fly dresser of South Windham, Maine. The fly is preferred for landlocked salmon early in the season.

NINE-THREE STREAMER (Plate X)   *(As dressed by the originator)*
HEAD: Black
BODY: Medium flat silver tinsel
WING: A small bunch of white bucktail extending beyond the end of the hook (or hooks, if in tandem), over which are three medium green saddle hackles *tied on flat,* over which are two natural black hackles tied on upright. All hackles and the bucktail are of the same length.
CHEEKS: Jungle cock

Originated by Dr. J. Hubert Sanborn, of Waterville, Maine, to imitate a smelt,

346

which is the favorite bait fish of landlocked salmon and trout in many Maine lakes. This is one of the most popular Maine streamer flies; it got its name because Dr. Sanborn's first salmon caught with it weighed nine pounds and three ounces. The fly is often dressed on tandem hooks, used for trolling. It is also dressed on long-shanked hooks in small sizes for trout. Of it, Dr. Sanborn says: "I designed the Nine-Three to imitate a smelt as it looks in the water, with dark back, lighter below, and with silver belly and jungle cock eyes. The fly looks rough, but when wet it forms together evenly. The green feathers are tied on flat instead of edge-wise, which gives the fly a motion in the water that the others don't have. I have told many commercial fly tyers about this but nobody will tie it this way because it looks rough. We believe it the best fly year round for trout, togue, salmon, perch, and bass. I have also caught Atlantic salmon on it."

ORANGE STEELHEADER BUCKTAIL (Plate IV)   *(As dressed by the originator)*

HEAD: Black

TAIL: A small bunch of polar bear hair, dyed hot orange, rather long

BODY: Wound with silver wire of at least 22 gauge over a foundation of black thread, size B. Both thread and wire should be lacquered (see instructions in Chapter 10).

WING: A bunch of light orange polar bear hair over which is a bunch of hot orange polar bear hair, both extending to the end of the tail. The thread is passed under each of the two bunches before tying the head, in order to raise and separate the hair.

Originated by Fred A. Reed, of Nevada City, California. This fly has been one of the most popular for steelhead in the northwest and is also used extensively on inland lakes and streams for all varieties of western trout. Reed dresses it on a 1/0, 2/0, or 3/0 hook, 2X or 3X heavy, 1X or 2X long. When tied as a triple-wing fly, an additional wing of hot orange is tied in midway of the hook, which in this case has an extra-long shank. Bucktail may be substituted for the polar bear. An easier way to dress the body than to use silver wire is to use three-amp lead fuse wire covered with silver tinsel. This method is less permanent than that of using the silver wire.

ORDWAY STREAMER   *(As dressed for the originator)*

HEAD: Yellow

BODY: Medium flat silver tinsel

THROAT: A small bunch of white bucktail, slightly longer than the hook

WING: Four white neck hackles, the two of each pair curving outward to make a V

SHOULDERS: Each a red goose body feather, about one-third as long as the wing and curving outward to allow greater action to the wing

This fly is almost identical to the Colonel White, the main difference being in the splayed dressing of the feathers to give the fly greater action in the water. In this it is very similar in construction to many saltwater streamer flies and, if dressed on noncorrosive hooks, would be an excellent saltwater pattern. It was designed by George T. Ordway, of Franklin, New Hampshire, and was tied and named for him by the Percy Tackle Company, of Portland, Maine. Both the Ordway and the

347

Colonel White seem to have influenced the Bonbright Streamer, which is the most elaborate pattern in this color combination.

OWL EYED OPTIC (Plate IV)
  See Chapter 10.

PAINT BRUSH BUCKTAIL   (As dressed by the originator)
HEAD: Black
TAIL: A very small and very long bunch of dark red bucktail
BODY: Wound with silver wire, or with copper wire covered with medium flat silver tinsel (see instructions in Chapter 10)
WING: A small bunch of yellow bucktail, over which is a small bunch of bright red bucktail topped with a few hairs of brown bucktail dyed red. The wing extends to the end of the tail. In applying the two parts of the wing, turns of thread are taken under both the yellow and the red bucktail to raise the wing to an angle of about forty degrees. In the three-wing pattern the rear wing is bright red bucktail (dressed on a very long-shanked hook) and the lower part of the front wing is yellow bucktail, dressed fairly full, with the upper wing dark red bucktail. All three wings extend to the end of the long tail. Polar bear hair may be substituted for the bucktail if desired.
THROAT: (Dressed as a "spike" as explained above on page 274.) A small bunch of yellow bucktail. This generally is omitted, particularly in the two-wing dressing.

Originated by Peter J. Schwab, of Yreka, California, in 1927. This is one of a series of steelhead flies listed in the comments on the Princess Bucktail, and in notes in Chapter 7.

PARMACHENEE BEAU STREAMER (Plate IX)   (As dressed by the author)
HEAD: Black
TAIL: Two tiny sections of red-and-white swan wing feathers, married together with the red at the top. Both are rather long and thin, and curve upward. (A section of barred wood duck or mandarin duck body feather occasionally is substituted.)
BODY: Medium flat silver tinsel
RIBBING: Narrow oval silver tinsel
THROAT: One red and one white neck hackle wound on mixed as a collar and gathered downward
WING: Four white saddle hackles. (The same wing often is used as called for in the Parmachenee Belle Streamer. In this case, the shoulders and horns called for here are eliminated.)
HORNS: Each a single strand from a red macaw tail feather, nearly as long as the wing
SHOULDERS: Married red and white sections of right and left goose wing feathers, alternating white, red and white. The shoulder is one-half as long as the wing and the three married sections are equal in width.
CHEEKS: Jungle cock

A bucktail wing frequently is used in dressing this fly, as described under the

348

Parmachenee Belle Streamer. The Parmachenee Beau is a popular adaptation of the Parmachenee Belle.

PARMACHENEE BELLE STREAMER (Plate XII)

(As dressed by Fin, Fur and Feather, Ltd.)

HEAD: Black

TAIL: Two tiny sections of red-and-white swan wing feathers, married together with the red at the top. Both are rather long and thin, and curve upward.

BUTT: Three or four turns of peacock herl (optional)

BODY: Wound with dark yellow wool, picked out slightly and shaped larger toward the head

RIBBING: Narrow oval silver tinsel

THROAT: One red and one white neck hackle wound on mixed as a collar and gathered downward

WING: Two wings, one each from right and left swan wing feathers. Each wing is composed of three married sections equally wide, white, red, and white, extending just beyond the tail.

CHEEKS: Jungle cock (optional)

Many dressers dispense with the difficulty of marrying the wing feathers by putting on white wings and adding a strip of red on the outside. Bucktail wings are a later version composed of a very small bunch of white bucktail, over which is a very small bunch of red bucktail, with a very small bunch of white bucktail over this. The fly is identical with the trout fly of the same name except that it is dressed as a streamer. It was originated prior to 1890 by Henry P. Wells, of Providence, Rhode Island, and was named for Parmachenee Lake and the Parmachenee Club, in the Rangeley section of Maine. A similar fly, dressed with a silver body, is known as the Parmachenee Beau.

The Parmachenee Belle, when dressed as a bucktail, is excellent as a steelhead fly on Washington, Oregon, and California rivers. In the Eel River of California, and on many others, it is popular for Chinook salmon and for silver salmon as well as for steelhead. The hook used is heavy iron, size 1, 2X short. The tail is a small bunch of mixed red-and-white bucktail. The body and throat is as given above, with the throat long and fully dressed. The wing, in the steelhead version, is a very small bunch of red bucktail, over which is a very small bunch of white bucktail, over which is a very small bunch of red bucktail, all of equal length and very long, extending slightly beyond the end of the tail. Since the hook used is very short, part of the body may be applied as a tag, extending partway down the bend of the hook, before the tail is added. Jungle cock cheeks are not called for in the pattern but many anglers think that they enhance the value of the fly.

The Delaware Streamer, a variation of the Parmachenee Belle, which was originally called the Seth Brown, is a smallmouth bass fly first used in the headwaters of the Delaware River, in New York State. It has a gold tinsel tag, red wing-section tail, red chenille butt, heavily dressed yellow chenille body ribbed with oval gold tinsel, white hackle wing, red wing-section shoulders, and a throat of a wide red hackle palmered fairly heavily after the wing and shoulders have been applied.

349

PIN FISH

(As dressed by the originator)

HOOK SIZE: 8, 4X long (Allcock's #2811S)

HEAD: White

BODY: Fine flat silver tinsel

THROAT: A tiny bunch of red hackle fibers, very short

WING: A tiny bunch (only a few hairs) of white bucktail no longer than the hook. Over this are two gray or blue dun neck hackles, very thin, extending slightly beyond the bend of the hook.

CHEEKS: Gold eyes, or the very tips of jungle cock, or a bit of gold Mylar on each side. The head usually is painted white.

This slim fly, like the Sidewinder, is considered "fabulous" for landlocked salmon and trout. Its secret is its slimness. It was originated by the Rev. Elmer James Smith, of Prince William, New Brunswick, Canada. It imitates small bait fish, such as smelt. Both flies are excellent in stream mouths in spring when smelt are returning from spawning runs upriver.

PINK LADY BUCKTAIL *(As dressed by Herbert L. Howard)*

HEAD: Red (use red thread in tying)

TAG: Three or four turns of medium flat gold tinsel

TAIL: Seven or eight golden pheasant tippet fibers

BODY: Of pink wool, dressed medium thick and shaped slightly larger toward head. The wool is not picked out. (Silk may be substituted.)

RIBBING: Medium flat gold tinsel

THROAT: A small bunch of yellow hackle fibers, rather long

WING: A very small bunch of blue-gray bucktail, over which is a very small bunch of brown bucktail. Both extend slightly beyond the tail.

This is an adaptation of the Pink Lady dry fly originated by George M. L. La Branch, of New York City. The fly is used for brown and rainbow trout in the waters of central and northern New York State.

PINK LADY STREAMER *(As dressed by Herbert L. Howard)*

HOOK: Usually tandem in sizes 4 and 6, or on 4X long hooks, sizes 2 to 8

HEAD: Red

BODY: Oval or flat silver tinsel

WING: A sparse bunch of white nylon, over which are a few strands of peacock herl. Over this are two grizzly neck hackles, with a French blue (Blue Charm blue) neck hackle on each side, over which is an orange hackle on each side, in any desired lengths. The wing should be slim.

SHOULDERS: Each a pale gray-brown side feather, or wood duck, or dun spade hackles

CHEEKS: Jungle cock

This fly is popular in the northeast and in Canada for landlocked salmon and trout. It is said to be a cross between the Pink Lady and Carrie Stevens' Blue Devil.

The traditional Pink Lady has a red head, silver body, and a wing of white bucktail, over which are orange hackles, with grizzly hackles outside. The same shoulders and cheeks are used.

Another version of the above streamer which is widely used in Maine and offered by numerous fly dressers under the same name is:

HEAD: Red

BODY: Flat silver tinsel

350

THROAT: A small bunch of orange bucktail extending slightly beyond bend of hook

WING: A small bunch of white bucktail as long as the orange. Over this are two orange hackles with a dark grizzly hackle on each side, all of same length extending slightly beyond bend of hook.

SHOULDERS: Gray mallard, quite large (wood duck sometimes is substituted)

CHEEKS: Jungle cock

At times four red hackles are substituted for the above feathers in the wing. The pattern often is dressed in tandem with a trail hook dressed with a body of silver tinsel.

PLYMOUTH STREAMER *(As dressed by Fin, Fur and Feather, Ltd.)*

HEAD: Black

TAIL: A section of a red duck, goose, or swan wing feather, narrow and long

BODY: Medium flat silver tinsel

RIBBING: Narrow oval silver tinsel (optional)

THROAT: A Plymouth Rock hackle applied as a collar and separated to accommodate the wing

WING: Four Plymouth Rock saddle hackles

This is one of the simplest of the streamers. The body dressing is standard for many similar patterns having different throats and wings.

POLAR CHUB BUCKTAIL (Plate I) *(As dressed by the originator)*

HOOK SIZE: All sizes, 4X long

HEAD: Painted brown on top, pale green underneath

TAIL: A fairly large bunch of white polar bear hair, nearly half as long as the hook

BODY: Prepare a slightly tapered floss base and coat it with heavy lacquer. While this is wet, wind the body with large silver oval tinsel. Lacquer this and let it dry before applying the wing.

WING: Three small bunches of polar bear hair, each extending to the end of the tail; white, over which is olive green, over which is dyed brown (or brown bear hair)

CHEEKS: Jungle cock, short and wide

This freshwater or (on stainless-steel or nickel hooks) saltwater fly was originated in 1955 by E. H. (Polly) Rosborough, a prominent angler and professional fly dresser of Chiloquin, Oregon. Rosborough previously had originated the popular Silver Garland Marabou patterns, but feels that this fly is easier to cast. It represents several types of bait fish, particularly small chubs (roaches). It is a popular bucktail for many species of game fish both in fresh and in salt water.

351

PRINCESS BUCKTAIL *(As dressed by Peter J. Schwab)*

HEAD: Black

TAIL: A small bunch of hot orange polar bear hair, very long

BODY: Wound with brass or gold-plated wire (see instructions in Chapter 10, and below)

WING: A small bunch of yellow polar bear hair, over which is a small bunch of hot orange polar bear hair. In applying the two parts of the wing, turns of thread are taken under both bunches of polar bear hair to raise the wing to an angle of about forty degrees. (Bucktail may be substituted for polar bear hair in this dressing.) The wing extends to the end of the tail.

This is one of a series of wire-bodied steelhead flies popularized by Peter J. Schwab, of Yreka, California. The set includes the Bellamy, Bobby Dunn, Brass Hat, Paint Brush, Princess, Queen Bess, Van Luven, and Wood Pussy; all were originated by Schwab except for this one, which is attributed to Charles H. Conrad, of San Francisco, California. The Princess was named for Schwab's granddaughter, Ginnie Lobb. Schwab says of it, "The Princess was tied to meet the demand for a bucktail of predominantly orange hue, but note that the orange is hot orange, which is about two-thirds yellow and one-third red, and that yellow is used on the underwing. It is a beautiful fly whether tied with polar bear hair or bucktail. Although it usually is tied with a brass or gold-plated wire body, I like it best when the wire is covered with plain gold tinsel and ribbed with oval gold tinsel. Mark my words and see if some 'inventor' doesn't come along and give the fly a colored floss body and introduce it as his very own 'killer.' It is pretty with almost any kind of body."

QUEBEC STREAMER   *(As dressed for the originator)*

HEAD: Black
TAIL: A short golden pheasant crest feather, curving upward
BUTT: Three or four turns of bright yellow silk
BODY: Maroon wool, medium thick and picked out slightly
RIBBING: Narrow oval gold tinsel
THROAT: A maroon saddle hackle tied on as a collar and then gathered downward
WING: Two matched sections of purple goose or swan side feathers, covered by two matched sections of bronze mallard side feathers, all slightly longer than the tail

This fly was originated by Alexander Learmonth, of Montreal, in 1931 and dressed for him by Frier Gulline, of Fin, Fur and Feather, Ltd., of Montreal. It is one of the most popular flies for trout and bass in Canada, and it is used frequently for landlocked salmon.

QUEEN BEE STREAMER   *(As dressed by the originator)*

HEAD: Black
BODY: Medium flat silver tinsel
THROAT: A small bunch of red hackle fibers
WING: A small bunch of yellow bucktail, over which is a small bunch of white bucktail, with four medium brown saddle hackles over this. The bucktail and the hackles are of the same length, extending beyond the barb of the hook.
CHEEKS: Jungle cock

352

Originated by Dr. J. Hubert Sanborn, of Waterville, Maine, for trolling for squaretail trout in Maine lakes. The fly usually is tied on tandem hooks. With it,

Dr. Sanborn has taken many large trout, including one of seven pounds which qualified him for Maine's famous "The Big One That Didn't Get Away Club."

QUEEN BESS BUCKTAIL *(As dressed by the originator)*

HEAD: Black

TAIL: A small bunch of California gray squirrel, rather long, showing the black bar and white tip

BODY: Wound with silver wire, or with copper wire covered with medium flat silver tinsel (see instructions in Chapter 10)

WING: A small bunch of yellow bucktail, over which is a small bunch of California gray squirrel. The wing extends to the end of the tail. In applying the two parts of the wing, turns of thread are taken under the bucktail and under the squirrel to raise the wing to an angle of about forty degrees.

This is one of a series of wire-bodied steelhead flies originated by Peter J. Schwab, of Yreka, California, and is the one which he considers his favorite for taking steelhead on the Klamath River. He named it in honor of his wife. The fly usually is dressed in the double-wing version described above. In the three-wing dressing a longer shank hook is used and the rear wing is yellow bucktail with the front wings as given above. The addition of a throat of golden pheasant tippet is optional. Detailed notes on the dressings and use of these steelhead bucktails, as evolved by Mr. Schwab after many years of experience, are given in Chapter 10. He considers them of national value in taking all species of trout. His comments, as taken from his article in the June 1946 issue of *Sports Afield* magazine, are: "Previously I tied it with flat silver tinsel over a thinly padded body with a tail of barred wood duck and a spike [this differs from a throat, as explained in Chapter 10] of small paired golden pheasant tippets. In this combination it is still more beautiful. If I were limited to one bucktail it would be the Queen Bess. It is a highly successful lure for trout and bass everywhere. The only changes made in the original pattern were the substitution of wire for the yarn padding immediately upon the discovery of the added value of this feature; the substitution of the dyed goose tail after I ran out of barred wood duck; and the omission of the spike after I ran out of pheasant tippets! Just so we gave the fish that seductive flash of silver, yellow, and gray they were fully satisfied.

"We renamed the fly on the Klamath River last October 22 when five of us made big catches with it, including a ten-pounder landed by Queen Bess (my wife) herself. It had previously proved itself the full equal and the one possible superior of the Van Luven as an all-purpose all-weather fly. Use it on dark days or bright days, in clear or murky water. If the fish will strike at all, they will strike the Queen Bess."

After the above was printed, Schwab wrote me: "The only significant change has been the substitution of hair tails for feather tails, using gray squirrel in Queen Bess. The hairs outlast feathers and are equally effective."

QUILL-BODY MINNOW *(As dressed by Thomas W. Cooney)*

HOOK SIZE: 8, 3X long or longer

THREAD: Transparent for body; red for head

TAIL: The tips of two splayed white neck hackles, or bucktail of any desired length

BODY: The base of a quill shaft from a goose or other large bird. Over this is fitted a sleeve of silver Mylar tubing.

HEAD: Wound heavily with red thread, with white eye and black pupil

This pattern is reminiscent of the Quilby Minnow famous after World War II, which was made without the Mylar overbody and which sometimes was weighted by filling the quill cavity with low-melting-point alloy. This body was white, with a large red head, plus eye and pupil. The tail often was yellow hair or hackle.

To dress the Quill-Body Minnow cut a base quill section slightly shorter than the hook shank and slit the underside so it can be fitted over the hook shank. Apply the tail and wind the thread up and down the shank, then apply lacquer. Fit the quill carefully over the prepared shank and wrap it thoroughly, again applying lacquer. Slide the Mylar tubing over the wet lacquered quill. (Be sure the quill is of the right size to comfortably fit the tubing.) Tie down the Mylar at both ends, optionally leaving a longer end to fringe as part of the tail. Lacquer the body and finish the head. Include a throat, if you wish.

This quill body will float unless weighted. It is an excellent fly to use as a miniature "plug" for bass and other surface-feeding species, especially pond fish. Its dressing colors can be altered to imitate various bait fish. A nymph or other small sinking pattern could be used on a dropper for added results.

RAILBIRD STEELHEAD BUCKTAIL (Plate IV)   *(As dressed by C. Jim Pray)*

HEAD: Black

TAIL: An Amherst pheasant crest feather, very long. (A small bunch of claret or scarlet hackle fibers may be substituted. Yellow is used on some variations.)

BODY: Of claret wool, fairly thin, palmered with claret hackle, medium thick and fairly long. (This fly usually is dressed on a heavy No. 1 hook, very short.)

THROAT: A yellow hackle tied on as a collar, moderately heavily dressed and as long as the palmered claret hackle

WING: A small bunch of gray fox tail hair, very long, extending beyond the tail

CHEEKS: Jungle cock, dressed high and rather long

Originated by John S. Benn, an Irish fly dresser who emigrated to California. This popular pattern was first tied about 1900 with wings of railbird flight feathers, for which barred sprig or gadwall (taken from under the wings of the bird) later were substituted. The fly always has been famous for taking steelhead and many other species of western trout, particularly on the Eel and Klamath rivers. The above variation, adapted by C. Jim Pray, is now more popular than the earlier versions with feathered wings, and is used successfully from California to Alaska.

The early pattern of the Railbird Steelhead is as given above except that the wing is dressed with black-and-white-barred teal flank feather strips instead of the gray fox. Although there is reason to believe that the above historical facts are true, A. J. McClane, formerly fishing editor of *Field & Stream* magazine, wrote about the Railbird Steelhead as follows: "One of the old-time patterns developed in or about 1915. As with many good patterns, its conceptions came about through pure chance. Jim Hutcheson, a steelhead veteran of long standing, was fishing the Breakwater Pool on the Eel River, taking some nice steelhead on a fly called the Kate. Several friends working the same piece of water were doing very badly, and they asked Jim what fly he was using. Being in a Puckish frame of mind, he replied that the fly was a 'railbird,' local argot that referred to people who sat in front of the cigar store. He passed out samples and one fellow who wanted some extras sent the fly to Martha Benn [a San Francisco tyer of that period]. Fly-tying materials were hard to get in those days, so Martha improvised, making the fly as near to the original as she could. It was none too close, so she dubbed it the Humboldt Railbird. The Railbird has been changed many times since, but this dressing is still standard.

"There is a popular California variation of the Railbird originally tied by C. Jim Pray for Fred Bair of Klamath Lodge, which is dressed as follows: Bair's Railbird —Body: flat silver tinsel; Tail: claret or wine hackle tip; Throat: yellow hackle (eight or ten turns); Wings: barred black and white teal flank; Cheeks: jungle cock."

RAY BERGMAN BUCKTAIL   *(As dressed by the originator)*

HEAD: Black
BODY: Medium embossed silver tinsel
THROAT: A very small bunch of red hackle fibers, rather short
WING: A very small bunch of white polar bear fur over which is a very small bunch of pale yellow bucktail. The wing is sparsely dressed.
SHOULDERS: Each the tip of a red body feather from a macaw, one-third as long as the wing

Originated by Ray Bergman, of Nyack, New York, in 1925. He said of it: "At the time we called all flies of this type streamers. It would be termed a bucktail now. I do not consider this fly of any particular interest except that it was one of the early ones." The fly often is known as the R. B. Streamer.

RED FIN STREAMER (Plate XI)   *(As dressed by the originator)*

HOOK SIZE: 6 and 8, 6X long
HEAD: Black
TAIL: A very few fibers of bright red marabou, cut off vertically above end of bend of hook
BODY: Wound with pink floss, slightly tapered
RIBBING: Flat gold tinsel
THROAT: A very few fibers of bright red marabou, cut off vertically to be same size as the tail
WING: Two black saddle hackles, on each side of which is a golden badger saddle hackle, all of same length and extending slightly beyond the tail
CHEEKS: Jungle cock, small and short

This is another of the natural imitation patterns of the late Lew Oatman, of Shushan, New York. It was not included in the notes given me by Oatman, but was provided by Keith Fulsher, of Eastchester, New York, who was a close friend of Lew's and a collector of his original patterns. Fulsher says, "Lew Oatman was trying to catch the colors of the red fin shiner. Like many of Lew's patterns, it takes advantage of the lateral stripe offered by the badger saddle hackles. I think the fly was originated about 1952. Originally the tail and throat were made very long with red marabou, the throat extending beyond the hook bend and the tail streaming

355

far out behind. Later, Lew clipped both tail and throat short and preferred this later style."

RED GHOST   *(As dressed by Ray Salminen)*
HOOK SIZE: 2 to 10, 4X long, or tandem 1/0 to 4, regular, 5X strong, Mustad
  #7970
HEAD: Red
BODY: Dressed thin, with red silk, lacquered
RIBBING: Narrow flat silver tinsel, lacquered
THROAT: Four or five strands of peacock herl, under which is a very small
  bunch of red bucktail, both extending beyond the barb of the hook. The
  peacock is as long as the wing and the bucktail only slightly shorter. Under
  these is a golden pheasant crest feather nearly as long as the wing, curving
  upward.
WING: A tiny bunch of white bucktail, quite long, over which are four bright
  red saddle hackles
SHOULDERS: Each a Ripon's silver pheasant body feather, one-third as long as
  the wing, and very wide
CHEEKS: Jungle cock

This is the famous Gray Ghost in red instead of gray. It was adapted by Ray Salminen, of Acton, Massachusetts, who prefers it as a trolling fly with hooks in tandem. Ray, who dressed flies professionally, said that this fly was so popular that it accounted for fifty percent of his business, which was mainly for flies for casting and trolling for trout and landlocked salmon in northeastern lakes.

When I wrote *Streamer Fly Tying & Fishing* in 1966, its reputation for accuracy and authenticity in fly dressings was such that it was considered the "bible," which was used to settle all arguments. As has been noted, one angler, however, remarked that the Gray Ghost (reproduced herein in Color Plate II) showed the fly with a wing of a pinkish cast. (This was true and was due to the fading of the original pattern over the years.) Many anglers who copied the fly also copied the pinkish tint of the wing and found it to be at least as effective as the original. Thus the Pink Ghost was born! On the theory that if pink was better, red must be best, this adaptation became popular.

REDHEAD BUCKTAIL (Plate X)   *(As dressed by the originator)*
HOOK SIZE: 8 to 12, 4X long
HEAD: Red
TAIL: The tip of a small Amherst pheasant crest feather, about as long as the
  gap of the hook, and curving upward
BODY: Medium flat gold tinsel
RIBBING: Medium oval gold tinsel
WING: A very small bunch of white capra hair (Asian goat), over which is a very
  small bunch of red squirrel tail hair. The wing is dressed sparsely.

356

Originated by A. I. Alexander III, of Andover, Massachusetts, who says, "This resembles a multitude of small bait fish in our local trout waters, and is for casting with a light, delicate rod in small water. Small streamers and bucktails have a good record of hooking fish with me. There are no short strikes, as there can be with the big No. 2 and No. 4 patterns. When a fish grabs a small fly, he has hold of the iron."

RED HORSE STREAMER (Plate XI)   *(As dressed by the originator)*
HOOK SIZE: 6 and 8, 6X long
HEAD: Black
TAIL: The tips of two yellow hackles, on each side of which is an orange hackle, all of same length and very short
BODY: Wound with white wool, slightly tapered
RIBBING: Oval silver tinsel
THROAT: The same as the tail
WING: Two olive green saddle hackles, on each side of which is a gray-blue dun saddle hackle; all of the same length and extending well beyond the tail
CHEEKS: Jungle cock

This is another pattern by Lew Oatman, of Shushan, New York. Oatman says, "This pattern was designed for bass in waters where the red horse sucker is common. There are many rivers, in Colorado for instance, where trout feed on them."

RED PHANTOM STREAMER (Plate IV)   *(As dressed by the originator)*
HEAD: Black bead head with white eye with black pupil
TAIL: A very small bunch of red hackle fibers
BODY: Wound with bright red wool shaped heavier toward the head. The wool is not picked out.
RIBBING: Medium flat silver tinsel
WING: A bunch of strands from a white marabou feather extending just beyond the tail of the fly

Originated by E. H. (Polly) Rosborough, of Chiloquin, Oregon, in 1948. This marabou streamer is considered to be one of the best flies for steelhead and is excellent for bass and squaretail trout as well. The white marabou wing makes it extremely active and visible in the most turbid of waters. The body can be weighted if desired.

RED SQUIRREL GOLD STREAMER   *(As dressed by the originator)*
HEAD: Black
BODY: Medium embossed gold tinsel
THROAT: The tip of a very short golden pheasant crest feather dyed red
WING: A very small bunch of fox squirrel tail hair over which are two honey badger hackles of the same length as the squirrel tail hair
CHEEKS: Jungle cock, very short

This is one of a series of three streamers originated by Ray Bergman in 1933. These flies should be dressed sparsely in small sizes. They are excellent for all species of trout.

357

RELIABLE STREAMER   *(As dressed by the originator)*
HOOK SIZE: 6 to 10, 4X long
HEAD: Black

TAIL: A very small bunch of orange-red hackle fibers tied in over the tip of the barb of the hook and extending slightly beyond the bend

TAG: Two turns of flat gold tinsel. (This is continued for the ribbing.)

BODY: Wound with red chenille

RIBBING: Flat gold tinsel

THROAT: A very small bunch of orange-red hackle fibers

WING: A very small bunch of natural cream-colored polar bear hair extending just beyond the end of the tail. Over this on each side is a fairly wide wing, of the same length as the hair, cut from a golden pheasant tail feather (or feathers). This conceals most of the hair and slants upward slightly.

Originated by Paul Kukonen, professional fly dresser and fly-casting champion of Worcester, Massachusetts. Kukonen says, "This fly originally was tied with sections of turkey wing feather(s). It imitates nothing, but is exceptionally good for casting or trolling for trout, especially after the water cools off in September and October. The wing sections are matched rights and lefts, from a fourth to half an inch wide, depending on the size of the fly." Several turkey-wing flies are dressed similarly in various color combinations, such as Stewart's Hawk, which is included in this book.

ROGAN ROYAL GRAY GHOST STREAMER (Plate IX) *(As dressed by the originator)*

HEAD: Black

TAG: Four or five turns of fine silver wire, begun at the bend of the hook, forward of which are several turns of light yellow silk, dressed thin, about three times as long as the silver

TAIL: A moderately long golden pheasant crest feather, curving upward, over which is a golden pheasant crest feather dyed red and cut off to one-half the length of the one below

BUTT: Four or five turns of black ostrich herl. The butt is moderately heavily dressed.

BODY: Dressed very thin with orange silk

RIBBING: Narrow oval silver tinsel, rather widely spaced

THROAT: Five peacock herls extending to the tip of the tail, below which is a very tiny bunch of white polar bear hair of the same length, with a long golden pheasant crest feather below this curving upward with the tip touching the tip of the tail of the fly

WING: Four gray shoulder hackles extending to the tip of the tail

TOPPING: Two golden pheasant crest feathers, both laid on as one, extending to the tip of the tail to balance the throat feather. The curves of these feathers should match the curve of the wing.

SHOULDERS: Each a section of a barred wood duck feather wide enough to cover the wing and one-third as long

358   The Rogan Royal Gray Ghost is a glorification of the Gray Ghost described elsewhere in this book. This adaptation is the work of Alex Rogan, the renowned salmon-fly dresser formerly of New York City, and is an attempt by him to enhance the beauty of the famous Gray Ghost by making it as nearly like a salmon fly as possible and still having it remain technically a streamer. This fly is dressed on a 5X long Limerick hook. Rogan also dressed the Rogan Royal Gray Ghost as a

salmon fly by using a salmon hook and making the fly somewhat shorter. In this version, horns of blue macaw and cheeks of blue chatterer are added, with a few strands of a teal body feather added to the tail. The wood duck shoulder is longer, extending two-thirds the length of the wing. The head is wound with several turns of black ostrich herl, the tip of the head being painted red. Added comment about Rogan is included in the notes on the Golden Rogan Bucktail. These two of Alex Rogan's flies are more "exhibition patterns" than sensible flies to fish with.

ROSE OF NEW ENGLAND BUCKTAIL   (As dressed by Judge Lee Parsons Davis)

HEAD: Black

TAG: A few turns of narrow embossed silver tinsel

TAIL: One or two very short golden pheasant crest feathers, curving upward

BUTT: Two turns of red wool

BODY: Medium embossed silver tinsel. Just behind the head is another butt of red wool of the same size as the butt at the rear.

RIBBING: Narrow oval silver tinsel

WING: A tiny bunch of yellow bucktail, over which is a tiny bunch of red bucktail, over which is a tiny bunch of yellow bucktail, with a tiny bunch of brown bucktail over this. All four bunches are of the same size. Care should be taken not to have the fly overdressed.

CHEEKS: Jungle cock

This fly was originated by Everett Price, a guide on the Miramichi River in New Brunswick. It was introduced by Judge Lee Parsons Davis, of White Plains, New York, who wrote me: "The above dressing is in accordance with the original patterns, with some refinements which do not change the pattern. While I did not originate the fly, I do claim to have introduced it to the fly-fishing fraternity, and many years ago I got Abercrombie & Fitch Company to catalog it. I discovered it while fishing in the early spring on the Miramichi River, near Doaktown, with Howard Lyons as guide. We were not having luck with the streamer flies at hand. One morning he took me into a barber shop run by Doris O'Donnell in Doaktown. Doris was quite a character. He weighed about three hundred pounds. At the time of my introduction he had a customer half shaved in the barber's chair. Lyons asked him to tie a Rose of New England for me. He left the customer to shift for himself while he tied two of them rather roughly. When I asked him what I owed him he replied, 'If you don't catch any fish today you don't owe me anything. If you do, fifty cents will square it.' I caught many fish that day on that fly and have used it constantly ever since. Tied on No. 12 hooks, it is as successful for trout as the larger sizes are for salmon." This fly was used for black salmon (kelts) and is included here only because it is well known.

ROXY'S FOX SQUIRRELTAIL   (As dressed by Lyon and Coulson, Inc.)

HEAD: Black

TAIL: A very small bunch of fibers from a mandarin duck breast feather

BODY: Wound very thin with red silk

RIBBING: Narrow flat silver tinsel

THROAT: A medium brown saddle hackle tied on as a collar and then gathered downward. The hackle is as long as the shoulder and rather sparsely dressed.

WING: A small bunch of fox squirrel tail hair

SHOULDERS: Each a white duck breast feather, about one-third as long as the wing

This fly was originated by Roxy Roach, of Tawas City, Michigan, who died in 1947. (See notes for Roxy's Gray Squirreltail.)

ROXY'S GRAY SQUIRRELTAIL   *(As dressed by Lyon and Coulson, Inc.)*

HEAD: Black

TAIL: A very small bunch of fibers from a mandarin duck breast feather

BODY: Wound very thin with olive-yellow silk

RIBBING: Narrow flat gold tinsel

THROAT: A narrow section of a red duck wing feather about one-third as long as the wing, over which is a Plymouth Rock saddle hackle tied on as a collar and then gathered downward. The hackle should be as long as the duck feather and should be sparsely dressed.

WING: A small bunch of gray squirrel tail hair

SHOULDERS: Each a white duck breast feather, about one-third as long as the wing

This pattern was originated by Roxy Roach, of Tawas City, Michigan. Roach was recognized as one of the most skillful anglers on Michigan's Au Sable River. He developed the Roxy's Gray Squirreltail and the Roxy's Fox Squirreltail for taking the large brown trout for which the lower reaches of this river are famous. He made these bucktails both weighted and unweighted in several sizes up to size 2, always dressed on long-shanked hooks.

ROYAL COACHMAN STREAMER (Plate IX) and BUCKTAIL (Plate IV)

HEAD: Black   *(As dressed by Fin, Fur and Feather, Ltd.)*

TAIL: A narrow but long section of a bright red duck or goose wing feather

BUTT: A few turns of green peacock herl

BODY: Wound very thin with scarlet silk

THROAT: A fairly long brown hackle wound on as a collar and gathered downward

WING: Two matched sections of white swan wing feathers extending slightly beyond the tail

This streamer is an adaptation of the trout fly of the same name—for generations one of the best and most historic of English wet and dry fly patterns. The dressing given above is the most popular one for the waters of eastern Canada. The fly is less popular in the eastern United States than on western coastal rivers, where most anglers include it (or a very similar pattern) as one of the most productive for steelhead, cutthroat, and all other species of large trout. This dressing occasionally is varied by shaping the body fatter toward the head and adding a ribbing of narrow oval silver tinsel. A tail of half a dozen strands of a golden pheasant tippet may be substituted for the section of red duck wing. Four white saddle hackles or a bunch of white polar bear, bucktail, or other white hair often is used instead of the swan wing sections (which are preferred rather than duck or goose because of their longer length).

The Royal Coachman used on western rivers nearly always is a bucktail rather than a streamer. Most of the western patterns call for a shorter hook than do the eastern versions, and a second butt of peacock herl (sometimes both butts are of black chenille) usually is added behind the throat. The bucktail wing often is twice as long as the hook and is heavily dressed. Normally there is no ribbing. The tail is composed of a small bunch of red hackle fibers rather than a section of wing feather. Many anglers consider it important to add jungle cock cheeks. In 1937 a Washingtonian named Jack Wallenschlaeger began using narrow strips of chamois for the tails of the Royal Coachman and the Yellowhammer and called them Shammy tails. This variation is popular for all trout in the northwest and in British Columbia. There, Royal Coachman streamers are preferred for crappie and bass, but the bucktail patterns are almost universally used for trout.

That the Royal Coachman is adapted to midwestern waters, as well as to those in the east and west, is indicated by a letter from Harold H. (Dike) Smedley, nationally known writer, angler, and distance fly caster, who wrote me: "Michigan's one-and-only is the Royal Coachman in streamer or bucktail patterns. The trout in Michigan streams react favorably to it in all sizes and materials and no one ever has used a fly that did any better. Michigan fishermen are quite well satisfied with it."

RUSSELL'S FANCY BUCKTAIL   *(As dressed by Judge Lee Parsons Davis)*
HEAD: Black
TAG: Four or five turns of medium embossed silver tinsel
TAIL: A golden pheasant crest feather, rather long and curving upward
BODY: Medium embossed silver tinsel
RIBBING: Narrow oval silver tinsel
THROAT: A very small bunch of white bucktail, extending to the barb of the
    hook
WING: A very small bunch of white bucktail, over which is a very small bunch of
    yellow bucktail, both as long as the tail
CHEEKS: Jungle cock, rather short

This fly, also called the Yellow Peril Bucktail, is named for Jack Russell, who owned Russell's Camps, on the Miramichi River, in New Brunswick. It is one of the well-known flies for black salmon and, in Maine and Canada, is a favorite for landlocked salmon. Elsewhere, it is good for bass and pond fish. It originated on the Miramichi River, and has been used there extensively since 1920.

SABBETH STREAMER   *(As dressed by Poul Jorgensen)*
HOOK SIZE: 2 to 10, 4X long
HEAD: Black
TAIL: A small bunch of Amherst pheasant fibers
BODY: Flat silver tinsel
WING: A small bunch of white polar bear hair (or white bucktail) extending to   361
    end of tail. Over this are two white saddle hackles with a black one on each
    side, extending slightly beyond end of tail.
TOPPING: About four strands of peacock herl
THROAT: A small bunch of red hackle fibers, applied as a beard
CHEEKS: Jungle cock, fairly long

Originated by Phil Johnson. The example which was dressed by Poul Jorgensen for this book lacked the throat, but it is called for in his book *Dressing Flies for Fresh and Salt Water* (Rockville Center, N.Y.: Freshet Press, 1973).

SAGUENAY STREAMER *(As dressed by the originator)*
HEAD: Black
TAIL: About six or seven fibers from a golden pheasant tippet, medium long
BODY: Medium embossed gold tinsel
THROAT: A yellow saddle hackle tied on as a collar and then gathered
downward. The throat is dressed sparsely and is of medium length.
WING: Two yellow saddle hackles between two Plymouth Rock saddle hackles.
They should be thin and should extend slightly beyond the tail.
CHEEKS: Jungle cock, small and rather short

Robert E. Coulson, of Lyon and Coulson, Inc., of Buffalo, New York, originated this fly in 1924. With the Lord Denby and the St. Ignace it makes up a set of three patterns which were designed for taking the large eastern brook trout on the Nipigon River in the Nipigon district of Ontario. This one was named for one of Coulson's Indian guides.

ST. IGNACE STREAMER *(As dressed by the originator)*
HEAD: Black
TAIL: About six or seven fibers from a golden pheasant tippet, medium long
BODY: Medium flat gold tinsel
THROAT: A honey badger hackle, tied on as a collar and then tied downward.
The throat is dressed sparsely and is of medium length.
WING: Four honey badger hackles. They should be thin and should extend
slightly beyond the tail.
CHEEKS: Jungle cock, small and rather short

This fly was originated by Robert E. Coulson, of Lyon and Coulson, Inc. in 1924. With the Lord Denby and the Saguenay it completes a set of three which were designed for taking the large eastern brook trout on the Nipigon River. The St. Ignace was named for St. Ignace Island at the mouth of the Nipigon River, around whose shallow shores large trout frequently are found in substantial numbers.

SANBORN STREAMER (Plate IX) *(As dressed by the originator)*
HEAD: Black
TAG: Four or five turns of narrow flat gold tinsel
BODY: Medium thick, wound with black silk
RIBBING: Narrow flat gold tinsel
THROAT: A small bunch of bright yellow hackle fibers
WING: Four bright yellow neck hackles
CHEEKS: Jungle cock

Designed by Fred Sanborn, of Norway, Maine, and originally tied for him by Gardner Percy of the Percy Tackle Company, of Portland, Maine. This fly essentially is the Black Ghost dressed in yellow and gold rather than in white and silver.

362

It is one of the favorites in Maine for trout and landlocked salmon. Many anglers also consider it an excellent bass fly.

SANDERS STREAMER   *(As dressed by the originator)*
HEAD: Black
BODY: Narrow flat silver tinsel
WING: A very small bunch of white bucktail extending well beyond the hook, over which are four grizzly saddle hackles, slightly longer than the bucktail
CHEEKS: Jungle cock

This fly is closely related to the primitive and haphazard early streamers of the Rooster's Regret type discussed in Chapter 2. It originally was tied to order by the Percy Tackle Company, for Sanders Brothers Store, leading outfitters in Greenville, Maine, for the backwoods fishing country of the Moosehead region of Maine.

SATIN FIN STREAMER (Plate X)   *(As dressed by the originator)*
HOOK SIZE: 10 to 2
HEAD: Black
TAIL: A very few fibers of yellow marabou, cut off vertically just beyond the bend of the hook
BODY: Wound with white silk floss, slightly tapered
RIBBING: Flat medium silver tinsel
THROAT: A very few fibers of yellow marabou, cut off vertically to the same length as the tail
WING: Two blue saddle hackles, on each side of which is an orchid saddle hackle, all of the same length and extending slightly beyond the tail
CHEEKS: Jungle cock, small

This beautiful streamer was originated by Keith C. Fulsher, of Eastchester, New York, as a trout and bass fly. Fulsher says, "This was originated in 1957 to imitate the satin fin minnow *(Notropis whipplii)* found in many streams and lakes in New York and surrounding states. This is a valuable food for trout, bass, and other game fish and is not uncommon in warm waters. I wanted a fly with the bluish purple coloring found not only in the satin fin itself but also in many other species of bait fish. The dominant yellow fins are particular to the satin fin, and this use of marabou for fins is very effective; adding not only color but also action to the fly. This is intended to represent the satin fin in its breeding colors."

SHANG'S FAVORITE STREAMER (Plate II)   *(As dressed by the originator)*
HEAD: Black, with red band
BODY: Wound thinly with red silk
RIBBING: Narrow, flat silver tinsel
THROAT: A very small bunch of white bucktail extending beyond bend of hook, under which is a small bunch of gray hackle fibers
WING: Four or five strands of green peacock herl, on each side of which are two grizzly saddle hackles. The hackles, peacock, and bucktail all are of the same length.
SHOULDERS: Each a red duck breast feather extending one-third the length of the wing. The two red feathers should cover the bases of the four grizzly

363

hackles and they should have very pronounced outside edges.

CHEEKS: Jungle cock, not quite as long as the shoulders

This fly was originated by Carrie G. Stevens, the famed fly dresser of Madison, Maine, and was named in honor of the Hon. Charles E. (Shang) Wheeler, former state senator of Stratford, Connecticut, and at one time amateur champion duck-decoy maker of the United States. Wheeler spent many summers at Upper Dam, on Mooselookmeguntic Lake, in the Rangeley section of Maine, where Mrs. Stevens and her husband, Wallace, had their summer camp, and he assisted Mrs. Stevens with suggestions for dressing many of her flies. In fact, it was Shang Wheeler who started Carrie Stevens in the fly-tying business when she remarked that she needed more to do than mere housekeeping to occupy her. He brought to her all the basic tools and materials needed to dress streamers, remarking that, having been a milliner, she should be good at it, and would find a ready market among the sportsmen who visited Upper Dam.

SHANG'S SPECIAL STREAMER (Plate II)　　　*(As dressed by the originator)*

HEAD: Black, with red band

BODY: Flat silver tinsel

THROAT: A small bunch of white bucktail extending slightly beyond the bend of the hook

WING: Four or five strands of green peacock herl, over which are two complete jungle cock neck feathers, one on each side of the herl. The herl, jungle cock, and bucktail all are of the same length.

SHOULDERS: Each a red duck breast feather one-third as long as the wing. The red feathers are wide and have a decided edge.

CHEEKS: Jungle cock, half as long as the shoulders

This fly was originated about 1930 by Carrie G. Stevens, and was named in honor of the Hon. Charles E. (Shang) Wheeler, who gave her the idea for the fly and who used it successfully for the big eastern brook trout in the famous Upper Dam Pool in the Rangeley section of Maine. The fly is most popular in sizes 6 and 8.

SHUSHAN POSTMASTER BUCKTAIL (Plate XI)　　　*(As dressed by the originator)*

HOOK SIZE: 6 to 10, 6X long

HEAD: Black

TAIL: A very small section of a brown mottled turkey feather, as long as the gap of the hook

BODY: Wound with light yellow floss, slightly tapered

RIBBING: Flat gold tinsel

THROAT: A few fibers from a duck wing quill, dyed bright red and as long as the tail

WING: A small bunch of fox squirrel tail hair, extending to the end of the tail

CHEEKS: Jungle cock, small and short

364

This bucktail was originated by Lew Oatman, of Shushan, New York, about 1953 and named for the postmaster of the town, who was one of Lew's favorite fishing companions on the Battenkill River, which flows from Vermont into New York State.

SIDEWINDER   *(As dressed by the originator)*

HOOK SIZE: 4 to 8, 6X long (Allcock's #2811S)
HEAD: Red
BODY: Fine flat silver tinsel (a very thin body)
WING: A tiny bunch of white bucktail only as long as the hook. Over this are
   two extremely thin brown neck hackles, both with concave sides together,
   about as long as the hook, so one side of the combined feathers is dull, the
   other shiny.

This simple fly is noted as being "fabulous" for landlocked salmon and brook
trout, as well as other species. Its secret is its slimness. If very thin neck hackles
are not obtainable try the tips of saddle hackles. The fly often is used without the
body—head and wing only. It imitates small bait fish, such as smelt. The Sidewinder was originated by the Rev. Elmer James Smith, of Prince William, New
Brunswick, Canada, and is a great favorite in New England.

SILVER AND ORANGE BUCKTAIL   *(As dressed by the originator)*

HEAD: Black
BODY: Medium embossed silver tinsel. The originator prefers to dress the fly
   on a 2X short turned-down ball-eye hook with 4X head, with size B
   lacquered thread. The tinsel is tied in close to the eye, wrapped back to the
   bend of the hook, lacquered, and then wrapped back to the start of the tie.
THROAT: Several turns of a hot orange hackle. The throat is as long as the hook
   and rather heavily dressed.
WING: A bunch of Kashu pine squirrel tail hair tied over the collar of hot
   orange hackle. (Kashu pine squirrel tail is of a very pale ginger color with a
   white tip.) The wing is slightly longer than the hook.

Originated by Fred A. Reed, of Nevada City, California. This is primarily a
steelhead fly for northern California and Oregon, but it also is popular for all other
species of trout. The wing may be tied with bucktail of a similar color. The fly is
also very successful if the wing is left off entirely.

SILVER DARTER STREAMER (Plate XI)   *(As dressed by the originator)*

HOOK SIZE: 4 to 12, 2X to 6X long
HEAD: Black
TAIL: A very small section from a silver pheasant wing quill, slightly longer
   than the gap of the hook
BODY: Wound with white floss, slightly tapered
RIBBING: Medium narrow flat silver tinsel
THROAT: Two or three fibers of a peacock sword feather, reaching about
   halfway to the point of the hook and curving toward it
WING: Two white-edged badger saddle hackles, extending slightly beyond the
   end of the tail
CHEEKS: Jungle cock, small and short

365

This is another of Lew Oatman's patterns. In sending it to me he said, "This
imitates the Cayuga minnow and is very effective for brook, brown, and rainbow
trout. It does well in heavily fished streams throughout the season, even in low,
clear water, and does equally well in wilderness areas. I often have taken trout with

it when I couldn't seem to pick a dry fly rising trout would strike. It should be a very slim fly in the water, and I like to use the slenderest hackles available."

SILVER DEMON BUCKTAIL   *(As dressed by the originator)*

HEAD: Black

TAIL: A very small bunch of orange hackle fibers of moderate length

BODY: Thinly wound with narrow oval tinsel, several turns of which are taken below the tail to act as a tag. On extra-long-shanked hooks, flat silver tinsel and silver ribbing may be used.

THROAT: Several turns of an orange saddle hackle applied as a collar and tied back but not gathered downward. The hackle is glossy, stiff, and of moderate length.

WING: A medium-sized bunch of badger hair extending slightly beyond the end of the tail. (Ground squirrel tail hair may be substituted and is to be preferred over gray squirrel because it is stiffer and more wiry. In the feather-winged version, sections of barred gadwall feathers are used. The two matched sections are fairly narrow and curve upward, extending between the end of the hook and the end of the tail.)

This is the steelhead dressing of the Silver Demon and is very similar to the Silver and Orange Bucktail. For additional information, see notes for the (Cains River) Silver Demon Streamer.

SILVER GARLAND MARABOU STREAMER (Plate VII)   *(As dressed by the originator)*

HEAD: Black (large black optic heads with white eyes and red, black, or orange pupils often are used)

BODY: Of special silver tinsel, as described below

WING: Two matched white marabou feathers, considerably longer than the hook

TOPPING: Four greenish blue ostrich herls, over which are four black ostrich herls

SHOULDERS: Four yellowish green ostrich herls on each side. All the ostrich herl is as long as the marabou.

CHEEKS: Jungle cock, rather long

This unusual type of dressing was originated by E. H. (Polly) Rosborough, of Chiloquin, Oregon, in 1936. The Silver Garland is one of the most famous and most productive of all marabou streamers, due principally to the unusual construction of the body. The body is fairly fat and heavy, dressed with tinsel (over a weighted body if desired) which is formed into a chenille-like fringe similar to Christmas-tree tinsel. This provides a brushlike metal body which should be lacquered to keep it bright. The value of the body is due largely to the added flash of reflected light which this type of tinsel provides. This makes the fly especially productive in high or discolored waters.

366

Silver Garland Marabous can be dressed with copper tinsel bodies, although the silver is more popular. The one described above is recommended for large trout especially, and particularly in chub-infested waters. The fly is tied with a large variety of wing color combinations, some of which are as follows:

For Trout and Steelhead
1. White marabou wing and black ostrich-herl topping
2. White marabou wing with black over olive green ostrich-herl topping
3. Hot orange marabou wing with black ostrich-herl topping
4. Hot orange marabou wing with black over white ostrich-herl topping (dressings 3 and 4 are especially recommended for steelhead)
5. An all-black marabou wing with peacock-herl topping

For Bass and Other Spiny-Rayed Fish
6. Yellow marabou wing with black ostrich-herl topping
7. White marabou wing with royal blue ostrich-herl topping
8. White marabou wing with seal brown ostrich-herl topping

For Chinook, Silver, Landlocked, and Atlantic Salmon and All
Other Saltwater Fish Which Feed on Herring and Smelt
9. White marabou wing with royal blue over Silver Doctor blue ostrich-herl topping

<u>SILVER MINNOW</u> (The Incredible) (Plate I)   *(As dressed by Maury Delman)*
HEAD: Built up to minnow-head shape with oo nylon thread, painted silver. Small painted black eyes, with yellow dot in center.
TAIL: A small bunch of gray stripped mallard herl or grizzly hackle
BODY: Wound tightly with lead wire. The wire body is covered and tapered with silk floss of any color. This is covered completely by a double overlay of embossed flat silver tinsel or silver Mylar piping.
THROAT: A small bunch of long crimson rooster hackles, the longest ones extending to the point of the hook
WING: A very small bunch of white bucktail, over which is a very small bunch of blue (dyed) impala hair. Over this is a gray mallard flank feather tied on flat on top of the hair so that it surrounds all of the hair. The elements of the wing extend half again as long as the hook. Recommended hook size is 6, 2X long.

Tie the tail material onto the shank of the hook just ahead of the barb. Wrap the shank with lead wire, leaving it bare for an eighth of an inch at the end and a quarter of an inch back from the eye. This will provide for a tapered body. Silk floss is wound on to give an underlay for a smooth wrap of silver tinsel or piping. Double-wind the tinsel overlay, starting from the eye, wrapping spirally to the tail and returning to the eye. The hair is sparsely tied in as above. The mallard flank feather is laid on top of the hair and folded in at the sides. Do this so the feather won't flare out at the sides. Tie in the red rooster throat. Finally, wind on a full head of thread. Lacquer the head three times. Then apply two coats of silver paint. Paint on eyes as above.

This fly was dressed by Maury Delman, prominent outdoor writer from Flushing, New York, as tied by its originator, Al Giradot, of Detroit, Michigan. In an article in the March 1965 issue of *Sports Afield,* Maury says, "Properly fished, the Silver Minnow is the quintessence of deadliness. In Labrador I coaxed landlocked salmon from their white-water lies when all other flies failed completely. In Iceland the fly evoked hard strikes from sea trout. Manitoba's heralded God's River gave up lunker brook trout in heavy water. It has given me furious action from small-mouths and educated trout in eastern streams—and even walleyes. When Al first tied the fly he did not weight the body, so the streamer momentarily floated, requiring vigorous stripping-in to sink it. He wanted a minnow mimic that would travel the route of natural bait. By adding the lead and tinsel, he got precisely what he wanted."

SILVER MINNOW BUCKTAIL (Plate VII) *(As dressed by Don C. Harger)*
HEAD: Red. The head is properly dressed by adding a hollow brass bead painted red with a small yellow eye with a red pupil.
BODY: Medium flat silver tinsel over a thin padding of a base of fine wire
RIBBING: Medium oval silver tinsel
THROAT: A few fibers of a red hackle, of medium length
WING: A very small bunch of white bucktail, over which is a small bunch of gray squirrel tail hair of the same length
TOPPING: Four or five strands of peacock herl as long as the wing

This fly originated in British Columbia, where it was tied to imitate sea-run bait fish, particularly the candlefish and the smelt. It is particularly effective in estuaries and salt chucks in Washington and British Columbia rivers for sea-run cutthroat, silver salmon, and steelhead. The fly is dressed in several variations in the sections where it is most used, but this basic dressing usually remains the same. Some anglers eliminate both the bead head and the throat. Others eliminate the gray squirrel part of the wing and use a greater amount of peacock herl. The fly is almost identical with several eastern dressings, and its similarity in appearance to a bait fish should make it universally successful.

SILVER SALMON STREAMER *(As dressed by the originator)*
HEAD: Black
TAIL: The tips of two bright yellow saddle hackles, very thin and of moderate length
BODY: Dressed very thin with medium yellow silk
RIBBING: Medium flat silver tinsel
THROAT: Applied as a collar; several turns of a bright yellow saddle hackle of moderate width, separated at the top to accommodate the wing
WING: Four thin white saddle hackles
CHEEKS: Jungle cock of moderate length, dressed high

This fly was originated by Horace P. Bond, of Bangor, Maine, for fishing for landlocked salmon and squaretail trout in Maine lakes. Since it usually is used for trolling it normally is dressed on a very long hook. Another very similar Maine streamer is the Silver Ghost, which has a body of flat silver tinsel ribbed with oval silver tinsel but which otherwise is identical to this one. The Silver Ghost was first tied by Gardner Percy, of Portland, Maine, in a desire to try the Black Ghost streamer with a silver body.

368

SILVER TIP BUCKTAIL (Plate X) *(As dressed by the originator)*
HOOK SIZE: 6 or 8, 4X long
HEAD: Black, with a fine red lacquered ring at the base
TAIL: A strand of bright red wool, cut off above the bend of the hook

BODY: Four to six strands of fine gold oval tinsel tied in together and wrapped solidly up the hook shank. The body should be fairly thin.

WING: A small bunch of silver tip grizzly bear hair extending slightly beyond the end of the tail. The hair should be well marked with a dark brown base and light amber tips. The wing should be sparsely dressed.

Originated by Keith C. Fulsher, of Eastchester, New York. Fulsher says, "This fly was originated in 1955, and two things are dominant about it. The bright yellow tinsel, put on in this fashion, provides many little reflecting surfaces to make the fly glitter brightly in the water. The silver tip grizzly hair with the light translucent tips gives the impression of a little minnow's tail flicking as it swims. The fly is designed to imitate general species of bait fish. The name comes from the wing material used. The red added to the head provides a flash of gill coloring. This is an early-season fly for discolored water. It has been successful throughout the northeast and middle west. It is a good salmon fly when dressed on salmon-wet-fly hooks, with a collar of sparse yellow hackle added."

SKYKOMISH SUNRISE BUCKTAIL   *(As dressed by the originator)*

HEAD: White

TAG: Three or four turns of narrow flat silver tinsel

TAIL: A very small bunch of red hackle fibers, over which is a very small bunch of yellow hackle fibers, rather long and not mixed

BODY: Fairly heavily wound with red chenille

RIBBING: Narrow flat silver tinsel

THROAT: Three or four turns each of a red and a yellow hackle, wound on mixed as a collar and not tied downward. The hackles are fairly wide.

WING: A small bunch of white polar bear hair, slightly longer than the tail and dressed fairly high on the hook. The hook should be 2X long.

George McLeod of Seattle, Washington, originated this fly in 1938, and named it for the Skykomish River in northern Washington. In the opinion of many older Washington anglers this fly is more successful than all of the other patterns combined for steelhead and cutthroat trout. McLeod has taken several summer-run steelhead of over twenty pounds on it. In recent years its popularity has been dimmed by newer patterns, not necessarily any more effective.

SOO FLY BUCKTAIL   *(As dressed by the originator)*

HEAD: Black

TAG: Narrow flat gold tinsel. The tag is rather long, extending partway down the bend of the hook.

TAIL: The tips of two red hackles, rather long and splayed outwardly

BODY: Rear two-thirds is medium embossed silver tinsel. Front third is wound with peacock herl.

THROAT: Two turns of a red hackle, applied as a collar and gathered downward

WING: A bunch of yellow bucktail, over which is a bunch of black and red bucktail, mixed equally. The wing extends to the end of the tail and is rather sparsely dressed so that it will sink rapidly.

CHEEKS: Jungle cock

369

Originated by Earl Leitz, of Sault Ste. Marie, Michigan, for taking the large rainbows, or "Soo" trout, in the rapids of the St. Mary's River at the outlet of Lake Superior. Since these trout are large, these flies usually are dressed on No. 2 hooks. Ray Bergman, who fished with Leitz, stated in his columns in *Outdoor Life* that the Soo Fly is dressed in various ways, and he gives the following dressing as one of the variations:

BUTT: Yellow chenille (like an egg sac). (Although Bergman does not mention it, there probably is a tag of narrow flat gold tinsel, since many of the other flies used in these waters have it.)

TAIL: Tips of two barred Plymouth Rock hackles, dyed a deep Montreal claret. They should be rather long and splayed outwardly.

BODY: Medium embossed silver tinsel

RIBBING: Medium flat silver tinsel

WING: A bunch of claret red bucktail, over which is a bunch of yellow bucktail, over which is a bunch of brownish or faded black bucktail

CHEEKS: Jungle cock

Leitz states that the first dressing is the most popular of the several flies preferred for fishing the St. Mary's rapids. Other popular flies for this purpose are the Bali Duck Streamer, the Leitz Bucktail, and the Scotty. The second dressing given above is very similar to the Rose of New England, which also should be a good fly for these waters.

SPENCER BAY SPECIAL STREAMER (Plate X)   *(As dressed by the originator)*

HEAD: Black

TAIL: Eight or ten strands of a golden pheasant tippet, long enough to show a black band

BODY: Very thin, of medium flat silver tinsel

RIBBING: Narrow oval silver tinsel

THROAT: Applied as a collar; a pale yellow hackle forward of which is a small number of turns of a Silver Doctor blue (light blue) hackle, the two being moderately bushy and of average width. The collar is separated at the top to accommodate the wing.

WING: Two light blue saddle hackles with a cream badger neck hackle on each side. The badger hackles have a very pronounced black band, very wide at the butt.

CHEEKS: Jungle cock of moderate length, dressed high

The fly was originated by Horace P. Bond, of Bangor, Maine, for trolling for landlocked salmon. It was named in honor of Amory Houghton, owner of the Spencer Bay Camps on Moosehead Lake, in Maine. The fly is a favorite for land-locked salmon and big trout in Maine waters. Usually it is dressed on a very long hook.

370

SPRUCE STREAMER (Plate IV)   *(As dressed by E. H. Rosborough)*

HEAD: Black

TAIL: Four or five peacock sword fibers, about half an inch long when dressed on an average-sized hook (regular-length hooks should be used for this fly)

BODY: Rear quarter is red wool, not picked out, but built up toward the peacock. Front three-quarters is wound with peacock herl, rather heavily dressed.

THROAT: A silver badger hackle, wound on as a collar, fairly bushy, applied after the wing has been put on

WING: Two silver badger hackle tips, tied on back to back so that they splay out in the form of a V, extending slightly beyond the tail of the fly

The Spruce, listed prominently among northwestern trout patterns, is a fly of the Improved Governor type, ascribed to Albert and/or Clarence Milo Godfrey, who lived in Seaside, Oregon. It was designed in 1918 or 1919 primarily to take the summer and fall runs of cutthroat trout ("harvest" or "blueback" trout) in Oregon streams. The Spruce probably was made to imitate an insect found in stands of Oregon spruce timber, but it is now considered to be a streamer fly, regardless of the original reason for its dressing. While it is most successful as a cutthroat fly, it also is favored for brown and rainbow trout. Originally, the fly was called the Godfrey Special or Godfrey Badger Hackle. Regarding this, a California gentleman who knew Godfrey wrote to the fishing editor of *Field & Stream*: "This is a fly I have fished with great success for all trout, including steelhead. I found it especially deadly on Yellowstone cutthroat. I tied the fly for years and called it the Godfrey Special after its originator. I began to see a great many of them appearing in Portland, where they were sold for the coastal streams. Fishing Paulina Lake several years ago I met an angler using what I had heard of but had not seen up to that time—a Spruce fly. It was the Godfrey badger hackle tip wing fly. This last season, fishing the lower Klamath, a native asked me to tie him a pattern called the Kamloops. He had to go to Orich to get a sample. It was the Godfrey Special, or Spruce. He swore it would take twice as many 'creek' trout (cutthroat) as any other fly."

A variation of the Spruce Streamer is the Spruce Bucktail, tied with a small bunch of badger hair instead of with a badger hackle wing. The rest of the dressing is the same. A variation known as the Silver Spruce is used primarily for brown trout and rainbows, and is identical except that it has a silver tinsel body instead of the red wool and peacock. It first was tied by E. H. Rosborough of Chiloquin, Oregon, at the suggestion of Al Kellogg, manager of the Meier and Frank Company of Portland, Oregon. This fly, tied with a wing consisting of a small bunch of badger hair, of the same length as the feather wing, is popular on the Nehalem, Trask, and Nestucca rivers of Oregon. White-tipped squirrel tail occasionally is substituted for the badger. Then it is known as the Silver Spruce Badger.

Another variation is the Red Spruce, tied with a red wool body, fairly heavy but not picked out, and ribbed with narrow, flat silver tinsel. Other parts of the dressing are the same as the Spruce, except that a red hackle is placed inside the badger hackle on each side of the divided wing. All hackles are of the same length. Regarding it, E. H. Rosborough, who is famed as a dresser of western flies, wrote me: "The Red Spruce was designed for eastern brook trout. I first saw it at the Meier and Frank Company of Portland, Oregon, in the summer of 1943. I believe it was brought out by a husband-and-wife combination working under the name of Smith-Ely, of Blue River, Oregon, who at that time furnished most of Meier and Frank's flies. I am responsible for the Silver Spruce in both the feather- and hair-wing versions. A lot of tyers will use golden badger hackle in all of its color variations when the silver is hard to get, but not me! There are too many variations

371

now. The value of the Red Spruce is not as high as the others, except possibly for eastern brook trout.

"Although the Spruce was tied primarily for large sea-run cutthroat, it does very nicely on steelhead. It is dressed in sizes all the way down to No. 12 for trout fishing. In size 10 on a long-shank hook it took many steelhead on the Klamath during the 1946 season. The action of the turned-out wings on a slow, jerky retrieve makes it deadly in still-water stretches."

STEVENSON'S SPECIAL BUCKTAIL   *(As dressed by Don C. Harger)*

HEAD: Red
TAIL: A small bunch of guinea hen body feather fibers dyed red
BODY: Rear half is medium oval gold tinsel. Front half is wound with black chenille.
THROAT: A guinea hen body feather applied as a collar and tied back but not gathered downward. The throat is fairly long and rather heavily dressed.
WING: A bunch of fine yellow bucktail, extending to the end of the tail and dressed rather high on a large steelhead hook 2X long
CHEEKS: Jungle cock (optional)

The fly was originated by Clive N. Stevenson, of Roseburg, Oregon, who has taken a large number of record steelhead with it on several western coastal rivers.

STEWART'S HAWK STREAMER (Plate X)   *(As dressed by the originator)*

HOOK SIZE: 6 or 8, 5X or 6X long
HEAD: Black
TAIL: A very small bunch of white bucktail, about half the length of the hook shank
BODY: Embossed silver tinsel
THROAT: A very small bunch of red hackle fibers, about half as long as the hook
WING: A very small bunch of medium blue polar bear hair or bucktail extending to the end of the tail. On each side and joined over the front are two fairly wide sections of gray-brown and white hawk wing feathers selected for good markings. These are pointed at the ends and extend to the end of the tail. (Since most species of hawks are protected in most regions, turkey wing sections or other large wing feathers of similar color may need to be substituted.)
CHEEKS: Jungle cock, very small

This fly was originated by Austin S. Hogan, of Cambridge, Massachusetts, and named for his friend and angling companion Clarence "Cak" Stewart, of Fonda, New York. Mr. Hogan says, "This fly has been used very successfully for small-mouth bass in the north Atlantic states. The wing feathers, selected for softness, move inward and outward on intermittent retrieve. A similar pattern calls for a yellow chenille body with wing of white bucktail covered by sections of white goose or swan wing feathers." (Another similar fly of this type is the Reliable.)

372

SUMMERS GOLD BUCKTAIL   *(As dressed by Herbert L. Howard)*

HEAD: Black
TAIL: The tip of a golden pheasant tippet, tied in just below the second black band

BODY: Medium flat gold tinsel

THROAT: A red hackle feather, tied on as a collar, medium heavy and rather long

WING: A small bunch of white bucktail, over which is a small bunch of medium brown bucktail, both slightly longer than the tail

Dr. Orrin Summers, of Boundbrook, New Jersey, first tied this fly in 1912 and first used it on the Raritan River, near Nauright, in New Jersey. It is a universally useful bucktail for all freshwater game fish in all parts of the country, including bass and panfish, and for many saltwater species as well.

SUNFISH STREAMER   *(As dressed by the originator)*

HOOK SIZE: 6, 4X long

HEAD: Black

TAIL: A golden pheasant topping over which is a very small and shorter bunch of red hackle fibers

BODY: Yellow floss

RIBBING: Palmered dark furnace hackle

WING: A very small bunch of mixed red, green, and yellow bucktail extending to end of red part of tail, over which are two orange saddle hackles with one dark furnace hackle on each side, extending slightly beyond end of tail

THROAT: Two or three turns of a very wide dark furnace hackle

CHEEKS: Jungle cock, fairly long

This excellent streamer was originated by Poul Jorgensen, author of *Dressing Flies for Fresh and Salt Water,* and other books on fly dressing. Poul is one of the world's most outstanding fly dressers. He lives in Columbia, Maryland.

SUPERVISOR STREAMER (Plate XII)   *(As dressed by the author)*

HEAD: Black

TAIL: A thin section of red wool, rather short

BODY: Medium flat silver tinsel

RIBBING: Narrow oval silver tinsel (optional)

THROAT: A small bunch of white hackle fibers (optional)

WING: An extremely small bunch of white bucktail, over which are four very light blue saddle hackles. The bucktail is nearly as long as the hackles, both extending well beyond the tail.

TOPPING: Six or seven strands of peacock herl, as long as the wing (optional—see below)

SHOULDERS: Each a pale green shoulder hackle, two-thirds as long as the wing and fully as wide. (Correct shoulder hackles are short and stubby, with a creamy green center and a brighter green edge. They should be extremely pale in color.)

CHEEKS: Jungle cock

373

The Supervisor usually is considered to be one of the most important of the Maine-type streamer flies, especially for trout and landlocked salmon in waters where smelt exist. The idea for its dressing was conceived by Warden Supervisor Joseph S. Stickney, of Saco, Maine, while fishing at Moose Pond in Maine in 1925. Warden Supervisor Stickney originated it to imitate the finger smelt which the large squaretail (eastern brook) trout were pursuing at the time. The fly is named for Stickney's title. Since Stickney did not dress his own flies, he had other dressers make them for him, and he gave several of these to me; I was his annual fishing companion until his death in 1945.

Originally, Stickney had the Supervisor dressed without peacock topping. Later, he added this, calling the fly the Supervisor Imperial. This new version was so much more successful than the former one that Stickney chose to discard the former and to call the Supervisor Imperial simply the Supervisor. He preferred ribbing for dark days or murky water, but thought it too bright for casting on the sunlit clear water of lakes. Some of the flies he used were tied with the white throat and some were not. He preferred the fly sparsely dressed to more closely imitate the conformation of a smelt, and he was very particular about the color and shape of the shoulders.

It is probable that this fly was an original creation of Stickney's, although it may have been influenced (or vice versa) by one of the Hardy Brothers Terror Streamers, which were dressed similarly except that the shoulders were of barred gray hackles and there was no peacock, bucktail, or jungle cock. In England, the Terror Streamer is favored for salmon, sea trout, and the trout of inland waters.

TAP'S TIP BUCKTAIL   *(As dressed by the originator)*
HOOK SIZE: 4 to 8, 2X to 6X long
HEAD: Black (built up to conform to size of body); white eye with black pupil
BODY: Silver Mylar piping
WING: Four very small bunches of bucktail, white under green under red under black, all of the same length; half again as long as the hook

This simple but effective bucktail is one of the favorites of the famed author, angler, and gunner H. G. "Tap" Tapply, of Alton, New Hampshire, who is known to every sportsman as one of the editors of *Field & Stream.* It is named for his monthly column in that magazine, "Tap's Tips." It is an excellent fly for trout, landlocked salmon, and smallmouth bass. Tied on noncorrosive hooks, it also is an excellent fly for many species of saltwater game fish.

TARBOO SPECIAL   *(As dressed by the originator)*
HOOK SIZE: 4, 3X long, turned-up eye, standard salmon
HEAD: Black
BODY AND TAIL: Medium silver Mylar tubing, twice as long as the body. Fray the Mylar ends after tying the tubing down over the barb to form the tail.
THROAT: A sparse bunch of white polar bear hair, or bucktail, as long as the tail
WING: A sparse bunch of polar bear hair dyed olive, extending slightly beyond end of tail

374   Originated about 1976 by Steve Raymond, of Seattle, Washington, to imitate the three-spined stickleback, a common food fish in the estuaries of Puget Sound and the British Columbia coast. This pattern was designed especially for sea-run cutthroat trout, but is effective for other saltwater varieties. Polar bear hair gives a lifelike sheen and sparkle, but substitutes can be used. The tubing gives the fly

a substantial look, and its sparseness provides compactness for casting into the wind.

THOR BUCKTAIL (Plate IV)   *(As dressed by the originator)*

HEAD: Black
TAIL: A very small bunch of rather stiff orange hackle fibers of medium length
BODY: Medium thick, wound with dark red chenille
THROAT: Several turns of a mahogany saddle hackle, applied as a collar and tied back but not gathered downward. The hackle should be stiff, glossy, and rather long.
WING: A medium-sized bunch of white bucktail, extending to the end of the tail. White polar bear hair often is used.

This fly, one of the most famous of western steelhead patterns, was originated by C. Jim Pray, of Eureka, California, on Christmas Day of 1936. It is tied both as a bucktail and in the more conventional short pattern. The Thor first was used by Walter Thoreson, also of Eureka, who took an eighteen-pound steelhead with it to win first prize in the 1936 *Field & Stream* contest (western rainbow fly division) on the day it first was tied. It was named from the first four letters of Mr. Thoreson's name. In 1938, also on Christmas Day, Gene Sapp, of Ferndale, California, took a seventeen-and-three-quarter-pound steelhead with the Thor to win *Field & Stream's* first prize for that year.

Pray wishes to make it clear that "Harry Van Luven [see Van Luven Bucktail] tied a fly very closely resembling this pattern probably earlier than I tied the Thor. It was essentially the same except that it had a silk body instead of chenille and it was spiraled with oval silver tinsel. In my shop the Thor outsells any other fly for most streams, particularly the Klamath. It has traveled widely through the nation and in Alaska and British Columbia; wherever large fish are to be found."

THUNDER CREEK BUCKTAIL SERIES (Plate I)

The eight patterns in this unusual series originated by Keith C. Fulsher, of Eastchester, New York, are described, with dressing instructions, in Chapter 8.

TRI-COLOR BUCKTAIL   *(As dressed by the originator)*

HOOK SIZE: 2 to 8, 4X long
HEAD: Black
BODY: Flat silver tinsel
RIBBING: Oval silver tinsel
THROAT: A small bunch of straight white bucktail extending slightly beyond bend of hook
WING: A small bunch of straight orange bucktail, over which is a small bunch of straight green bucktail, both the same length as the white
CHEEKS: Jungle cock

375

This fly was originated about 1955 by Bud Wilcox, formerly a game warden and guide of Rangeley, Maine. The colors imitate a crayfish—back shell of green, orange claws, and white belly. It is a popular pattern in the Rangeley region. It should be fished close to the bottom in areas where crayfish should be.

TROUT FIN STREAMER (Plate X)   (*As dressed by the originator*)

HEAD: Black

TAIL: A section of a red goose or swan wing feather, long, thin, and curving upward

BODY: Medium flat silver tinsel

RIBBING: Fine silver cord

THROAT: A cream badger hackle wound on as a collar and gathered downward. The throat is rather long and of moderate fullness.

WING: Two opposite matched sections of married swan or goose wing feathers, fairly soft, in red, black, and white. The lower part of the wing is red, married to black in the middle and white on top. The red is twice as wide as either the black or the white. The wing extends just beyond the end of the tail.

CHEEKS: Jungle cock, fairly short. (This is optional and usually is not included.)

There are three streamers in the Trout Fin series: the Harlequin, in blue, black, and white; the Trout Fin, as dressed above; and a second version of the Trout Fin, with orange substituted for the red. All were originated by B. A. Gulline, of Fin, Fur and Feather, Ltd. The orange and red versions first were tied in 1929 for B. A. Gulline by Frier Gulline. The orange version differs from the red version in that it has a throat of red hackle fibers rather than the cream badger. Gold cord occasionally is substituted for the silver as a ribbing, and a few turns of either may be added as a tag. Anglers with whom these patterns are favorites prefer the red version for fishing in Canada, in the belief that it more closely approximates the color of the Canadian trout, which often are called "red trout" because of their high coloration. The orange version usually is used in the United States, where the trout ordinarily are less pronounced in color.

The proportions of the wings are highly important. The red (or orange) should be as thick as both the black and white together, and the black and white should be equal in thickness, so that the married wing is composed of one-half red (or orange), one-fourth black, and one-fourth white. Slightly more or less of the red or orange may be used in proportion if the color of the feather is much lighter or darker than normal.

Since a brook trout's fin has been a popular bait for many years, it is natural that others would imitate it in flies. Thus, Robert H. Cavanagh, Jr., of Woburn, Massachusetts, independently developed an almost identical pattern for fishing at Grand Lake Stream, Maine. His version calls for a tag of three or four turns of yellow floss, a tail of a short golden pheasant crest feather, curving upward, a butt of peacock herl, and a throat of guinea hen hackle. Other elements are the same. Those with the skill and patience to handle married wings will find this fly so beautiful that it seems a shame even to get it wet. Bob Cavanagh dressed a few for me several years ago. Two remain in my fly book and, while chewed almost beyond recognition by scores of trout, they are still highly effective.

376

TROUT PERCH STREAMER (Plate XI)   (*As dressed by the originator*)

HOOK SIZE: 2 to 10, 3X long

HEAD: Gray-tan, to match the upper wing

TAIL: A very small bunch of fibers from a blue dun hackle, slightly longer than the gap of the hook

BODY: Wound with white floss, slightly tapered

RIBBING: Medium flat silver tinsel

THROAT: The same as the tail, and of the same length

WING: A small bunch of summer sable tail hair, extending to the end of the tail. Over this are two fibers of pink dyed ostrich, of the same length. On each side of the hair and ostrich is a chinchilla saddle hackle of the same length.

CHEEKS: Jungle cock, small and short

This imitator pattern was designed by Lew Oatman, of Shushan, New York. He says, "Pike perch will feed heavily on schools of trout perch, especially during the spawning season when these little minnows run toward and into the creeks. This pattern, the Ghost Shiner, and the Silver Darter are fine when fly-fishing for the pike perch."

TWO-EGG SPERM FLY (WHITLOCK)   *(As dressed by the originator)*

HOOK SIZE: 2 to 8, Atlantic salmon (Mustad #3658D)

HEAD AND THREAD: Herb Howard's fluorescent orange

TAG: Fine flat gold Mylar, from above barb to point of hook

TAIL: A golden pheasant crest feather extending slightly beyond bend of hook

BUTT (REAR): Fluorescent pink chenille wound on to form a ball, like a salmon egg

BODY: Fine flat gold Mylar, about as long as the chenille egg is wide

BUTT (FORWARD): Same as rear butt, applied close to head

THROAT: One turn of a hackle of same color as the chenille; fairly long and very sparse

WING: One tip of a white marabou feather, extending to end of tail

This rather unorthodox pattern was originated by Dave Whitlock, of Cotter, Arkansas, about 1963 for fishing in Alaska and the Pacific northwest where salmon, steelhead, and trout feed on salmon eggs. It has a streamer wing and usually is fished along the bottom on a dead drift. The dressing incorporates an improvisation of the milt or skein of the egg sacs, as well as the eggs, and has met with such great success that it has been written about in *Fly Fisherman* magazine and other publications. The fly also has taken Atlantic salmon as well as salmon and steelhead in the Great Lakes fishery.

Since variations depend on the colors of the natural eggs, the fly's butts and throat (or collar) can be dressed in bright, dull, or fluorescent orange, yellow, or green. It sometimes is weighted with several turns of lead wire.

UMPQUA SPECIAL BUCKTAIL (Plate IV)   *(As dressed by Don C. Harger)*

HEAD: Red

TAIL: A very small bunch of white bucktail of moderate length

BODY: The rear one-third is yellow wool or silk, front two-thirds is red chenille or wool. The body is shaped more fully toward the head.

RIBBING: Narrow oval silver tinsel from tail to head

WING: A small bunch of white bucktail extending just beyond the end of the tail

SHOULDERS: Each a narrow strip of a red goose feather laid along the

377

midsection of the wing and nearly as long. A tiny bunch of red bucktail sometimes is substituted for each of the shoulders.

THROAT: A dark brown hackle tied on as a collar after the wing and shoulder have been applied. The hackle is of moderate length and fullness and is not gathered downward.

The Umpqua Special, sometimes known as the Rogue River Special, is claimed by several fly dressers, but seems to have been the result of variations of several old patterns. It contains a body similar to the Van Luven, the red-and-white wing of the Parmachenee Belle, the hackles of the Royal Coachman, and a touch of yellow present in any of a score or more of well-known flies. Prominent in its past is Clarence Gordon, of the North Umpqua, who is credited with part of its distinctiveness as a pattern. Early in its career a variation of it was known as the Wharton Red, tied with an all-red body. F. D. Colvin had a similar steelhead fly dressed to the order of Frank Youngquist, of Coos Bay, California, with the same body and a wing of salmon pink and white bucktail. Colvin later changed the fly to add yellow to the body and substituted yellow for the salmon pink bucktail in the wing. This is called the Colvin's Rogue River Special, and is one of the many accepted variations. When the description of the pattern was published in *Field & Stream* magazine, more than twenty fly dressers sent in supposedly correct versions, no two of which were exactly alike. Regardless of these details, the fly became so successful on the North Umpqua River that it later became best known as the Umpqua Special. Anglers on the Rogue River prefer it with small double hooks and jungle cock cheeks and know this adaptation as the Rogue River Special. The Umpqua Special frequently is tied on No. 8 or 10 hooks for low-water summer fishing. In its larger sizes it is extremely popular as a steelhead fly, particularly on northern California and Oregon waters.

VAN DE CAR BUCKTAIL   *(As dressed by the originator)*

HEAD: Black

TAIL: About a dozen strands of a red saddle hackle, rather long

BODY: Medium flat gold tinsel

RIBBING: Medium oval gold tinsel

THROAT: A red saddle hackle of moderate length wound on as a collar and tied downward

WING: A small bunch of fox squirrel tail hair

CHEEKS: Jungle cock, fairly short

The fly was originated by Tom Van De Car, of Hutchinson, Kansas. It is a favorite western trout fly, particularly on the Gunnison River of Colorado. Usually it is dressed in the smaller sizes, such as 6, 8, and 10.

VAN LUVEN BUCKTAIL   *(As dressed by Peter J. Schwab)*

378

HEAD: Black

TAG: Three or four turns of medium flat silver tinsel. (This is optional and is not used by Schwab and many other fly dressers.)

TAIL: A small bunch of red polar bear hair, rather long. (In early dressings a tail of a section of a red goose wing feather, of moderate width and rather long, was used, but the hair tail is now considered superior.)

BODY: Of red silk or wool, fairly thick. This can be applied over copper wire if it is desired to have the fly weighted (see instructions in Chapter 10).

RIBBING: Narrow oval silver tinsel

THROAT: A brown hackle wound on as a collar, fairly long and heavy

WING: A small bunch of white polar bear hair, extending to the end of the tail. Over this it is optional to place an extremely small bunch of yellow polar bear hair of the same length. Bucktail may be substituted for all polar bear hair called for in this dressing. As in most steelhead flies, two or three turns of thread should be taken under the wing to raise it to an angle of about forty degrees.

This is one of the most popular of all western steelhead flies. Peter J. Schwab, who was a famous writer and angler of Yreka, California, wrote about it in the July 1946 issue of *Sports Afield* magazine as follows: "This fly was named by me during the winter of 1926–1927 after my old friend and mentor, Harry Van Luven, of Portland, Oregon. It was originally tied on plain hooks as a hair fly with standard short wings, but we found it even better as a bucktail with wings one and a half times the length of the hook. Harry used the white hair from the tail of the western black-tailed deer for the smaller hair fly, but he preferred the longer white hair of eastern deer tails for the bucktail version. He tied six of the 'red flies' every night in his little cabin near Ennis Riffle on the Rogue River, and it was the only fly I ever knew him to use. The pattern was evolved by a simple process of elimination starting with the great Royal Coachman. Harry first omitted the easily torn peacock herl. Finding this good, he wanted still more red so he added the red tail. Finally after much experimenting, in collaboration with Jack Myers, both men were satisfied and they replaced the white goose wings with wings of white bucktail. Certainly this simple fly is one of the greatest of steelhead and rainbow trout flies, even as its co-authors were two of the greatest fishermen on the West Coast. I still use the Van Luven as my standard of comparison."

E. H. (Polly) Rosborough, of Chiloquin, Oregon, developed a popular adaptation called the Silver Admiral, which differs from the Van Luven only as follows: The dressing is fluorescent except for hook, tinsel, and head. The throat (tied as a collar) is heavy, long fluorescent bright red hackle. The wing is of white fluorescent polar bear hair slightly longer than the tail. The recommended hook is 1X long, 2X stout nickel. The Silver Admiral is preferred for turbid, roily water, especially for winter steelhead fishing before sunrise and at dusk. For this type of fishing the fly is dressed with an underbody wound with .015 lead fuse wire.

WARDEN'S WORRY BUCKTAIL (Plate XII)   *(As dressed for the originator)*

HEAD: Black

TAG: Three or four turns of narrow flat gold tinsel

TAIL: A narrow section of a red duck or goose wing feather, moderately long

BODY: Orange-yellow spun fur or wool applied loosely or picked out to make it fuzzy. The body is of medium fullness.

RIBBING: Narrow oval gold tinsel

THROAT: Three or four turns of a yellow hackle, wound on as a collar and gathered downward

WING: A small bunch of light brown bucktail, extending just beyond the end of the tail

379

This fly was originated about 1930 by Warden Supervisor Joseph S. Stickney, of Saco, Maine, from whose title the Warden's Worry and the Supervisor took their names. It is a favorite for trout, landlocked salmon, and many other game fish in all sections of the United States. It is often fished behind a spinner for walleyed pike. The dressing is from a fly given to me by Warden Stickney.

WELCH RAREBIT STREAMER (Plate XII)   *(As dressed by the originator)*
HEAD: Black
TAIL: Extremely narrow sections of duck or goose wing feathers in red, yellow, and blue plus two strands of a peacock sword feather. All four colors are of equal and normal length, with the blue and yellow married together on one side (with the yellow at the top) and the red and peacock on the other side.
BODY: Medium flat silver tinsel
RIBBING: Narrow oval silver tinsel
THROAT: A small bunch of fibers from a guinea hen body feather
WING: One wine red (dark red) saddle hackle on each side of which are two white saddle hackles
TOPPING: Nine strands of bright green peacock herl, as long as the wing

This is one of the best known of the Maine streamers. It was originated by Herbert L. Welch, of Haine's Landing, Maine, to imitate a smelt, which is the principal food fish in many Maine lakes. The name Rarebit is often misspelled. Welch dressed this fly without jungle cock cheeks.

WESLEY SPECIAL BUCKTAIL   *(As dressed by Herbert L. Howard)*
HEAD: Black
TAIL: A very small bunch of strands from a golden pheasant tippet
BODY: Medium flat silver tinsel
RIBBING: Narrow oval silver tinsel
THROAT: A few turns of a black hackle, of medium length gathered downward
WING: A small bunch of white bucktail, over which is a small bunch of blue-gray bucktail, both slightly longer than the tail
CHEEKS: Jungle cock

This is one of the patterns obtained by Herbert L. Howard of New Rochelle, New York, for Ray Bergman's book *Trout.* It is popular on the Rifle River and in the Au Sable River area of Michigan, particularly as a trout fly.

WINNIPESAUKEE SMELT   *(As dressed by Jim Warner)*
HEAD: Black
TAIL: A small bunch of golden pheasant tippet fibers, usually set upright
BODY: Flat silver tinsel
RIBBING: Oval silver tinsel
THROAT: A small bunch of red hackle fibers
WING: A bunch of white marabou, with a topping of about six black ostrich herls
SHOULDERS: Jungle cock body feathers, fairly long

This is a popular New England pattern named for the big New Hampshire lake famous for landlocked salmon fishing. Maine's Percy Tackle Company, which sells

380

many of this pattern, simplifies it by eliminating all but the body and wing. The fly is not unlike the famous Ballou Special, which also imitates a smelt.

WIZARD STREAMER (Plate II) *(As dressed by the originator)*
HEAD: Black, with red band
BODY: Thinly wound with red silk
RIBBING: Narrow flat silver tinsel
THROAT: A few strands of peacock herl, beneath which is a small bunch of white bucktail, both extending well beyond the bend of the hook. Beneath this is a small bunch of white neck hackle fibers.
WING: Two black saddle hackles with a yellow saddle hackle of the same length on each side. The wing is as long as the peacock and bucktail of the throat.
CHEEKS: Jungle cock

Originated by Carrie G. Stevens. This fly is a favorite in Maine waters for trout.

WOOD PUSSY BUCKTAIL *(As dressed by the originator)*
HEAD: Black
TAIL: A small bunch of black skunk hair, very long
BODY: Wound with silver wire, or with copper wire covered with medium flat silver tinsel (see instructions in Chapter 10)
WING: A small bunch of white polar bear hair or white skunk hair, over which is a small bunch of black skunk hair. The wing extends to the end of the tail. In applying the two parts of the wing, turns of thread are taken under both the white and the black hair to raise the wing to an angle of about forty degrees.

This fly was originated by Peter J. Schwab, of Yreka, California, in 1927. This is one of a series of steelhead flies listed in the comments on the Princess Bucktail and in notes in Chapter 10. The series is dressed with wire bodies to assist them in sinking in the swift and deep western coastal rivers, such as the Klamath, where they were first used. In either the weighted or unweighted types they are consistently valuable in all parts of the country for all species of game fish.

WOOLY LEECH (WHITLOCK) *(As dressed by Dave Whitlock)*
HOOK SIZE: 2 to 8, Atlantic salmon (Mustad #3658D)
THREAD: Black
TAIL: A bunch of olive marabou fibers as long as the hook, applied after the end of a section of stiff monofilament (.018–.025-inch diameter) has been tied in for a weed guard
HEAD: Two large bead-chain eyes applied in usual figure-eight fashion, with lead wire wound on in the same way to make a head which fills in between the eyes. This later is covered by body material lashed down similarly.
BODY: Orlon wool the same color as the tail, over which are palmered two soft, webby saddle hackles with bright sides out, of the same color. (The wool also covers the head.) After finishing the head tie in the other end of the monofilament to complete the weed guard, as explained in Chapter 9.

381

This fly represents many large swimming leeches as well as other slippery-skinned creatures such as tadpoles and salamanders. Thus, it can be tied in any color to match leeches, which are of a dirty black, brown, or muck color, as well as light to olive tan. The weed guard is important in using the fly around rocks where leeches so often collect. The weighted head balances the fly and causes it to dive, jig-fashion. The bead-chain eyes are fairly large, usually used in silver color, but sometimes in gold, or they can be painted. The fly should be fished slowly and erratically along the bottom. This is an excellent type for many species of game fish, especially bass, trout, and landlocked salmon.

Many famous anglers have developed leech patterns because of their great success in hooking big trout, particularly in the northwest, where the big ones are less rare than in the northeast. The "hot" flies often are leech imitations, descended from the well-known Wooly Worm type, but with longer, more leechlike tails to provide more appropriate shape. Mohair is superior to chenille, and marabou better than neck or shoulder hackles. I have given one of the best patterns, and the inclusion of others (all quite similar) seems superfluous.

YELLOW BREECHES STREAMER   *(As dressed by the originators)*

HEAD: Yellow
BODY: Medium oval silver tinsel
THROAT: The tip of a red hackle tied in vertically; of medium length
WING: A yellow marabou feather tip, over which is a bunch of herl from a light
    brown marabou feather. The bunch of brown marabou is of the same
    volume and length as the yellow marabou feather.
SHOULDERS: Three herls of a peacock feather on each side, tied in to separate
    the two colors of the wing. The peacock is of the same length as the wing.
CHEEKS: Jungle cock

This fly was originated by R. W. McCafferty and Charles Fox, of Hershey, Pennsylvania, for fishing in Yellow Breeches Creek in Pennsylvania. McCafferty writes about the fly as follows: "For a number of years I've used marabou streamers of one-inch and two-inch lengths and find that they take more trout than the longer ones, although the longer ones often cause more excitement in the fish. The Yellow Breeches Streamer resembles the minnows found in Yellow Breeches Creek, but the fly has been successful in many other places. We also like a Black Marabou Streamer because of its visibility in dark or dirty water. We have found that the angler can see the Black Marabou better than lighter colors under those conditions and so can the fish. In this section we have limestone streams which are always murky. In this milky water the black color almost always is good."

McCafferty's Black Marabou Streamer is dressed like the Yellow Breeches, except that the yellow and brown marabou is replaced by two black marabou feathers.

YELLOW JANE CRAIG STREAMER   *(As dressed by the originator)*

HEAD: Black
BODY: Medium flat silver tinsel
RIBBING: Narrow oval silver tinsel
WING: Four bright yellow saddle hackles
TOPPING: Six or seven strands of bright green peacock herl, as long as the wing
CHEEKS: Jungle cock

This is a later version of the Jane Craig Streamer, dressed with yellow hackles instead of white to give the fly greater visibility on dark days or in discolored water. It was originated by Herbert L. Welch, of Haine's Landing, Maine, in about 1923 and was named for Jane Craig, a vaudeville actress of the team of Dalton and Craig which toured the Keith Circuit of theaters at that time. In addition to the change in colors, this fly differs from the Jane Craig in that it has no throat. Also, it is ribbed, while the Jane Craig is not.

YELLOW MAY STREAMER (As dressed by Robert J. Stone)
HEAD: Black
BODY: Wound with yellow silk, shaped slightly in the middle
RIBBING: Narrow flat gold tinsel
THROAT: A small bunch of yellow saddle hackle fibers, rather long
WING: Four bright yellow saddle hackles

The Yellow Sally Streamer is identical to the Yellow May Streamer except that it is not ribbed. Both flies may be dressed with hair wings, although the feathered wings are more common. Both flies were adapted from the trout flies of the same names.

YELLOW PERCH STREAMER (Plate XI) (As dressed by the originator)
HOOK SIZE: 1 to 6, 3X to 6X long
HEAD: Black
TAIL: A very small bunch of fibers from a yellow hackle about as long as the gap of the hook (Oatman did not always dress the tail)
BODY: Wound with pale cream or amber floss, slightly tapered
RIBBING: Medium flat gold tinsel
THROAT: A very small bunch of yellow hackle fibers edged outwardly with four or five orange hackle fibers
WING: Two grizzly hackles dyed yellow, on each side of which is a yellow saddle hackle, all of the same length and extending slightly beyond the tail. (The grizzly hackles should be selected with wide dark bands.)
TOPPING: Several peacock herls, as long as the wing
CHEEKS: Jungle cock, rather small

This excellent imitative pattern was originated by the late Lew Oatman, of Shushan, New York. In sending the dressings and fly samples to me many years ago, Lew wrote about this one, "This fly was designed for largemouth bass which feed on the schools of small perch, and also for some lakes especially in the Westchester [New York] area where rainbow trout have been planted and are known to feed on these little fish. I have found that this streamer and the Golden Shiner will take bass during the day when they are not interested in the noisier lures."

YERXA BUCKTAIL (As dressed for the originator)
HEAD: Black
TAG: Four or five turns of narrow flat gold tinsel
BODY: Yellow wool or dubbing dressed rather full and picked out to make it fuzzy

RIBBING: Narrow flat gold tinsel

THROAT: A yellow neck hackle tied on as a collar and then gathered downward to make a full and bushy throat

WING: A bunch of white bucktail

CHEEKS: Jungle cock

This pattern was originated by Jack Yerxa, of Square Lake Camp, Square Lake, Maine, and was named for him by Gardner Percy, who tied flies for his camp. The fly was first used in 1928, and the original pattern caught over one hundred landlocked salmon in Square Lake during that year.

YORK'S KENNEBAGO STREAMER *(As dressed by the originator)*

HEAD: Black

TAG: Three or four turns of narrow flat silver tinsel

TAIL: A very short golden pheasant crest feather, curving upward

BUTT: Two or three turns of scarlet silk

BODY: Medium flat silver tinsel

RIBBING: Narrow oval silver tinsel

THROAT: A small bunch of red hackle fibers

WING: Four golden badger saddle hackles with a pronounced black stripe. The wing is longer than average.

TOPPING: A small bunch of red hackle fibers

CHEEKS: Jungle cock

This streamer was originated by Bert Quimby, one of Maine's most expert streamer fly dressers. He named it for T. Lewis York, who was the owner of York's Camps on Kennebago Lake, in Maine. It was dressed primarily to imitate the bait fish in Kennebago Lake, and is popular there as a spring fly.

Index

389

393

A NOTE ABOUT THE AUTHOR

Colonel Joseph D. Bates, Jr., was born in West
Springfield, Massachusetts. He was educated at the
Massachusetts Institute of Technology and was an
advertising agency vice-president until his retirement.
His military career covered twenty-seven years,
including service in the South Pacific during World
War II. He is the preeminent authority on the history
of fly patterns and the author of fourteen books on
angling, among them three books on spinning that
popularized that technique in the United States, and
an important book on Atlantic Salmon fishing. He
lives in Longmeadow, Massachusetts.

A NOTE ON THE TYPE

The text of this book was set via computer-driven
cathode ray tube in a type face called Baskerville. The
face is a facsimile reproduction of types cast from
molds made for John Baskerville (1706–75) from his
designs. The punches for the revived Linotype
Baskerville were cut under the supervision of the
English printer George W. Jones.
    John Baskerville's original face was one of the
forerunners of the type style known as "modern face"
to printers—a "modern" of the period A.D. 1800.

Composed by Com Com, a division of Haddon
Craftsmen, Allentown, Pennsylvania
Printed by The Murray Printing Company,
Westford, Massachusetts
Designed by Jacqueline Schuman

BOOKS BY JOSEPH D. BATES, JR.

Spinning for American Game Fish

Trout Waters and How to Fish Them

Streamer Fly Fishing in Fresh and Salt Water

Spinning for Fresh Water Game Fish

Spinning for Salt Water Game Fish

The Outdoor Cook's Bible

Streamer Fly Tying & Fishing
(with a subscribed limited edition of 600 copies)

Elementary Fishing

Atlantic Salmon Flies & Fishing
(with a subscribed limited edition of 600 copies)

Reading the Water

Fishing

How to Find Fish and Make Them Strike

The Atlantic Salmon Treasury

Streamers and Bucktails: The Big Fish Flies